Object-Oriented Design Heuristics

Object-Oriented Design Heuristics

Arthur J. Riel

ADDISON-WESLEY PUBLISHING COMPANY, INC.

Reading, Massachusetts • Menlo Park, California • New York • Don Mills, Ontario
Wokingham, England • Amsterdam • Bonn • Sydney • Singapore
Tokyo • Madrid • San Juan • Seoul • Milan • Mexico City • Taipei

The publisher offers discounts on this book when ordered in quantity for special sales.

For more information, please contact:

Corporate & Professional Publishing Group
Addison-Wesley Publishing Company
One Jacob Way
Reading, Massachusetts 01867

Library of Congress Cataloging-in-Publication Data

Riel, Arthur J., 1962-
    Object-oriented design heuristics / Arthur J. Riel.
        p.   cm.
    Includes bibliographical references and index.
    ISBN 0-201-63385-X (hardcover : alk. paper)
    1. Object-oriented programming (Computer science)   I. Title.
QA76.64.R54   1996
005.1—dc20

95-48396
CIP

ISBN 0-201-63385-X

Text design by Wilson Graphics & Design (Kenneth J. Wilson)
Text printed on recycled and acid-free paper.

1 2 3 4 5 6 7 8 9-MA-99989796
First Printing, April 1996.

For Armand and Marie Riel,
who started this project some 34 years ago,

and for Susana Cumplido,
without whose help I could not have finished this book.

Contents

Preface   xi

Acknowledgements   xvii

1   The Motivation for Object-Oriented Programming   1

   1.1   Revolutionists, Evolutionists, and the Object-Oriented Paradigm   1

   1.2   Accidental Versus Essential Complexity à la Frederick Brooks   3

   1.3   The Waterfall Model   4

   1.4   The Iterative Model   5

   1.5   Same- Versus Different-Language Prototyping   6

   1.6   Software Reusability   7

   1.7   Corporate Hierarchies of Good Designers   8

**2   Classes and Objects: The Building Blocks of the Object-Oriented
Paradigm**   11

   2.1   Introduction to Classes and Objects 11

   2.2   Messages and Methods 15

   2.3   Class Coupling and Cohesion 18

   2.4   Dynamic Semantics 21

   2.5   Abstract Classes 22

   2.6   Roles Versus Classes 24

3   Topologies of Action-Oriented Versus Object-Oriented Applications   29

   3.1   Differences in Application Topologies 29

   3.2   When the Action-Oriented Paradigm Goes Right 32

   3.3   The God Class Problem (Behavioral Form) 32

   3.4   Another Example of Poor System Intelligence Distribution 37

   3.5   The God Class Problem (Data Form) 39

3.6   The Proliferation of Classes Problem 41

3.7   The Role of Agent Classes 45

3.8   Examining the Use of Separate Entity and Controller Classes 48

4   The Relationships Between Classes and Objects   53

4.1   Introduction to Class and Object Relationships 53

4.2   The Uses Relationship 53

4.3   Six Different Ways to Implement the Uses Relationship 54

4.4   Heuristics for the Uses Relationship 56

4.5   Refining the Amount of Collaboration Between Two Classes 58

4.6   The Containment Relationship 60

4.7   Semantic Constraints Between Classes 64

4.8   Attributes Versus Contained Classes 66

4.9   More Containment Heuristics 67

4.10   A Relationship Between Uses and Containment? 69

4.11   Containment by Value Versus Containment by Reference 71

5   The Inheritance Relationship   75

5.1   Introduction to the Inheritance Relationship 75

5.2   Overriding Base Class Methods in Derived Classes 79

5.3   The Use of the Protected Section of a Base Class 81

5.4   The Width and Depth of Inheritance Hierarchies 83

5.5   Private, Protected, and Public Inheritance à la C++ 85

5.6   A Real-World Example of Specialization 88

5.7   Heuristics That Trade Off Design Complexity and Flexibility 89

5.8   A Real-World Example of Generalization 92

5.9   The Mechanism of Polymorphism 93

5.10   A Problem with the Use of Inheritance as a Reusability
       Mechanism 98

5.11   An Inheritance Solution to an Interrupt-Driven Architecture 102

5.12   Inheritance Hierarchies Versus Attributes 103

5.13   The Confusion of the Need for Inheritance Versus an Object's
       Dynamic Semantics 105

5.14   Using Inheritance to Hide the Representation of a Class 107

5.15   Mistaking Objects for Derived Classes 108

5.16   Mistaking Object Generalization for the Need to Build Classes at Runtime 110

5.17   The Attempt to NOP a Base Class Method in Its Derived Class(es) 113

5.18   The Implementation of Optional Parts of Objects 117

5.19   A Problem with No Optimal Solution 118

5.20   Reusing Components Versus Reusing Frameworks 123

6   Multiple Inheritance   **131**

6.1   Introduction to Multiple Inheritance 131

6.2   The Common Misuse of Multiple Inheritance 132

6.3   A Valid Use of Multiple Inheritance 135

6.4   Accidental Complexity In Languages That Do Not Support Multiple Inheritance 136

6.5   Frameworks That Incorporate Multiple Inheritance 137

6.6   The Use of Multiple Inheritance in the Design of Mixins 137

6.7   DAG Multiple Inheritance 139

6.8   Accidental DAG Multiple Inheritance via Poor Implementation of Optional Containment 140

7   The Association Relationship   **143**

7.1   Introduction to Associations 143

7.2   Associations Implemented Through a Referential Attribute 144

7.3   Associations Implemented Through a Third-Party Class 146

7.4   Deciding Between a Containment and an Association Relationship . 147

8   Class-Specific Data and Behavior   **151**

8.1   Introduction to Class-Specific Versus Object-Specific Data and Behavior 151

8.2   Using Metaclasses to Capture Class-Specific Data and Behavior 152

8.3   Using Language-Level Keywords to Implement Class- Versus Object-Specific Data and Behavior 153

8.4   Metaclasses à la C++ 153

8.5   A Useful Abstract Class That Is Not a Base Class? 156

9   Physical Object-Oriented Design   159

   9.1   The Role of Logical and Physical Object-Oriented Design   159

   9.2   The Construction of Object-Oriented Wrappers   163

   9.3   Persistence in an Object-Oriented System   166

   9.4   Memory Management Issues in an Object-Oriented Application   169

   9.5   Minimal Public Interfaces for Reusable Components   170

   9.6   Implementing Safe Shallow Copies   175

   9.7   Concurrent Object-Oriented Programming   177

   9.8   Implementing Object-Oriented Designs in Nonobject-Oriented
       Languages   179

10   The Relationship Between Heuristics and Patterns   183

   10.1   Heuristics Versus Patterns   183

   10.2   Transitivity Among Design Transformation Patterns   186

   10.3   The Reflexive Property of Design Transformation Patterns   189

   10.4   Other Design Transformation Patterns   192

   10.5   Future Research   196

11   The Use of Heuristics in Object-Oriented Design   199

   11.1   The ATM Problem   199

   11.2   Choosing a Methodology   201

   11.3   A First Attempt at Producing an Object Model for the ATM   203

   11.4   Adding Behavior to Our Object Model   204

   11.5   Explicit Case Analysis Due to Accidental Complexity   209

   11.6   Messaging Objects in Different Address Spaces   211

   11.7   The Processing of the Transaction   211

   11.8   Returning to the Domain of the ATM   212

   11.9   Other Miscellaneous Issues   214

   11.10 Conclusion   217

A   Heuristics Summary   219

B   Memory Leakage in C++   225

C   Selected C++ Examples   245

Bibliography   369

Index   373

Preface

In the process of teaching object-oriented analysis, design, and implementation to several thousand students, it became clear to me that the industry was in serious need of guidelines to help developers make proper decisions. Since 1987 I have scoured the literature in search of productivity and complexity metrics that can be applied at different levels of development to improve an object-oriented application. I added my own "homemade" guidelines to those found in the literature and came up with approximately 60 guidelines, several of which are tongue-in-cheek yet no less important than any others. I briefly considered calling them the "Sixty Golden Rules of OOA/D," but I recalled Dykstra's legendary "Goto Considered Harmful" paper, which branded users of goto statements heretics who should be burned at the stake in the company courtyard. That paper was important in that it provided an industry rule that stopped the users of goto statements who were destroying, wittingly or unwittingly, the maintainability of their systems. Unfortunately, the side effect of such a rule was the breeding of a group of pathological authors who, for the past 25 years, have published articles stating that the judicious use of a goto statement in some picky little piece of an application is more readable than a corresponding piece of structured code. Of course, these papers were followed up by a half-dozen rebuttal papers, which were themselves rebutted ad nauseam.

In order to prevent the same pathology from occurring, I refer to these 60 guidelines as "heuristics," or rules of thumb. They are not hard and fast rules that must be followed under penalty of heresy. Instead, they should be thought of as a series of warning bells that will ring when violated. The warning should be examined, and if warranted, a change should be enacted to remove the violation of the heuristic. It is perfectly valid to state that the heuristic does not apply in a given example for one reason or another. In fact, in many cases, two heuristics will be at odds with one another in a particular area of an object-oriented design. The developer is required to decide which heuristic plays the more important role.

This book does not invent yet another object-oriented analysis or design methodology, though the idea of creating "Riel's OOA/D Methodology" was tempting. The industry already has enough methodologies offering similar or overlapping advice, using a completely different vocabulary for common concepts. The typical problem of the object-oriented developer—which has not been seriously addressed—occurs once a design has been completed, regardless of the methodology used. The developer's main question is, "Now that I have my design, is it good, bad, or somewhere in between?" In asking an object-oriented guru, the developer is often told that a design is good when "it feels right." While this is of little use to the developer, there is a kernel of truth to such an answer. The guru runs through a subconscious list of heuristics, built up through his or her design experience, over the design. If the heuristics pass, then the design feels right, and if they do not pass, then the design does not feel right.

This book attempts to capture that subconscious list of heuristics in a concrete list backed up by real-world examples. The reader will become immediately aware that some heuristics are much stronger than others. The strength of a heuristic comes from the ramifications of violating it. The reader does not get a prioritized ordering of the heuristics. It is my feeling that in many cases the sense of priority is defined by a combination of the application domain and the user's needs and cannot be quantified here. For example, a common area of design where two heuristics might request opposite directions are those that trade complexity with flexibility. Ask yourself which attribute a software designer desires most, increased flexibility or decreased complexity, and you begin to see the problem of prioritizing heuristics.

The design heuristics are defined on a backdrop of real-world examples focusing on the area of design to which each heuristic belongs. The foundation of real-world examples provides an ideal vehicle for explaining the concepts of object-oriented technology to the novice. The end result is that this book is appropriate to the newcomer who would like a fast track to understanding the concepts of object-oriented programming without having to muddle through the proliferation of buzzwords that permeates the field. Yet, at the same time, it appeals to the experienced object-oriented developer who is looking for some good analysis and design heuristics to help in his or her development efforts.

The first chapter looks at the motivation for object-oriented programming, starting with several issues which Frederick Brooks argued in his "No Silver Bullet" paper published in 1987 [1]. My perspective on object-oriented programming is that it is a natural progression or evolution from action-oriented development. As software has become more complex, we are required to remove ourselves one more level away from the machine in order to maintain the same grasp we have on the software development process. Just as structured methodologies removed one level from bottom-up programming, object-oriented technology removes one level from structured methodologies. It is not that bottom-up programming or structured methodologies are wrong and object-oriented programming is right. Bottom-up programming is perfectly valid when there exists only 4K of memory to develop, just as structured methodologies are perfectly valid when only 256K of memory exists. With the advent of increasingly cheaper and more powerful hardware, the complexity of software has skyrocketed. Developers of the early 1980s did not have to consider the complexity of graphical user interfaces and multithreaded applications; simpler menu-driven, single-threaded systems were the norm. In the very near future, no one will buy a software product unless it incorporates multimedia with moving video and voice recognition. The more complex systems require a greater level of abstraction, which the object-oriented paradigm provides. This is no revolution in software development; it is simply an evolution.

Chapter 2 discusses the concepts of class and object, the basic building blocks of object-oriented technology. They are viewed as the encapsulation of data and its related behavior in a bidirectional relationship. The notion of sending messages, defining methods, and inventing protocols are explored through real-world examples. This is the first chapter to list heuristics. Given the small subset of the object paradigm with which to work, these heuristics are fairly simple but no less useful than the more complex heuristics of subsequent chapters.

The third chapter examines the difference between an action-oriented topology and an object-oriented topology. The different topologies of these methodologies contain the kernel of truth behind object-oriented development. Action-oriented development focuses largely on a centralized control mechanism controlling a functionally decomposed set of tasks, while object-oriented development focuses on a decentralized collection of cooperating entities. I am convinced that the notion of a paradigm shift is the change in thinking required to move from a centralized to a decentralized control model. The learning curve of object-oriented development is an equally large unlearning curve for those of us reared in the world of action-oriented development. The real world in which we live is more attuned to the object model than to a centralized control mechanism. The lack of a paradigm shift manifests itself in systems that consist of a central godlike object that sits in the middle of a collection of trivial classes. These systems are built by developers stuck in the mindset of an action-oriented topology. This chapter proposes numerous heuristics for developing optimal application topologies.

Chapters 4 through 7 examine each of the five main object-oriented relationships: uses (Chapter 4); containment (Chapter 4); single inheritance (Chapter 5); multiple inheritance (Chapter 6); and association (Chapter 7) through a series of real-world examples. Most of the heuristics of interest to the object-oriented designer can be found in these chapters. The chapters on inheritance include many examples of the common misuses of the inheritance relationship. This information is vital in reducing the proliferation of classes problem, such as designing too many classes for a given application. The class proliferation problem is a major cause of failure in object-oriented development.

Chapter 8 examines the role of class-specific data and behavior, as opposed to object-specific data and behavior. The invoice class is used as an example of an abstraction that requires class-specific data and behavior. Both the SmallTalk metaclass and the C++ keyword mechanisms are illustrated. In addition, the notion of C++ meta-classes (i.e., templates) is compared and contrasted to the SmallTalk notion of metaclasses.

Chapter 9 examines the role of physical object-oriented design in the development of object-oriented systems. While there is much to say about physical design in general, many issues overlap those discussed in the action-oriented paradigm. Issues such as the granularity of efficient implementation (e.g., look at replacing hardware, then compilers, then mechanisms, and then algorithms, before examining individual language statements to speed up an application) are discussed in great detail in the literature. This text examines physical design issues either that are unique within the object-oriented paradigm or for which the object-oriented paradigm offers unique solutions. These include the notion of software wrappers to hide hostile (i.e. non-object-oriented) subsystems from an object-oriented problem domain, persistence in time versus persistence in space, object-oriented versus relational database management systems, memory management and garbage collection, reference counting, minimal public interfaces, concurrent object-oriented programming, and implementing object-oriented designs in nonobject-oriented languages.

In 1987 I attended a small workshop at the OOPSLA conference which discussed the past, present, and future of the object-oriented paradigm. During this conference, Kent Beck discussed research Christopher Alexander published in the area of architecture (constructing buildings, not software). Alexander felt that all architecture had an as-yet undescribed quality, which he tried to capture in entities he called patterns. Kent discussed the possibility of looking for patterns, that is, domain-independent solutions to known problems or interesting structures, in object-oriented architectures. Recently, much of the research performed in this area is exploding into the forefront of the object community. This has led me to ask the question, "What is the relationship between heuristics and patterns?" They are obviously related in that they are found in much the same manner. We examine any structure or problem that arises in many different domains. We then try to encapsulate the entity in either a heuristic or a design pattern format. Chapter 10 of this text discusses design patterns and their relationship to design heuristics. I believe the most interesting relationship between patterns and heuristics is that heuristics tell a designer when it is time to apply one of several design patterns. Patterns are too large for the average designer to know, through some intuition, that it is time to apply a pattern. Heuristics, on the other hand, are rarely more than two sentences of text and can be easily applied. The combination of the two can be extremely effective. This chapter also illustrates several interesting properties that design patterns and heuristics share.

The reader should avoid the temptation to criticize the early examples in this text as being too trivial or not within the computer science domain. It is common to hear, early in the lecture, a small percentage of attendees of my courses muttering statements such as, "This information is not useful because I do not program fruit baskets, dogs with tails, or alarm clocks." While it is true that a large part of this book deals with everyday items from the real world, I offer a reasonable explanation. If design heuristics and patterns are truly domain-independent, then why not choose a simple domain in which to teach them? In the design courses I have taught, it is common to hear a design group shouting out, "This is the core-the-apple problem," or "This is the dog-with-an-optional tail" problem. Once a heuristic is understood, it is a simple matter to expand its use to any domain, regardless of the domain's complexity.

I have added Chapter 11 of this book for those who wish a design example with more "meat." Chapter 11 provides an analysis and design problem revolving around the automatic teller machine (ATM) domain. The ATM problem has been widely published in various texts dealing with the object-oriented paradigm. In this case it was chosen because it provides a familiar example that illustrates the use of design heuristics and patterns in a more computer science-like domain. In addition, since it is a distributed system (the ATM and the Bank live in different address spaces), it allows for the illustration of a design technique called "design with proxies." This design technique allows a system architect to ignore the distributed facet of an application at logical design time, deferring these problems until much later in design. This is important since many of the design problems associated with distributed systems can be traced to early convolution due to addressing of distributed processing before a logical design is complete.

On a final note, in all of my courses I have noticed that the class divides into two camps. The first camp likes to live in the realm of abstraction, discussing design for design's sake with little discussion of implementation. The second camp has difficulty understanding the abstractions, but if you show the members of that camp a fragment of code, the picture becomes very clear to them. When this book was sent to reviewers, I asked each reviewer to specify whether this book should illustrate the design examples with C++ implementations. Two reviewers stated that it was obvious that this book requires C++ examples, because the abstract concepts would be difficult to understand without them. Another two reviewers stated that this is a design book and as such has nothing to do with C++, or any programming language for that matter. The other two reviewers were relatively neutral. This leaves me with the obvious dilemma of satisfying both camps. My solution is to provide an appendix to the text with a collection of selected C++ implementations of design examples viewed within that chapter. If you tend to be an abstractionist, you will most likely want to ignore the appendix. If you are the type of person who learns by examining the implementation of abstractions (I live in your camp most of the time), you may want to check the implementation of certain design problems in the appendix. It is my hope that this satisfies those desiring implementations without cluttering the design information with code.

Note: All C++ examples were compiled and tested under Borland C++ 4.5 on a Pentium 100 Mhz IBM PC clone. They should work on your favorite C++ compiler as well.

Acknowledgements

This text is the product of a large number of innovative people who, knowingly or unknowingly, contributed to my study of design heuristics and patterns. I wish to give my first thanks to Dr. Lee McKnight of AT&T Bell Laboratories, who began my journey down this path, and Dr. Karl Lieberherr, who later instructed, pushed, shoved, dragged, and otherwise navigated me through the object-oriented paradigm. Without these two individuals, this book would never have been started, let alone finished.

I wish to acknowledge Brian Foote and Ralph Johnson, who refined my thoughts on design heuristics in their paper, "Designing Reusable Classes," *Journal of Object-Oriented Programming* **1**, no. 2 (1988). Five of the heuristics in this text were collected from this paper. The work of Frederick Brooks serves as a basis for much of Chapter 1's discussion on accidental versus essential complexity. Brooks continues to author some of the best literature in the field of software development.

I thank several classes of students at Northeastern University (1986–1987) for suffering through the meal example in lectures immediately before lunch. Their work on object-oriented design projects at a time before there were any formal methodologies proved invaluable to this text as well as to my own understanding of the object-oriented paradigm. My thanks to John Carter and John Cooper, with whom I worked on a C++ class library in 1987–1989. Their collaboration produced the discussion on reuse problems in the presence of inheritance (Section 5.10) and minimal public interfaces for reusable components (Section 9.5). In addition, John Carter is responsible for the wooden door example in Section 6.3.

I thank Cathryn Szekely, David Bardolini, and a lively group of C++ students at Chipcomm for motivating the "dogs and their tails" discussion in Section 5.17. Craig Hilsenrath and Tom Connors of Greenwich Capital Markets were the inspiration for the securities example in Section 5.16—I thank them for showing me how nasty the domain of securities can get. My thanks to several employees at Bell Northern Research who motivated numerous examples related to the domain of telephony. In particular, Todd Hansen and Gordon Grimes, for an interesting discussion concerning the trade-offs between data-driven and behavior-driven analysis and design. This discussion is presented in Chapter 11 of this text. The airplane example in Section 6.2 was taken from a very early work of Weiner and Pinson. Much thanks to Paul Sadlek and his group at Santa Clara Plastics, from whom the discussion on the relationship between uses and containment was initially derived (Section 4.10).

I wish to thank an employee of Bankers Trust who motivated heuristic 9.1 in a public seminar I gave in 1991; my apologies that I couldn't find your name in any of my records and properly acknowledge you. Likewise for the individual who discussed the Fortran waveform engine wrapper in a panel discussion at a conference in 1987 (Section 9.2). Thanks to Paul Hidy and group at Network Equipment Technologies. Some of your early work in this field contributed to the discussion in Section 9.2 on moving objects from one machine to another. I hope you are glad to see your early problems were indeed large, relevant problems. CORBA and its kin are still wrestling with your problem. My thanks to John Zak, Bruce Hyre, and many others at Traveler's Insurance who motivated the example in Section 9.2 on wrappers for PC/Unix clients to mainframe servers.

Special thanks to Bobbi Heath, James McQueston, and Michael Wissner of Avid Technologies for the media case study in Section 3.7. Gene Thomas and his group at BNR were the inspiration for the telephony example in Section 4.9. Thanks for all of the questions on containment that helped me refine my ideas in this area. More thanks to Craig Hilsenrath for the economy case study in the same section. Special thanks to Jenaline Low, Monica Tan, Stuart Woodward, and my other Singaporean friends, for interesting design discussions and my first durian.

Chapter 10, discussing the relationship between heuristics and patterns, was motivated by several discussions I had with other speakers at a conference in Germany (Devcon '94), including Kent Beck, James Coplien, Jon Hopkins, Meiler-Page Jones, and Larry Constantine. Thanks for the insight!

I wish to thank the reviewers of this text who pointed out many issues in its earlier drafts. They include Kent Beck, Tim Born, Karen Ellison, Gordan Grimes, Todd Hansen, Howard Harkness, Craig Hilsenrath, Doug Lea, Robert Martin, and Keven McGrath. I wish to acknowledge particularly thorough jobs by Robert Martin (on an earlier draft and the final manuscript) and Donald Firesmith (on an intermediate draft). Their constructive criticism undoubtedly made this a much better book. On the publishing side, I wish to thank Kate Habib and Kim Dawley, who convinced me at OOPSLA '93 to write this book, and my editors, John Wait and Mike Hendrickson, for their help in getting this book published and their patience in getting their hands on the manuscript.

I wish to thank those who have supported my research over the years, including Paul Kalaghan, Sheila Scott, Beth McFadden, Paul Hidy, Kelly Hart, Tim Korson, Edward Bernardon, John Macgregor, and Robert Scarlatelli.

A very special thank you to my office manager, Tina Young, who is constantly sweeping up the problems that inevitably drop on the floor and organizes such trivial things in life as schedules, budgets, and taxes. This work would not have been possible without her.

Thanks to Robert Flory, with whom I worked on the process control project at Draper Laboratories (sec. 5.20).

Last, but by no means least, I wish to acknowledge the thousands of students at Northeastern University, and companies too numerous to name here, who have participated in discussions and debate concerning object-oriented analysis and design in my courses on C++ and OOA/D from 1985 to the present. Many of your comments and insights have been incorporated into this text.

Chapter 1

The Motivation for Object-Oriented Programming

1.1 Revolutionists, Evolutionists, and the Object-Oriented Paradigm

In the process of learning about the object-oriented paradigm and all that it encompasses, you will first become aware of the many divisions within our community. Each division implies two or more camps who are generally very religious about their point of view. One of the first divisions of importance is the revolutionists versus the evolutionists. The revolutionists believe that a group of developers woke up at 3 o'clock one morning and realized that we have been developing software the wrong way all along. They believe they have found the solution to the software crisis, and the name of that solution is object-oriented programming. As the reader may have surmised, I fall into the camp of the evolutionists.

The evolutionists feel that object-oriented programming is no revolution in software development. It is simply the next logical step in a long series of steps that take the software developer further and further away from the machine details. A software crisis does not come about because we are incorrectly developing software. A software crisis comes about because our paradigm of programming is no longer sufficient to handle the complexity of problems we are asked to solve. Using octal and/or hexadecimal opcodes to write programs is a great paradigm when there are only 8 instructions and 1K of memory in our machine, of which 90 percent is used up by our operating system. I have no trouble using this method of programming when there are only 8 opcodes to remember and 30 lines of code to write. When my hardware becomes more sophisticated and I begin getting problems that require 64K of memory, remembering opcodes then starts creating a level of complexity I cannot handle. At that time, I begin using assembly-language mnemonics. This works great until a point where the complexity of my problems outgrows this paradigm. I similarly upgrade to using a high-level language whose instructions each replace many assembly-language mnemonics, allowing me to think at a higher level. Aside from reducing the language complexity, I also seek out a better way of thinking about my problem. Instead of stringing instructions into small functions and small functions into programs, I use a structured method for breaking my problem into smaller pieces, each of which is manageable.

We are currently at a point in software development where structured, top-down design methods are no longer sufficient for handling the complexity of problems possible with today's hardware. We need to find a paradigm of software development that can handle the added complexity. Very recently—in 1985—menu-driven systems were the norm. Today, a software application must have a graphical user interface if it is to be marketable. Within the next few years, the consumer will demand multimedia applications that talk to them, listen to them, and display moving video across the screen. Why is the object-oriented paradigm generating so much interest as a method for handling these more complex applications?

One of the biggest reasons for moving to the object-oriented paradigm for developing complex applications is that it allows designers more closely to model the real world. What do we find in our day-to-day lives that, I am sure everyone agrees, can be very complex? We find many machines, which interact with each other in a very decentralized fashion. There is no central control mechanism to which everyone reports, gets orders, fulfills them, and returns for more work. Structured methods are built on the idea of centralized control. The strength of a decentralized architecture is the fact that any one problem will affect one area of the application, which, in a good design, will be loosely coupled to the other areas of the application. This limits the impact of change on our system should there be a problem with one application area, or should we wish to extend the same. If decentralization allows the real world, with all of its complexities, to operate, shouldn't we attempt to handle complex software problems in the same way?

The newcomer to object technology will face suggestions such as "Before you can truly be an object-oriented developer, you will have to undergo a **paradigm shift**." While this sounds a bit dramatic, there is a kernel of truth to the notion of a paradigm shift. The software developer needs to think in a decentralized fashion, rather than follow the typical centralized control of the structural approach. Since successful real-world entities interact in a decentralized manner, I argue that there is as much an *unlearning curve* as a learning curve. You are unlearning the centralized control on which you have learned to rely in the action-oriented model of software development.

Regardless of where you stand on the revolution/evolution argument of object-oriented programming, the first annoyance you will encounter in learning the object-oriented paradigm is the proliferation of buzzwords that permeates the field. For example, a fairly straightforward concept that we will discuss in this book is called *polymorphism*, which is a simple concept hidden behind a Greek root word. Add to this synonyms such as *dynamic binding* and *runtime-type discrimination*, and modifying adjectives such as *pure* polymorphism and *true* polymorphism, and one can easily get caught up in a web of confusion. The buzzword problem is common in young fields. It takes a considerable amount of time for a technology to mature to the point where it has captured its concepts in a standard vocabulary. The problem is compounded in the object-oriented field in that many different subfields within computer science are approaching the object paradigm with their own vocabulary. While one group may be perfectly happy talking about containment and inheritance relationships, another group may already be calling these concepts has-a and a-kind-of relationships (respectively). I suspect that this problem will stay with us for the near future but will become a nonissue as the field matures. In the interim, I will attempt to avoid the use of synonyms in this book unless they are truly necessary to emphasize a particular point to a user.

1.2 Accidental Versus Essential Complexity à la Frederick Brooks

Frederick Brooks published a very interesting article in the October 1987 issue of *IEEE Computer*, titled "Conceptual Essence of Software Engineering or There Is No Silver Bullet" [1]. Frederick Brooks is the author of *The Mythical Man-Month* [2], a must-read text concerning his experiences managing software development projects, including a two-year stint as project manager of the IBM360 project. In his text he discusses what went right in his projects, what went wrong, and why. Anyone involved with producing software, particularly managers, should consider this text required reading. The "No Silver Bullet" article is a follow-up on his insights for software engineering. In it he discusses why we have a software crisis, why there is no magic methodology that will cure all of our problems, and what promising techniques we can use in the future to lessen the crisis.

A fundamental point the article makes is that there are two types of complexity feeding the software crisis; **accidental complexity** and **essential complexity**. Accidental complexity occurs due to a mismatch of paradigms, methodologies, and/or tools in our application. This type of complexity can be eliminated given sufficient resources to build or buy tools that complement one another. Object-oriented programming helps to eliminate accidental complexity by providing a consistent paradigm for software development that encompasses analysis, design, and implementation. This is not to say that object-oriented software projects do not contain accidental complexity. The MIS (management information science) world and other domains are faced with a particular type of accidental complexity. These groups have invested large sums of money in relational database technology and are now moving from the action-oriented to the object-oriented paradigm. Relational database schema languages are not expressive enough to describe in a direct manner the complex relationships between data and behavior in the object-oriented world. The result is that object-oriented designers need to translate these complex relationships down to the simplistic relationships found in relational databases. This translation creates accidental complexity, which most MIS companies are willing to live with considering the alternative of purchasing object-oriented databases that are not nearly as thoroughly tested as their relational counterparts. Even in these cases, the object-oriented paradigm allows for the control of this complexity through the use of *wrappers*, which are abstractional layers that isolate the piece of the application with accidental complexity from the rest of the application. We will talk more about the wrapper mechanism in Chapter 9, which covers physical design issues of the object-oriented paradigm.

The real culprit of the software crisis is essential complexity. Essential complexity revolves around the fact that software is intrinsically complex, and no methodology or tool is going to eliminate this complexity. There are several reasons why software possesses essential complexity:

1. Software applications, for their size, are the most complex entities that humans build.

2. Software is intangible and, for the most part, invisible.

3. Software does not wear out in the traditional sense of machinery with moving parts wearing out. However, software is constantly being used in ways its authors never expected (often uncovering errors), and end users are constantly demanding extensions to their software.

1.3   The Waterfall Model

The old paradigm of treating the software development process as an assembly line is no longer valid. Consider the traditional **waterfall model** of software development (see Figure 1.1). In this model, analysis, design, coding, testing, and maintenance form five discrete steps, each having a well-defined input and a well-defined output. At each transition the outputs become deliverables that allow managers to assess the project's progress. It became apparent rather quickly that software wasn't exactly an

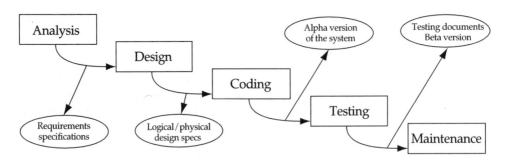

Figure 1.1 The waterfall model of software development.

assembly-line process. Consider the best course of action on an assembly line if one link in the chain is slowing down the rest of the assembly line. For example, what should we do if our assembly line is constructing dolls and the person putting on the arms is slowing down the line? Obviously, we should put another person on the line to help with the arms. This will eliminate the bottleneck. Try this technique with software engineering, and the results are often disastrous. If coding is running late, a project manager cannot simply add a few members to the development team. The current members of the team will see a decrease in productivity as they take the time necessary to train the newcomers. Nevertheless, many companies have continued to use the waterfall model for project development.

The waterfall model may be understandable, traceable, and desirable to managers, since they can easily track progress with a set of well-defined deliverables. However, it does not work well for developers of large systems. In fact, I doubt that developers have ever really used the model. It works great when designing your fifteenth mailing list program. You have already built 14 of them. Now you need only tweak the analysis and design models you already have, implement the new one (which looks an awful lot like the other 14), and test it. I cannot imagine taking the same mailing list developers, giving them a requirements specification for creating a real-time process control system to fold men's suit sleeves with a robot, and watching them use a waterfall process to get a good application. I have too many developer friends who, when asked how they cope with the waterfall model on unfamiliar domains, answer, "Oh, I write specs to keep managers happy and then code the thing the way I want." Of course, having the wrong specifications is worse than having no specification at all. Why not create a process for software development which maps to the real world, including the need to go back and modify design, add new requirements, test new ideas, etc.? Such a process is called the iterative model of software development.

1.4 The Iterative Model

The **iterative model** of software development is basically a waterfall model, except we allow software developers to move in two directions along the flow of the project (see Figure 1.2). If we detect a design flaw while coding part of the application, we can move back to the design phase and correct it. Or if we detect the need for a new system requirement while testing part of the application, we can move back to the analysis phase and repair the problem. This model of software engineering causes many problems in the action-oriented paradigm. Action-oriented software often has many hidden dependencies between data and behavior. Combine that with a centralized control mechanism, and you run into a situation where you touch an existing application and the whole world crumbles into dust. The thought of adding a new requirement or changing the design when 90 percent of the application has been coded is not an option. The object-oriented paradigm corrects this problem by providing its developers with a decentralized form of flow control and the ability to

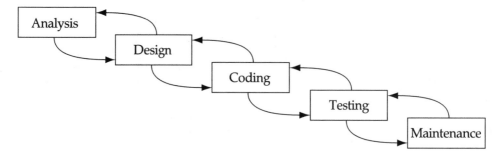

Figure 1.2 The iterative model of software development.

prevent hidden dependencies between data and behavior. For these reasons, the iterative model of software development is becoming the process of choice among object-oriented developers.

The iterative model is not without its problems, however. While I believe that the model accurately reflects the development process from a system architect's point of view, it presents a large problem to the project manager. In short, the model currently lacks a series of well-defined development milestones. This does not imply that a project manager needs to wait until the day before a software system is to be shipped to customers before he or she receives any feedback. It implies that we need new iterative milestones that can provide the necessary feedback without the burden of casting large portions of the application in concrete.

One such deliverable is known as the **software prototype**. The field of prototyping comes from the realization that complex entities in the real world are grown and not built. Many developers are looking to prototyping as a method for controlling the essential complexity of modern-day software. Through prototyping, an application can be grown a layer at time, each layer being thoroughly tested before moving on to the next layer. In this way, design flaws can be detected early enough to facilitate inexpensive corrections, while the working prototype can also serve as a productivity metric. By measuring the amount of functionality in the prototype versus the amount of smoke and mirrors, we can track progress.

1.5   Same- Versus Different-Language Prototyping

The field of prototyping is divided into two main philosophies. These revolve around the argument as to whether a prototype should be written in the same language as the final product (**same-language prototyping**) or a different language (**different-language prototyping**). In same-language prototyping, the advantages seem almost too good to pass up. The development team need only use one language, which implies one set of tools, one set of books, one learning curve, and one set of training. Not surprisingly, same-language prototyping is the more common of the two types.

The final prototype essentially becomes the product. The major disadvantage to this model of development is that during prototyping, the writing of garbage code that lacks any bells/whistles, efficiency, robustness, or extensibility is allowed, if not encouraged. After all, the purpose of prototyping is to test design ideas and requirements' feasibility, not to implement a final product. In this domain, many developers may be tempted to make statements such as, "I know this code lacks any of the above-mentioned features, but this is only the prototype. I'll be back later to rewrite this section of the application." Of course, six months later the project is running behind schedule, "later" never comes, and the garbage code is shipped with the product.

Another issue with same-language prototyping is that language issues may cloud a designer's judgment at a time in system development where software platforms are not supposed to be in the forefront. For example, C++ developers often run into design problems because their language is a **multiparadigm language** as opposed to a **pure object-oriented language** (e.g., SmallTalk). A multiparadigm language allows its users to develop easily in both the object-oriented and action-oriented paradigms. A pure object-oriented language coaxes its users to use the object-oriented paradigm. One disadvantage of using a multiparadigm language for object-oriented development is that the developers can easily fall back into a straight action-oriented development process. If a developer is using a pure language, he or she can guarantee the use of object-oriented development constructs. (Note: Do not equate "object-oriented" with "good." Our pure-language developer might be a lousy object-oriented developer and may thus end up with an unmaintainable system, but it will have been built using object-oriented constructs. It should come as no surprise that the object-oriented paradigm will allow its users to build bad systems. No technology will prevent this from happening.)

In different-language prototyping, we can swap the advantages and disadvantages discussed above. The overhead of two learning curves, set of tools, and so on can be prohibitive. Also, convincing your manager, and yourself, that writing 5,000 lines of code and throwing it into the trash can is a good thing. I will be the first to argue that the code was not interesting; it was the intangible design distilled from the code that was useful. However, it is still a psychological difficulty, especially in a corporate environment that still uses the amount of code written as a measure of productivity. The advantage of never "accidentally" shipping garbage code, coupled with being able to work in a pure object-oriented environment regardless of the application's target language, has been enough to win over many companies to this philosophy of prototyping. A typical language combination is SmallTalk for the prototyping and C++ for the target language of the application.

1.6 Software Reusability

Another method for controlling the essential complexity is to avoid the development of software all together. Instead of building software, why not buy it? Our MIS developers do not build their relational database; they buy one. If you need a spreadsheet, you will not build your own; you will buy it from Lotus, Microsoft, Borland, or some other vendor. The advantage of buying software is that it is cheaper than building the software, especially when maintenance costs are considered. The major disadvantage is that you get whatever functionality you are given. The software you build yourself meets exactly your specifications, while the software you buy probably does not.

Instead of the term "buying software," many people are now referring to "reusing software." The term "software reuse" has become a major buzzword in the object-oriented community. Why all the excitement with reusing software in the object-oriented world? We have always had software reuse. How many developers have used an `if` statement in their favorite programming language? How many C programmers have used `printf`? How many Pascal programmers have used `writeln`? Why the renewed discussion on software reusability? As it turns out, there is an inverse proportion between the size (or granularity) of the code we reuse and its flexibility. `If` statements are very small and very flexible, while Lotus 1-2-3 is a much larger level of reuse, but it has a specific purpose. It is thought that the types of constructs found in the object-oriented paradigm find a happy medium between the granularity of the software and its flexibility. Unfortunately, the level of software reuse achieved in object-oriented applications has been disappointing for many developers. There are several reasons for this disappointment, which we will explore in the relevant sections of this text that deal with the specific object-oriented constructs responsible.

1.7   Corporate Hierarchies of Good Designers

A last topic Brooks mentions in his "No Silver Bullet" article as a method for controlling essential complexity is to create a corporate hierarchy of great software designers, giving them a large pool of junior designers from which they can groom their replacements. The analogy to management is provided in that senior managers sit at the top, grooming their replacements from a broad base of junior managers. This cuts to the heart of the "art versus science" argument among software developers. Is software development something we learn or is it a talent with which we are born? I refuse to get dragged into this argument, but I will draw a potential analogy. If someone put a gun to my head and told me I had to learn to play the piano in one year (and I play no musical instrument), I wouldn't be too worried. If my life depended on it, I have no doubt I can learn to play the piano. If the person then told me that in three years I had to be a great concert pianist, I'd be a dead man!

Regardless of whether great designers are born or built, I think there is a serious flaw in creating a hierarchy of great designers. It is the same flaw that we find in some of corporate management today. From what sources do new ideas generally come? New ideas are traditionally the product of grass-roots movements starting at the lowest levels. By creating hierarchies, we risk stagnation. As evidence of this, I found it both surprising and interesting that much of structured design and stepwise refinement started in academia and was forced on a fairly reluctant industry, while much of object-oriented programming was founded in industry and research laboratories and forced on a reluctant academia (with a healthy set of notable exceptions). I believe the reluctance to offer object-oriented programming to undergraduates in academia stemmed from a hierarchy of people who have preached the merits of action-oriented development. The object-oriented community did not help by saying, "We have been building software wrong for the last 30 years; here is object-oriented programming—it is the right way to do it."

We are now entering an era where software development has become too complex for structured methodologies to handle. The future only promises additional complexity as hardware evolves at its exponential pace. The question is, can we produce a software development methodology that offers a chance to eliminate accidental complexity and, at least, control essential complexity? I believe that the object-oriented paradigm, with its decentralized control flow, bidirectionally related data and behavior, implicit case analysis (i.e., polymorphism), and information-hiding mechanisms, coupled with rapid prototyping and an iterative model of software development, offer the best chance for achieving this goal. The remainder of this text will discuss a myriad of issues about this achievement and how it can be improved and tracked.

Glossary of Terms

Accidental complexity   The complexity in an application resulting from the use of mismatched tools or paradigms of software development.

Different-language prototyping   A philosophy of prototyping in which the language used for the prototype is different from the language used for the application.

Essential complexity   The complexity of an application due to the intrinsic qualities of the software itself.

Multiparadigm language   A programming language that supports both the object-oriented and action-oriented paradigms.

Paradigm shift   The movement toward a new model of programming from an older model.

Programming paradigm   A model of developing software.

Pure object-oriented language   A programming language that supports only the object-oriented paradigm.

Same-language prototyping   A philosophy of prototyping in which the language used for the prototype is the same as the language used for the end product.

Software prototype   A model of an application built to test the feasibility of a software design, implementation, or solution. It often omits features of extensibility, efficiency, and robustness in favor of a speedy implementation.

Software prototyping   The act of producing an example of an end-product application in order to test or prove the feasibility of a particular software design, implementation, or solution.

Iterative model (of software development)   A flexible model of designing software which recognizes that software development is an iterative process that must allow its practitioners the ability to modify existing results in order to fix earlier mistakes.

Waterfall model (of software development)   A rigid model of designing software which focuses on milestones with well-defined deliverables. The development process is one-way, i.e., once a milestone is reached, earlier process steps cannot be revisited.

Chapter 2

Classes and Objects: The Building Blocks of the Object-Oriented Paradigm

2.1 Introduction to Classes and Objects

The object-oriented paradigm uses the concepts of class and object as basic building blocks in the formation of a consistent model for the analysis, design, and implementation of applications. These concepts can best be explained through a real-world example. Given a room full of people, if you were to ask, "How many people in this room could build an alarm clock if given all the pieces?" at best one or two individuals would raise their hand. If the same room of people were asked, "How many people in this room could set an alarm clock to go off at 9 a.m.?" it is a safe bet that most people would raise their hand. Isn't it absurd that so many people claim to be able to use an alarm clock when they can't even build an alarm clock? The immediate response to this question is, "Of course not! *Your* question is absurd!"

There are many things in the real world that we are capable of using without knowing anything about their implementation: refrigerators, cars, photocopy machines, and computers, just to name a few. The reason they are easy to use without knowledge of their implementation is that they are designed to be used via a well-defined public interface. This interface is heavily dependent on, but hides from its users, the implementation of the device. This design strategy is what allows the alarm clock manufacturer the freedom to replace the 60 tiny components currently being used in the construction of alarm clocks for three subcomponents made overseas without any offense to the users of alarm clocks.

Another example of public interface versus implementation can be seen within the domain of automobiles. Very few users of automobiles cared when car manufacturers went from mechanical ignition systems (i.e., distributor, points, condenser, etc.) to

11

electronic ignition systems. Why? The public interface remained the same; only the implementation changed. Imagine, however, that you go to a car dealer to buy a new car and the dealer hands you a key and tells you to test drive the car. You sit in the driver's seat and look for the key hole of the ignition. You check the steering column, the dashboard, and the immediate area to no avail. You ask the dealer how to start the car, and he or she says, "Oh, with this model you use the key to open the trunk and inside the trunk you'll find a red button. Just push the red button and the car will start." Now you are upset because the car maker modified the public interface you have come to associate with automobiles.

One of the basic ideas in the object-oriented paradigm is exactly this philosophy. All implementation constructs in your system should be hidden from their users behind a well-defined, consistent public interface. Users of the construct need to know about the public interface but are never allowed to see its implementation. This allows the implementor to change the implementation whenever he or she desires, so long as the public interface remains the same. As a frequent traveler, I can assure you that the benefits of being able to use alarm clocks without knowledge of their implementation are great. I have stayed in many hotels using a wide assortment of alarm clocks; electric, windup, battery operated, in both digital or analog models. Not once have I sat on a plane worrying that I wouldn't be able to use the alarm clock in my hotel room.

Most readers immediately understood what I meant by the term "alarm clock" even though there probably wasn't an alarm clock nearby. Why is that? You have seen many alarm clocks in your life and realized that all alarm clocks share certain attributes such as a time, an alarm time (both displayed in terms of hours and minutes), and a designation as to whether the alarm is on or off. You also realize that all alarm clocks you have seen allow you to set their time, set their alarm time, and turn the alarm on and off. In effect, you now have a concept, called alarm clock, which captures the notion of data and behavior of all alarm clocks in one tidy package. This concept is known as a **class**. The physical alarm clock you hold in your hand is an **object** (or instance) of the alarm clock class. The relationship between the notion of class and object is called the **instantiation relationship**. An alarm clock object is said to be **instantiated** from the alarm clock class, while the alarm clock class is said to be the generalization of all alarm clock objects you have encountered (see Figure 2.1).

If I were to tell you that my alarm clock jumped off my nightstand, bit me, then chased after the neighbor's cat, you would almost certainly consider me mad. If I told you my dog did the same things, it would sound quite reasonable. This is because the name of a class not only implies a set of attributes, it also denotes the behavior of the entity. This bidirectional relationship between data and behavior is a cornerstone of the object-oriented paradigm.

An object will always have four important facets:

1. its own identity (This might only be its address in memory.);

2. the attributes of its class (usually static) and values for those attributes (usually dynamic);

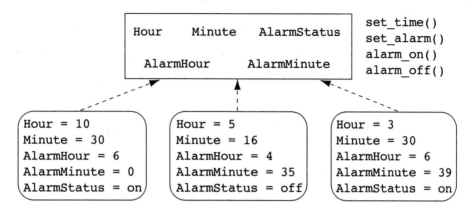

Figure 2.1 An alarm clock and its objects.

3. the behavior of its class (the implementor's view);

4. the published interface of its class (the user's view).

To put this discussion in the perspective of software development, a class can be implemented as a record definition with the important addition of the list of operations allowed to work with that record definition. In a procedural language it is easy to find data dependencies on a given function. Simply examine the implementation of the function and look at the data types of all parameters, return values, and local variable declarations. If, however, you want to find the functional dependencies on a data definition, you are required to examine all of the code, looking for functions dependent on your data. In the object-oriented model, both types of dependencies (data to functions and functions to data) are readily available. Objects are variables of a class data type. Their internal details should be visible only to the list of functions associated with their class. This limiting of access to the internal details of objects is called **information hiding**. It is optional in many object-oriented languages, which leads to our first and most important heuristic.

Heuristic 2.1

All data should be hidden within its class.

The violation of this heuristic effectively throws maintenance out the window. The consistent enforcement of information hiding at the design and implementation level is responsible for a large part of the benefits of the object-oriented paradigm. If data is made public, it becomes difficult to determine which portion of the system's functionality is dependent on that data. In fact, the mapping of data modifications to functionality becomes identical to that in the action-oriented world. We are forced to

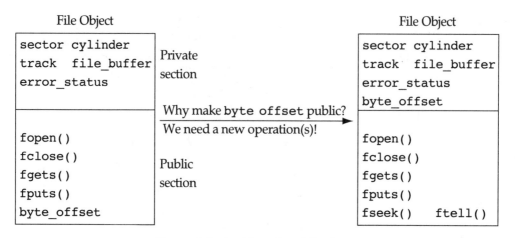

Figure 2.2 Accidental public data.

examine all of the functionality in order to determine which is dependent on the public data.

From time to time, a developer will argue, "I need to make this piece of data public because . . . ." In this case, the developer should ask him or herself, "What is it that I'm trying to do with the data and why doesn't the class perform that operation for me?" In all cases the class is simply missing a necessary operation. Consider the File class in Figure 2.2. The developer accidentally thought that the byte_offset data member should be global to allow for random-access I/O, but what was really needed was an operation(s) to perform that task. (Note to non-C programmers: The functions fseek and ftell are standard C library routines for handling random-access file I/O.) Beware of developers who boldly state, "We can make this piece of data public because it will never change!" One of Murphy's laws of programming will see to it that it is the first piece of data that needs to change.

We can further illustrate the benefits of data hiding by considering an example of a point class whose implementation is in rectangular coordinates (see Figure 2.3). The naive designer might argue that we can make the x- and y-coordinates of the point

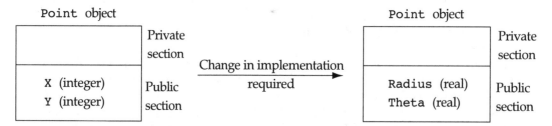

Figure 2.3 The danger of public data.

public because that implementation will never change. Inevitably, some new requirement will force a change to polar coordinates, thereby affecting any user of the class point. Had we made the data hidden, then only the implementors of the class would have needed to modify their code.

2.2   Messages and Methods

Objects should be treated as machines that will carry out operations in their public interface for anyone who makes an appropriate request. Due to the independence of an object toward its user, and the syntax of some of the early languages that implemented object-oriented concepts, the term "sending a message" is used to describe the execution of an object's behavior. When an object is sent a message, it must first decide it if understands the message. Assuming it understands the message, the object maps the message to a function call passing itself as an implied first argument. Deciding the understandability of a message is done at runtime in the case of an interpreted language and at compile time in the case of a compiled language.

The name (or prototype) of an object behavior is called a **message**. Many object-oriented languages support the notion of **overloaded functions** or operators. This construct states that two functions in the system can have the same name as long as their argument types differ (intraclass overloading) or they are attached to different classes (interclass overloading). The alarm clock class might have two `set_time` messages, one that takes two integers and one that takes a character string. This would be an example of intraclass overloading.

```
void AlarmClock::set_time(int hours, int minutes);
void AlarmClock::set_time(String time);
```

Alternately, alarm clocks and watches might both have a `set_time` message that takes two integers. This would be an example of interclass overloading.

```
void AlarmClock::set_time(int hours, int minutes);
void Watch::set_time(int hours, int minutes);
```

It is important to note that a message consists of the function name, argument types, the return type, and the class to which it is attached. This is the primary information that a user of a class needs to know. In some languages and/or systems, additional information may be presented, such as the types of exceptions thrown from the message as well as any relevant concurrency information (e.g., whether the message is synchronous or asynchronous). The implementors of a class are required to know how a message is implemented. The implementation of a message—the code that implements a message—is called a **method**. Once the thread of control is inside a method, all reference to the data members of the object to which the message was sent is through the implied first argument. This implied first argument of the method is called the **self object** in many languages (C++ prefers to call it the "this" object). Finally, the list of messages to which an object can respond is called its **protocol**.

There are two special messages to which classes/objects can respond. The first is an operation that users of a class call in order to construct objects of the class. This is called a **constructor** of the class. A class may have many constructors, each taking a different set of initialization parameters. For example, we may be able to construct alarm clocks by giving the class five integer arguments specifying the hours, minutes, alarm hours, alarm minutes, and alarm status; *or* we may want to pass two strings and an integer argument. Each string would be of the form "hour:minutes," signifying the time and alarm time, respectively, while the integer would specify the alarm status. Some classes have a dozen or more constructor functions.

The second special message to which classes/objects can respond is an operation that cleans up an object prior to its removal from the system. This operation is called a **destructor** of the class. Most object-oriented languages have only one destructor per class since any decisions that need to be made at runtime can be stored as part of the object's state. There is no need to pass additional arguments into the method. We will refer to both constructors and destructors during various topics within this text. Consider them the initialization and clean-up mechanisms of the object-oriented paradigm.

Heuristic 2.2

> **Users of a class must be dependent on its public interface, but a class should not be dependent on its users.**

The rationale behind this heuristic is one of reusability. An alarm clock might be used by a person in a bedroom (see Figure 2.4). The person is obviously dependent on the public interface of the alarm clock. However, the alarm clock should not be dependent on the person. If the alarm clock were dependent on its user, namely the person, then it could not be used to build a timelock safe without attaching a person to the safe. These dependencies are undesirable, since we want to be able to lift the alarm clock out of its domain and deposit it into another domain with no user dependencies. It is best to view the alarm clock as a little machine having no knowledge of its users. It simply performs the behaviors defined in its public interface for whoever sends it a message.

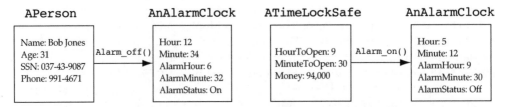

Figure 2.4 The use of alarm clocks.

Heuristic 2.3

Minimize the number of messages in the protocol of a class.

The exact opposite of this heuristic was published some years back. The claim was that if a class implementor can think of some operation for a class, then someone will want to use it in the future. Why not implement it? If you follow this heuristic, then you will love my `LinkedList` class—it has 4,000 operations in its public interface. The problem is that you want to execute a merging of two `LinkedList` objects. You assume the `LinkedList` class must have this operation so you scan its alphabetized list of messages. You cannot find an operation called merge, union, combine, or any other known synonym. Unfortunately, it is an overloaded plus operator (`operator+` in C++). The problem with large public interfaces is that you can never find what you are looking for. This is a serious problem with reusability in general. By keeping the interface minimal, we make the system easier to understand and the components easier to reuse.

Heuristic 2.4

Implement a minimal public interface that all classes understand [e.g., operations such as copy (deep versus shallow), equality testing, pretty printing, parsing from an ASCII description, etc.].

If the classes that a developer designs and implements are to be reused by other developers in other applications, it is often useful to provide a common minimal public interface. This minimal public interface consists of functionality that can be reasonably expected from each and every class. The interface serves as a foundation for learning about the behaviors of classes in a reusable software base. We will discuss specific items for this minimal public interface in more detail in Chapter 9.

Heuristic 2.5

Do not put implementation details such as common-code private functions into the public interface of a class.

This heuristic is designed to reduce the complexity of the class interface for its users. The basic idea is that users of a class do not want to see members of the public interface which they are not supposed to use. These items belong in the private section of the class. A common-code private function is created when two methods of a class have a sequence of code in common. It is usually convenient to encapsulate this common code in its own method. This method is not a new operation; it is simply an implementation detail of two operations of the class. Since it is an imple-

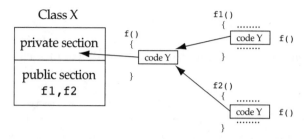

Figure 2.5 Example of a common-code private function.

mentation detail, it should be placed in the private section of the class, not the public section (see Figure 2.5).

In order to get a more real-world feel for common-code private functions, consider the class X to be a linked list, `f1` and `f2` to be the functions `insert` and `remove`, and the common-code private function `f` to be the operation for finding the location in the linked list for an insertion or removal.

Heuristic 2.6

Do not clutter the public interface of a class with items that users of that class are not able to use or are not interested in using.

This heuristic is related to the previous one in that any common-code functions placed in the public interface are only cluttering that interface since users of the class do not want to call such functions. They are not new operations of the class. Some languages, such as C++, allow for the erroneous inclusion of other types of functions in the public interface of a class. For example, it is legal in C++ to place the constructor of an abstract class in the public interface of that class even though the user of the class will receive a syntax error if he or she attempts to use such a constructor. The more general heuristic (2.6) is included to preclude these problems.

2.3   Class Coupling and Cohesion

A number of heuristics deal with coupling and cohesion between/within classes. We strive for tight cohesion within classes and loose coupling between classes. This runs parallel to heuristics in the action-oriented paradigm which attempt to achieve the same goals with functions. Tight cohesion in a function implies that all the code making up the function is closely related. Loose coupling between functions implies that when one function wishes to use another, it should always enter and exit the function from one point. This leads to action-oriented heuristics such as, "A function should be structured such that it has only a single return statement."

In the object-oriented paradigm, we mirror the goals of loose coupling and tight cohesion at the class level. There are five basic forms of coupling between classes: nil coupling, export coupling, overt coupling, covert coupling, and surreptitious coupling. **Nil coupling** is the best, as it implies two classes that have absolutely no dependency on one another. You may eliminate one of the classes without affecting the other class. Of course, it is not possible to have a meaningful application built with only nil coupling. The best we can produce with only nil coupling is a class library, a collection of stand-alone classes that have nothing to do with one another. **Export coupling** states that one class is dependent on the public interface of another class, that is, it uses one or more published operations of another class. **Overt coupling** occurs when one class uses the implementation details of another class with permission. A good example of overt coupling can be found in the "friend" mechanism in C++. A C++ class X can grant friendship to another class Y, thereby granting the methods of class Y access to the private implementation details of class X. **Covert coupling** is the same as overt coupling except no permission is granted to the class Y. If we invent a language that allows a class Y to state, "I am a friend of class X and will take access to its private implementation," then the classes X and Y are covertly coupled. The last form of coupling, surreptitious coupling, states that a class X knows the internal details of class Y through some means. If a class X uses a public data member of class Y, then X is said to be surreptitiously coupled to class Y. This is the most dangerous form of coupling because it creates a strong implicit dependency between the behavior of Y and the implementation of X.

Heuristic 2.7

> **Classes should only exhibit nil or export coupling with other classes, that is, a class should only use operations in the public interface of another class or have nothing to do with that class.**

All other forms of coupling allow a class to give away implementation details to other classes, thereby creating implied dependencies between the implementations of the two classes. These implied dependencies always cause future maintenance problems when one of the classes wishes to change its implementation.

Class cohesion strives to ensure that all of the elements of a class are strongly related. A number of heuristics apply to this property.

Heuristic 2.8

> **A class should capture one and only one key abstraction.**

A **key abstraction** is defined as a main entity within a domain model. Key abstractions often show up as nouns within requirements specifications. Each key abstraction should map to only one class. If it maps to more than one class, then the designer is probably capturing each function as a class. If more than one key abstraction maps to the same class, then the designer is probably creating a centralized system. These classes are often called **vague classes** and need to be split into two or more classes that capture one abstraction each. In Chapter 3 we will explore these two degenerate designs in more detail.

Heuristic 2.9

Keep related data and behavior in one place.

A violation of this heuristic will cause a developer to program by convention. That is, to accomplish some atomic system requirement, he or she will need to affect the state of the system in two or more areas. The two areas are actually of the same key abstraction and therefore should have been captured in the same class. The designer should watch for objects that dig data out of other objects via some "get" operation. That type of activity implies that this heuristic is being violated. Consider a user of a stove class trying to preheat an oven for cooking. The user should only send the stove an `are_you_preheated?()` message. The oven can test if the actual temperature has reached the desired temperature, along with any other constraints concerning the preheating of ovens. A user who decides if the oven is preheated by asking the oven for its actual temperature, its desired temperature, the status of its gas valve, the status of its pilot light, etc., is violating this heuristic. The oven owns the information of temperature and gas cooking apparatus; it should decide if the object is preheated. It is important to note the need for "get" methods (e.g., `get_actualtemp()`, `get_desiredtemp()`, `get_valvestatus()`, etc.) in order to implement the incorrect preheat method.

Heuristic 2.10

Spin off nonrelated information into another class (i.e., noncommunicating behavior).

The developer should look for classes with a subset of methods that operate on a proper subset of the data members. The extreme case is a class where half of the methods work on one half of the data members and the other half of the methods work on the other half of the data members (see Figure 2.6).

For a more real-world example, consider a dictionary class. For small dictionaries the best implementation is a property list (a list of words and their definitions), but for larger dictionaries a hash table is better (i.e., faster). Both dictionary implementations require the ability to add and find words. A design of a dictionary class that exhibits noncommunicating behavior is shown in Figure 2.7.

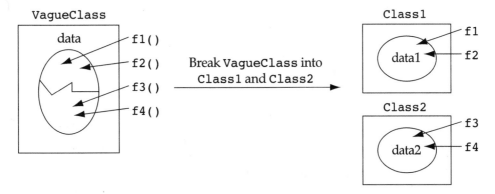

Figure 2.6 A class with noncommunicating behavior.

This solution assumes that the users of the dictionary class will have knowledge of how large the dictionary is going to be; they are required to make the decision between hash table and linked list implementations. In general, displaying implementation details in the class name and allowing users to make such decisions are bad ideas. A better solution to this problem is shown in Chapter 5 since it requires the inheritance relationship. In that solution a single dictionary class hides its representation as an internal detail. The dictionary class decides to change its representation when the size of the dictionary reaches a predetermined threshold.

2.4 Dynamic Semantics

In addition to fixed data and behavioral descriptions, objects have local state (i.e., a snapshot) at runtime of the dynamic values of an object's data descriptions. The collection of all possible states of a class's objects, along with the legal transitions

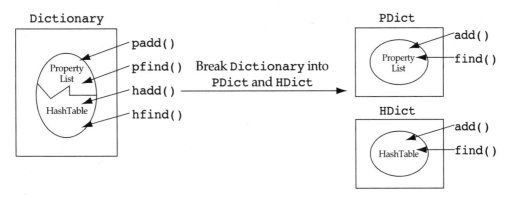

Figure 2.7 Noncommunicating behavior (real-world example)

from one state to another, is called the **dynamic semantics** of the class. Dynamic semantics allow an object to respond differently to the same message sent at two different times in the life of the object. Consider the following abstract example:

```
Method junk for the class X
        if (local state #1) then
            do something
        else if (local state #2) then
            do something different
    End Method
```

The dynamic semantics of objects are an integral part of any object-oriented design. In general, any class with interesting dynamic semantics should have those semantics documented in a state-transition diagram (see Figure 2.8). Classes with interesting dynamic semantics include those classes having a finite number of states, with well-defined transitions from one state to another. The state-transition diagram in Figure 2.9 details the dynamic semantics of the processes in an operating system. It shows that processes can be in a runnable state, the current process state, the blocked state, the sleeping state, or the exited state. In addition, processes can be created only in the runnable state; they can be destroyed only in the exited state; they can exit only if they are in the current process state; and they can become the current process only if they are first a runnable process. This information can be very useful for creating test suites for our class and its objects. Some designers accidentally model dynamic semantics as static semantics. This mistake leads to a proliferation of classes, a serious problem in the object-oriented paradigm. We will explore this problem and its avoidance in Chapter 5 when discussing the inheritance relationship.

2.5   Abstract Classes

In addition to the classes we have discussed so far, there is an important type of abstraction we need to explore. Consider the following questions: Have you ever eaten a fruit? How about an appetizer? What about a dessert? Many people answer yes to all three questions. In the event that you answered yes to any of these questions, consider these questions: What does a fruit taste like? How many calories are in a dessert? How much does an appetizer cost?

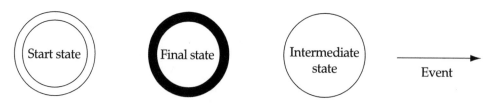

Figure 2.8 State-transition diagram notation.

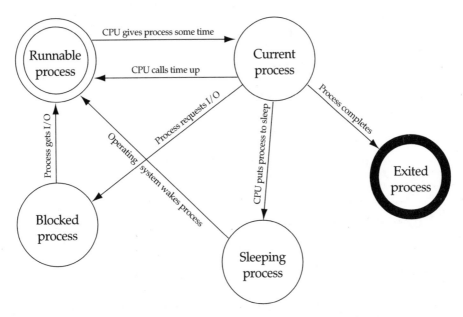

Figure 2.9 State transitions of processes in an operating system.

I claim that nobody has eaten a fruit. Lots of people have eaten apples, bananas, and oranges, but nobody has eaten a .3-pound red fruit. Likewise, a waiter approaches you in a restaurant and asks you what you would like for dinner. You answer, "an appetizer, an entree, and a dessert." If the waiter simply walks away, you've got a problem since you like shrimp cocktail but hate melon (two potential appetizers). We agree that there is no such thing as a fruit, appetizer, or dessert object, but these terms do capture useful information. If I held up an alarm clock and said, "What do you think of my fruit?" you would think I was crazy. If I held up an apple and asked the same question, you would consider me sane. The notion of fruit captures useful information even though you cannot create objects of it. It is, in effect, a class (concept) that does not know how to instantiate objects of its type.

> Classes that do not know how to instantiate objects are called **abstract classes**.
> Classes that do know how to instantiate objects are called **concrete classes**.

Watch out for the commonly used term **abstract data type**, or **ADT**. It is sometimes used as a synonym for class with no distinction between abstract class and concrete class.

An important use of abstract classes in the object-oriented paradigm is to facilitate the construction of inheritance hierarchies, that is, they connote the notion of category headings (see Figure 2.10). We will discuss their usefulness in Chapter 5.

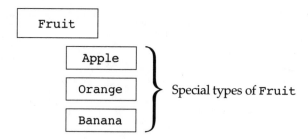

Figure 2.10 Classes capturing category information.

2.6   Roles Versus Classes

Heuristic 2.11

> **Be sure the abstractions that you model are classes and not simply the roles objects play.**

Is Mother or Father a class, or are they the roles that certain Person objects play? The answer depends on the domain that a designer is modeling. If, in the given domain, Mother and Father have different behavior, then they should probably be modeled as classes. If they have the same behavior, then they are different roles that objects of the Person class play. For example, we can view a family as an object of the class Father, an object of the class Mother, and several Child objects. An alternative might be to think of a family as a Person object called father, a Person object called mother, and an array of Person objects called children (see Figure 2.11). The distinction depends on differing behavior. Before creating separate classes, be sure the behavior is truly different and that you do not just have a situation where each role is using a subset of the Person functionality. Remember, there is nothing wrong with an object using a subset of its class's behavior.

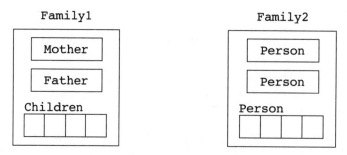

Figure 2.11 Two views of a family.

Some designers test if a member of a public interface cannot be used in a given role. If it cannot be used, this implies the need for a different class. If it is simply not being used, then it is the same class used in multiple roles. For example, if an operation of mother is `go_into_labor()`, then mother is best implemented as a separate class since fathers are incapable of going into labor. However, if our family lives in a sexist society where only mothers are to execute the `change_diaper()` method, then mother is simply a role of the person class. This decision is made because fathers could execute the `change_diaper()` method if necessary. This point gets convoluted in more abstract domains where it is not clear what cannot be executed versus what a designer or domain chooses not to execute.

During the design process, object-oriented designers are clearly drawn to make or not make a particular role into a class. This implies that there is a missing heuristic waiting to be discovered. The preceding paragraph gives a best guess to this heuristic, but I am not yet satisfied that it will apply to all domains.

Glossary of Terms

Abstract class   A class that does not know to instantiate objects of itself.

Class   The encapsulation of data and behavior in a bidirectionally related construct. Correlates to a concept in the real world. Synonyms include abstract data type or ADT.

Concrete class   A class that knows how to instantiate objects of itself.

Constructor   A special operation of a class that is responsible for building/initializing objects of the class.

Destructor   A special operation of a class that is responsible for destroying/cleaning up objects of that class.

Dynamic semantics   The collection of all possible states that an object of a class can have, along with the allowable transitions from one state to another. Often documented through a state-transition diagram.

Information hiding   The ability of a class to hide its implementation details from the users of objects of that class.

Instantiation relationship   The relationship between a class and its object(s). Classes are said to instantiate objects.

Key abstraction   A key abstraction is defined as a main entity within a domain model. Key abstractions often show up as nouns within the domain vocabulary.

Message   The name of an operation defined on a class. In strongly typed languages, a message may include the name, return type, and argument types of the operation (i.e., its prototype).

Method   The implementation of a message.

Object   An example member of a class consisting of its own identity, the behavior of the class, the interface of the class, and a copy of the class's data. Also called an instance of the class.

Overloaded function   The ability to have two functions with the same name so long as their argument types differ (intraclass overloading) or they are attached to different classes (interclass overloading).

Protocol   The list of messages to which a class can respond.

Self object   The reference to the object to which a message is sent, when it is within the method.

Summary of Heuristics

Heuristic 2.1   All data should be hidden within its class.

Heuristic 2.2   Users of a class must be dependent on its public interface, but a class should not be dependent on its users.

Heuristic 2.3   Minimize the number of messages in the protocol of a class.

Heuristic 2.4   Implement a minimal public interface that all classes understand [e.g., operations such as copy (deep versus shallow), equality testing, pretty printing, parsing from an ASCII description, etc.].

Heuristic 2.5   Do not put implementation details such as common-code private functions into the public interface of a class.

Heuristic 2.6   Do not clutter the public interface of a class with things that users of that class are not able to use or are not interested in using.

Heuristic 2.7   Classes should only exhibit nil or export coupling with other classes, that is, a class should only use operations in the public interface of another class or have nothing to do with that class.

Heuristic 2.8   A class should capture one and only one key abstraction.

Heuristic 2.9 Keep related data and behavior in one place.

Heuristic 2.10 Spin off nonrelated information into another class (i.e., noncommunicating behavior).

Heuristic 2.11 Be sure the abstractions that you model are classes and not simply the roles objects play.

Chapter 3

Topologies of Action-Oriented Versus Object-Oriented Applications

3.1 Differences in Application Topologies

It is very helpful to think of object-oriented software development as the next logical step in removing the details of the machine away from software developers. However, a learning curve is associated with this removal of details, due mostly to the different topology that the object-oriented paradigm enforces on the software development process. While action-oriented software development is involved with functional decomposition through a very centralized control mechanism, the object-oriented paradigm focuses more on the decomposition of data with its corresponding functionality in a very decentralized setting. It is this decentralization of software that gives the object-oriented paradigm its ability to control essential complexity. It is also the cause for much of the learning curve. When the object-oriented community talks about the need for designers to undergo a paradigm shift, it is this decentralization to which they refer.

In the following examples we will discuss the worst-case action-oriented topology contrasted with the best-case object-oriented topology. We will then examine what happens when the action-oriented paradigm goes right and when the object-oriented paradigm goes wrong. In any event, many developers believe that the average action-oriented development leans toward the worst-case scenario while the average object-oriented development tends toward the best-case result (especially in the presence of important design heuristics). Consider the symbolic functional decomposition displayed in Figure 3.1.

As the figure shows, an application has been broken down into five functions. As an afterthought, underlying data structures are created as part of the implementation

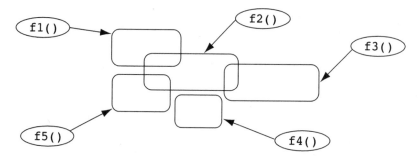

Figure 3.1 A typical action-oriented topology.

of these functions. The developers of these data structures have realized that some functions can share parts of their underlying data (e.g., f1() and f2() are sharing part of the data structure). In the action-oriented world, it is easy to find data dependencies simply by examining the implementation of functions. Given the union of the formal parameter types, local variable types, and any accessed global variable types, the developer knows exactly the data on which code is dependent. However, we have a problem if we wish to know the functional dependencies on a piece of data in the system. In the action-oriented paradigm, there is not an explicit relationship between data and functionality. Consider a change to the data structure marked X in Figure 3.2.

Based on the diagram, we can state that only the functions f1() and f2() will require modification if the data marked X is modified. However, last weekend another developer created f6() without your knowledge (see Figure 3.3). It is also dependent on the data marked X. You make all of your changes to the data X and the functions f1() and f2(). You compile, link, and run the resultant executable, and things do not work properly. You spend the next *n* days trying to find out what went wrong. Anyone who has developed any application of reasonable size has undoubtedly run into this problem. Most action-oriented systems have these undoc-

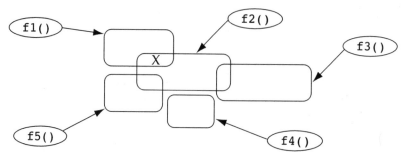

Figure 3.2 A typical action-oriented topology.

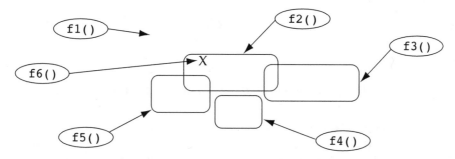

Figure 3.3 A typical action-oriented topology.

umented data/behavior dependencies due to their unidirectional relationship between code and data. Most action-oriented systems have a spaghetti-like underlying
data structure on which all developers hang their code. If version 1 of a system does
not have it, version 2 will be likely to have it (read Frederick Brook's *Mythical Man-
Month* book for an interesting discussion on the dangers of version 2 of a system).

How does object-oriented programming control this complexity? Consider an object-
oriented solution to the above problem (see Figure 3.4). Many developers correctly
claim that the action-oriented paradigm focuses only on the functionality of a system
and typically ignores the data until it is required. They then claim that the object-
oriented paradigm focuses exclusively on the data, ignoring the functionality of the
system until it is required. This is not possible, because the behavior of a system
often drives the decomposition of data. It is preferable to think of the object-oriented
paradigm as keeping data in the front of a developer's mind while keeping functionality in the back of his or her mind. The result of this process is the decomposition
of our system into a collection of decentralized clumps of data with well-defined
public interfaces. The only dependencies of functionality on data are that the operations of the well-defined public interfaces are dependent on their associated data
(i.e., implementation). In Figure 3.4, the classes D1 and D2 use one another to carry

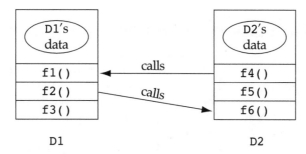

Figure 3.4 A typical object-oriented topology.

out the functionality. The action-oriented picture is not always so bleak, nor the object-oriented picture so rosy.

3.2   When the Action-Oriented Paradigm Goes Right

When first exposed to the action-oriented solution to the preceding problem, many people state that they do not build action-oriented software in this way. They place each data structure of their system in a separate file in which they include any functions in the system relying on that data structure. It is true that this makes the system more maintainable, but what is the file they have created? It is the bidirectional relationship between data and behavior, namely, a class, in object-oriented terminology. What the object-oriented paradigm does is to replace the convention of encapsulating data and behavior using the file system with a design-language-level mechanism. In short, it takes programming by convention carried out by the best programmers and replaces it with a lower-level mechanism. This allows the average programmer to take advantage of good design/implementation techniques without fully understanding the principles behind them. The main problems of programming by convention is that first a given developer has to understand it and second, he or she must stick with it. The latter constraint is the toughest to enforce.

We see that when action-oriented programming goes right, it takes on the attributes of the object-oriented paradigm. This makes sense, since the object-oriented paradigm is really an evolutionary step from the action-oriented paradigm. Does that imply that the object-oriented paradigm is the panacea that will eliminate the software crisis? If it isn't, where does the object-oriented paradigm go wrong? There are two very distinct areas where the object-oriented paradigm can drive design in a dangerous direction. The first is a problem of poorly distributed system intelligence, while the second is the creation of too many classes for the size of the design problem. We refer to these pitfalls as **the god class** problem and **the proliferation of classes** problem. The god class problem manifests itself in two forms, the behavioral form and the data form. The proliferation of classes problem is produced by a number of factors. We will examine each of these problems in the following sections.

3.3   The God Class Problem (Behavioral Form)

The behavioral form of the god class problem is caused by a common error among action-oriented developers in the process of moving to the object-oriented paradigm. These developers attempt to capture the central control mechanism so prevalent in the action-oriented paradigm within their object-oriented design. The result is the creation of a god object that performs most of the work, leaving minor details to a collection of trivial classes. There are a number of heuristics that work together cooperatively toward the avoidance of these classes.

Heuristic 3.1

Distribute system intelligence horizontally as uniformly as possible, that is, the top-level classes in a design should share the work uniformly.

Heuristic 3.2

Do not create god classes/objects in your system. Be very suspicious of a class whose name contains `Driver`, `Manager`, `System`, or `Subsystem`.

Heuristic 3.3

Beware of classes that have many accessor methods defined in their public interface. Having many implies that related data and behavior are not being kept in one place.

Heuristic 3.4

Beware of classes that have too much noncommunicating behavior, that is, methods that operate on a proper subset of the data members of a class. God classes often exhibit much noncommunicating behavior.

Violations of these heuristics imply the creation of a behavioral god object. As Heuristic 3.2 states, watch out for classes with names like `Driver`, `System`, the `BlahBlahManager`, the `BlahBlahSystem`, the `BlahBlahSubsystem`, etc. Another symptom of this problem is the creation of many get and set functions in the public interfaces of your applications' classes. These get and set functions are called **accessor methods**. While it may be reasonable to walk up to an apple and ask for its weight, many such functions imply that some larger class is getting a great deal of data from other classes, performing computations on this data, and then setting the states of many objects to reflect the updated information. These classes are examples of behavioral god classes. Their design also violates the heuristic (heuristic 2.9) stating that related data and behavior should be kept in one place.

To further illustrate this point, I refer to a discussion that ensued on an Internet forum that normally deals with **design patterns**. This particular discussion revolved around the role of accessor methods and started with an entry that lamented the fact that a point class that has `get_x()`, `set_x()`, `get_y()`, and `set_y()` methods is giving away implementation details. Other entries answered that this is true, unfortunate, but necessary. I chimed in that, first of all, by definition methods cannot possibly give away implementation details. Are `get_x()` and `get_y()` simply returning data members, or are they multiplying a radius by the cosine or sine of some angle theta (i.e., is the point stored in rectangular or polar coordinates)? Who knows? The fact that a point can give you its position in rectangular coordinates is no reflection on the actual representation. Now, if you tell me that when the implementation of a point is modified you will modify the gets and sets in the public interface of the class, then I agree that your accessor methods are giving away implementation details. However, it is your convention, and not the accessor methods themselves, that is giving away the implementation details.

Second, accessor methods are not dangerous because they give away implementation details—they are dangerous because they indicate poor encapsulation of related data and behavior. Why is someone getting the *x*- and *y*-values of the point, what are they doing with them, and why isn't the point class doing the work for them? It is clear that the behavior working on the results of `get_x()` and `get_y()` is related to the point class, but it is not attached to that class. Why not? Often, the class whose method is using the point's accessor methods is a god class. It is capturing centralized control and requires data from the mindless point class. There are two reasonable explanations for the need for accessor methods. Either the class performing the gets and sets is implementing a policy between two or more classes, or it is in the interface portion of a system consisting of an object-oriented model and a user interface.

The first reasonable explanation can be best illustrated by looking at an example from a course-scheduling system domain. In this domain we have course objects, course offering objects, and student objects. The course class captures static information about the course objects (e.g., their number, description, duration, minimum and maximum numbers of students, list of prerequisites). The course offering class captures static and dynamic information related to a particular section of a given course (e.g., the course being offered, the room and schedule for the course, the instructor, the list of attendees). The student class captures information such as the student's name, social security number, and the list of courses he or she has taken.

As Figure 3.5 shows, one of the operations on the course offering is `add_student()`. The course offering is given a student and told to add it to the attendee list. The

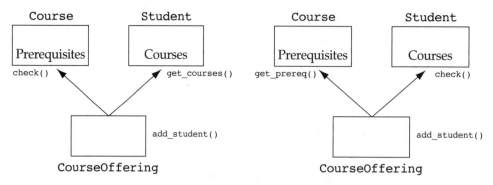

Figure 3.5 Two designs for checking student prerequisites.

course offering would like to check that the student has fulfilled the necessary prerequisites. How does it perform this function? The problem is that the student knows which courses he or she has taken, but the course knows the prerequisites required. We now have a piece of policy information that requires the data of two classes to make a decision. At a minimum, we need to get the information from one class and give it to the other class. The course offering could ask the student for its list of courses and give them to the course, asking, "Is this course list sufficient to fulfill your prerequisites?" Or the course offering could ask the course for its list of prerequisites and give it to the student, asking, "Have you fulfilled the necessary prerequisites?" In either case, we need an accessor method on either the student class or the course class.

It is interesting to note that both of these designs are in direct violation of heuristics implied by Jacobson's Objectory methodology (i.e., an object-oriented analysis/design methodology) [3,4,5]. This methodology argues that **policy** information should not be placed inside of classes involved in the policy decision because it renders them unreusable by binding them to the domain that set the policy. The methodology's solution is either to have the course offering get both lists of courses and perform the check, or to create a `PrerequisiteChecker` class to do that operation. The `PrerequisiteChecker` class is a special type of class called a **controller class** (see Figure 3.6). By definition, such classes only contain behavior. They get their data from outside the class and are used to decouple classes from their policy. While it is true that controller classes do render their host classes more reusable, it is because those classes are mindless. What do a student and course do if we remove all policy information from them? Nothing but get and set operations. The host classes become clumps of mindless data with an interface of gets and sets while the controller classes possess all of the behavior. I view this type of design as the artificial separation of data and behavior into separate classes. The object-oriented paradigm strives to keep both data and behavior in a bidirectionally related package. It is true that there may exist classes possessing lots of meaningful, domain-independent behavior with a small amount of policy behavior that would lock them into one domain. In these

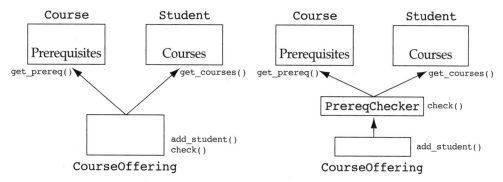

Figure 3.6 Designs involving controller classes.

cases, a controller class is clearly a useful facility; however, I believe these cases to be fairly rare outside of our second rationale for having accessor methods.

The second rationale for using accessor methods revolves around domains whose architecture involves an object-oriented model interacting with a user interface. By definition, user interfaces display the internals of a model, allow a user to update those internals, and put the internals back into the model. The heuristic here is that a model should be independent of its user interface. In order to accomplish this goal, the interface must be allowed to extract and replace details from the model via accessor methods. The use of the accessor methods should be restricted to classes within the interface portion of the code. It is important to note that the model classes of these types of systems rarely have any interesting behavior. Typical of information management-type systems, they revolve around a model of getting a record, chewing it up, and spitting it out in some new form. This is not to trivialize the development of information management systems. I have seen many very complex, difficult systems within these domains, but the complexity is in the area of data modeling and user interface design, not interesting behaviors between classes in the model.

Heuristic 3.5

In applications that consist of an object-oriented model interacting with a user interface, the model should never be dependent on the interface. The interface should be dependent on the model.

For example, consider a course-grading system that maintains many courses each having a number of students, a number of assignments, etc. while each of the assignments has a grade for each student. The user of such a system clearly would like to view/change grades for assignments, add/delete/modify assignments with respect to courses, and add/delete students to/from courses. If we want to follow the heuristic of keeping data and behavior in one place, then it seems clear that we need to have the assignment, course, and student classes display their data on a screen and take values from the user to be used for modifying the states of the respective classes. Of course this would violate Heuristic 3.5, which is concerned with modifying or replacing the interface without affecting the model. In order to follow this heuristic, we need to have classes in the interface portion of the design getting and setting the states of objects in the model. This need for accessor methods is unfortunate, but no less necessary. Although the classes of the model will have accessor methods, the other classes in the model should not use them. That portion of a class's public interface should be reserved solely for the classes in the user interface portion of the design.

The literature is only beginning to reflect the inherent dangers of controller classes in object-oriented design. See the article by Rebecca Wirfs-Brock on the two very different designs for a brewery control system as an example [6].

3.4 Another Example of Poor System Intelligence Distribution

Another example of system intelligence distribution can be drawn from the domain of a forced hot water, oil-fired home heating system as described in Booch's book on object-oriented design [7]. One portion of the requirement specification discusses the contents of each room in the house as consisting of a desired temperature input device, an actual temperature sensor, and an occupancy sensor. A heat flow regulator is responsible for sensing when each room needs heat. If any of the rooms needs heat, the heat flow regulator turns on the furnace, waits for the water to heat up, and then tells the room that heat is available. The method of determining if a room needs heat is to find the difference between the desired and actual temperatures. If there is a person in the room, then heat should be provided as soon as the actual temperature is less than the desired temperature. If there is no person in the room, then the actual temperature is allowed to drop to five degrees less than the desired temperature before heat is supplied.

The first mistake that might be made is to create only the classes `HeatFlow-Regulator`, `DesiredTempDev`, `ActualTempDev`, and `OccupancySensor`. The `HeatFlowRegulator` sends messages to the other three classes in order to determine if the room needs heat (notice that the room class is conspicuously absent from the design in Figure 3.7). The `HeatFlowRegulator` is a god class in this design. It performs most of the work while the three classes with which it shares lexical scope perform relatively little work. This design violates Heuristic 3.1 on distributing system intelligence horizontally.

Due to the real-world domain of the home heating system, many designers immediately consider the room to be a reasonable class. Since each room object contains an object of each sensor, the room can encapsulate the three objects to facilitate the construction of more rooms. The typical error that occurs in this design is that the public interface of room is given operations such as `get_actual_temp()`, `get_desired_temp()`, `is_occupied()`, `set_desired_temp()`, etc. The `HeatFlowRegulator` then asks the room for the actual temperature, the desired temperature, and whether or not someone is in the room. After collecting this information, the `HeatFlowRegulator` computes whether or not a room requires heat.

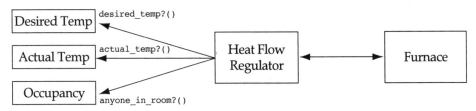

Figure 3.7 Home heating system without encapsulation.

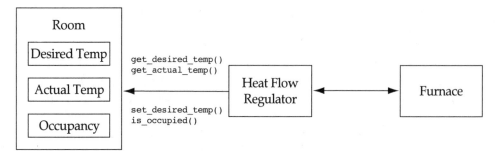

Figure 3.8 Home heating system with encapsulation.

The problem with this design is that the `HeatFlowRegulator` is still a god class in that it performs most of the system's work, and the designer has failed to keep related data with its behavior. As stated earlier in this chapter, whenever a get or set function appears in an object-oriented design, it is important for the designer to ask, "What is it I'm doing with this data and why doesn't the class do it for me?"

The best solution to this particular problem is to let the room class decide when it needs heat (see Figure 3.8). It has all of the necessary data encapsulated within it, so it is the likely candidate for performing this calculation. Either the `HeatFlow-Regulator` asks each room if it requires heat (see Figure 3.9) or, as some designers prefer, the room objects demand heat from the `HeatFlowRegulator`. We will later see that logical design does not care one way or the other. Physical design, for example, choice of software/hardware platform or efficiency, will most likely dictate one message direction over the other.

A last tongue-in-cheek heuristic for finding god classes in your system is to write down all of the classes on a sheet of paper. Ask each developer which $n - 1$ of the n classes he or she would be willing to write. If everyone avoids one class, then that is the god class you are looking for. For example, of the five classes in the first design of the home heating system, everyone will avoid the `HeatFlowRegulator` since it

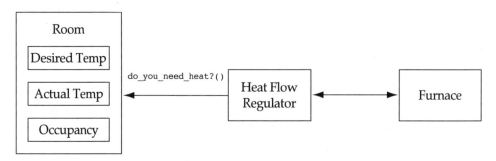

Figure 3.9 Home heating system with distributed intelligence.

is the most complicated. It is important to note that a workaholic in your group will spoil the results of this test.

Heuristic 3.6

Model the real world whenever possible. (This heuristic is often violated for reasons of system intelligence distribution, avoidance of god classes, and the keeping of related data and behavior in one place.)

Heuristic 3.6 is motivated by the desire for a maintenance person (i.e., the author of the software three months later when he or she cannot remember what they did or why!) to be able to directly relate to the architecture of the system. When the home heating system problem is used in a design course as an exercise, many groups have a heated discussion concerning the room. Some members of the groups argue that rooms do not do anything in the real world and, therefore, should not be a class. Other members argue that a room class is necessary for encapsulation and intelligence distribution. I tend to side with the latter. The modeling of the real world is desirable, but not nearly as important as the other heuristics. Some designers reconcile this problem by renaming the room class to something more benign, such as roomcontroller, thermostat, or roommechanism. In a design critique it is important that individuals realize when they are arguing about some interesting and important design decision and when they are only arguing about the name of a class. I do not mind arguing six hours over the name of a class so long as I understand that is the sole ramification of the argument. Many hours of design critique are wasted by confusion between design issues and other matters such as class names.

3.5   The God Class Problem (Data Form)

The second form of the god class problem occurs very often when a designer is migrating a legacy system to a new object-oriented design. There is an enormous interest in finding a good process for this migration, since it is rare that a software developer gets to design a new system from the beginning. The legacy system is often fraught with many existing problems which need to be addressed. While examining a development process for migrating legacy systems is outside the scope of this text, it is within our interest to examine one of the problems such a process must address.

The high-level design shown in Figure 3.10 was taken from a legacy system that dealt with telephone call processing. The topology of this system consisted of a large global data structure, which I will call the `CallProcessingBlock`, and a number of call processing functions. The data structure contained all of the data that the many call processing functions need in order to fulfill their requirements. Each of the call processing functions used the data it needed directly from the global data

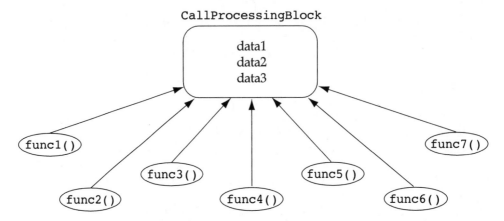

Figure 3.10 A legacy call processing system.

structure. (The names of the individual data members and call processing functions is left abstract so as not to convolute the example.)

When the design team decided to migrate this system, they first encapsulated the `CallProcessingBlock` in a class and added accessor methods for each of the data members to the public interface of this new class (see Figure 3.11). The functions were then grouped together into controller classes. The controller classes would then use the accessor methods of the `CallProcessing` class to collect the necessary data. While such a system is certainly an improved migration from the original, it is not a good object-oriented design. The `CallProcessing` class is a god class that holds

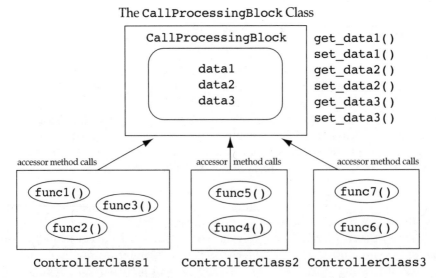

Figure 3.11 A poor migration for the call processing system.

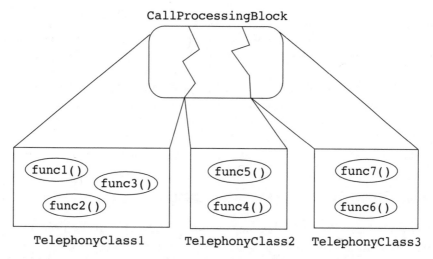

Figure 3.12 A better migration for the call processing system.

all of the data, while the controller classes violate the rule of keeping data and its behavior together. I would argue that controller classes are popular because it makes it seemingly easy to migrate legacy systems which possess this topology. The correct migration is to split the `CallProcessingBlock` into pieces based on collections of the call processing functions (see Figure 3.12). The collections of call processing functions and their portion of the data are grouped together based on the subset of the `CallProcessingBlock` data used. This leads to an object-oriented design that possesses the qualities of decentralization and bidirectionally related data and behavior.

3.6   The Proliferation of Classes Problem

We will see many heuristics in this book discussing trade-offs and improvements of one design over another. Many of these are small tweakings on a design and are local in nature. A single violation rarely causes major ramifications on the entire application. We will examine a group of 10 heuristics that focus on a particularly nasty pitfall in the design of object-oriented software. This pitfall is known as the proliferation of classes problem. At a conference some years back, a speaker brought out the interesting point that there is no way to get spaghetti code in an object-oriented system—you get ravioli code instead. Consider the solution to our fictitious problem consisting of `f1()` through `f5()`. In our object-oriented solution, we developed a design consisting of `D1` and `D2`. Imagine the problems if our solution to this tiny problem had 18 classes, or 180 classes. This is the notion of class proliferation. Our extensibility problem is no longer, "I need to change this data, now whom do I need to tell . . . ? OOPS!" In the object-oriented paradigm, the problem has been transformed into, "I want to add this feature to my system, which 54 classes of the

16,786 classes in my system need to be modified . . . . ? OOPS!" You have the same maintenance problem; it just manifests itself differently. Of the 10 known places that proliferation occurs, three are intuitively obvious at design time because they lead to an exponential explosion in the number of classes. We will examine all 10 within the area of the paradigm that they occur (many occur through the inheritance relationship). For those wishing to look ahead, the heuristics in question are 2.11, 3.7, 3.8, 3.9, 3.10, 4.9, 5.14, 5.15, 5.16, 5.18. Three of these heuristics are discussed below.

Heuristic 3.7

Eliminate irrelevant classes from your design.

An irrelevant class is one that has no meaningful behavior in the domain of your system. These are usually detected by looking for classes that have no operations besides set, get, and print type functions. The reason `sets`, `gets`, and `prints` are not counted as meaningful behavior is that all too often they operate solely on the descriptive attributes of a system. The fact that a car will give you its color field is generally not interesting behavior in the domain of a system. There are notable exceptions to using get and set operations in the detection of irrelevant classes. Sensors and transducers often have meaningful get and set operations, namely, getting is the behavior of sensors and setting is the behavior of transducers. When we discuss eliminating irrelevant classes, we do not necessarily remove the information from our design. Typically, the class is demoted to an attribute.

Heuristic 3.8

Eliminate classes that are outside the system.

This heuristic is really a special case of the previous heuristic. If a class is outside the system, it is irrelevant with respect to the given domain. Classes outside the system are not always easy to detect. During successive iterations of design, it eventually becomes clear that some classes do not require any methods to be written for them. These are classes that are outside of the system. The hallmark of such classes is an abstraction that sends messages into the system domain but does not receive message sends from other classes in the domain. I have seen this to be a problem in three case studies, including the following:

> A company was building a product registration system for processing consumer-purchased equipment such as blenders, toasters, televisions, etc. A question arose as to whether the blender should be a class. One group argued that it should be since blenders do have methods like whip, chop, puree, liquify, etc. If blender is a class, what about the person who fills out the registration card, the registration card itself, and the information on the registration card? While all of these abstractions have behavior, only the data on the card has behavior in this domain. Our

system should not care if someone filled out the card or if a squirrel arrived carrying it in his mouth. The only interest in the domain of the system is that there exists product registration information, and we somehow received it. It is important to note that although the blender is not a class in this domain, it will most likely appear as the value of an attribute in the product registration information that will be modeled as a card.

It is important not to laugh at any pitfall discussed in these designs, lest you tempt the fates and bring the same problem to your design.

Another company I dealt with listened to my discussion of the pitfall that the first company ran into, and they stated they would never fall into such a design flaw. The second company collected large quantities of automobile engine test data from specialized hardware including various dynamometers. They were designing a report generation system where a user would describe the report layout and the number of test points he or she wanted to see. In their initial design, they began discussing operations on the dynamometer. Dynamometers clearly have a well-defined public interface; unfortunately, it is not used in their domain. Like the first company, they chose to model a class outside their system. The collected data was interesting in their domain and should be modeled as a class, but the method of collection is uninteresting to report generators. They do not care if a squirrel is typing in data behind the computer or if fancy million-dollar machines are collecting it. They simply report what they have. If a process control system was being designed to run the dynamometer, then clearly the dynamometer should be modeled as a class. Watch out for the seduction of physical devices that are outside the system. Of all the irrelevant classes, they are the most frequently modeled.

The third case of classes outside the system occurred in the design of the automatic teller machine. This has become somewhat of a standard problem for design textbooks to model. If we consider the top-level classes one needs to model in order to facilitate a user withdrawing and depositing money, we might consider the ATM itself, the bank it will need to talk to, and the customer. Clearly, there are some other classes like deposit slots, keypads, display screens, etc. For now let us assume they are contained somewhere in the top-level classes (e.g., the ATM). If you claim the customer is a class, then a good question to ask is, "What does the customer do in your system?" A typical answer might be, "The customer sends a message to the ATM asking the ATM to withdraw $100." It turns out that sending messages is not meaningful behavior in a given domain. You must receive messages and, therefore, define messages/methods in order to be meaningful. What message does the ATM send to the customer? If the answer is none, then the customer is a class outside the system and should not be modeled. If an appropriate answer can be found, then by all means model the customer.

Heuristic 3.9

Do not turn an operation into a class. Be suspicious of any class whose name is a verb or is derived from a verb, especially those that have only

one piece of meaningful behavior (i.e., do not count **sets**, **gets**, and **prints**). Ask if that piece of meaningful behavior needs to be migrated to some existing or undiscovered class.

Figure 3.13 Classes which should be operations.

Violations of this heuristic are a leading cause of proliferation of classes. Be on the lookout for any class that has only one piece of meaningful behavior. Ask, "Should this class be an operation on one of my other classes, or is it really capturing some key abstraction?" Watch out for designers who request, "I need a class that does . . . ." The word "does" sounds too much like a behavior, not a request for an abstraction. Is it a violation of this heuristic or a slip of the language? It is certainly worth examining. Classes whose names are verbs, or are derived from verbs, are especially suspect. Newcomers to the object-oriented paradigm are especially prone to violations of this heuristic. These developers are accustomed to functions being the entity of decomposition and often capture each method in a single class. They have not yet made the leap to the larger granularity of abstractions found in the object-oriented paradigm.

A telecommunications project with which I was recently involved introduced the two classes shown in Figure 3.13 to the object-oriented design of their system. These two classes are really modeling operations on a class that is yet to be discovered. If we were to look at the public interfaces of these two classes, we would very likely find a single method. This method is the implementation of one piece of functionality that the undiscovered class requires. The better design is shown in Figure 3.14.

It is important to note that not all classes whose names are verbs need to be eliminated. In the context of a design course, some students who are asked to design an ATM system from a set of requirement specifications often produce the partial design contained in Figure 3.15.

The **deposit**, **withdraw**, and **balance** classes are good candidates for operations that have been accidentally turned into classes. The names of these classes are verbs,

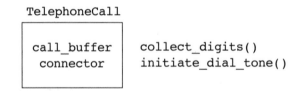

Figure 3.14 A better design for telephone services.

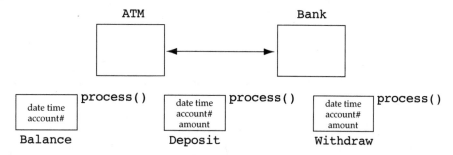

Figure 3.15 Partial ATM solution.

and they have only one meaningful operation in their public interface. Many students criticize the design and state that the ATM system should be designed as in Figure 3.16.

If we only consider logical design information, then the second design is more desirable. Why have three additional classes with only one operation each when we can simply give the bank class three additional methods? A problem with the second design is encountered when a requirement is added stating that the bank is responsible for printing monthly statements for its customers. The bank customers do not want to simply see their balance for the month; they want an itemized list of their transactions. This implies that deposits, withdrawals, and balance requests are persistent, that is, they must be stored for future use by the system. The fact that these entities are persistent implies that they should be modeled by a class. For that reason we defer back to the first design and model withdrawal, deposit, and balance as classes.

3.7   The Role of Agent Classes

Another interesting point to consider can be summarized in the following riddle posed at a conference several years ago by Meiler Page-Jones (OOPSLA '87):

> On an object-oriented farm there is an object-oriented cow with some object-oriented milk. Should the object-oriented cow send the object-oriented milk the un-

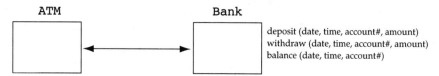

Figure 3.16 A better partial ATM solution?

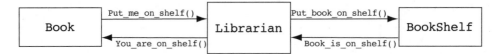

Figure 3.17 Object-oriented librarian: example agent class.

cow yourself message, or should the object-oriented milk send the object-oriented cow the unmilk yourself message?

While this sounds a bit silly, it brings up an interesting point. One group in a design course that I taught laughed at this riddle, but then spent 30 minutes during a design exercise arguing over the design of a library system. They could not decide if a book should send the bookshelf the `book_yourself` message or if a bookshelf should send the book the `shelf_yourself` message. The problem in both these examples is the same. There is a key element missing, namely, the object-oriented farmer and the object-oriented librarian. Are these abstractions classes?

During analysis it is common to model the real world whenever possible. The design process then modifies this real-world model in favor of heuristics like distributing system intelligence and avoiding god classes. The object-oriented farmer and librarian are examples of special classes called **agents**. Agents are often modeled as classes during analysis in a form such as that shown in Figure 3.17.

At design time we need to ask ourselves, "Of what use is the object-oriented librarian?" It is often the case that agent classes are irrelevant classes. The librarian class simply accepts messages from book and bookshelf and resends them to the desired target. Why not eliminate the librarian and reduce the number of classes and collaborations in our design (see Figure 3.18)?

In many cases this is exactly what we want to do. But what if the librarian has other useful behavior like checking the due data of books, sending out library fine notices, ordering new books? We could add this additional functionality to the `Book` and `BookShelf`; however, it often occurs that these two classes become increasingly complex. Based on the need for distribution of system intelligence, we use the agent class

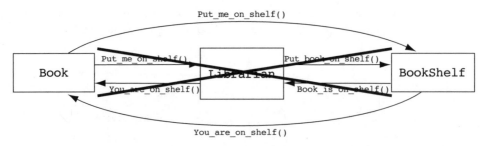

Figure 3.18 Eliminating irrelevant agents.

to offload some of the work. There is nothing wrong with leaving agent classes in a design if they capture a useful abstraction. Keeping irrelevant agents in a system overly complicates the design, with no benefit to the designer.

During a critique of the design in Figure 3.18, it is common for two designers to get into a long discussion as to whether the Book or the BookShelf should initiate the message. These arguments are often unsolvable since the logical design of the system often sees zero trade-off between the two choices. Physical design (i.e., considerations of efficiency with regard to software and hardware platforms) often shows one solution to be more expensive than the other. If that is not the case, then designers can simply flip a coin to settle the discussion.

Another common example of useless agents invading a system can be seen in the domain of an automatic teller machine. Many designers first view the ATM domain as having three high-level classes: the Bank, the Network, and the ATM itself. The Network is placed in the design since it is a good candidate for a key abstraction of the system. The designer later realizes that the Network does nothing except transfer messages between the ATM and the Bank. For this reason, the Network is often thrown out as a useless agent. The Bank and ATM send messages directly between each other. Much later in low-level design, the system designer realizes that methods sent by the ATM to the Bank need the use of some external network. Not wishing to be dependent on one type of network, the system designer creates a network wrapper class to shield the classes of the domain model (i.e., the key abstractions) from the physical network being used by the system. This network wrapper class is considered an implementation class. It is not needed to model the system. It was created solely for physical design reasons, flexibility in this case. Object-oriented designers often state that implementation-level classes should be kept completely separate from domain model classes to avoid confusion.

Heuristic 3.10

Agent classes are often placed in the analysis model of an application. During design time, many agents are found to be irrelevant and should be removed.

This heuristic is in violation of Jacobson's methodology, which argues that the library agent class is decoupling books from bookshelves and should therefore be kept in the system. It is fair to state that we have made the bookshelf class less reusable, and more bound to one domain, because the policy of placing books on bookshelves in a library has been encoded into the bookshelf class. If I want to reuse the bookshelf in my living room, I will have a problem because I do not want my books sorted via the Dewey decimal system. I want to sort my books as computer books on the first shelf, science fiction on the second, cookbooks and gardening books on the third shelf, and everything else on the fourth shelf. However, what will a bookshelf do if I place the policy of placing books on the shelf in a librarian? It simply has gets and sets, it is reusable because it is a mindless class, no more interesting than a linked list. The librarian has only behavior, no data. The bookshelf has only data, no meaningful behavior. We have separated data and behavior under the guise of software reuse. While the thought of books putting themselves on shelves seems very disturbing, the disturbance is due to the real-world nature of the domain. When we examine the design of the automatic teller machine in Chapter 11, we will see agent classes no less interesting than the librarian tossed out of the system with no such disturbance. This will be due to the domain being more abstract.

3.8   Examining the Use of Separate Entity and Controller Classes

The object-oriented community needs to examine carefully the roles of controller and agent classes in object-oriented design. While it is easier to migrate legacy systems using a technique of separating the entity classes (model) from their behavior (controller), in practice it leads to the artificial separation of data and behavior. This separation should be considered a violation of a fundamental principle of the object-oriented paradigm, namely, data and behavior are bidirectionally related as a conceptual block. The artificial separation is often encouraged by the fact that in business modeling, it often occurs that different applications will use the same data model differently. This often leads the designer to create entity classes to model the data and separate controller classes which work with the data model in different ways.

Consider the design of a media-based framework for a company with which I have recently worked. This company has many applications that work on an abstraction known in the media industry as a composition. The composition class contains a number of different items which together describe an edited work of film, or more generally, media. The data model can be easily reused in all of the applications. The problem is that it performs different functionality from one application to another. For example, when used by the editing application, it needs to support the functionality X, Y, Z; but when used by the playing application, it needs to support the functionality P, Q, R. As Figure 3.19 shows, the design of such a system via controller classes would argue for entity classes to support the composition class and its pieces and hierarchies, and two controller classes for handling the different functionality.

The problem with this design is that I can no longer examine a piece of data and ask, "Who is dependent on you?" I will now need to examine each of the controller classes to determine dependencies. How does this differ from having a behaviorless database schema and a collection of applications that possess all of the behavior? I argue that the popularity of controller classes is directly related to their semantic proximity to the action-oriented paradigm. In fact, they have some of the same problems as that paradigm, such as undefined data/behavior dependencies.

A better design is to state that the composition class has six behaviors in its public interface (i.e., P, Q, R, X, Y, and Z); see Figure 3.20. The fact that a given application

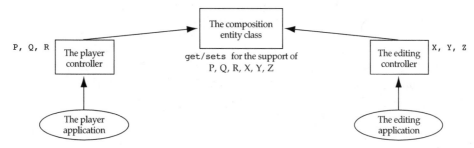

Figure 3.19 Reuse of entity classes via controller classes.

uses only half the public interface is irrelevant. There is no heuristic stating that a user of class needs use its entire public interface. I have a linked list class with 30 operations. It is not an error if you only want to use insert, delete, and traverse. What is relevant is that each application does not want to pay for the object code of operations it does not use. This is not a design issue (logical design) but a source-code maintenance issue (physical design). Do not throw away a better logical design for a simple physical design issue.

A more subjective reason for avoiding the entity/controller form of design is that humans do not like controllers in the real world. When is the last time you misplaced the controller for your refrigerator, stove, car, or overhead projector? We cannot misplace them, because data and behavior are encapsulated into the same package. Of course, there are real-world examples that do separate the controller from the data. I argue that all of these cases are not because of human preference but because of cost. The classic example is the videocassette recorder and its prerecorded tapes. We buy a VCR player (the controller) and then purchase or rent the VCR tapes (the entities) separately. I believe that this is due to the fact that the controller is extremely expensive (a physical design issue) and not by choice. Humans would prefer that each tape come with its own player, thereby encapsulating the controller and entity information in one package. At times when traveling, I would like to rent a movie but cannot because I left my controller at home.

In a recent lecture, the VCR explanation caused one skeptic to shout that the thought of each VCR tape having its own controller was ridiculous. Another student re-

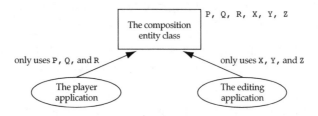

Figure 3.20 A better design for the composition class.

sponded that it was almost as ridiculous as the thought of people wanting a camera (a controller) and its film (the entity) in one neat little package. (Today the demand for disposable cameras is rising as the price decreases.) Several hours after the controller class discussion, the lightbulb of the overhead project burnt out and we needed to wait 15 minutes for a replacement. This led one of the students to comment that I would probably prefer that each overhead have its own behavior rather than relying on an external controller. I would have to agree!

Glossary of Terms

Accessor methods   Methods that perform get and set operations on the data members of a class.

Agent classes   Classes whose sole purpose is to decouple two or more additional classes. Characterized by delegating its methods to messages on other classes.

Controller classes   Agent classes that have behavior only and no data. Any necessary data is extracted via accessor methods on other classes.

Design patterns   Generic solutions to known problems that traverse multiple domains, often completely domain-independent.

Logical object-oriented design   The facet of object-oriented design that includes finding classes, their public interfaces, and their relationships.

Physical object-oriented design   The facet of object-oriented design that includes the effect of hardware and software platforms on the logical design of the system, efficiency, portability, and future requirements' needs.

Policy   The portion of an application that discusses domain-dependent computations based on the information from one or more class(es).

Summary of Heuristics

Heuristic 3.1   Distribute system intelligence horizontally as uniformly as possible, that is, the top-level classes in a design should share the work uniformly.

Heuristic 3.2   Do not create god classes/objects in your system. Be very suspicious of a class whose name contains `Driver`, `Manager`, `System`, or `Subsystem`.

Heuristic 3.3   Beware of classes that have many accessor methods defined in their public interface. Having many implies that related data and behavior are not being kept in one place.

Heuristic 3.4   Beware of classes that have too much noncommunicating behavior, that is, methods that operate on a proper subset of the data members of a class. God classes often exhibit a great deal of noncommunicating behavior.

Heuristic 3.5   In applications that consist of an object-oriented model interacting with a user interface, the model should never be dependent on the interface. The interface should be dependent on the model.

Heuristic 3.6   Model the real world whenever possible. (This heuristic is often violated for reasons of system intelligence distribution, avoidance of god classes, and the keeping of related data and behavior in one place.)

Heuristic 3.7   Eliminate irrelevant classes from your design.

Heuristic 3.8   Eliminate classes that are outside the system.

Heuristic 3.9   Do not turn an operation into a class. Be suspicious of any class whose name is a verb or is derived from a verb, especially those that have only one piece of meaningful behavior (i.e., do not count `sets`, `gets`, and `prints`). Ask if that piece of meaningful behavior needs to be migrated to some existing or undiscovered class.

Heuristic 3.10   Agent classes are often placed in the analysis model of an application. During design time, many agents are found to be irrelevant and should be removed.

Chapter 4

The Relationships Between Classes and Objects

4.1 Introduction to Class and Object Relationships

An object-oriented design requires that the developer first find some of the key abstractions of the system along with their well-defined public interfaces. The second step consists of describing the relationships between these key abstractions. In the object-oriented paradigm, we discuss these relationships as falling into one of four categories:

- the uses relationship (object-based);
- the containment relationship (object-based);
- the inheritance relationship (class-based);
- the association relationship (object-based).

The term "object-based versus class-based" does not describe the method in which a relationship is defined, namely, with objects or with classes (respectively). It denotes whether or not all objects of a class have to obey the relationship. We will see that this is not the case with uses, containment, or association, but it is true for inheritance. An object-oriented design is made up of the classes, their protocols, and a description of the four relationships just listed (minimally). Each relationship has its own characteristics and can be dangerous when used in the wrong area of design. With this in consideration, each has its own heuristics governing its correct use.

4.2 The Uses Relationship

The first relationship in our list, as well as the first relationship that most developers come across, is called the **uses relationship**. Simply stated, if an object of one class

53

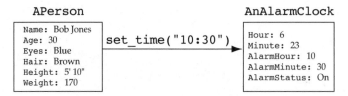

Figure 4.1 A person using an alarm clock.

sends a message to an object of another class, the first class is said to have a uses relationship with the second class. For example, consider Figure 4.1, in which an object of class `Person` is sending a message to an object of class `AlarmClock` to set its time to 10:30. The `Person` class is said to use the `AlarmClock` class. Does this imply that all objects of class `Person` send messages to objects of class `AlarmClock`? Of course not. This is why we claim that the uses relationship is object-based, that is, not all objects of the class are required to obey the relationship.

4.3   Six Different Ways to Implement the Uses Relationship

Let us consider how the uses relationship is implemented. If an object wants to send a message to another object, then the first object must know the name of the second object. How can it know its name? Consider the automatic teller machine. Somewhere in the process of a customer withdrawing money, the ATM requires the cash dispenser to hand the customer his or her money. This implies that the ATM is not capable of carrying out all of the work necessary to withdraw money. It uses a `CashDispenser` object to perform some of the work (along with a lot of other objects as well: `Bank`, `CardReader`, `DisplayScreen`, `Keypad`, etc.); see Figure 4.2.

How does the ATM know the name of the `CashDispenser` object? In this case we will find that the actual relationship is one of containment, not uses. A jump of intuition is necessary to determine that ATMs contain as one of their data members an object of class `CashDispenser`. It knows the name of this data member implicitly; therefore, it can send it a message with no further work. We will see that many uses relationships are refined into containment relationships. Likewise, all containment relationships are first and foremost uses relationships. Many object-oriented gurus claim that finding uses relationships is an analysis activity while refining uses

Figure 4.2 ATM using a cash dispenser for a user.

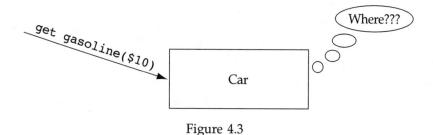

Figure 4.3

into containment constitutes a design activity; others disagree. Since we follow an iterative model of software development in the object-oriented paradigm, the line between analysis and design is blurred, leaving arguments along these lines solely for academic purposes.

If a uses relationship is not a containment relationship, then how does the first object (the sender) know the name of the second object (the receiver)? Consider the relationship between a car and a gas station. It doesn't make sense to say that a car contains a gas station; however, cars do ask gas stations to give them gasoline. How does the car know the name of the gas station (see Figure 4.3)? There are five implementations of the uses relationship aside from using a containment relationship.

The number one implementation of the uses relationship (aside from uses via containment) is that the car is given the name of the gas station as a formal parameter of the message (see Figure 4.4). Consider a higher-level object sending the car the `get_gasoline()` message passing the name of a gas station as an argument—"Car get gasoline at the gas station G, which exists at location . . . ."

Another possibility is that the car asks a third-party class (a map) for the name of an appropriate gas station (see Figure 4.5). Of course, this only postpones our problem. How do we know the name of the map object?

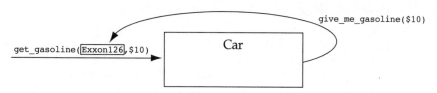

Figure 4.4 Car receiving gas station as a parameter.

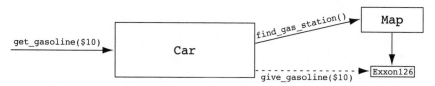

Figure 4.5 Car receiving gas station from a third-party class.

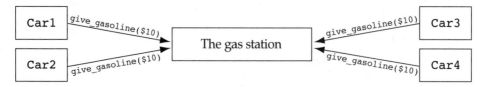

Figure 4.6 All cars use a global gas station.

A third possibility is that all cars in the world go to one global gas station and we all know its name by convention (see Figure 4.6). This is actually a special case of the first method, since global data are considered implicit parameters to a method.

The fourth method is for the wealthy. Whenever our car needs gasoline, we pull over onto the side of the road, buy the land that's there, build a gas station, use the gas station, and destroy the gas station when we leave. In short, the `get_gasoline()` method for the car class builds a gas station as a local object, uses it, and then destroys it on exiting the method (see Figure 4.7). While this is not appropriate for the car/gas station domain, there are many domains where building a local object to perform some functionality is useful.

The fifth and last method for implementing the uses relationship is that "god" tells a car, when it is built, who its gas station is. The car stores this information in a special type of attribute called a **referential attribute** for later use in the `get_gasoline` method. We will discuss more about this method of implementation in Chapter 7.

4.4   Heuristics for the Uses Relationship

The typical relationship among the main, top-level objects in an application is the uses relationship. In an optimal object-oriented design, none of these uses relationships can be refined into containment. A main problem to watch for is uses relationships that should have been refined into containment but were not. There is a heuristic that can help identify these.

Figure 4.7 Car building a gas station for use.

Heuristic 4.1

Minimize the number of classes with which another class collaborates.

This heuristic claims that the list of classes another class uses should be kept to a minimum. In the worst case, an object-oriented design will consist of a collection of primitive, simplistic classes, all of which use each other. The top-level design will be very difficult to comprehend. Notice that our heuristic of avoiding a god class is not violated here. We may have distributed system intelligence very uniformly among the large group of top-level objects. The solution is to look for places in the uses relationship graph where one class communicates with another group of classes and ask, "Can I replace this group of classes with one class containing the group, thereby reducing the number of collaborations?" There will be many such tests of which only a percentage will answer yes. These should be wrapped in containing classes to reduce complexity. For example, consider the restaurant patron and types of food shown in Figure 4.8. A better solution is to wrap the food in the containing class "meal" in order to reduce the number of collaborations at the top level of the design.

One can argue that we have actually increased the number of uses relationships from three to four, but thanks to data hiding we do not count uses relationships inside the meal class. They are invisible to the restaurant patron and are simply implementation details of the meal. We will see later in this chapter that containment is the simplifying relationship of the object-oriented paradigm. Whenever we can contain one item in another, it implies that we can ignore the contained object at some high level of design.

It is important to note that once an object of a class sends a message to an object of another class, a collaboration exists between the two classes. Some developers have tried to quantify the collaboration minimization heuristic to state that a class should not collaborate with more than six classes. These developers are trying to build complexity metrics based on short-term memory restrictions. While this information is applicable to containment and inheritance relationships, I am not convinced that the short-term memory constraint applies in this case. In order to understand a single requirement (e.g., scenario, use case) in an application, one does not have to concep-

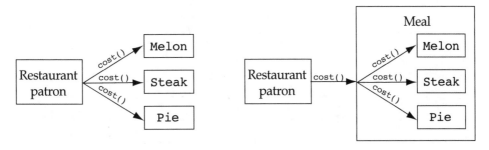

Figure 4.8 Finding containing classes from uses relationships.

tualize all of the collaborations of a class. Since understanding a class is usually accomplished by analyzing its roles in an application's requirements, developers rarely analyze all of the collaborations outside the scope of a single requirement.

4.5   Refining the Amount of Collaboration Between Two Classes

From the viewpoint of logical design, once a collaboration exists between two classes, a certain level of complexity has been added to the system. It does not matter whether two different messages are sent between the two classes or one hundred messages are sent. The complexity is constant. If we view the system from its implementation standpoint (e.g., physical design), we find some other interesting forms of complexity. Consider these questions and their associated diagrams in Figure 4.9.

1. What is the effect on the complexity of a system if a class has many message sends to a collaborating class instead of just one? For example, how do we compare the complexity of a class X, which has a method f1() that sends a class Z an f10() message, to a class Y, which has six methods f2(), f3(), f4(), f5(), f6(), and f7(), each of which sends Z the f10() message? At logical design time we simply state that X uses Z and Y uses Z. Intuitively, the class Y seems more complex because more of its implementation is tied to Z. If there is a problem with the f10() method of Z, then will more code need

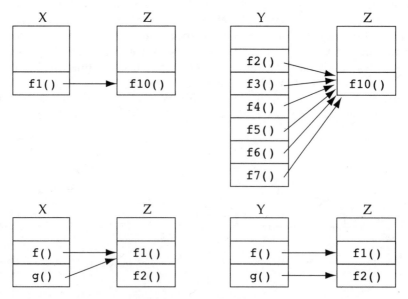

Figure 4.9 Additional collaboration complexities: which designs are more complex?

to be examined in the case of class Y? Since we do not know the relative complexities of `f1()` to `f2()`, `f3()`, etc., we cannot readily answer what initially seems intuitive.

2. What is the effect on the complexity of a system if a class sends different messages as opposed to the same message? For example, a class X sends the class Z the `f1()` message from two of its methods versus class Y, which sends Z the `f1()` and `f2()` messages each once. Both examples involve two message sends, but we only state the generic "X uses Z and Y uses Z" at logical design time. Again, class Y intuitively seems more complex because it is dependent on two methods of Z instead of just one. We could say that Y collaborates more with Z than does X. We certainly wish to minimize the amount of collaboration in addition to the number of collaborators.

3. What about limiting the amount of fanout that a class exhibits, that is, the product of the number of methods and the messages they send? If a class has seven methods, each of which sends out 10 messages, then that class has a fanout of 70. Should we limit this value? Again, we can certainly see that complexity increases with fanout.

The moral of the story is that each of these examples/questions adds complexity to the design, but they are small correction factors compared to the original concern of too many collaborating classes. We should minimize the number of message sends between two collaborating classes, the number of different ways the classes collaborate, and class fanout. I do not believe we can construct quantitative heuristics to deal with these issues, although several authors have offered them. Heuristics that state "facts," like "fanout should be limited to 50," give little rational explanation for the magic number 50. There is certainly a difference in complexity between a class X that has 2 methods, each of which sends 25 messages to the class Z, and a class Y that has 10 methods, each of which sends 5 messages to the class Z. Why not limit fanout to 45 or 55 or 70? I believe that the qualitative metrics are best provided with no guess as to their quantification.

Heuristic 4.2

Minimize the number of message sends between a class and its collaborator.

Heuristic 4.3

Minimize the amount of collaboration between a class and its collaborator, that is, the number of different messages sent.

Heuristic 4.4

Minimize fanout in a class, that is, the product of the number of messages defined by the class and the messages they send.

If these heuristics are considered equal to the collaboration minimization heuristic (Heuristic 4.1), then we would be implying that there is some break-even point between adding more message sends between classes and adding a new collaboration. For example, we might argue that rather than letting a method of the person class use a new alarm clock message, it might be better for the person class to collaborate with some entirely new class. This is never true, because the big hit in complexity for the uses relationship comes at the class level, not the object level. The fact that the person class is dependent on two classes rather than one is the overriding concern. The amount of coupling between the objects of a class is a much smaller problem.

4.6   The Containment Relationship

The meal class that we created in Figure 4.8 to reduce the number of collaborations between the restaurant patron and the pieces of the meal is a good example of the **containment relationship**. Containment occurs whenever a class has as one of its attributes an object of another class. In our example, we claim that a meal contains a melon. Does this imply that all melons are contained inside meals? Of course not—there are melons contained in grocery stores, fields, and garbage cans. This makes containment an object-based relationship, since not all objects of the classes have to obey the relationship.

Heuristic 4.5

If a class contains objects of another class, then the containing class should be sending messages to the contained objects, that is, the containment relationship should always imply a uses relationship.

The rationale behind this heuristic is that contained objects that are not sent messages by the containing class are useless information (since data hiding precludes their use by others), or else there is some get method to return the contained object for use by others. The latter is a violation of keeping related data and behavior in one place, except in the case of **container classes**. Container classes are generic classes used as a temporary holding space for other objects. Their interesting behavior is the insertion and removal of other objects. Unless we are dealing with a container class, the contained object needs to be removed and placed in its appropriate abstraction. That is, the data decomposition model is flawed at this point in the design.

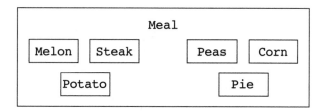

Figure 4.10 A broad and shallow meal class.

Consider the design of a meal class shown in Figure 4.10. It is an example of a broad and shallow containment hierarchy, namely, lots of data members in the class but little depth.

An alternative design for the meal class is shown in Figure 4.11. It is an example of a narrow and deep containment hierarchy.

The key question is, "Which design is better?" There are always two groups to consider when asking such a question: the users of a class and the implementors of a class. For the users of the meal class, which design is better? If you answer design #1, you are wrong, and if you answer design #2, you are wrong. Why? As a user of the meal class, you should not care which design is used. If you have a preference, it means that you are dependent on the implementation of the meal class, a clear violation of data hiding. It has been my experience that this question will solicit many votes for design #1. This shows the typical action-oriented designer's obsession with knowing implementation details when designing a high-level design, a cause of many extensibility problems. In the object-oriented world, if a user of a meal object wants to know the cost of the meal, he or she simply sends the cost message to his or her object. Any other knowledge of the containment hierarchy will cause maintenance problems.

Now ask the same question to the implementors of the class. Again, the question solicits many votes for design #1. Why? In most procedural languages, the heuristic

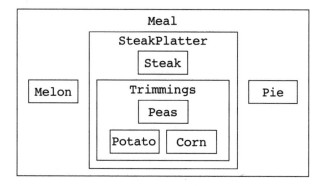

Figure 4.11 A narrow and deep meal class.

has been to favor broad and shallow data structures as opposed to deeply nested structures. Developers were concerned with memorizing the path names to get access to a particular piece of data. They did not want to write statements like `"obj1.first.x.p.q.mydata = 10;"`. Instead, they wanted to write statements like `"obj1.mydata = 10;"`. This inconvenience is not a problem in the object-oriented world. Users of data structures never access data directly. Thanks to data hiding, we can nest structures as deeply as we wish without increasing the complexity for our users. Given that we have removed the perceived advantage of shallow over deep structures, why are deep structures better? Consider the following heuristics.

Heuristic 4.6

Most of the methods defined on a class should be using most of the data members most of the time.

If this is not true for a given class, then it is probable that the designer has captured two or more abstractions in one class. A class should capture only one meaningful abstraction within a domain. In the grossest violation, half of a class's methods will use half the data members while the other half of the methods are using the other half of the data members. The class should be split along these lines due to it having too much noncommunicating behavior. For an example of this construct, see the dictionary example in Chapter 2 (Section 2.3).

Heuristic 4.7

Classes should not contain more objects than a developer can fit in his or her short-term memory. A favorite value for this number is six.

The rationale behind this heuristic is that most of the methods defined on a class should be using most of the data members most of the time. Assuming this is true, implementors of a method will need to think about all of the data members while writing the method. If the developer cannot keep all of the data in his or her short-term memory, then items will be omitted and bugs will creep into the code. The standard number of seven plus or minus two is widely accepted in the world of psychology as the number of items most people can keep in their short-term memory. We choose six to take into consideration people with poor short-term memories and the fact that most methods take an argument or two, which must be considered in addition to the data members. In short, this heuristic is a complexity metric on a class. (Emphasizing a point: If few methods use most of the data members most of the time, then we have a noncommunicating class that may need to be split.) [8]

How does one reduce the number of data members within a class? When a class contains more than six items, it is time to start grouping logical collections of the data members within a new containing class. In the case of the meal, we determine that the steak platter class can contain the steak, potato, peas, and corn. Likewise, the trimmings class can further reduce the complexity by encapsulating the potato, peas, and corn. Consider the implementor of the cost function for the first meal. He or she is thinking about six items, while the implementor of the second meal considers only three. Imagine the result if our meal gets more interesting; for example, we may decide that the meal contains an appetizer (melon or shrimp cocktail), an entree (steak platter or shrimp platter), and a dessert (pie, cake, or jello). The implementor of the cost method for the first meal is now thinking, "If the appetizer is a melon, add 75 cents to the sum; but if it is a shrimp cocktail, then count the number of shrimp in the shrimp cocktail, multiply by 65 cents, then check if there is cocktail sauce because we charge 15 cents extra for sauce . . . ." Our lazy object-oriented implementor simply asks the appetizer, entree, and dessert for their cost and sums them up. It is true that someone has to decide which appetizer is in the meal, and if that appetizer happens to be a shrimp cocktail, then they need to perform some functionality to compute its cost. But at least in this stage of implementation, we can put off the work of thinking about that portion of the problem. It has been my experience that lazy programmers have the easiest time producing narrow and deep containment hierarchies. They simply pretend that any work that can be spun off into another class is not their responsibility.

Heuristic 4.8

Distribute system intelligence vertically down narrow and deep containment hierarchies.

This heuristic goes together with distributing system intelligence horizontally across the top-level classes. Both are important heuristics, although horizontal distribution is more important than vertical distribution. An improper horizontal distribution affects the entire application, while an improper vertical distribution affects only the implementation of the class in question.

One perceived problem with the narrow and deep hierarchies is that of efficiency. Computing the cost of the broad and shallow meal amounts to the overhead of seven function calls, while the narrow and deep design has a total of nine function calls. The impact of function call overhead is greatly exaggerated. If the language of implementation is an interpreted language (e.g., Smalltalk, CLOS), then this level of efficiency has been thrown out the window. If you are dealing with a compiled language, in particular C++, by definition you are worried about efficiency. In languages such as these, mechanisms known as inline functions are usually available to eliminate the function call overhead of tiny (one line) functions. In short, either you do not care about the overhead, or you do care and your language provides an escape.

A side benefit of narrow and deep hierarchies is that you get more hooks for software reuse. Let us assume we want to build a turkey dinner for some other domain. It is natural for us to look to the meal for reuse. We realize the entire meal class cannot be reused, but maybe we can find some interesting items inside its black box. We open the black box of the first design and lots of little pieces fall out. We pick up the potato, peas, and corn, realizing that we will need them in the turkey dinner as well. Now we try to strip out the method code that deals exclusively with these three data members. We quickly find that it is a frustrating job trying to break up the abstraction, so we throw the whole mess away and build our abstraction from scratch. Using the second design, we open the black box and find three other black boxes. We discard the melon and pie as useless in our new domain, but we find the steak platter interesting. We open its black box and find another black box called trimmings, which captures the abstraction we need for our turkey dinner. Now we can grab the trimmings structure with its methods and look no further into the design. The ability to reuse a particular section of a containment hierarchy can be very beneficial toward the development of new designs.

4.7   Semantic Constraints Between Classes

It is very common for containment hierarchies to have **semantic constraints** imposed upon them. In the case of the meal class, we wanted the appetizer to come first, the entree second, and the dessert third. We captured this information in the definition of the class. This is the preferable method for capturing semantic constraints because it makes it impossible for a user of the class to build objects that violate the semantic constraint. However, it is not always possible to implement constraints in this way. Consider another semantic constraint of the meal class. We expand the definition of trimmings to state that a trimming object is a potato and two vegetables. Let us assume that there are four possible vegetables: peas, corn, squash, and asparagus. The semantic constraint is that peas and corn is a disallowed combination of vegetables. If we follow our previous implementation of semantics constraints, we will attempt to capture the information in the class definition. We create the `Squash-SquashMeal`, the `SquashPeasMeal`, the `SquashAsparagusMeal`, the `Squash-CornMeal`, the `AsparagusAsparagusMeal`, the . . . fourteen different combinations of vegetables, each encapsulated as a separate meal class. We leave out definitions for the `PeasCornMeal` and the `CornPeasMeal`. This is an obvious proliferation of classes. Adding another choice of vegetable leads to 16 more classes, the next gives us 32 classes, etc. We end up with $2^n - 2$ classes for n vegetables.

Implementors will avoid this proliferation of classes by implementing the constraint in the behavior of the class. The typical place to implement the constraint is in the constructor of a class, that is, the operation of a class that builds its objects. In this way the class refuses to build objects that violate the semantic constraint. Whose constructor should check the constraint in this example? It depends on the domain of the application. Are all trimmings with peas and corn illegal, or is it just when they are used in a steak platter, or just when used in a meal? The class demanding the constraint is the one whose constructor tests the constraint. In general, designers try to place the constraint as low in the containment hierarchy as possible.

An alternative to capturing the constraint in the constructor of the class is to allow for the creation of illegal objects with respect to the constraint, but then check the state of the object in each method. For example, we may state that the relationship between a car class and an engine class is that of containment, namely, the car contains an engine. Does this imply that any car can contain any engine? We know that this is not possible. We first try to capture the constraint within the class definition by defining the `ChevyChevelle454`, the `ChevyChevelle318`, etc. We find a proliferation of classes, so we attempt to implement the constraint in the behavior of the class. Do we want to model the constraint in the constructor disallowing the creation of illegal objects, or do we want to allow for the creation of illegal objects but have the methods of the car class perform state tests on the object? It depends on our domain. Do we want it to be impossible for a mechanic to put the wrong engine in a car, or do we want to allow for that, leaving a car that will not work completely? If we want it to be impossible for a mechanic to put the wrong engine in a car, then we will test the semantic constraint in the constructor of the car class. If we want the latter design, then the constructor allows illegal cars to be built. The illegal cars might execute the `start_engine` method with no problems, but when sent the `drive()` message, they exhibit no behavior, due to the bad internal state of the car.

Consider the semantic constraint itself. The car needs to know which car/engine combinations are legal. How does the car get this information? It could be maintained in each type of car; for example, the `ChevyChevelle` class contains a list of allowed engines. This is a distributed design with respect to semantic information. People who have changed their own oil and needed to find the appropriate oil filter know of this solution. They pick up each type of oil filter and look for their car's make and model on the back of the filter. Another solution is to place a table of car and engine types in the car class. The cars method(s) can check for legal combinations in this way. Others feel that this clutters the car class a bit too much, so in order to distribute the system intelligence, they push the table into a third-party catalog class. A catalog object is consulted by the appropriate method(s) of the car class. Both of these solutions are equivalent to our do-it-yourselfer looking for his or her oil filter in a table or catalog that describes the allowed oil filters for each make and model of car. Either a distributed or a centralized solution to the implementation of the semantic constraint information may be more applicable than the other in a given domain. In general, a centralized solution is better in domains where existing constraint information is volatile, while stable constraint information allows for a more distributed model.

Heuristic 4.9

When implementing semantic constraints, it is best to implement them in terms of the class definition. Often this will lead to a proliferation of

classes, in which case the constraint must be implemented in the behavior of the class—usually, but not necessarily, in the constructor.

Heuristic 4.10

When implementing semantic constraints in the constructor of a class, place the constraint test in the constructor as far down a containment hierarchy as the domain allows.

Heuristic 4.11

The semantic information on which a constraint is based is best placed in a central, third-party object when that information is volatile.

Heuristic 4.12

The semantic information on which a constraint is based is best decentralized among the classes involved in the constraint when that information is stable.

4.8   Attributes Versus Contained Classes

When designing a containment hierarchy, keep in mind that most classes have attributes. Most attributes are descriptive in nature: the color of a car, the weight of a fruit, the length of a house. These are not considered containment relationships, since the contained data does not have behavior associated with it. For example, which of the following sentences make sense?

1. An engine contains pistons.

2. An engine contains maximum horsepower.

3. An engine has pistons.

4. An engine has maximum horsepower.

Most people consider sentence number 2 to be inappropriate. Notice that the verb "to have" is less descriptive than the verb "to contain." Why is there a semantic difference between sentences 1 and 2? A piston has behavior and is therefore modeled as a class, while maximum horsepower is simply a descriptive attribute and has no behavior. In some cases, several pieces of data may be encapsulated together and still called an attribute. Consider the role of a bank card in the domain of the automatic teller machine. It encapsulates the account and pin number but has no meaningful behavior. At best, it defines `get_account()` and `get_pin()`, but we do not count `gets` and `sets` on descriptive attributes as meaningful behavior. Many object-oriented designers refer to this entity as an attribute. This extended definition causes some confusion, especially among MIS developers, who have a more restrictive definition of attribute. They often ask, "What is the bank card an attribute of?" The object-oriented designer responds, "The bank card is an attribute of the system."

4.9   More Containment Heuristics

Heuristic 4.13

A class must know what it contains, but it should not know who contains it.

This heuristic is important if a designer wishes to reuse his or her abstractions. Consider the relationship "`BedRoom` contains `AlarmClock`". It is necessary that the `BedRoom` object knows about its contained `AlarmClock` object, but the `AlarmClock` should have no dependencies on the `BedRoom`. The main reason is reusability. I want to be able to take the `AlarmClock` out of the `BedRoom` and use it in the design of a `TimeLockSafe`. If the `AlarmClock` is dependent on the `BedRoom`, then the `BedRoom` goes wherever the `AlarmClock` goes. This implies that the `Bed`, `SleepingHuman`, `NightStand`, `Bureau`, `Trunk`, etc. also go where the `AlarmClock` goes since they are contained together in the `BedRoom`. Objects of the `TimeLockSafe` class are now dependent on `NightStands`, `Beds`, `Trunks`, etc.

Heuristics 4.14

Objects that share lexical scope—those contained in the same containing class—should not have uses relationships between them.

Objects that share lexical scope are objects that are contained in the same containing class. The reason they should not be using each other is anchored in both reusability and complexity issues. Consider Figure 4.12's fragment of an automatic teller machine design, which focuses on an ATM attempting to get a pin number from its user. The card reader has detected that it has a legal bank card. The system now needs to get a pin number for verification. A typical solution is for the card reader to ask the ATM's display screen to display a prompt to the user, followed by the card reader asking the keypad to get a pin number.

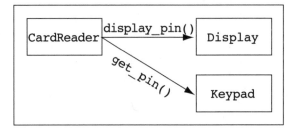

Figure 4.12 Example of objects sharing lexical scope and using each other.

The problem in this design is initially a reusability issue. Card readers have nothing to do with display screens and keypads outside of the domain of automatic teller machines. If I want to reuse the card reader in a security door, I have to place a display screen and keypad in the door because card readers are dependent on them. This clearly hinders the reuse of the class sending the messages.

Even if a developer decides that he or she does not care about reusability, there is a serious complexity issue that needs resolution. The automatic teller machine contains all three objects, which implies that there are uses relationships between the ATM and card reader, the ATM and display screen, and the ATM and keypad. The ATM can handle any coordinated activity between these three classes. By adding a uses relationship between the card reader and display screen, we are adding complexity to the design whose functionality is already available in the ATM machine. A better solution is to allow the ATM to find that it has a card, prompt the user via its display screen, and get a pin number from its keypad (see Figure 4.13). In general, the containing class should use its existing uses relationships to accomplish the behavior that the lexical scope sharing objects are duplicating.

There is a notable area of design where a designer will violate Heuristic 4.13. This occurs when a number of different classes are dependent on one another in complex ways. Rather than have all of these complex dependencies, the designer wraps the

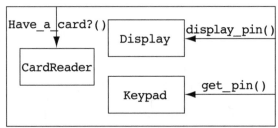

Figure 4.13 A better solution to the objects sharing lexical scope problem.

related classes in a containing class. Each contained object sends messages to the containing class, which then broadcasts the message to the rest of the contained objects or a preselected list, depending on how the designer wants to distribute the system intelligence between the containing class and its contained pieces. In all of these designs, the designer is violating the heuristic in order to satisfy Heuristics 4.1 and 4.14. In short, having a contained object that knows about its container is preferable to a large number of uses relationships. Three case studies illustrate this violation of Heuristic 4.13:

> The first example can be found in the domain of the securities industry. In a particular securities trading application, the designer found himself with a number of different types of objects that fell under three categories: price providers (databases, real-time pricing information, economic models), markets (U.S. Treasuries Market, Madrid Stock Exchange, New York Stock Exchange), and analyzers (domain-defined or homemade analytics for securities). Objects of these classes are all dependent on one another, in that, if one changes it could have an impact on any of the other objects. Rather than creating a uses relationship from each of the classes to each of the others, the designer chose to wrap all of the objects in a new containing class which he called an economy. If any of the contained objects changed state, they could inform the economy, which propagated the changes to each of the other contained objects. They, in turn, could produce further changes, of which the economy object could be informed. This design proved extremely flexible and substantially less complex had the designer elected to enforce Heuristic 4.13.

> A second example of a proper violation of Heuristic 4.13 can be found in the domain of telephony. A development team was implementing a maintenance application for telephone service hardware. In such a domain, there are many devices which the development team named features. There are many different types of features, some of which can be dependent on each other. Rather than have many different features sending messages to each other, or even knowing whether the other class was available, all message sends were to a containing class called the unit. The unit class was responsible for reducing the coupling between its contained pieces, by mapping requests between the sender and receiver. It could also handle the complexity of deciding whether or not the desired entity was available.

> The third case is the widely published dialog box example. In graphical user interfaces, dialog boxes are often viewed as collections of objects of a number of different types. These different objects often communicate with each other to achieve some goal. Rather than have each contained object know about the existence of the other contained objects, we allow the dialog box to handle the communication. As in the two previous domains, each contained object sends messages to the containing class (in this case the dialog box class) and the containing class broadcasts the request to its pieces.

4.10   A Relationship Between Uses and Containment?

Another topic related to the containment relationship involves an interesting intermediate relationship that falls somewhere between uses and containment. I first discovered this distinction while performing a design critique at a process control company that was writing software to control semiconductor chip processing hardware. The hardware looked very much like a restaurant steam table with three robots hanging off of it. The "steam table" was made up of a number of small stainless steel tanks, each containing treatment baths for racks of etched silicon wafers. Some of the baths were acidic treatments, some were alkaline treatments, and some were rinsing water baths. The control software was to run a rack of wafers through a "recipe" whose steps placed the rack in a particular tank for a certain amount of time. The movement of the racks was performed via one of the three robots. To better understand their problem, the system architects used the clever real-world analogy of a traveler. The racks were the travelers, the tanks were hotels, and the robots were airplanes. A discussion quickly divided the design team into two camps. This discussion revolved around the relationship between hotels and their guests, that is, the racks of wafers and the acid, alkaline, and water baths. One camp stated that the relationship between the two is a uses relationship, while the other argued that it is a containment relationship. The camp arguing for containment made the mistake of stating that the relationship was not the uses relationship. This position became impossible to defend since the containment relationship implies the uses relationship. The result was a significant loss of time as the two camps argued.

Since this first discussion, the problem has manifested itself repeatedly in my design courses. If you ask a group of people the relationship between a classroom and its students, over 80 percent will typically say containment. If you ask those people to keep their hands up as long as they agree with containment, and then ask for the relationship between a parking lot and its cars, a few will drop their hands. If you then ask for the relationship between a gas station and its cars, then almost all of the hands will drop. Why? It is clear that these relationships are equivalent. Where does this temporal dependence originate? To make the problem worse, consider the relationship between a car and its engine. Almost all designers agree that this is containment, but the engine can be removed from the car in much the same way that people are removed from classrooms and cars from gas stations.

The solution to these problems requires that designers understand that there are three, and not two, relationships involving uses and containment. The first is clearly a uses relationship and is never confused with containment. A good example is "person uses an alarm clock." There is no hint of containment here. Then there is the car and its engine example. This is clearly containment (which implies uses). However, a third relationship lies between these two extremes. This is the domain of the parking lot and its cars, the classroom and its students, and the gas station and its cars. Some groups simply consider this intermediate category as a uses relationship since it does not exhibit the design-simplifying attribute of a true containment relationship: This relationship does not guarantee that we can ignore the contained objects at some high level of design. The important thing is to understand the three concepts; what we call them is irrelevant. Some groups with which I have dealt refer to them as composition, containment, uses, respectively; others call them containment, uses, uses; others call them containment, containment, uses; and still others have called them strong containment, weak containment, and uses. A good test for knowing whether you have the strong or weak form of containment is to ask yourself the following question: "If I remove the contained object, is the behavior of the containing class modified?" If the answer is yes, then you have the strong form of containment (composition?); if the answer is no, then you have the weak form. If I remove a student from a classroom, is the behavior of the classroom affected? No. If I remove the engine from a car, is the behavior of the car affected? Yes.

4.11 Containment by Value Versus Containment by Reference

The last topic related to containment is a language-dependent distinction between **containment by value** and **containment by reference**. Containment by value implies that an object contains another object; containment by reference implies that an object contains a pointer to another object. Containment by value requires that an object lives and dies together with another object. Containment by reference allows for optional pieces of objects (a shrimp cocktail may or may not contain cocktail sauce), the sharing of one object by a group of other objects (i.e., object sharing), containment of an abstract class (e.g., meal contains appetizer), and the weak form of containment discussed above. Languages that do not distinguish between these two flavors of containment support containment by reference only. While this issue typically does not affect designers since they do not care about the particular implementation of a containment relationship, I mention it here since many case tools that are commercially available have icons that demonstrate the distinction. These case tools are more interested in the distinction because they need to generate C++ code than for any real architectural purpose (C++ allows for the explicit distinction between containment by value and containment by reference).

Glossary of Terms

Attribute   A single piece or a collection of data that does not possess behavior.

Classed-based relationship   An object-oriented relationship between two classes in which all objects of the classes involved obey the relationship.

Container class   A class whose main purpose is the storage of other objects. Often implemented as a homogeneous-looking list of heterogeneous objects, namely, a polymorphic list.

Containment by reference   A containment relationship in which the contained object is indirectly linked to the containing class, usually via a pointer or referential attribute.

Containment by value   A containment relationship in which the contained object is directly linked to the containing class, that is, the objects involved in the relationship are born and die together.

Containment relationship   An object-based relationship between two classes in which one of the classes has as its attribute an object (directly or indirectly) of the other class. Additionally, the contained object must not be visible outside of the containing class.

Descriptive attribute   An attribute that contains a descriptive piece of data concerning the objects of a class.

Object-based relationship   An object-oriented relationship between two classes in which all objects of the classes involved do not obey the relationship.

Referential attribute   A special type of attribute through which one object can retrieve another object.

Semantic constraint   An application-specific constraint imposed on an object-oriented relationship restricting its scope or behavior, most often associated with the containment relationship.

Uses relationship   An object-based relationship between two classes in which one class references a public operation(s) of the other class.

Summary of Heuristics

Heuristic 4.1   Minimize the number of classes with which another class collaborates.

Heuristic 4.2   Minimize the number of message sends between a class and its collaborator.

Heuristic 4.3   Minimize the amount of collaboration between a class and its collaborator, that is, the number of different messages sent.

Heuristic 4.4   Minimize fanout in a class, that is, the product of the number of messages defined by the class and the messages they send.

Heuristic 4.5   If a class contains objects of another class, then the containing class should be sending messages to the contained objects, that is, the containment relationship should always imply a uses relationship.

Heuristic 4.6   Most of the methods defined on a class should be using most of the data members most of the time.

Heuristic 4.7   Classes should not contain more objects than a developer can fit in his or her short-term memory. A favorite value for this number is six.

Heuristic 4.8   Distribute system intelligence vertically down narrow and deep containment hierarchies.

Heuristic 4.9   When implementing semantic constraints, it is best to implement them in terms of the class definition. Often this will lead to a proliferation of classes, in which case the constraint must be implemented in the behavior of the class—usually, but not necessarily, in the constructor.

Heuristic 4.10   When implementing semantic constraints in the constructor of a class, place the constraint test in the constructor as far down a containment hierarchy as the domain allows.

Heuristic 4.11   The semantic information on which a constraint is based is best placed in a central, third-party object when that information is volatile.

Heuristic 4.12   The semantic information on which a constraint is based is best decentralized among the classes involved in the constraint when that information is stable.

Heuristic 4.13   A class must know what it contains, but it should never know who contains it.

Heuristic 4.14   Objects that share lexical scope—those contained in the same containing class—should not have uses relationships between them.

Chapter 5

The Inheritance Relationship

5.1 Introduction to the Inheritance Relationship

The **inheritance** relationship is one of the more important relationships within the object-oriented paradigm. It is best used to capture the a-kind-of relationship between classes, such as `ChevyChevelle` is a-kind-of `Car`, `Dog` is a-kind-of `Animal`. Its primary purpose is twofold: It acts as a mechanism for expressing commonality between two classes (**generalization**), and it is used to specify that one class is a special type of another class (**specialization**). The terms "specialization" and "generalization" are generally considered synonyms of "inheritance." They are used often during object-oriented design critiques to discuss the process under which inheritance was found, that is, did the designer have the more general class first (specialization) or the more specific class first (generalization)? If an inheritance hierarchy is simply shown to a developer, there is no way that he or she can determine whether specialization or generalization was used to find the inheritance relationships. Many object-oriented designers have found that generalization is the more difficult, and less frequently discovered, form of inheritance.

Generalization usually tends to be more common in version 1 of a system. During the design process, the system architects decide that two or more classes have something in common, namely, data, behavior, or just a common interface. This common information is collected in a more general class from which the two or more classes can inherit. Undiscovered generalization relationships will result in duplicate abstractions and implementations, that is, data, code, and/or public interfaces. Many generalizations are found toward the end of the object-oriented design process. These generalizations can be added late in the process with little or no effect on the other members of the design team.

In contrast, specialization tends to be more common in successive versions of a particular system. As the system adapts to added functionality, some classes will inevitably require special treatment. Inheritance is ideal for implementing these special cases. It is especially useful for adapting standard components for use in application-specific areas. For this reason, inheritance is called the reusability mechanism of the object-oriented paradigm.

It is very important to note that a major stumbling block while learning the object-oriented paradigm is that developers confuse the containment and inheritance relationships in their designs. The information in this chapter is meant to prevent this problem. We will begin with an abstract example of inheritance in order to discuss the vocabulary and semantics of the mechanism. We will then examine many real-world examples of specialization, generalization, and the many misuses of inheritance. Consider the example in Figure 5.1, where class B inherits from class A.

First a little vocabulary. If a class inherits from another class, it is called a **subclass**. If a class is inherited by another class, it is called a **superclass**. The inventor of C++, Bjarne Stroustrup, realized that these terms are ambiguous (for reasons we will see in the following discussion). He decided to rename superclass as **base class** and subclass as **derived class**. In this example, class A is considered a superclass or base class of class B, and class B is considered a subclass or derived class of class A.

If a class inherits from another class, then the inheriting class should be a special type of the inherited class. In this abstract example, class B is a special type of class A, meaning all B objects are first and foremost A objects. This implies that inheritance is a class-based relationship since all objects of the class must obey the relationship.

The first semantics of the inheritance relationship that one notices is that all derived classes (their objects) get a copy of the base class's data (see Figure 5.2). This does not necessarily imply that methods of the derived class can see the data of their base class; that is a matter for some debate. It implies that a subclass will always have a superset of its superclass's data (a proper superset if the subclass has any data of its own). Many newcomers to the paradigm argue that the terms "superclass" and "subclass" are backwards with regard to the set of data of each class. In fact, the terms "superclass" and "subclass" do not refer to the set of data in each class; they refer to the set of objects under each class. Since all B objects are legal A objects by definition, class A will always have a superset of B's objects (a proper superset if there

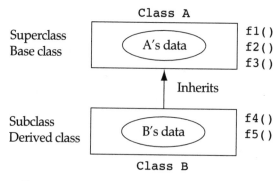

Figure 5.1 Class B inherits from class A.

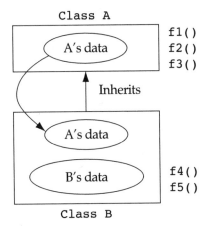

Figure 5.2 Class B inherits from class A: inheritance of data.

are any A objects at all). It is this situation that Stroustrup found ambiguous and which led him to create the terms "base class" and "derived class."

We discussed in Chapter 2 the fact that classes have two access areas, public and private. Within the framework of inheritance, it makes sense to consider a third level of access: protected. All three access areas can contain data as well as function members. The private area of a class is available only to the implementors of the class, that is, those who write methods for the class. The public area of a class is available to all implementors and users of the class. We have argued that no data should be placed in the public section since that would create an undesirable relationship between the users of the class and its implementation. The protected section of the class is something between public and private. It looks like private access to all users of the class except the implementors of derived classes. In our example in Figure 5.3, anything in the protected section of A would be visible to implementors of A (obviously) and implementors of B since B is a derived class of A. It would be invisible to other users of A as well as to the users of B. The main question is, "Should an implementor of B be allowed to see A's data?" Before we answer the question, we need to know a bit more about the semantics of inheritance.

If inheritance only implied getting a copy of the base class data in the derived class, then the relationship would be useless. The containment relationship has the exact same semantics. There would be no difference between "class B inherits from class A" and "class B contains class A." There must be some other difference that sets inheritance apart from containment. Since classes capture data and behavior, and we have already covered inheritance of data, it must be the behavior that is of interest. When a class inherits from another class, it not only gets a copy of the base class data, it also gets access to the base class functionality. This is what sets the containment and inheritance relationships apart. When a class contains another class, the containing class does not get the functionality of its contained class as part of its

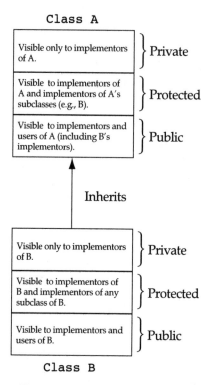

Figure 5.3 Class access rules.

public interface. For example, the meal class contains a melon and the melon class has a peel operation that returns a rind. Does this imply that meals have a peel function defined in their public interface? The answer is no! Implementors of meals can send the contained melon the peel message as part of the implementation of a method for the meal class, but meals themselves do not get the operation for free. If the meal class inherited from the melon class, then the meal class would receive the peel function as part of its public interface. This would be necessary since we would be arguing that meals are special kinds of melons. If a class is a special type of another class, then it must behave like the other class.

In our abstract example, objects of class B would be allowed to process the messages f1, f2, and f3 since B objects are special types of A objects. Normally, if a B object were sent the message f1, the system would ask, "Do B objects know how to f1?" If the answer is no, error! Within the presence of inheritance, the system asks the same question, but if the answer is no it then asks, "Does B inherit from someone who does know how to f1?" If the answer is no, it is again an error. If, however, the answer is yes, then the system uses the inherited method to execute the message f1. If inheritance is being used to model a specialization hierarchy—and it should be—then the derived class is not allowed to eliminate any of the functionality of the base class. Otherwise anything could be made a special type of anything else by simply eliminating all behavior of the base class and adding all new behavior to the derived class; for example, a monkey is a special type of banana except it doesn't `peel`, `turn_yellow`, or `chop`; it does `jump`, `squeal`, and `swing_from_trees` though.

The inheritance of functionality and data creates an extremely powerful extensibility mechanism. It allows a designer to create a special type of an existing class which has additional data and function members and to guarantee that the new type is behaviorally compatible with the old type. This implies that I can change each base class object into a new derived class object and guarantee that the system will run exactly as it did before. This fact is easy to prove. Any message being sent to objects of the base class will be inherited from the base class by the new derived objects. These messages access data of the base class only; therefore, we have the same code running on the same data, providing behavioral compatibility (see Figure 5.4).

5.2 Overriding Base Class Methods in Derived Classes

In many cases, the object-oriented designer uses inheritance to add a specialization relationship that is not behaviorally compatible to the superclass. This implies that the user wishes to override the definition of a base class message with his or her own algorithm. This is allowable within the framework of specialization and is called an **overriding method**. For specialization, the derived class cannot eliminate messages of the base class but the derived class can change the method that defines them (see Figure 5.5). Most object-oriented languages support the calling of the base class

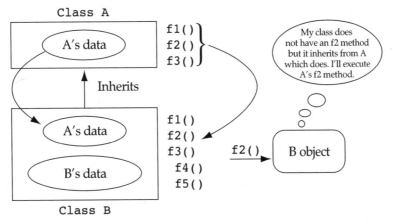

Figure 5.4 Class B inherits from class A: inheritance of behavior.

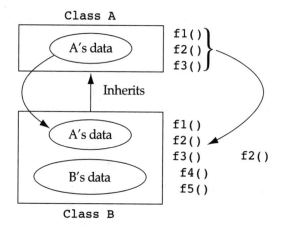

Figure 5.5 Class B inherits from class A: overriding base class behavior.

method from the overriding derived method. This is important since many times a designer has added data members to the derived class and wishes to handle their functionality at the derived class level. After handling the new data, the designer delegates up to the base class to let it handle its own data.

Inheritance is *transitive* in that if class B inherits from class A and class C inherits from class B, then class C inherits (via transitivity) class A (see Figure 5.6). This hierarchy demonstrates that a class can be both a derived class and a base class simultaneously. For example, class B is a base class of class C but a derived class of class A. One should think of inheritance as capturing a categorization hierarchy or taxonomy of the classes involved.

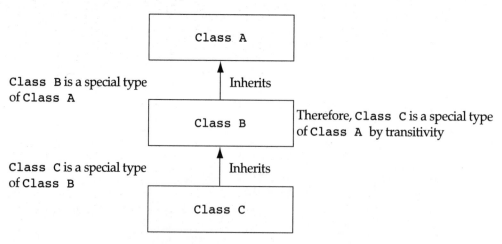

Figure 5.6 The transitivity of inheritance.

Heuristic 5.1

Inheritance should be used only to model a specialization hierarchy.

The containment relationship defines a black-box design where users of a class need not know about the implementation-dependent, internal classes. On the other hand, the inheritance relationship is a white-box design due to the inheritance of functionality. In order to know which messages can be sent to a derived class, I need to see the classes it inherits. If a white-box design is used where a black-box design would work as well, then we have needlessly opened our implementation to users of a class. Specialization cannot be effectively shown with a black-box design. Therefore, the opening of design details is allowable for this type of abstraction. For example, if I told you that I was a special type of XYZ, it would be useless until you understood what an XYZ is and what it does. Base classes are often used to convey high-level category information to readers of the design. In the winter of 1994, I taught a C++/object-oriented design course to a group in Singapore. Someone in the class asked me if I knew what a durian was. I told the attendee that I had no idea. She told me it was a tropical fruit unique to Southeast Asia. I still didn't know exactly what a durian was, but I had a good idea of some of its attributes and expected behaviors.

Heuristic 5.2

Derived classes must have knowledge of their base class by definition, but base classes should not know anything about their derived classes.

If base classes have knowledge of their derived classes, then it is implied that if a new derived class is added to a base class, the code of the base class will need modification. This is an undesirable dependency between the abstractions captured in the base and derived classes. We will see a much better solution to these types of dependencies when we discuss the topic of polymorphism later in this chapter.

5.3   The Use of the Protected Section of a Base Class

Getting back to our question on protected data, let us add some real-world names to our classes A and B. Let us say that A is the class `fruit`, which has, as its data members, a real number called `weight` and a string called `color`. In addition, all fruit have a print operation that outputs strings like, "Hi, I'm a .3-pound red fruit." That is the best the `fruit` class can do for a good default print function. Assume that class B is an apple that contains the additional data member `variety`. Should apple objects be able to see their own weight? Another way of asking the question is, "Should the `weight` data member of the `fruit` class be in the protected section?"

At first glance, this seems perfectly reasonable. If you do make `weight` a protected data member, then you are stating that if the `weight` data member needs to change in the future, you are willing to examine all methods of derived classes as well as the methods of the base class. This is a weakening of data hiding that should be avoided.

Heuristic 5.3

All data in a base class should be private; do not use protected data.

Just as I argued against those designers who favored public data, the designers should ask themselves the question, "What am I doing with the protected data, and why doesn't the class that owns the data (namely the base class) do it for me?" When asking the analogous question concerning public data, there is never a good answer. The designer is clearly missing an operation on the class through which he or she wants access to the data. In the case of protected data, there may be a valid answer. Why do I want to make the weight of fruit protected? Because the apple class is overriding the print method of fruit with its own print method. This method prints strings like, "Hi, I'm an apple and I weigh .3 pounds." In order to define this function at the apple level, I need access to the weight. Why not let the fruit class handle this behavior? Because the fruit class is not supposed to know of any derived class-specific data (Heuristic 5.2). When stuck in these cases, it is best to create a protected access function called `get_weight`, which simply returns the weight data member. In this case, the methods of `apple` are dependent only on the protected interface of `fruit` and not on the implementation of `fruit`. The protected interface of `fruit` is much easier to maintain than the implementation. While I railed against public accessor methods in Chapter 3 which often demonstrate a design flaw, there is nothing wrong with defining protected accessor methods. They are allowing derived class implementors access to base class data in an implementation-safe way. The implementors of derived classes have a right to access the data of their base class; however, the users of a class do not have a right to the data of the class they are using.

Beware of the class designer who claims that the weights of fruits have been a real number since time immemorial; therefore we can make the data member protected since we know it will never change. Murphy's 79th law of programming will see us eating fruit on 30 different planets 20 years from now, and the `weight` data member will no longer be a real number but an object of type `planetweight` that contains a mass and an acceleration. Our protected access function could easily be updated to accommodate the new implementation, but the direct users of protected data will have to examine each of the methods on their derived classes for possible modifications.

Similarly, watch out for the class designers who claim that they are willing to look at the methods of only three additional classes (`apple`, `banana`, and `orange`) in order to win the right to make `weight` protected (see Figure 5.7). Twenty years from now, if the `fruit` class is worth anything, there will be many derived classes hanging

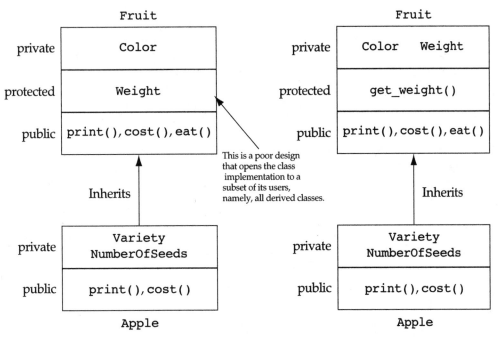

Figure 5.7 Eliminating protected data with accessor methods.

off it. These designers will find themselves looking at the kiwi, which inherits from TropicalCitrusFruit, which inherits from CitrusFruit, which inherits from Fruit. Without a doubt, this assumption could become very dangerous, with formidable expense at maintenance time.

Some languages do not support the notion of a protected class access mechanism. These languages are deficient in that they compensate for the missing access protection either by making private access behave as protected, or by forcing the user to put all protected members in the public interface. The first solution opens up the implementations of all base classes to their derived classes, resulting in numerous maintenance headaches. The second solution forces the user to place implementation details in the public interface of the class, thereby forcing the user to violate Heuristic 2.5, which states that class designers should never put in the public interface items that users of the class do not require. In either event, such a language is not expressive enough to capture what we are trying to describe at design time.

5.4   The Width and Depth of Inheritance Hierarchies

What can we say about heuristics on the width and depth of inheritance hierarchies? For containment, we claimed that the width of the hierarchy should be limited to six classes. Is this reasonable for inheritance as well? No. The heuristic exists for containment because the addition of data members to a class increases the complexity of the methods of the class. Adding a new derived type of fruit to our inheritance hierarchy does not increase the complexity of the existing classes, since each derived class is independent of the other, and the base class should be independent of all derived classes (Heuristic 5.2). If there is any heuristic on the width of an inheritance hierarchy, it should be that the wider the hierarchy, the better (assuming the inheritance relationships are valid). A wide hierarchy implies that many classes are taking advantage of the abstraction captured in the base class. Each inheritance link is removing redundant design and implementation effort. However, it is important to note that many of the inheritance pitfalls we will discuss in this chapter manifest themselves as wide inheritance hierarchies.

Heuristic 5.4

In theory, inheritance hierarchies should be deep—the deeper, the better.

The motivation behind this heuristic is that by having a deep taxonomy of abstractions, a new derived class can descend the hierarchy, taking on more refined abstractions the deeper it travels. For example, it is better to have a kiwi inherit from TropicalFruitFromThePacificRim, which inherits from TropicalFruit, which inherits from Fruit, than to just have a kiwi inherit from Fruit. The kiwi can capture more and more abstractions as it is categorized by the deeper hierarchy.

Heuristic 5.5

In practice, inheritance hierarchies should be no deeper than an average person can keep in his or her short-term memory. A popular value for this depth is six.

Several projects' developers used the "deeper is better" philosophy when designing their object-oriented systems, only to find implementors getting lost in their deep inheritance hierarchies (which, in the case studies, were between 12 and 17 levels in depth). These developers redesigned their systems to take a less refined collection of abstractions with inheritance hierarchies that were only five to seven levels in depth. All projects' developers found these depths to be better. Like the heuristic involving the width of containment hierarchies, the number six is widely regarded as the number of items the average person can keep in short-term memory. Some designers have pointed out that this problem is due to a lack of tools. If a designer has a graphical user interface that allows him or her to point and click on a derived class, resulting in the display of the class with all of its inherited data and interface, then the theoretic heuristic is clearly the more appropriate of the two. Lacking such a tool implies that the pragmatic heuristic is more appropriate.

5.5   Private, Protected, and Public Inheritance à la C++

If you are, or will be, a C++ programmer, there is a note of caution pertaining to inheritance relationships. The C++ language has implemented relationships called **private inheritance**, **protected inheritance**, and **public inheritance**. The public inheritance relationship is synonymous with the definition of inheritance in the object-oriented paradigm. The private and protected inheritance relationships are used to capture the notion of "inheritance for implementation." The semantics of these relationships are such that the derived class gets a copy of the base class data (with the same access rules of public inheritance); the implementors of the derived class get access to the public section of the base class; but the users of the derived class do not get access to the public section of the base class. In short, private and protected inheritance are the containment relationship. They do not capture the notion of either specialization or categorization. The difference between private and protected inheritance is that protected inheritance allows implementors of grandchildren (derived classes of the derived class) to use the public section of the base class; private inheritance does not.

Since classes can be inherited only once in C++, these relationships are actually a warped form of containment in that the containing class can contain only one object of the specified type. A good heuristic for C++ is to avoid the use of private and protected inheritance, using containment via data members instead. While I can find many C++ programmers who will argue that they know what they are doing and want to use C++'s inheritance relationship to implement containment, they are doing a great disservice to their maintenance people (which is probably them three months later when they cannot remember what they implemented). A serious pitfall in the object-oriented paradigm is confusing the use of containment and inheritance relationships. Using an inheritance syntax to implement containment muddies the waters all the more. In the name of readability, only public inheritance should be used in the C++ language.

The following facts are true, independent of the form of inheritance used (i.e., private, protected, or public inheritance) in the example in Figure 5.8).

1. Anything in the private section of a class can be accessed only by implementors of that class, that is, only the implementors of `Fruit` can access `weight` and `color` in the private section of `Fruit`; only the implementors of `Apple` can access `taste` and `seednum` in the private section of `Apple`; and only the implementors of `MacintoshApple` can access the `OrchardLocation` in the private section of `MacintoshApple`.

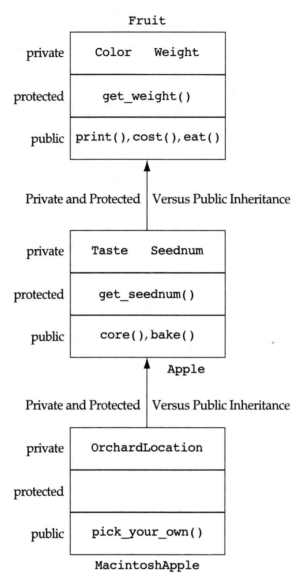

Figure 5.8 The differences between public, protected, and private inheritance.

2. Anything in the protected section of a class can only be accessed by implementors of that class or a derived class, that is, the `get_weight` method of `Fruit` can be accessed by implementors of `Fruit`, `Apple`, or `MacintoshApple`; the `get_seednum` method of `Apple` can be accessed by implementors of `Apple` or `MacintoshApple`.

3. Anything in the public section of a class can be accessed by implementors of that class or direct users of that class, that is, the `print`, `cost`, and eat methods of `Fruit` are visible to implementors and users of `Fruit`; the `core` and `bake` methods of `Apple` are visible to implementors and users of `Apple`; and the `pick_your_own` method of the `MacintoshApple` is visible to implementors and users of `MacintoshApple`.

4. Anything in the public interface of a class can be accessed by implementors of its immediate derived class, that is, the `print`, `cost`, and `eat` methods of `Fruit` are visible to implementors of `Apple`; the `bake` and `core` methods of `Apple` are visible to implementors of `MacintoshApple`.

The only remaining questions are the following:

Can users of `Apple` access the public interface of `Fruit`?

Can users of `MacintoshApple` access the public interface of `Apple`?

Can implementors of `MacintoshApple` access the public interface of `Fruit`?

If we use public inheritance, whose semantics state that the public interface of the base class appears to be copied into the public interface of the derived class, then the answer to all three questions is yes. If we use protected inheritance, whose semantics state that the public interface of the base class appears to be copied into the protected section of the derived class, then the users of `Apple` and `Macintosh-Apple` cannot access the `eat`, `cost`, and `print` operations since users of a class cannot access the contents of the protected section of a class. However, implementors of `MacintoshApple` can access the protected section of `Apple` so they can use the public methods of `Fruit`. Therefore, the answers to the three key questions are no, no, and yes. Lastly, if we use private inheritance, whose semantics state that the public interface of the base class appears to be copied into the private section of the derived class, then the answer would be no to all three questions since only the implementors of a class can see the private members of a class.

If all of this appears confusing, you are in good company. Private and protected inheritance are simply warped forms of containment and should be avoided. The fact that C++ has implemented these concepts warrants their treatment in this text. All future references to inheritance in this text are synonymous with public inheritance in C++. The reason I balk at creating heuristics telling designers to avoid using private and protected inheritance is that I want the heuristics to be language-independent. Also, both of these constructs have a well-founded theoretic backing (inheritance for implementation). The real problem with their use is understandability on the part of a system architect who is looking at code which uses these constructs. He or she is likely to think about the semantics of specialization when seeing the syntax of private inheritance, when in fact he or she is examining containment.

```
+-----------------------------+  taxes ()
|         Salary              |  benefits ()
|        Sicktime             |
|        MedicalPlan          |
|                             |
+-----------------------------+
```

Figure 5.9 The `NewEmployee` class.

5.6   A Real-World Example of Specialization

Now that we have seen an abstract model of inheritance, discussed the general semantics of the relationship, and developed some useful heuristics, let us look at some real-world examples of specialization and generalization. Assume we are starting a new company. We might decide that we are all new employees and each new employee gets a salary, sick time, and a medical plan. A couple of methods applicable to new employees is taxes (to compute taxes from salary) and benefits (to handle the sick time and medical plan). Such a class could be diagrammed as shown in Figure 5.9.

Six months go by and our start-up company is doing well because all of the employees work 80-hour weeks. We decide that anyone that has been employed by the company for six months should be considered a full employee with additional benefits over new employees. These benefits include a dental plan, vacation, and company car. Such a class is shown in Figure 5.10.

We notice that the data members of the full employee are the same as the new employee except for the additional benefits. Likewise, as we discuss the taxes and benefits functions for the full employee, we find that the taxes function is identical to the new employee (we assume nontaxable benefits in this example) and the benefits function is the same except for some additional code to handle the dental plan, vacation, and company car. In short, we realize that the full employee is really just a special kind of new employee. Since inheritance is the relationship responsible for modeling specialization, we claim that there is an inheritance relationship between the full and new employee classes with full employee being a derived class of new employee (see Figure 5.11).

```
+-----------------------------+  taxes()
|         Salary              |  benefits()
|        Sicktime             |
|        MedicalPlan          |
|        DentalPlan           |
|         Vacation            |
|           Car               |
+-----------------------------+
```

Figure 5.10 The `FullEmployee` class.

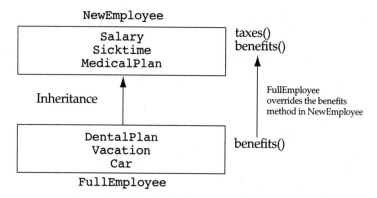

Figure 5.11 Using inheritance to create a better employee design.

5.7 Heuristics That Trade Off Design Complexity and Flexibility

Heuristic 5.6

All abstract classes must be base classes.

If a class cannot build objects of itself, then that class must be inherited by some derived class that does know how to build objects. If this is not the case, then the functionality of the base class can never be accessed by any object in the system, and therefore the class is irrelevant in the given domain. (There is one degenerate case where an abstract class that is not a base class can exist. We will examine this degenerate case in Chapter 8.)

What about the opposite heuristic—do all base classes have to be abstract? After examining the new and full employee example above, the answer is obviously no. Both the new and full employee classes are concrete classes (i.e. they know how to build objects of themselves) and the new employee is a base class. However, there is a heuristic that captures this desirable design trait.

Heuristic 5.7

All base classes should be abstract classes.

This heuristic implies that all the roots of an inheritance tree should be abstract, while only the leaves should be concrete. Why is this a heuristic? Consider our inheritance model for the new and full employees. Our company has been so successful that it takes new employees five months to learn who to see for maintenance, purchase-order signatures, sick time issues, health insurance, etc. The company decides that it is necessary for new employees to have a one-day orientation session to reduce this learning curve. Obviously, full employees already know all of these details, so they do not need an orientation session. In our current design, can we add an orientation to the new employee class without adding it to the full employee class? The answer is no; we cannot add anything to the new employee class without also adding it to the full employee class. This is the danger of inheriting from a concrete class. The fear is that the specialization link between the two classes will not hold up under extension or refinement of the design. How could we have avoided this problem? Instead of claiming that full employees are special types of new employees, we could have claimed that new employees and full employees have something in common. This common information could have been captured in an abstract base class called `All Employees`, with the new and full employee classes becoming derived classes of this new abstract class (see Figure 5.12).

In order to understand the strength of a heuristic, it is necessary to understand the ramifications of violating it. In this case, the necessary changes to our system were brought about by violating the heuristic. We had to rename all occurrences of `NewEmployee` to `AllEmployee`—a global name change. This is the worst that can happen to a designer who violates this heuristic. In fact, if the designer can live with the name of the concrete class as the name of the new abstract class (renaming the concrete class to something different), then he or she may be able to avoid the name change in some languages. For example, name the abstract class `NewEmployee` and rename what used to be `NewEmployee` as `NewNewEmployee`. Typically, and this example is no exception, the name of the concrete base class is too specific to use as the name of the new abstract class.

Given that violations of this heuristic can force a designer to rename classes globally, shouldn't we always turn inheritance from a concrete class into inheritance from an

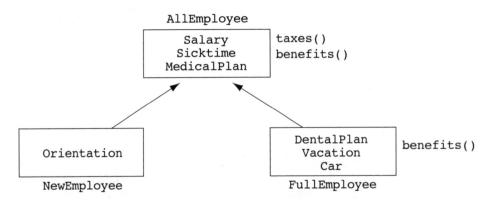

Figure 5.12 A better `Employee` inheritance hierarchy.

abstract class (using the `Employee` classes as a model)? The answer would appear to be yes, except that another heuristic gets in our way. Consider the case where we cannot see any change to the base class that we would not want carried into the derived class. As Figure 5.13 shows, the `NewEmployee` class could still inherit from `AllEmployees`, but it would be empty—no data and no behavior. All of its attributes would be derived from the abstract base class. This `NewEmployee` class is an irrelevant class since it adds no meaningful behavior to our system. Therefore, it should be removed, based on Heuristic 3.7.

This is a case where one heuristic tells the designer to go in one direction and another heuristic tells the designer to go in the exact opposite direction. Which direction should we choose? If there is only one place in the design where the choice needs to be made, then it does not matter. One irrelevant class will not ruin a design, nor will one area of the design that may require a global name change. Unfortunately, most designs have many places where this decision needs to be made. I would not want 50 irrelevant classes in my system, nor would I want 50 potential name changes. The typical solution is to attempt to find which of the 50 cases are most likely to change. Add an irrelevant derived class for these. The others are left as inheritance from a concrete class. It is important to realize that finding the classes most likely to change is not an easy task. Imagine a designer in our employee domain standing up in a design critique and stating, "We would never give anything to a new employee that a full employee would not want as well." The assumption here is that everything a new employee gets is good. The designer has not considered orientation, layoff notices, probationary periods, etc. In languages that allow for type aliasing (e.g., the `typedef` statement in C and C++), a reasonable solution is to create the inheritance hierarchy with just the full and new employees (no abstract class) and alias the `NewEmployee` class to the `AllEmployee` class wherever applicable. This allows for easy global name changes should it ever become necessary.

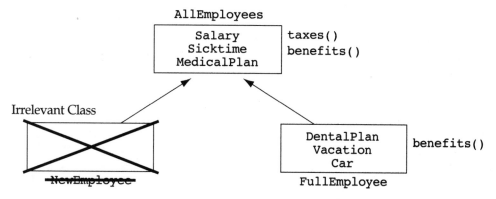

Figure 5.13 `NewEmployee` as an irrelevant class.

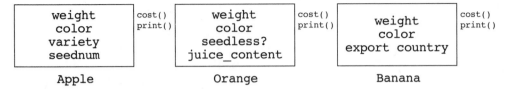

Figure 5.14 Finding commonality among classes.

5.8   A Real-World Example of Generalization

We consider the preceding example to be specialization because we started with a base class and added a new derived class to our system. Consider the three classes displayed in Figure 5.14. It is obvious that they have some things in common. First, all three contain a weight and a color. This in itself is not enough to constitute an inheritance relationship. If two or more classes share only common data, that is, no common messages, then that common data should be encapsulated in some new class. The two (or more) classes that share the common data can each contain the new class. Since the object-oriented paradigm encapsulates data and behavior in a bidirectional relationship, common data usually implies common behavior. In these cases, an inheritance relationship is required to capture the common abstraction. In our example in Figure 5.14, each of the three classes also has a print and cost function (i.e., common messages). Upon further inspection, we find that the apple and orange classes also have the same implementation for the print function (i.e., common methods). The result is the need to create a common base class called Fruit to capture the common abstractions (see Figure 5.15).

Since we started with derived classes and then found the base class, this is called **generalization**. While this real-world example makes it look easy to generalize, in practice many of the common abstractions are not found until the late stages of software development. This is not a serious problem since new base classes can be

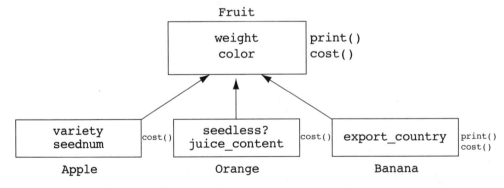

Figure 5.15 Generalization of Apple, Banana, and Orange to Fruit.

added to the system very late in development with little impact on the system. In this example, even if there were many users of `Apple`, `Orange`, and `Banana`, we could easily add the abstract `Fruit` class with no effect on these users. The users of these classes are sending messages to apples. They do not care if `apple` defines the method directly or steals it from a base class. As long as `apple` prints itself when it is told, the user is happy. Of course, in these situations there is a chance that the implementor of `Apple` named the method `print()` but the implementor of `Orange` named the equivalent method `write()`.

Heuristic 5.8

Factor the commonality of data, behavior, and/or interface as high as possible in the inheritance hierarchy.

The point of this heuristic is to allow as many derived classes as possible to take advantage of a common abstraction. A violation of this heuristic implies that a particular abstraction will need to be redesigned and implemented in each of the derived classes, rather than once in the base class [9]. It is important that all derived classes in the hierarchy share the common abstraction, since the abstraction cannot (or should not) be eliminated by a derived class. See Section 5.17 for details of this common pitfall.

The heuristic also allows users of a derived class to decouple themselves from that class in favor of a more general class. For example, rather than depending on the `Apple` class, a user could depend on some fruit class, which may be an apple.

5.9   The Mechanism of Polymorphism

The fruit example, as written, assumes a domain where apples, oranges, and bananas are used separately. They just happen to have a common abstraction (fruit). Let us consider a domain where someone would like to walk up to a fruit, not knowing what type of fruit it happens to be, and tell it to compute its cost. The fruit basket object/class shown in Figure 5.16 is an example where this type of operation might be applicable.

For some of the operations on the fruit basket, it is convenient to think of a fruit basket as a list of fruit. Operations like `how_many()` do not care what types of fruits have been placed in the fruit basket. Other operations, such as `cost`, need to know the explicit type of fruit in the fruit basket since apples cost 50 cents, bananas cost 40 cents, and oranges cost 60 cents. In action-oriented programming, this type of construct is usually implemented as a structure-embedded union (in C) or variant record (in Pascal) (see Figure 5.17).

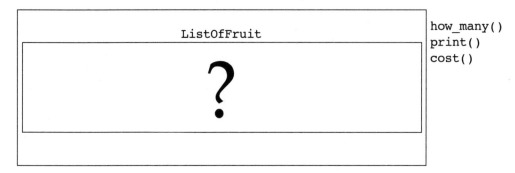

Figure 5.16 The `FruitBasket` class.

A design that uses variant records to implement the fruit basket inevitably requires explicit case analysis (e.g., a `case` statement, nested `if-then-else` statements) to determine which type was stored in the variant record. For example, the `cost` function for the variant record `fruit` would look like the following pseudocode:

```
Function fruit_cost(fruit f)
    perform case analysis on the type field of f
        case Apple:   return 50
        case Banana:  return 40
        case Orange:  return 60
    End
```

The problem with explicit case analysis is that if we decide to add a new type of fruit, we need to add a new case to the case statement. When we modify existing code, we risk introducing new bugs into that code. Watch out for the designer who claims that nothing can go wrong since there is only one added case statement. In reality, there is never one added case statement; there are usually many of them sprinkled throughout the code. The probability of forgetting to add the appropriate case to one of them is high [10].

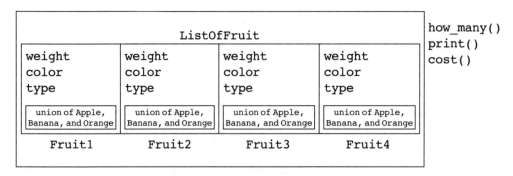

Figure 5.17 The `FruitBasket` class.

The object-oriented paradigm solves this problem through a mechanism known as **polymorphism** or **dynamic binding**. The idea behind polymorphism is that a group of heterogeneous objects (e.g., apples, oranges, bananas) can be made to look homogeneous (e.g., a bunch of fruit), but can then be distinguished based on their own specific type at runtime. If you do not mind believing in magic, then imagine the ability to walk up to any fruit and tell it to give you its cost. You know the object to which you sent the cost message is not a fruit object because there is no such thing as a fruit object (fruit is an abstract class). Therefore, it is an apple, or a banana, or an orange masquerading as a fruit (see Figure 5.18). When the message is sent, the system figures out (magic) which type of fruit you are actually sending the message to and calls the appropriate method, i.e., the cost method of `Apple`, or the cost method of `Banana`, or the cost method of `Orange`.

If you do not like believing in magic, there is an explanation as to how polymorphism is implemented. In the object-oriented community, you may hear people talk about true polymorphism versus polymorphism. The argument here revolves around the implementation of polymorphism. Interpreted languages generally make all message sends polymorphic by definition of the language (e.g., SmallTalk). The typical implementation is for the system to ask the object for its type at the time the message is sent (see Figure 5.19). The object gives the system a string with the name of its type, e.g., "Apple." The system hashes this string with the string containing the name of the message, e.g., "cost." This gives the system an index into a hash table where the address of the cost method for the apple class lives. It then jumps to this address, which completes the message send. This is often called **true polymorphism**.

Compiled languages such as C++, which are concerned with higher levels of efficiency, allow the implementors of a class to decide which functions should be polymorphic (or dynamically bound) and which should be **monomorphic** (or **statically bound**). These languages typically build jump tables for each class containing poly-

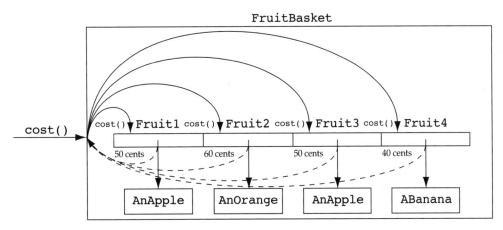

Figure 5.18 The `FruitBasket` and polymorphism.

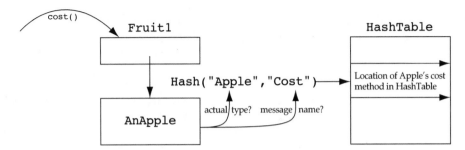

Figure 5.19 The implementation of polymorphism (SmallTalk).

morphic functions. As is illustrated in Figure 5.20, a hidden pointer is added to each object, which points at its particular jump table. The address of this jump table maintains the particular type of the base class we are examining, e.g., apple objects point at the apple jump table even if they are being viewed as fruit. At runtime, when a derived class is built, its constructor points the hidden pointer at the appropriate jump table. In order to execute a polymorphic function call, the system need only

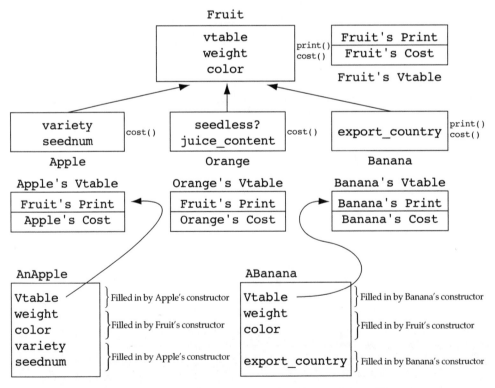

Figure 5.20 The implementation of polymorphism (C++).

jump into the jump table with the constant offset defined by the name of the message. No hashing of strings or hash table problems (e.g., collisions) need to be addressed at runtime.

There is another refinement to polymorphism, called **pure polymorphism**. A pure polymorphic function has no default definition in the base class. Derived classes that inherit a pure polymorphic function are said to be inheriting for interface, that is, they are inheriting messages, not methods. In the fruit example, we state that the `print` message for the `Fruit` class has a good default method. The best a fruit can do is print, "Hi, I'm a .3-pound red fruit." If a derived class does not define its own `print` function, then it can at least get this default through inheritance. On the other hand, the `cost` function has no good default. The `Fruit` class wants to state that all derived classes of `Fruit` must define a cost method, but it has no clue as to what the algorithm should be. This is the role of pure polymorphism. We say that `print` for `fruit` is polymorphic, and `cost` for `fruit` is pure polymorphic. In C++, an abstract base class is implemented either as a class that has one or more pure polymorphic functions and/or as a class that has no public constructor.

Heuristic 5.9

> If two or more classes share only common data (no common behavior), then that common data should be placed in a class that will be contained by each sharing class.

Heuristic 5.10

> If two or more classes have common data and behavior (i.e., methods), then those classes should each inherit from a common base class that captures those data and methods.

Heuristic 5.11

> If two or more classes share only a common interface (i.e., messages, not methods), then they should inherit from a common base class only if they will be used polymorphically.

The last heuristic refers to the fact that inheritance for interface does not buy you anything unless the derived objects will be required to perform a runtime type discrimination. If all valves turn on and turn off, but each valve does it differently, then the base class "valve" is not useful unless there exists some place in the application where a generic valve will need to decide which it is at runtime. If water valves are always used in one place, and oil valves are always used in another place, then runtime-type discrimination is unnecessary and the base class "valve" adds no interesting perspectives to the design. Of course, a designer is free to argue that the objects are likely to be polymorphic in the future, thereby justifying the existence of the base class through extensibility concerns.

Heuristic 5.12

> **Explicit case analysis on the type of an object is usually an error. The designer should use polymorphism in most of these cases.**

If a designer creates a method that states, "If you are of type1, do this; else if you are of type2, do this; else if are of type3, do this, else if . . . ," he or she is making a mistake. The better approach is to have all of the types involved in the explicit case analysis inherit from a common class. This common class defines a pure polymorphic function called do_this, and each type can write its own do_this method. Now the method the designer creates need only send the do_this message to the object in question. The polymorphism mechanism can perform the case analysis implicitly, eliminating the need to modify existing code when a new type is added to the system.

5.10   A Problem with the Use of Inheritance as a Reusability Mechanism

One role of polymorphism is in the creation of reusable, standard components that can be derived into custom components. Beware of the marketing hype that claims that object-oriented designers can take standard components from a reusable library, inherit from them, and produce custom components that optimally reuse the code of the standard component. The following case study is taken from a C++ class library project in which I participated several years ago. In the process of designing a linked list class, I considered the fact that the library was also going to have a sorted linked list class. Early in the design process, I realized that sorted linked lists are special types of linked lists (which are unsorted). I wondered how to get optimal reuse of code from this inheritance relationship, and came up with the design in Figure 5.21.

I then realized that it was not the insert and delete methods that were different—it was where I performed the insertion and deletion that differed. I abstracted out this difference into a polymorphic function called find and made the function protected. The reason for the protected status is that the find method is not an operation for users of the classes, and so it should not be in the public interface, but the derived class (SortedLinkedList) needs to override it. Thus, it cannot be private. The resultant hierarchy, shown in Figure 5.22, produced optimal reusability of the base class code (or at least as optimal as I could imagine). In the actual library, the

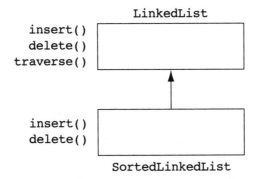

```
                          LinkedList
        insert()
        delete()
        traverse()



        insert()
        delete()



                      SortedLinkedList
```

Figure 5.21 The reuse of abstractions through inheritance.

LinkedList class consisted of 40 pages of code and documentation, whereas the SortedLinkedList class had only 2 pages, most of it documentation.

It is very common to see protected, polymorphic functions being called from monomorphic functions in the base class (in languages that allow implementors a choice between polymorphic and monomorphic functions). Some developers like to call them the "reusability hooks" of a class. Examples of this type of binding can be viewed through examples of a linked list and a sorted linked list inserting a number. The examples assume a compiled language that supports implementor choices between monomorphic and polymorphic functions.

> When a linked list wishes to insert a value, the compiler, at compile time, asks the linked list class, "Do you know how to insert into objects of your class?" The answer is yes (see Figure 5.22), so hardwire the function call to insert for linked list. This method always takes a reference to a linked list as the implied first argument. However, that reference may be referring to a derived object of linked list (namely a sorted linked list object). At runtime, the insert for linked list method is directly called, and execution continues until the call to the find method. The

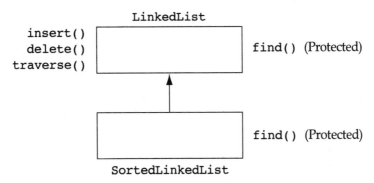

```
                      LinkedList
        insert()
        delete()                          find() (Protected)
        traverse()



                                          find() (Protected)

                  SortedLinkedList
```

Figure 5.22 Optimizing the reuse of code and abstractions.

find message is polymorphic, so the system must ask the implied first argument, "I know you look like a linked list object, but what are you really?" The object replies, "I'm a linked list!" The system then transfers control to the protected find method for linked list, which returns the desired result for linked list objects and `insert` continues.

When a sorted linked list wishes to insert a value, the compiler, at compile time, asks the sorted linked list class, "Do you know how to insert into objects of your class?" The answer is no since sorted linked lists do not define an insert method. The compiler then asks, "Do you inherit from someone who does know how to insert?" The answer is yes—the linked list class. The compiler then hardwires the call to `insert` for linked list. At runtime, the insert for linked list method is directly called, and execution continues until the call to the find method. The find message is polymorphic, so the system must ask the implied first argument (which is a reference to a linked list), "I know you look like a linked list object, but what are you really?" The object replies, "Okay! You caught me. I'm a sorted linked list object masquerading as a linked list." The system then transfers control to the protected find method for sorted linked list, which returns a result very different from the find method of linked list, and `insert` continues.

It appeared that the marketing hype was true. I took a standard component (`LinkedList`) and created a custom component (`SortedLinkedList`) with optimal code reusability (see Figure 5.23). Given this fact, it would be possible to sell the library as a collection of class definitions (header files) and object code consisting of the compiled class methods. Customizers of my standard components would not need to know the implementation of my base classes in order to customize them. My balloon suddenly burst when I decided to add a linked ring class to my class library. I realized quickly that linked rings are really just special types of linked lists except the tail pointer of the list points back at the head. I was disappointed to find out that I got zero code reusability. When I implemented the methods of linked list, I iterated over the list by using a conditional test that checked to see if the current pointer into the list was `nil` (or `NULL`, i.e., zero, for C++ programmers). If it was `nil`, then I knew I was at the end of the list. By definition, the linked ring abstraction

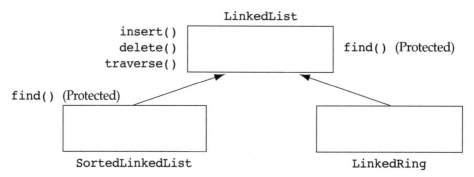

Figure 5.23 A problem with optimal reuse of standard components.

will never see a `nil`. Even an operation as simple as `traverse()`, which prints the elements of a list, was unusable. Given a linked list with the values 10, 20, and 30, `traverse` would print "`( 10 20 30 )`." A linked ring of the same value would print "`( 10 20 30 10 20 30 . . .)`" ad infinitum.

Proponents of the marketing hype argue that the problem is mine, not that of inheritance. Their heuristic is that *every* separate idea within a method of a base class should be encapsulated in a protected, polymorphic function. It is true that if you follow this heuristic you will always get optimal code reusability. You will also go insane if you try to debug or maintain a base class designed in such a manner. The biggest problem is deciding what constitutes a separate idea. Is dynamically allocating a node of a list, perhaps as part of a copy method, a separate idea? It is not, given the classes we have discussed so far. The picture changes when one starts thinking about doubly linked lists, which contain `double_nodes` instead of `nodes`. In short, a derived class is what defines separate ideas in the base class methods. Therefore, unless you know about the derived classes, you cannot provide the necessary hooks in the base class methods. This is the bad news. The good news is that optimal reusability can be achieved with some changes to the implementation details of the base class. The important point is that a customizer needs access to the implementation of a base class. The fact that most, if not all, class libraries are sold in source-code format attests to this fact.

In this example we need to abstract out the testing for the end of lists in the base class methods into a protected polymorphic method called `at_end()`. The `at_end` method will simply check against `NULL` for the `LinkedList` objects and the `SortedLinkedList` objects (via inheritance; see Figure 5.24). However, the `LinkedRing` class will override this method with its own `at_end` method, which will test the current pointer against the head pointer.

The only party affected by the new polymorphic `at_end` function is the implementors of the `LinkedList` class. The users are unaffected, and they are the group we worry about most. Many designers point out that as a class gets older, it picks up more and more of these polymorphic hook functions, which makes it easier to get

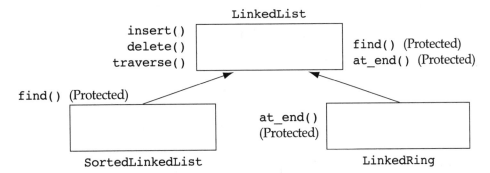

Figure 5.24 Providing optimal reusability through inheritance.

optimal reuse for free. This is entirely true and is called the **maturing** of the base class. Consider a sorted linked ring class. All of the necessary code is already defined in the existing classes. We simply take the `at_end` method of `LinkedRing` and the find method of `SortedLinkedList`. It is important to note that a new derived class may require more than one polymorphic hook function to get optimal reusability. In our class library, the doubly linked list class required five additional polymorphic hook functions in order to incorporate its abstraction optimally with that of the linked list class. Once we found the necessary abstractions, we had all of the necessary hooks for `SortedDoublyLinkedList`, `DoublyLinkedRing`, and `SortedDoublyLinkedRing`. In any event, these hooks are always implementation details of the base class.

5.11   An Inheritance Solution to an Interrupt-Driven Architecture

Recall Heuristic 4.13 on the containment relationship. It stated that a contained object should not have knowledge of the class that contains it. We stated that this heuristic is important if a designer wishes to reuse his or her abstractions. If the contained object knows its containing class, then it cannot be reused in a domain that does not have the container and everything else in that container.

Following this heuristic often becomes a problem when dealing with interrupt driven devices. Consider the problem where `ATM` contains a `CardReader`. A use case of this system states that the user puts a card in a `CardReader`, which activates the `ATM`. The most intuitive design for such a system might look like the diagram in Figure 5.25. The main problem with this design is that `CardReader` cannot be reused outside the domain of the `ATM`. What if we wish to build a new class called `SecurityDoor` which contains a `CardReader`? This design would not allow it.

A better solution is to use the inheritance relationship to generalize the `ATM` to some device (see Figure 5.26). This uses the inheritance relationship to state that an `ATM` is a special type of device, and it uses the containment relationship to state that `CardReader`s are contained in some device, not necessarily an `ATM`. This reduces the constraint from "`CardReader`s must be used inside an `ATM`" to "`CardReader`s

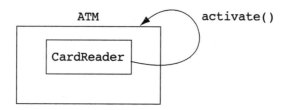

Figure 5.25 The `ATM` and `CardReader` problem.

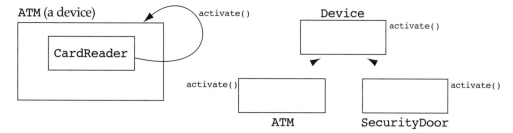

Figure 5.26 ATMs as special types of devices.

must be used inside some device, of which `ATM` is one of many." This solution implies that multiple inheritance might be necessary. If the `ATM` contains two such interrupting devices and wishes to use this generalizing solution, then it will need to inherit from two abstract classes. This inheritance will be easy to live with since the abstract classes will contain only a pure polymorphic interface closely coupled with the contained data object (in this case, the `CardReader`).

An even better design (from the viewpoint of logical design), which removes all constraints, is to modify the way we look at interrupt-driven systems. In one design course, a participant said, "Everything is a polling system. The difference between polling and interrupt-driven is your point of view. When we poll in hardware, we like to call it interrupt-driven." With this in mind, let us think of the `CardReader` as a polled device. Even if it is physically interrupt-driven, we can use the interrupt to change the state of the `CardReader` object. The `ATM` can poll for a change in this state. This design allows any object or class to ask the `CardReader` if it has a card (see Figure 5.27). When it has a card, the client object can react any way it likes. This design offers the needed flexibility when dealing with containment hierarchies. The reader should note that this design might not be practical for physical design reasons, such as efficiency. The fact that an `ATM` does not do anything while waiting for a card allows us to use the polling solution.

5.12   Inheritance Hierarchies Versus Attributes

An interesting problem arises due to confusion between attributes versus the need for an inheritance hierarchy. A design philosophy advocated by Weiner, Wilkerson,

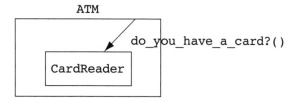

Figure 5.27 A better solution to the `ATM` problem.

and Wirfs-Brock [10] includes examining the parts of speech associated with the English description of the system (a requirements specification). They state that nouns are good candidates for classes and objects, verbs are good candidates for operations on these classes and objects, and adjectives tend to signal inheritance. I like their methodology because it gives designers a starting point when they have no idea what their classes/objects, operations, or inheritance should be. I dislike their methodology because it starts designers off with a long list of candidates that must be refined. It puts them on a dangerous path toward the proliferation of classes, one of the more serious problems in the object-oriented paradigm. At this time, let us focus on the adjectives portion of their methodology. I have a requirements specification with the following sentence in it:

> In our system, there exist red balls, green balls, and yellow balls.

Which of the designs in Figure 5.28 is a better model of the class `Ball`?

Many designers choose the first model, where there exists one class called `Ball`, which has color as an attribute. Unfortunately, the requirements specification describes a domain in which red balls bounce twice as high as green balls and yellow balls do not bounce at all. Also, if you eat a red ball you die, a yellow ball makes you sick, and a green ball makes you stronger. Now which design is better?

Another question that demonstrates the same problem can be extracted from the fruit hierarchy described earlier. Why is it considered reasonable to have a variety attribute in the `Apple` class but not in the `Fruit` class? There are different types of fruit, and we modeled that abstraction as an inheritance hierarchy. However, there are also different types of apples, and we implemented that abstraction as an attribute. Why is there a difference?

The deciding question is "Does the value of an attribute affect the behavior of the class?" If the answer is yes, then most of the time we want inheritance. If the answer is no, then we want to model the abstraction as an attribute that can take on different values. There are cases where differing values of attributes should not imply inheritance. We will discuss this class of problems a bit later in this chapter.

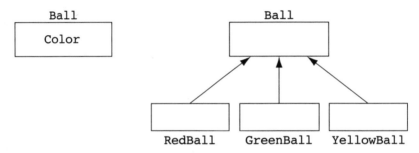

Figure 5.28 Two designs for the `Ball` class.

What would inform a designer that he or she is making a mistake if the error is to model an abstraction as an attribute when it should have been modeled as an inheritance hierarchy? As the designer begins to model methods of his or her class, he or she will notice that some methods are performing explicit case analysis on the values of attributes. This implies that inheritance might be necessary.

What would inform a designer that he or she is making a mistake if the error is to model an abstraction as an inheritance hierarchy when it should have been modeled as an attribute? All meaningful behavior on the derived classes will be the same, so it will migrate to the abstract base class. This implies that all of the derived classes lack meaningful behavior of their own and should be eliminated as irrelevant classes. The first case is much more common. As a design proceeds through many iterations and more information is gathered, it is often the case that attributes end up defining an inheritance hierarchy.

Beware of behaviors defined on derived classes which could be factored into a single behavior of the base class through parameterization via the value of a base class attribute. An example would be a designer who argues that the `RedBall`, `GreenBall`, and `YellowBall` classes need to exist because the `print` function for `RedBall` prints "`Hi, I'm a red ball!`"; the `print` function for `GreenBall` prints "`Hi, I'm a green ball!`"; and the `print` function for `YellowBall` prints "`Hi, I'm a yellow ball!`" The bounce function of `ball` mentioned earlier might fit into this category. Maybe the `Ball` class should have an attribute called `Bounce-Factor`, which would be zero, one, or two.

Heuristic 5.13

> **Explicit case analysis on the value of an attribute is often an error. The class should be decomposed into an inheritance hierarchy, where each value of the attribute is transformed into a derived class.**

5.13 The Confusion of the Need for Inheritance Versus an Object's Dynamic Semantics

Let us examine a new inheritance hierarchy that was discovered through application of Heuristic 5.13. While examining a `Stack` class, a designer realized that the `pop` method was performing case analysis on the value of the `Stack_pointer` data member. If it was zero, the stack could not pop, and if it was greater than zero, it had an algorithm for popping. The design was further substantiated when he or she realized that empty stacks know how to push but nonempty stacks know how to both push and pop (see Figure 5.29). That is, the `pop` method is really an added functionality.

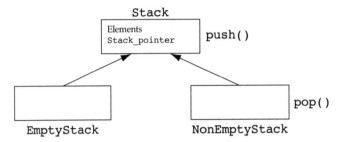

Figure 5.29 The `Stack` inheritance hierarchy.

What do you think of this design? Everything seems satisfactory until we think about the life of a stack object. It is created as an empty stack object; someone executes a push operation and the empty stack object is converted to a nonempty stack object. Later, someone executes a pop operation and the nonempty stack object turns back into an empty stack object. The object keeps toggling its type at runtime. In most object-oriented implementations, changing the type of an object at runtime is an expensive operation. It requires constructing an object of the new class using a constructor for the new class which accepts an object of the old class as an argument. The old object must then be destroyed upon return from the constructor.

What has caused this problem? It turns out that explicit case analysis on the value of an attribute is sometimes the implementation of the dynamic semantics of an object (i.e., its states and their transitions). If a designer attempts to capture these dynamic semantics using the static semantics of inheritance, a toggling of types is the result. Whenever an object would have changed its state in the old design, an object of one derived class must be changed to an object of another derived class in the new design. This is highly inefficient and confusing. The modeling of an object's legal states as classes is another cause of proliferation of classes, albeit a trivial one. The designer usually detects this toggling problem at design time, and certainly at implementation time. While the stack class in Figure 5.29 does not look like a serious proliferation problem, consider the state-transition diagram in Figure 2.9 for the class `Process` (of an operating system). If each state of the `Process` class is modeled as its own distinct class, then we would be adding five new classes to our system. In addition, many objects would be toggling their types at runtime. In any event, users of a class should not be aware of the mechanics of its states and/or their transitions. These items are implementation details of the class.

Heuristic 5.14

Do not model the dynamic semantics of a class through the use of the inheritance relationship. An attempt to model dynamic semantics with a static semantic relationship will lead to a toggling of types at runtime.

How do we implement dynamic semantics? The preferred method is to perform explicit case analysis on the values of the attributes that capture the state information. While explicit case analysis is undesirable, at least this case analysis is used only by implementors of the class. Explicit case analysis on the types of objects is often performed by the users of a class, a much nastier maintenance problem. Also, it is much more likely for applications to get a new type than for a class to get a new state. James Coplien's letter/envelope idiom can be used to provide an interesting polymorphic solution to this problem [11]. I call this solution a **dynamic semantic wrapper** and display it in Figure 5.30. The idea is to capture the states of a class in an inheritance hierarchy internal to the class. A state field of the class will toggle types, but since the state class does not contain data, type changes are extremely cheap (one-integer assignment in the case of C++).

The problem with this solution is that inheritance hierarchies tend to get a bit unruly in large applications. Having each class with interesting dynamic semantics contain its own inheritance hierarchy adds complexity to the design. Many developers do not feel this added complexity is a good trade-off considering they only get out of explicit case analysis in the hidden implementation of the class. However, as Coplien correctly points out, some classes have very complex state behavior that certainly benefits from the distributive effects of the inheritance solution.

5.14 Using Inheritance to Hide the Representation of a Class

Recall our `Dictionary` class from Chapter 2's (Section 2.3) discussion on class cohesion and coupling. In that example, we took a dictionary that contained a property list and hash table with the four operations **hadd**, **padd**, **hfind**, and **pfind** and converted it into two classes called `PDictionary` and `HDictionary`, each having "add" and "find" operations. This solution eliminated the weak coupling and noncommunicating behavior found in the `Dictionary` class but required the builder of `Dictionary` objects to decide which implementation of dictionaries he or she wanted. In some domains, leaving this decision to the users is appropriate. If the

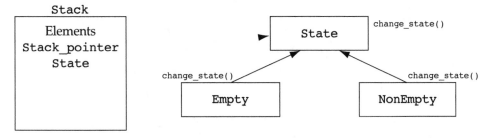

Figure 5.30 Dynamic semantic wrappers.

builder of a dictionary understands how he or she will use the dictionary, then perhaps he or she should be the one to make the implementation decision. Some may object to my concatenating the name of a data type to the word "dictionary," but that is just an argument of class naming. If we called them `SmallDictionary` and `LargeDictionary`, most objectors would disappear.

(Side note: I am constantly surprised at the amount of time wasted during design critiques when two parties think they are arguing about some important design issue when, in fact, they are arguing only about the name of a class. Some of these discussions are due to the learning curve, and some are intrinsic to design in general. I think I have become faster at catching these cases, but I am amazed at how often I get dragged into such discussions. I am tempted to add this tongue-in-cheek heuristic: "If two parties who know what they are talking about argue for a long period of time during a design critique, flip a coin to resolve the situation." The argument implies that the two camps are in a design situation where there does not exist a clear trade-off between the two contested designs. The "who know what they are talking about" clause is very important. Sometimes critique arguments go on for a long period of time because neither party knows what they are talking about. I do not mind arguing for six hours over the name of a class as long as I understand that, at the end of the argument, all I stand to win or lose is a class name.)

In many domains it is not appropriate for the users of a class to decide a class's representation. The class implementors are expected to decide the best representation for the class, based on its current state. Whenever the state changes, the class implementors are required to examine the change and determine if the representation still adequately reflects the best solution for the given use of the object. If the representation becomes inappropriate, the implementors are expected to effect the necessary representational changes. In the case of dictionaries, the constraints may state that for dictionaries with less than 100 words, property lists are the best representation; for dictionaries with more than 100 words, hash tables become more appropriate. When a `Dictionary` object's user adds the 100th word to the object, the `Dictionary` class automatically changes its representation from a property list to a hash table. If a `Dictionary` object's word count drops below 100, the `Dictionary` class will change the representation back to a property list from the hash table. This change of representation is completely hidden from the users of the class (see Figure 5.31).

5.15 Mistaking Objects for Derived Classes

Consider the inheritance hierarchy shown in Figure 5.32. At first view the inheritance hierarchy looks correct. `GeneralMotors`, `Ford`, and `Chrysler` are all special types of car manufacturers. On second thought, is `GeneralMotors` really a special type of car manufacturer? Or is it an example of a car manufacturer? This is a classic error and it causes proliferation of classes. The designer of this hierarchy has accidentally

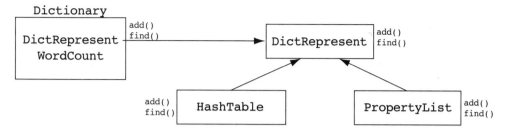

Figure 5.31 Dictionary with hidden, changing representation.

turned what should have been objects of a class into derived classes of the class. If you have made this mistake, it will certainly manifest itself as a derived class for which there is only one instance in your system. How many `GeneralMotors` objects are there? `Ford` objects? `Chrysler` objects? The answer for all three classes is one. In this case they should have been objects. Keep in mind that not all derived classes that have only one instance in your system are manifestations of this error, but many will be.

Heuristic 5.15

> **Do not turn objects of a class into derived classes of the class. Be very suspicious of any *derived* class for which there is only one instance.**

There is a temptation to state that in some domains the three objects of the class `CarManufacturer` should actually be derived classes due to some domain-specific reason. For example, perhaps `GeneralMotors` and `Ford` have very different accounting methods, and we feel this difference in behavior requires a polymorphic method (see Figure 5.33). Even in these cases, the three items in question are still objects. If the accounting methods are different, the developer is required to find some way of abstracting the differences into the data of the `CarManufacturer` class and to create a generic method that uses this data to manifest the appropriate behavior of each object. It makes no sense to create a derived class for which there can be only one object.

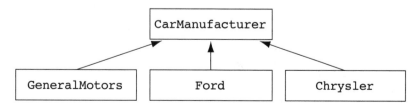

Figure 5.32 Creating classes from objects.

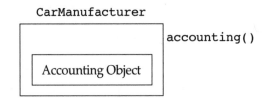

Figure 5.33 Using objects to generalize behavior.

5.16   Mistaking Object Generalization for the Need to Build Classes at Runtime

Another category of problem manifests itself through inheritance hierarchies. This problem occurs when a developer thinks that he or she needs to create new classes at runtime. The domain in which this problem presented itself was a case where a development team was designing a trading system for securities. One requirement of the system was to allow securities traders to build deals around a fixed set of securities set by the SEC and other government bodies. They designed the class hierarchy displayed in Figure 5.34 to model these securities.

A second requirement stated that traders want the ability to invent and trade new securities on a moment's notice. For example, a trader may decide to group a gold option with a taxfree municipal bond and call it a new security, say a Gmuni. Even worse, the trader may decide to take his or her new Gmuni security and combine it with Lotus Development Corp. stock and call this new security a GmuniLotus (see

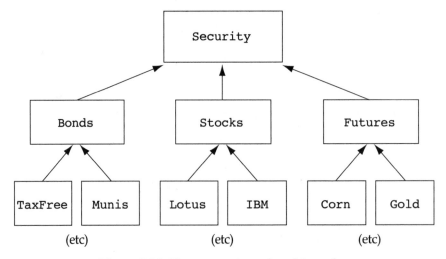

Figure 5.34 The Security class hierarchy.

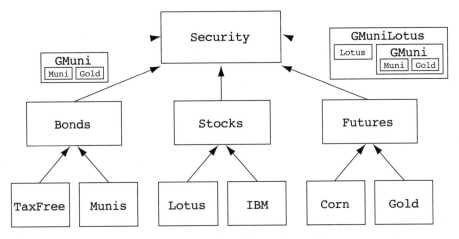

Figure 5.35 The `Security` class hierarchy with new securities.

Figure 5.35).* The possible permutations are endless. This led the developers to assume that they needed an interpreted language to carry out their goals, since compiled languages wouldn't allow them to create classes and inheritance relationships at runtime.

When faced with these situations, a designer needs to reconsider the problem. We should state, "We do not build classes at runtime; we build objects at runtime." The problem for us to solve is the generalization of the things we consider classes, but are really objects. The resulting generalization will be a new class that captures the abstractions within our problem. In this example, let us consider the `Gmuni`, `GmuniLotus`, and a number of other custom-built securities to be objects. What class would capture the abstraction to which these objects belong? In the most general case, these objects belong to a class that is a container of securities. This can be captured in the `BasketOfSecurity` class shown in Figure 5.36.

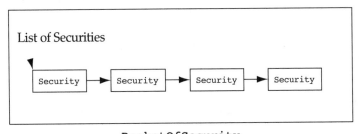

Figure 5.36 Solution to generalizing custom `Security` objects.

---

*Readers that are in the securities industry will find these examples unrealistic for the domain. The securities examples were selected for clarity across a wide audience, and are adequate for discussing the heuristic.

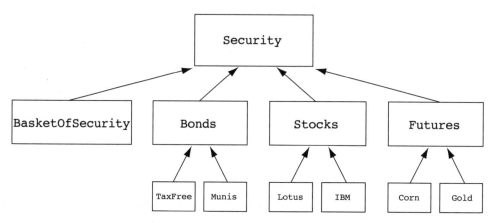

Figure 5.37 The new `Security` class hierarchy.

Figure 5.37 illustrates that not only does the `BasketOfSecurity` class contain a list of securities, but it is itself a security. This is an unusual, but not incorrect, case where a class contains and inherits from the same class. It is unusual only because containers of items are seldom a special type of the items that they contain. Another example of this construct can be seen in graphical user interface classes. A window can be viewed as a container of window items (buttons, sliders, borders, etc.). In addition, a window is a window item because windows can contain windows.

Consider a pure polymorphic function called `price()`. Each security in the hierarchy must define a price method describing the security's current value. If the price of any `BasketOfSecurity` is simply the sum of its components, then the method is trivial. We simply loop over the list of securities, summing the price of each. In the active world of securities, this simple scheme is inadequate. The traders of securities build new securities, which amount to hedged bets. By selling gold and buying silver in one security, the trader limits the potential for loss since gold and silver tend to rise and fall together. The trader is hoping the spread between the two increases in his or her favor. Some of these hedging structures can have complex pricing schemes. Beware of class designers who argue that since each `BasketOf-Security` knows how to price itself differently, each should be a different class with a polymorphic price method. The items in question are still objects. It is just that the problem of pricing them has gotten tougher to generalize. We need to come up with a pricing formula that is encapsulated in each `BasketOfSecurity` object (see Figure 5.38). A generic pricing method can then use this encapsulated formula to calculate the price of the new security.

Another case where this problem arose was in a group of developers designing a reporting system for automobile engine test data. The requirements of the system included the ability for end users to describe complex reports such as, "Show me the blah-blah-blah statistics averaged over every tenth point for the first two thousand data points then every fiftieth point for the next fifty thousand data points,

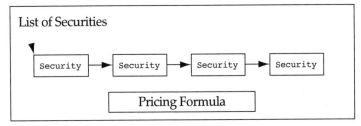

BasketOfSecurity

Figure 5.38 Solution to generalizing custom `Security` objects.

etc." These report descriptions could be extremely complicated. The initial assumption was that each report description represented a class. Again the problem was creating classes at runtime. The solution was to treat every report as an object and then find a good report class that generalized all of them. The data implementation of this class was fairly complex, but the generic methods were surprisingly easy. The main benefit was that only objects were built at runtime, not classes.

Heuristic 5.16

If you think you need to create new classes at runtime, take a step back and realize that what you are trying to create are objects. Now generalize these objects into a class.

5.17   The Attempt to NOP a Base Class Method in Its Derived Class(es)

Another interesting problem that arises in the construction of inheritance hierarchies occurs when the designer attempts to NOP a base method in the derived class, that is, define an empty method in the derived class. While teaching a C++ course at a telecommunications company, I introduced the following heuristic.

Heuristic 5.17

It should be illegal for a derived class to override a base class method with a NOP method, that is, a method that does nothing.

An attendee of the course objected, explaining that their developers did this all of the time. Rather than explaining the actual problem involving classes in their domain combined with a C++ binding for OSF Motif, the objecting person drew a real-world analogy. She stated that they had a situation in which there is an existing class called `Dog`. The behaviors that all `Dogs` know how to carry out is `bark`, `chase_cats`, and `wag_tail`. Later in development they discovered a special type of `Dog` (a derived class) called `DogNoWag`. This new class was exactly like a `Dog` except it didn't know how to wag its tail. They claimed that a good solution was to have `DogNoWag` inherit from `Dog` and override the `wag_tail` method with an empty C++ method (i.e., a NOP) (see Figure 5.39).

A number of other students in the class began to shout out supporting statements such as, "What about dogs with paralyzed tails?" "What about dogs with cut-off tails?" "What about dogs with broken tails?" and "What about stupid dogs who haven't learned to wag their tail?" I have encountered this phenomenon with increasing frequency. These questions imply a completely different design problem than the original, although the originators assume they are bolstering the same argument. There are at least two separate arguments being carried out here. I will create three separate arguments from these questions, in order to introduce a third concept.

The first argument is the one raised by the original problem. What is wrong with the design presented in Figure 5.39? The main objection is that the design does not capture a logical relationship. The design implies the following statements:

> All dogs know how to wag their tails.

> `DogNoWag` is a special type of dog.

> `DogNoWag` does not know how to wag its tail.

Obviously, the rules of classic logic are not being obeyed. Either all dogs do not know how to wag their tails or `DogNoWag` is not a special type of dog. Why should we preserve classic logic? My main argument is that a designer can now use inheritance without restriction. Anything could be considered a specialization of anything else by NOPing all of its base class public interface and adding a new derived public interface.

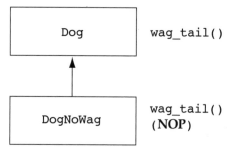

Figure 5.39 `Dogs` and their tails.

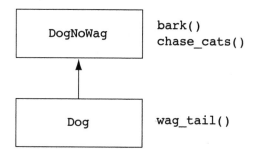

Figure 5.40 `Dogs` and their tails, corrected.

I have seen this NOPing problem entering many designs since the issue was first raised in this course. I believe the problem is psychological: It has always occurred in designs where a derived class is already present and a base class is being added. For whatever reason, designers tend to consider any new class added to a design as being a derived class of the existing classes. When the new base class is added, it is forced to inherit from something that should be its derived class. The result is to eliminate some of the functionality of the derived (acting as base) class via NOP methods. The correct design is found by flipping the hierarchy upside down, making the base class the derived class and the derived class the base class (see Figure 5.40).

However, in some cases, the `DogNoWag` class has some message/method that the `Dog` class does not have. In these cases, neither class is a derived class of the other; they simply have something in common. This common information is captured in an abstract class (e.g., `AllDogs`), and both classes inherit from the abstract class (see Figure 5.41). This latter solution always eliminates the problem of NOP functions.

A recently published introductory object-oriented text contained an example that argued against this heuristic. The domain was that of the animal kingdom, with a focus on platypuses. The author argued that the real world is more complex than that of simple inheritance. We like to categorize things with exceptions, making statements such as

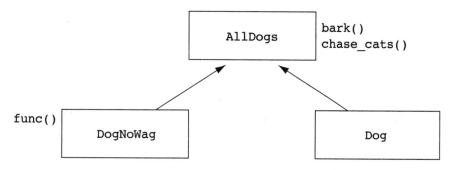

Figure 5.41 `Dogs` and their tails.

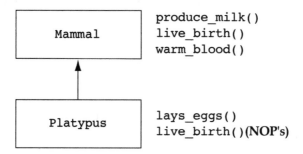

Figure 5.42 Mammals and platypuses.

All mammals have hair, nurse their young with milk, are warm-blooded, and give live birth to their young. Platypuses are special types of mammals that lay eggs instead of giving live birth.

Such a statement maps to the design in Figure 5.42 of mammals and platypuses.

This design is clearly equivalent with the dogs and their tails design: It violates classic logic. Either platypuses are not mammals, or not all mammals give live birth. But what if this is the way human beings like to think of the relationship between mammals and platypuses? Shouldn't we be allowed to model our domains in the way we like to think about them? I will argue against this type of justification. I do not think we can correctly think of a platypus as a special type of mammal unless we are willing to give up the notion that all mammals give live birth. What we really need to state is that mammals and platypuses have a lot in common. That common information needs to be stored in a new base class from which both `Platypus` and `Mammal` inherit (see Figure 5.43). This is the same solution we used for the dog example.

What about the stupid dogs, dogs with paralyzed tails, broken tails, cut-off tails? These are not special classes of dogs: They are dogs with bad state. They still have a `wag_tail` method, which checks the state of the dog, finds that the state is insuf-

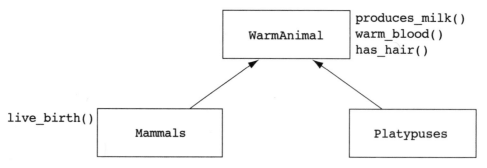

Figure 5.43 Mammals and platypuses, revised.

Dog

```
             IQ: 21            wag_tail()
                               {
                                   if (IQ > 45) {do behavior}
                               }
```

Figure 5.44 Dogs with bad state: stupid dogs.

ficient to manifest behavior, and terminates. This method is not a NOP—it has behavior. If these states were modeled as classes, we would get the same problem we had with the `Stack`, `EmptyStack`, and `NonEmptyStack` classes, namely, toggling types. Stupid dogs will learn to wag their tails and change their type from `StupidDog` to `Dog`. Later they might bump their heads into walls and be stupid again, necessitating a change in type (see Figure 5.44). Likewise, paralyzed and broken tails heal, cut-off tails are stitched back on, etc. You would not want to create classes like `CarWithDeadBattery`, `CarWithStolenBattery`, `CarWithBadStarter`, `CarWithCrackedBlock`, or `CarWithWrongEngine`. These are simply examples of cars with bad state.

5.18   The Implementation of Optional Parts of Objects

While dogs with their tails cut off can be described as dogs with bad state, they bring up an interesting design point. How do we handle optional components of a class? The tail of a dog is optional, the cocktail sauce on a shrimp cocktail is optional, etc. There are two main proposals for the design of optional components: inheritance and containment by reference. These designs are demonstrated in Figure 5.45 for both of the example domains.

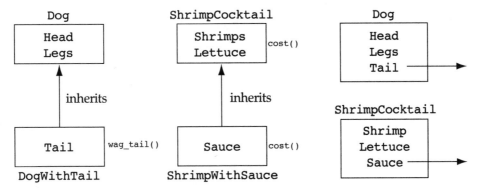

Figure 5.45 Designs for optional components.

Figure 5.46 Missing optional tails as objects.

At first glance, some C++ programmers would choose inheritance as a better model because C++ would use a NULL pointer to implement dogs without their optional tail (see Figure 5.46). This would imply that the wag_tail method would need to perform a conditional test on the pointer before sending a message. Since we try to eliminate explicit case analysis, inheritance seems to be a better choice. As any SmallTalk programmer would point out, the problem is not in the design but in the choice of a multiparadigm language. In a pure language, the NULL pointer could be an object that would be sent the necessary message without a conditional test. In addition, the inheritance solution introduces an extra class (i.e., it is more complex). This type of trade-off will take up incredible amounts of time in a design critique. Neither camp can get enough of an advantage to justify one design over another.

While the trade-offs between these two methods are minimal when there is only one optional component, this is not the case when there are two or more optional components. Consider a House class, which has a heating system, a cooling system, a plumbing system, and an electrical system. All four systems are optional components of a house. Using inheritance to model this design, we end up with 17 classes: 16 derived classes and the base class House. The beauty of this design is that every time we add an optional symbol to our House class, the number of derived classes doubles (approximately). Add an optional alarm system, and we end up with 33 classes instead of 17. Add an automatic sprinkler system, and we get 65 classes. This leads to an exponential, and obvious, proliferation of classes (see Figure 5.47).

The solution is to use containment by reference whenever there are two or more optional components (see Figure 5.48). In order to be consistent, most designers will use this choice when there is only one optional component.

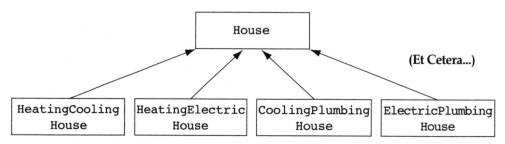

Figure 5.47 Class proliferation and optional components.

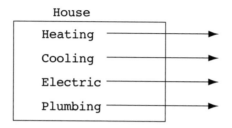

Figure 5.48 Nonproliferation through containment by reference.

Heuristic 5.18

Do not confuse optional containment with the need for inheritance. Modeling optional containment with inheritance will lead to a proliferation of classes.

5.19   A Problem with No Optimal Solution

All of the problems discussed thus far have a satisfactory solution(s). The following problem occurs often in design but has no satisfactory solution; all known solutions have some major drawback. Consider our previous example of a fruit basket (in Section 5.9) that can contain any number of apples, oranges, and bananas. We discussed the role of polymorphism in this example, and why it was to our advantage to design the fruit basket as containing a mixed list of fruit. It often occurs that this mixed-list design is useful for many operations defined for fruit baskets. However, at some later date we decide that one of the derived classes has a special behavior that the others do not. The designer wishes to iterate over all of the fruit in the list for some operations, but then would like to look only at the objects of a particular derived class. For example, consider the case where apples know how to core themselves, but "core" has no relevant meaning to the other types of fruit. Let us also assume that the designer wishes to iterate over the fruit list, telling just the apples to core themselves. How can this be accomplished? We cannot iterate over all the fruit, telling them to core themselves, since only certain fruit know the meaning of that operation. The two most popular solutions either warp the model of fruit by forcing all fruit to know how to core themselves or force the user of the `Fruit` hierarchy to perform a large amount of bookkeeping (see Figure 5.49).

It is important to be sure that the problem actually exists before discussing the possible solutions. This problem often occurs due to naming problems of methods. Consider the `Fruit` hierarchy shown in Figure 5.50.

If the designer wants to send the apples the **core** message, the oranges the **section** message, and the bananas the **peel** message, the real problem is found in the naming

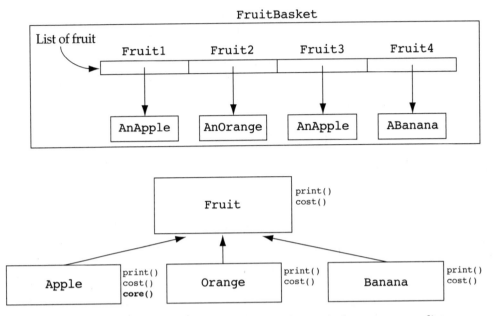

Figure 5.49 Distinguishing heterogeneous objects in homogeneous lists.

of the messages. A better solution would be to state that all fruit know how to prepare themselves, but there exists no good default method (i.e., `prepare` is a pure polymorphic function). The `core` message of apple, the `section` message of orange, and the `peel` message of banana are all renamed to `prepare`, and the problem is solved (see Figure 5.51).

Assuming that the problem really exists, our options are limited. A naive solution is to have each class in the hierarchy maintain a list of messages to which it can respond. At runtime, the developer asks each object for that list of messages. If the appropriate message is in the list, then the developer can send the right message. In this example, the developer would send each fruit object in the fruit basket a "tell me what you can do" message. He or she then checks to see if `core` is in the list. If

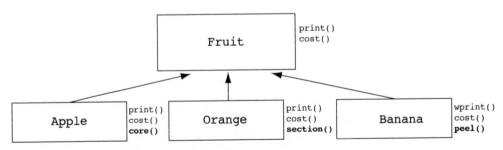

Figure 5.50 Misnamed homogeneous operations.

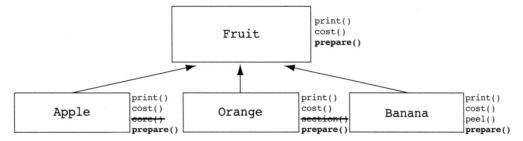

Figure 5.51 The solution for misnamed homogeneous operations.

it is, the `core` message can be sent to the object. The maintenance of the "tell me what you can do" method is the Achille's heel of this solution. Implementors will never be able to keep up with changes to the class due to the implicit, accidental complexity introduced by this solution. This solution is sometimes used appropriately in domains where all objects are restricted as to what operations they can perform/add.

A second, and to many designers the best, solution is to define a core method on the fruit class which is defined as a NOP (see Figure 5.52). The designer can now iterate over all of the fruit in the fruit basket, telling each object to core itself. If a fruit does not know how to core itself, it gets a NOP function for free. If it does know how to core itself, it overrides the default NOP function with its own `core` function.

While this solution is easy to implement, it has several problems. First, what if someone adds a pineapple, which also knows how to core itself. The original requirement was to walk through a fruit basket and core all of the apples. In this model, the pineapples would also be cored (unexpectedly). This is certainly an undesirable side effect of our design.

The second and larger problem with this design is that we have warped our model (the fruit hierarchy) to satisfy a warped user of the hierarchy. When the designer of the fruit basket decided to mix all of the fruit in a polymorphic list, he stated that he did not want to know the exact type of fruit at runtime and that he would use

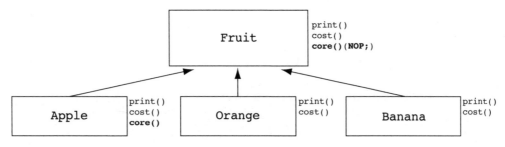

Figure 5.52 The most popular solution.

polymorphic functions of fruit to distinguish the different behaviors of each fruit type. In the next breath he reneged on this statement and stated that he needed to know which of the mixed fruit were `apple` objects, a major violation of his original model. By forcing `Fruit` to know about `core`, we are warping the polymorphic model for one user: Our base class now has derived class information (a clear violation of Heuristic 5.2). If many designers use this model, it is conceivable that each designer will run into a similar situation. If resolved in this manner, the `Fruit` class will become hopelessly convoluted with derived class-specific functions all defaulted to NOPs. This design choice is often called the "fat interface" solution.

Another solution is to force the designer of the `FruitBasket` class to take the responsibility for misusing the fruit abstraction. He or she must maintain a list of apples in addition to the list of mixed fruit in the fruit basket (see Figure 5.53). This maintains the proper abstraction of the `Fruit` hierarchy and puts the extra effort in the hands of the hierarchy users—those who are responsible for using it in a way for which it was not intended. However, this design is not without its problems. First of all, the bookkeeping job can get very complicated when several lists must be maintained. This can lead to errors of improper objects being added to the wrong lists or objects getting lost in the fruit basket. Second, how does the fruit basket know when the fruit object being added is an apple instead of an orange or a banana? The method `add_item` is taking a reference to a `fruit` as an argument, not an apple. One possibility is to create another method on the `FruitBasket` class called `add_apple`. The `add_item` method is responsible for all fruits other than apples. The problem here is that there is nothing to stop a user of a fruit basket from adding an apple via the `add_item` method, thereby putting the fruit basket in an invalid state with respect to its semantics. The alternative solution is to ask each fruit being added to the fruit basket its type. If its type needs special handling, as apples do in this example, then the fruit basket can handle that processing. Of course, this leads to explicit case analysis on the type of an object, another maintenance headache (and a violation of Heuristic 5.12).

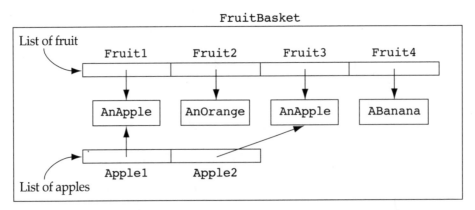

Figure 5.53 Another popular solution.

The moral to the story is that there is no optimal solution. All solutions have problems that need to be addressed. I tend to use the latter design where possible only because I do not believe that users of a hierarchy should cause them to be poorly designed. Many people choose the NOP method solution because it is the easiest to implement (no bookkeeping/case analysis), especially when they own the hierarchy and the class that uses it. In this case its a trade-off between warping *their* code or warping *their* code, so they choose the warping easiest to implement. Physical design may play a role in selecting the method. Imagine that the fruit basket is stored in a database where retrieval of each piece of fruit is slow. Clearly, the solution of maintaining a separate list of the apples is more appropriate since we do not want to waste the time of extracting a fruit from the database only to find out that it is an orange or a banana.

5.20   Reusing Components Versus Reusing Frameworks

Heuristic 5.19

When building an inheritance hierarchy, try to construct reusable frameworks rather than reusable components.

This heuristic illustrates the difference between system and domain analysis. **System analysis** attempts to find key abstractions from the particular application you are developing. The result is system-specific classes, which we call components. It is a designer's hope that they will become reusable in other applications. **Domain analysis** is the process of taking a step back and asking ourselves, "Can we create one design that satisfies the needs of a whole family of applications, of which our system is one member?" If the answer is yes, then the result is often reusable frameworks. In this context, a **framework** is defined as a class that contains a base class(es) by reference. Consider the design that wishes to place an object-oriented wrapper around the operating system in order to make the transition between hardware platforms easier. Someone performed system analysis and decided which operations an operating system needed in order to satisfy the given application. These became pure polymorphic functions on a base class called `OperatingSystem` (see Figure 5.54). The derived classes `DOS`, `Unix`, and `VMS` must define each of these methods in order to be useful in the application.

Given this hierarchy, it is possible to port our application to `OS/2` by creating a new derived class, `OS/2`, and implementing the necessary methods in this new operating system. While this is useful, domain analysis would have asked the question, "Can we take the reusable components `DOS`, `VMS`, `Unix`, and now `OS/2`, and find a reusable framework that models them more fully?" We can generalize these derived classes by realizing that all operating systems consist of a file system, a process system, and a device driver system (see Figure 5.55). Of course, there are different

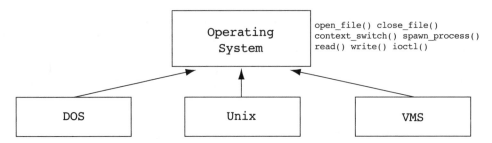

Figure 5.54 An operating system wrapper.

types of file systems, process systems, and device driver systems, each of which requires its own methods. However, we have now captured part of the design of an operating system. With luck we can continue to break down each piece into its generic pieces. Even though we never get any reusable code, we can get a reusable design. Reusable designs are often considered much more useful than reusable code. Do you want to be in a situation where you are told to create an OS/2 class with its 50,000 lines of code? Or would you prefer to be in a situation where you are told to create an OS/2 class with its 50,000 lines of code but it requires the following three pieces, each of which has the following pieces and interfaces, etc.? After creating several object-oriented systems, most developers agree that the production of a good design requires a great amount of effort for each system. Any reduction of that effort is very valuable and can save much more time than a simple reduction in code.

It is important to note that the OperatingSystem class shown in Figure 5.55 allows for an OperatingSystem object to be created from a UnixFS, a DOS_process, and a VMS_devicedriver. This is obviously an unworkable OperatingSystem object. This implies that there exists a semantic constraint between the objects contained in the OperatingSystem class. These semantic constraints are best captured in the class definition when possible. For this reason, many designers will bring back the derived classes DOS, Unix, and VMS for the sole purpose of maintaining the semantic constraints of operating systems. These derived classes usually capture the semantic constraint in their constructors, which build and pass the appropriate pieces of the framework to constructors higher in the hierarchy (see Figure 5.56).

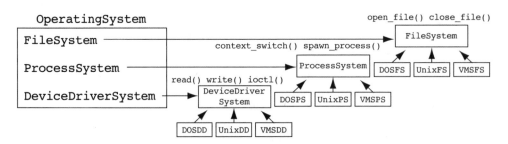

Figure 5.55 A framework for operating systems.

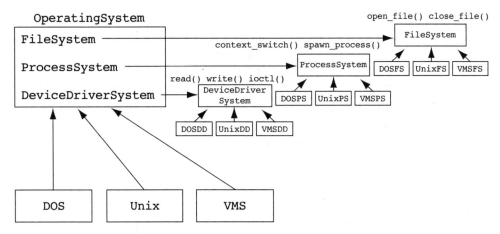

Figure 5.56 A framework for operating systems.

Many case studies demonstrate the benefits of reusable frameworks. In a process control project on which I worked at Draper Laboratories in the mid 1980s, our requirements were to development a system to fold men's suit sleeves with a robot. Instead, our development team took a step back and asked, "What do all process control systems (of which we are aware) require for design and implementation?" We designed a framework for process control architectures based on our answers to that central question. It was on this framework that we built our first representative application, namely, the robotic sleeve-folding system. As it turned out, the textile industry did not prove to be a steady source of funding for automation research and development. However, companies involved with composites manufacturing were in great need of automation. Our framework was used to create a new application, which wrapped kevlar around steel frames to simulate the manufacturing of airplane wings. The new system took less than two days to develop on top of the existing framework. It would have taken considerably longer to build a new system from the beginning, even if some of the existing code was reusable.

In another case study, I taught an object-oriented analysis and design course to a group of employees from The Travelers' Insurance Company. In this course, one-third of the attendees were working on a workmen's compensation insurance claim system, another third on a health insurance claim system, and the last third on an automobile insurance claim system. I argued that this was the perfect class to discuss domain analysis and framework design since clearly they were building three related systems. Several members of the class argued that these related segments of the insurance industry were completely different upon closer inspection. However, after several hours, we were able to produce a considerable collection of abstractions that were common to all three domains. A dissenting member of the class agreed that there were many abstractions in common but stated that upon implementation they differed significantly. She argued that it was not worth the time to create the abstractions if their eventual implementations were going to differ. While there may not be any code in common among the three designs, the fact that the designs overlap is very valuable information. Would you like to build a new system of 500,000 lines of code with nothing but its requirements to guide you? Or would you like to write 500,000 lines of code but know exactly how it is decomposed at the design level? After building systems, any developer will argue that the latter task is much easier than the former.

A third and last case study comes from Salomon Brothers. This company needed to build a collection of applications that dealt with reporting systems for securities trading. Instead of spending two team years building each of a number of systems, an enterprising executive allowed his group the extra time to construct a framework to support all of the applications. The result was that the first application took longer than the expected time, due to the need for framework design and construction. The remaining applications took a small fraction of the expected time, due to a high level of reuse achieved from the framework designed by the first group. This resulted in a substantial net savings in development time and effort as well as increased maintainability of the system. The latter is a result of the large amount of design and code sharing between the applications.

It is important to note that the development and use of a framework requires a front-end investment in time and money. The reward comes in reduced maintenance costs for the systems already developed and in reduced development costs for future systems. This type of cost structure must be supported by the top levels of management for the organization attempting the development of the framework. Unfortunately, there are surprisingly few companies willing to spend the extra time/money today to save significant amounts of both in the future.

Glossary

Base class   A class from which another class inherits.

Derived class   A class that inherits from another class.

Dynamic binding   A synonym for polymorphism.

Dynamic semantic wrapper   A construct used to encapsulate the states and transitions of a class in a local inheritance hierarchy.

Framework   A collection of classes and their relationships which may or may not capture reusable code, but always captures reusable portions of the design of an application family.

Generalization   A synonym for inheritance, it sometimes implies that the inheritance relationship in question was found by examining existing derived classes in order to find a new base class.

Inheritance   A class-based, object-oriented relationship that models specialization or a-kind-of relations.

Monomorphic function   A function whose address is decided at compile time. Also called a statically bound function.

Overriding method   A method in a derived class which has the same name and argument types as a method in its base class.

Polymorphic function   A function whose address is decided at runtime. Also called a dynamically bound function.

Private inheritance   An inheritance mechanism of C++ that allows a derived class to inherit only the data, and not the behavior, of its base class.

Protected inheritance   An inheritance mechanism of C++ that allows a derived class to inherit only the data, and not the behavior, of its base class. Protected inheritance is distinguished from private inheritance in that protected inheritance allows the descendent implementors (i.e., lower-level derived classes) to see the behavior of the base class; private inheritance does not.

Public inheritance   An inheritance mechanism of C++ that allows a derived class to inherit the data and behavior of its base class. The semantics of this mechanism are equivalent to the object-oriented paradigm's definition of inheritance.

Pure polymorphic function   A polymorphic function for which the base class has no meaningful default behavior.

Specialization   A synonym for inheritance, it sometimes implies that the inheritance relationship in question was found by adding a new derived class to an existing base class.

Static binding   A synonym for monomorphism.

Subclass   A class that inherits from another class.

Superclass   A class from which another class inherits.

True polymorphism   An implementation of polymorphism focusing on a global hash table of function addresses stored in the environment of the supporting language.

Summary of Heuristics

Heuristic 5.1   Inheritance should be used only to model a specialization hierarchy.

Heuristic 5.2   Derived classes must have knowledge of their base class by definition, but base classes should not know anything about their derived classes.

Heuristic 5.3   All data in a base class should be private; do not use protected data.

Heuristic 5.4   In theory, inheritance hierarchies should be deep—the deeper, the better.

Heuristic 5.5   In practice, inheritance hierarchies should be no deeper than an average person can keep in his or her short-term memory. A popular value for this depth is six.

Heuristic 5.6   All abstract classes must be base classes.

Heuristic 5.7   All base classes should be abstract classes.

Heuristic 5.8   Factor the commonality of data, behavior, and/or interface as high as possible in the inheritance hierarchy.

Heuristic 5.9   If two or more classes share only common data (no common behavior), then that common data should be placed in a class that will be contained by each sharing class.

Heuristic 5.10   If two or more classes have common data and behavior (i.e., methods), then those classes should each inherit from a common base class that captures those data and methods.

Heuristic 5.11   If two or more classes share only a common interface (i.e., messages, not methods), then they should inherit from a common base class only if they will be used polymorphically.

Heuristic 5.12   Explicit case analysis on the type of an object is usually an error. The designer should use polymorphism in most of these cases.

Heuristic 5.13   Explicit case analysis on the value of an attribute is often an error. The class should be decomposed into an inheritance hierarchy, where each value of the attribute is transformed into a derived class.

Heuristic 5.14   Do not model the dynamic semantics of a class through the use of the inheritance relationship. An attempt to model dynamic semantics with a static semantic relationship will lead to a toggling of types at runtime.

Heuristic 5.15   Do not turn objects of a class into derived classes of the class. Be very suspicious of any *derived* class for which there is only one instance.

Heuristic 5.16   If you think you need to create new classes at runtime, take a step back and realize that what you are trying to create are objects. Now generalize these objects into a class.

Heuristic 5.17   It should be illegal for a derived class to override a base class method with a NOP method, that is, a method that does nothing.

Heuristic 5.18   Do not confuse optional containment with the need for inheritance. Modeling optional containment with inheritance will lead to a proliferation of classes.

Heuristic 5.19   When building an inheritance hierarchy, try to construct reusable frameworks rather than reusable components.

Chapter 6

Multiple Inheritance

6.1 Introduction to Multiple Inheritance

I was one of the early C++ programmers who began with C++ version 1.2. At that time, there was a large group of C++ developers screaming for C++ version 2.0. Why? C++ version 2.0 implemented the **multiple inheritance** (MI) relationship, and version 1.2 did not. Multiple inheritance is the ability for a class to directly inherit from more than one base class. In retrospect, I believe that 49 percent of these screaming developers were screaming because they wanted to misuse multiple inheritance. Another 49 percent screamed because they heard the other 49 percent screaming and jumped on the bandwagon with no real knowledge of why they were screaming. Out of all the screaming developers, only 2 percent understood why they wanted multiple inheritance and were not misusing it. As proof of the multiple inheritance hype argument, I offer the following true story. In the process of peddling a C++ class library consisting of data structure classes, I would invariably be asked, "Does your library use multiple inheritance?" I would reply, "No, but where would you use multiple inheritance in linked lists, hash tables, and stacks?" Their response would be, "I don't know, but my manager said that all of our new tools must have multiple inheritance."

A sudden backlash against multiple inheritance erupted shortly after version 2.0 was released and lots of developers began using it. Statements such as "Multiple inheritance adds no expressive power to C++ and should be removed in the next release, if not sooner!" "Multiple inheritance destroys reusability; get rid of it!" and "I shot off my big toe with multiple inheritance!" were (are) commonplace. The C++ community spent over a year publishing papers debating the use and misuse of multiple inheritance, with no settlement in sight. The position presented and justified in this text is that multiple inheritance does add expressive power to the object-oriented paradigm (and C++ for that matter). It is also one of the most misused features of the object-oriented paradigm. If a design requires multiple inheritance and it is not available at the language level, then the result is accidental complexity. Later in this

131

chapter, we will examine the nature of this accidental complexity in the context of a real-world multiple inheritance example.

Heuristic 6.1

If you have an example of multiple inheritance in your design, assume you have made a mistake and prove otherwise.

This heuristic is not intended to brand MI as evil or even undesirable. It is meant to emphasize the large level of multiple inheritance misuse that exists in many object-oriented designs. When I attend an object-oriented design critique and see a lot of multiple inheritance in the design, I immediately assume that there is a mistake in that portion of the design. I am rarely disappointed in my assumption.

6.2 The Common Misuse of Multiple Inheritance

Since multiple inheritance misuse is so prevalent in object-oriented designs, it makes sense to investigate the reasons for this misuse and see why it is so dangerous. Let us assume that we have three classes: Wings, Fuselage, and Cockpit. We would like to construct an Airplane class from these three classes. We can accomplish the design using two different object-oriented constructs. We could have the Airplane class inherit from Wings, Fuselage, and Cockpit, or it could contain them. Since wings are made of aluminum and rivets, we can extrapolate our design to include them (see Figure 6.1).

Which method is better? Many designers will say that the use of multiple inheritance is wrong because Airplanes are not special types of Fuselages. So what? You took my word for it when I stated that inheritance should always model a specialization hierarchy. Why is it important to do this? Let us examine the data of the two Airplanes. What is the difference between the two designs? It turns out that there

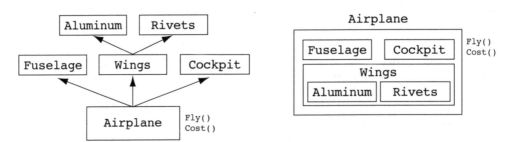

Figure 6.1 Two methods of designing an airplane.

is no difference in typical language implementations of multiple inheritance. The only difference in C++ is that the system names the Wings, Fuselage, and Cockpit objects in the first design and the developer names them in the second design. If the data is the same, then the difference must be in the behavior of the Airplane. In the second design, what can an Airplane do, that is, to which messages can it respond? If you guess fly and cost, then consider that rivets know how to heat themselves. Now what can an Airplane do? Of course, the Airplane does not get the heat message in the second design. Why? Because containing an object of a class does not imply that the interface of the containing class gets the interface of the contained class. This is an important characteristic of the containment relationship. The second design is a black-box design. You, the user of an Airplane, do not care how I, the implementor of the Airplane, created the internal design. It makes no difference to you if I broke down an Airplane into a narrow and deep hierarchy as it is pictured above or whether I designed my Airplane as a broad and shallow class containing 6,000 data members like needle gauge covers, oxygen mask cups, oxygen mask hoses, oxygen mask release levers, needle gauge needles, Naugahyde, seat belt buckles, seat belt clasps, etc. So long as the Airplane flies and computes its cost, the users of Airplane are happy. They do not care how the job is accomplished.

To which messages can the Airplane of the first design respond? This is the fundamental problem with using multiple inheritance to simulate containment. The user of the multiply inheriting derived class (i.e., the Airplane) must know how it was implemented in order to use it. This is an unnatural relationship and implies that the Airplane can perform any function that each of its pieces is able to perform. Inheritance is intrinsically a white-box design construct, while containment is intrinsically a black-box design construct. Whenever given the choice between white- and black-box design, always choose the black-box construct. The C++ developers who claimed that multiple inheritance was ruining their designs and their chances for creating reusable components were misusing multiple inheritance by using it in place of the containment relationship. If I thought multiple inheritance was necessary in a language for the implementation of the containment relationship, then I would have been screaming for C++ 2.0 as well.

Heuristic 6.2

Whenever there is inheritance in an object-oriented design, ask yourself two questions: 1) Am I a special type of the thing from which I'm inheriting? 2) Is the thing from which I'm inheriting part of me?

Is an airplane a special type of fuselage? No.

Is a fuselage part of an airplane? Yes.

Is an airplane a special type of flying device? Yes.

Is a flying device part of an airplane? No.

These two questions will get you out of trouble most of the time. The answers will be yes/no or no/yes, respectively. A yes to the first question and no to the second implies you need inheritance. The opposite answers imply that containment is the better choice. Watch out for accidental multiple inheritance. Consider the following statements checking for legal multiple inheritance.

Is an orange a special type of citrus fruit? Yes.

Is a citrus fruit part of an orange? No.

Is an orange a special type of food? Yes.

Is a food part of an orange? No.

Is this a valid example of multiple inheritance? No, because citrus fruit is a special type of food (assuming there do not exist inedible citrus fruit). Watch out for accidentally detecting the transitivity of the inheritance relationship and trying to model it as multiple inheritance (see Figure 6.2). Always ask yourself a third question, "Are any of my base classes derived classes of the other base classes?"

Heuristic 6.3

Whenever you have found a multiple inheritance relationship in an object-oriented design, be sure that no base class is actually a derived class of another base class.

Hierarchies that violate this heuristic have what is called **accidental multiple inheritance**.

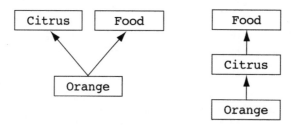

Figure 6.2 Accidental multiple inheritance.

6.3   A Valid Use of Multiple Inheritance

We have now seen the misuse of multiple inheritance. When is multiple inheritance a valid construct in an object-oriented design? Multiple inheritance is useful for capturing a relationship known as **subtyping for combination**. It is used to define a new class that is actually a special type of two other classes and those two base classes are from different domains. Consider the example in Figure 6.3, which describes one method for defining a wooden door.

We must first run through our three questions to ensure that our design is correct. Recall Heuristic 6.1, which states that if we have multiple inheritance in our design, we should assume we are making a mistake and should prove otherwise. In this example, our wooden door is made completely out of wood; do not worry about steel hinges and brass door knobs. We will look at that design of a door in the next example.

Is a wooden door a special type of door? Yes.

Is a door part of a wooden door? No.

Is a wooden door a special type of wooden object? Yes.

Is a wooden object part of a door? No.

And last but not least,

Is a wooden object a special type of door? No.

Is a door a special type of wooden object? No.

Since this design satisfies all of our heuristics, it is considered valid multiple inheritance.

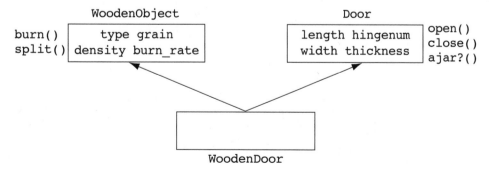

Figure 6.3 A wooden door: an example of a material object.

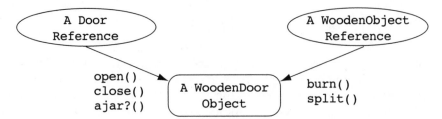

Figure 6.4 Multiple referencing of multiply derived objects.

Users of polymorphism should note that the wooden door designed above can only be viewed as a wooden object *or* a door via a given reference. If a wooden object reference is accessing the wooden door, then it knows about burn and split but has no knowledge of open and close. If a door reference is accessing the wooden door, then it knows about open and close, but not burn and split. For this reason, it is common for objects of classes derived from multiple classes to have access via multiple references of the different base classes (see Figure 6.4).

6.4 Accidental Complexity In Languages That Do Not Support Multiple Inheritance

What would happen to our design if we were forced to implement it solely with single inheritance? It would look like the model in Figure 6.5.

The designer is forced to contain all but one of the base classes and must provide **delegation functions** to these containing classes. The problem with this design is that when we add a new operation to the WoodenObject class, we must scan our design for any class that contains WoodenObject and check to see if it is true con-

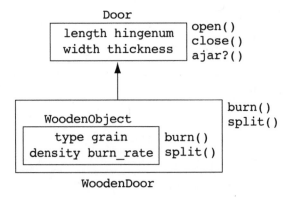

Figure 6.5 A single-inheritance WoodenDoor.

tainment or simply pseudo-inheritance. If it is pseudo-inheritance, we must add a delegation function to the containing class which simply calls the function on the contained `WoodenObject`. This would fall under Frederick Brook's idea of accidental complexity (see Section 1.2). If a developer does not have multiple inheritance at his or her disposal, he or she will get accidental complexity for these types of designs. Multiple inheritance, therefore, adds expressive power to the languages that implement it.

6.5   Frameworks That Incorporate Multiple Inheritance

Consider a modification to our notion of `WoodenDoor`, where we take into consideration the fact that doors have a body of some material (e.g., wood, steel, plastic), hinges of some material (e.g., brass, steel, gold), an optional window of some material (glass, plastic, Plexiglass), and a door knob of some material (e.g., steel, brass, wood). This implies that there is only one door class, but it is implemented as a framework (see Figure 6.6). The multiple inheritance is simply pushed down into the framework of the door.

Like all frameworks, this framework captures information relevant to the design of doors as well as the code that implements doors. By adding a new derived class to one of the contained base classes, we create the possibility for a number of different object constructions. For example, by adding a steel hinge to our domain, we create the possibility of having wooden doors with steel hinges, steel doors with steel hinges, etc.

6.6   The Use of Multiple Inheritance in the Design of Mixins

An interesting use for multiple inheritance is in the creation of **mixins**, which are inheritance hierarchies that abstract out certain properties from the classes that ex-

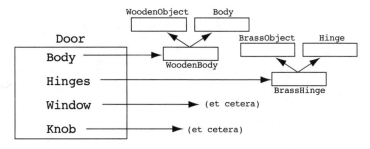

Figure 6.6 A framework for doors.

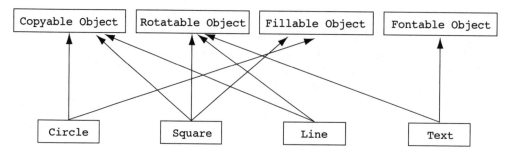

Figure 6.7 An example of mixins.

hibit them. Each class picks and chooses which of the properties its objects will possess. For example, we may have some objects that are copyable, fillable, editable, and fontable. Others may only be copyable and fillable; still others are only fontable, etc. The design for such a mixin might look like the model in Figure 6.7.

One problem with mixins is that they are very static due to their implementation via inheritance. What if text is rotatable only when it is contained within a frame object, but cannot exhibit this behavior outside of a frame object? What if lines can be copied only when they are in selected mode? For the implementation of behavior that depends on the state of an object, it is best to use containment with conditional testing on the state of the object at runtime. Object-oriented structures created in this manner are called **compositional mixins**. Our questions above imply that we want our design of lines and text to be as those shown in Figure 6.8. When a line is told to copy itself, it does not inherit this functionality from the `CopyableObject` class as it did in Figure 6.7. Instead, the `Line` class itself implements `copy` to check first the state of the `Line` object to see if the line is selected. It then makes sure that it contains the necessary `CopyableObject`. Only when all conditions are satisfied does the `Line` class send a `copy` message to the `CopyableObject`. The `Text` object is designed in a similar manner with respect to rotation. The trade-off between a traditional mixin and a compositional mixin revolves around ease of adding behavior versus flexibility. The traditional mixin maximizes ease of adding behavior but is not flexible, while

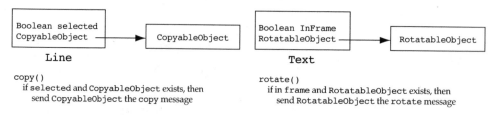

Figure 6.8 An example of a compositional mixin.

the compositional mixin increases the effort of adding new behavior but is more flexible.

6.7   DAG Multiple Inheritance

If an object-oriented design only uses single inheritance, the entire inheritance hierarchy can be displayed as a tree. If multiple inheritance is used, then a **directed acyclic graph** (i.e., a DAG) is needed to display the hierarchy. In some designs, the multiple inheritance hierarchy can produce a diamond-shaped structure, which overly complicates design as well as implementation. Consider Figure 6.9, the object-oriented design of a graduate student.

As suggested by the multiple inheritance heuristics, we first assume that we have made a mistake, and then we prove otherwise.

Is an instructor a special type of person? Yes.

Is a person part of an instructor? No.

Is a student a special type of person? Yes.

Is a person part of a student? No.

Is a graduate student a special type of student? Yes.

Is a student part of a graduate student? No.

Is a graduate student a special type of instructor? Yes.

Is an instructor part of a graduate student? No.

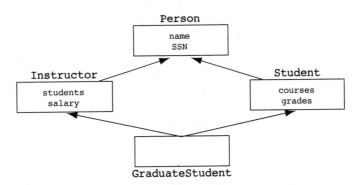

Figure 6.9   A graduate student: an example of DAG inheritance.

Is an instructor a special type of student? No.

Is a student a special type of instructor? No.

Now that we have fulfilled the necessary tests to ensure that multiple inheritance is a valid construct in this context, we are faced with a dilemma. How many names and social security numbers does a graduate student have in the real world? One, of course. Our graduate student has two, based on the semantics of inheritance, that is, a derived class gets a copy of its base class's data. This is an implementation problem for any language wishing to support multiple inheritance. It is important to note that we cannot always eliminate one copy of base class data when faced with class designs like the graduate student. Imagine that the person class had the data member's name and telephone number instead of name and social security number. As a graduate student I might be "Mr. Riel" with my office number when viewed as an instructor, but "Arthur Riel" with my home phone number when viewed as a student. This choice of design must be given to the users of any language supporting multiple inheritance.

In the C++ language, the keyword `virtual` is used with inheritance to distinguish those hierarchies willing to share the common base class (e.g., `Person`). Virtual inheritance in C++ creates a collection of unique problems for its users. Issues involving the order of constructor calls are particularly error prone. This form of inheritance complicates design and implementation, but it is necessary in some cases like the graduate student example. Designers should not be overly concerned with diamond-shaped multiple inheritance. This form of multiple inheritance is fairly rare in most object-oriented designs; therefore, the typical object-oriented designer will not have to deal with it often.

6.8   Accidental DAG Multiple Inheritance via Poor Implementation of Optional Containment

Poor object-oriented designers who accidentally implement classes with more than one optional component using inheritance will find themselves with a bad case of DAG multiple inheritance. The `House` class from the previous chapter (Section 5.18) was defined with four optional data members, a heating system, a cooling system, a plumbing system, and an electrical system. If a designer tries to capture these optional data members in an inheritance hierarchy, then he or she will find themselves in trouble (see Figure 6.10).

Of course, all of this is unnecessary. The actual solution is to use containment by reference to implement optional data members. (See Chapter 5, Section 5.18, for a description of this solution.)

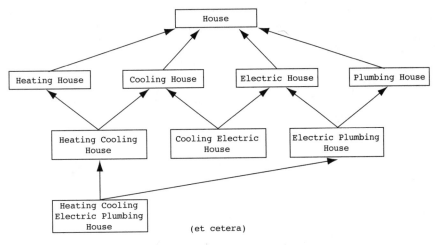

Figure 6.10 A bad house.

Glossary

Accidental multiple inheritance   The use of multiple inheritance to model what should have been modeled as a collection of transitive single-inheritance relationships.

Compositional mixins   The modeling of a class's properties through the containment of property classes.

DAG multiple inheritance   A multiple inheritance hierarchy whose representative graph contains a closure.

Delegation functions   Messages on a containing class whose sole purpose is to transfer the message down to a single contained object.

Mixins   Classes whose behaviors are inherited from a number of property classes.

Multiple inheritance   The object-oriented relationship that allows a derived class to inherit from more than one base class.

Subtyping for combination   A use of multiple inheritance that allows a single derived class to combine the abstractions from two or more different domains into a single domain.

Heuristics Summary

Heuristic 6.1   If you have an example of multiple inheritance in your design, assume you have made a mistake and then prove otherwise.

Heuristic 6.2   Whenever there is inheritance in an object-oriented design, ask your-self two questions: 1) Am I a special type of the thing from which I'm inheriting? 2) Is the thing from which I'm inheriting part of me?

Heuristic 6.3   Whenever you have found a multiple inheritance relationship in an object-oriented design, be sure that no base class is actually a derived class of another base class.

Chapter 7

The Association Relationship

7.1 Introduction to Association

As is typical within the object-oriented community, one needs to be careful with vocabulary. The same term can imply different things to different developers. In the behavioral-driven methodologies, such as those proposed by Wirfs-Brock et al., Booch, and Jacobson [9,7,3,4], the general overview is that designers first find classes and their protocols. This implies that the first relationship application designers find is the uses relationship. During design they refine some of these uses relationships into containment relationships and then examine the domain for inheritance hierarchies. At the end of this process, it is possible to find some classes that are related but the relationship is not uses, containment, or inheritance. If such a relationship exists, it is called an **association**.

In the data-driven methodologies, such as the one proposed by James Rumbaugh [12] et al., the general overview is that designers find classes, followed by associations between those classes. Many of these associations are then refined into uses, containment, or inheritance relationships. Those that cannot be refined to one of these three fall into a category called **simple associations**. Within this chapter, our use of the word "association" will correspond to a relationship between two classes which is not uses, containment, or inheritance. In short, the association relationship will be defined as a catch-all relationship between classes which cannot be refined to one of the three main relationships that we have discussed previously, namely, uses, containment, and inheritance.

What is the relationship between the car in your driveway and the *name* of the company that manufactured it? What about the relationship between the car in your driveway and the company that manufactured it? The first question is easier to answer than the second. The name of the company that manufactured your car is an attribute of your car. It is important to note that it is a more important attribute than other car attributes like color, mileage, and vehicle identification number. The latter three attributes hold descriptive information concerning the car class. They are often called **descriptive attributes**. The car manufacturer, on the other hand, provides access to an entire object (of the class `CarManufacturer`) that exists elsewhere in your domain. This type of attribute is called a **referential attribute**. We can say that the name of the company that manufactured your car is a referential attribute of the car.

What about our second question: "What is the relationship between the car class and the car manufacturer class?" Is this relationship inheritance? No, because your car is not a special type of car manufacturer, and car manufacturers are not special types of cars. What about containment? No, your car is not contained in a car manufacturer (it is in your driveway), nor does your car contain a car manufacturer. What about a uses relationship? This is a possibility. If the car sends a message to the car manufacturer or the car manufacturer sends a message to the car, then there is a uses relationship between the two classes. For the sake of argument, let us state that neither class sends a message to the other class. What is the relationship between the two classes? We can say that the car is "made-by" the car manufacturer. This is not very precise within the realm of the object-oriented paradigm. Notice that it is not one of the three standard object-oriented relationships (uses, containment, inheritance), yet there is some relationship between the two classes. This is an example of the association relationship.

There are several types of association relationships: one-to-one, one-to-many, many-to-one, many-to-many. In addition, the relationship can be required or optional. There are two main methods of implementing these associations: the use of a referential attribute and the use of a third-party class. The first method is the most popular for designing one-to-one or many-to-one required associations. The second method is the most popular for designing all others. Either method can be used in all cases, but one is generally easier to implement for a given association type. We will examine both implementations.

7.2 Associations Implemented Through a Referential Attribute

Since each car is made by one and only one car manufacturer (we go back in time 30 years when car parts were not produced all over the world), the type of association is a one-to-one required association. It is best implemented as a referential attribute. This attribute could simply be the name of the car manufacturer, or for better efficiency we may want a pointer to our associated car manufacturer. In either case, it is a referential attribute, the particulars being uninteresting implementation details.

It is of particular interest to C++ programmers that the car does not "contain by reference" a car manufacturer simply because it has a pointer to it. We claim that the car is associated with its car manufacturer through a referential attribute. This indicates that C++ does not draw a distinction between two very different object-oriented relationships, containment by reference and association through a referential attribute. Is this a problem? Not for developers who design a system and then go off and implement it. It simply implies that two things in which a designer is very interested at design time are implemented as the same construct in C++. It is a major problem for authors of reverse-engineering case tools for C++. In fact, it demonstrates that it is impossible for a developer to produce a fully automated reverse-engineering case tool for C++. Since several vendors claim to offer such tools, I invite you to give them the following code and ask them how they extract a design from it.

```
class ATM {
    Bank* bank;
    CardReader* cardreader;
};
```

The ATM does not contain a bank by reference; it is associated with its bank through a referential attribute. However, the ATM is not simply associated with its card reader—it contains it by reference. How do tools deal with this problem? The bad ones assume that since C++ does not distinguish the difference, the designer should not care about it. This is a serious deficiency. If a designer can say that a relationship is containment, then he or she can ignore the contained object at some level of design. If the relationship is only association, then he or she cannot ignore either class. In this example, we can focus on the relationship between the ATM and Bank, ignoring the CardReader (see Figure 7.1). If we assume no distinction in the two relationships, we are forced to consider all three classes at all levels of design. The better tools assume association (the simplest of the relationships) and allow a designer to update his or her picture to containment if necessary. The tool remembers the relationship once a designer assigns it by generating special comments in the code which the tool reads in when the code is reverse-engineered at a later time.

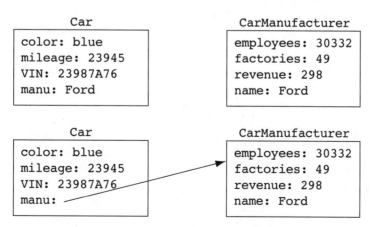

Figure 7.1 The association relationship between a car and its manufacturer.

If the car in Figure 7.1 does not use the car manufacturer, then what could be the possible use of the information stored by the referential attribute? It is true that most referential attributes are used to form uses relationships. This is a fifth variant on the implementation of the uses relationship, which we discussed in Section 4.3. In this case, we have assumed that the car is not using the car manufacturer, so of what possible use is the association information?

In all cases, the association relationship is used by some third-party class that performs an indirect uses relationship between the two classes involved in the relationship. Consider the `Recall` class shown in Figure 7.2. It uses the association between a car and its manufacturer in order to complete a recall operation for the car manufacturer.

A key question might be, "Why doesn't the car manufacturer perform the recall behavior? Recalls are clearly the responsibility of the car manufacturer." While it is true that car manufacturers should be performing the necessary recall, what if the car manufacturer class is growing too complex? Our heuristic for distributing system intelligence uniformly across our top-level classes may dictate that we push some of our complexity onto a new, third-party, top-level class. The `Recall` class could be such a class. It exists only for better distribution of system intelligence. The ramification was the translation of a direct uses relationship between `car` and `CarManufacturer` to an indirect uses via the `Recall` class. These situations are fairly rare, which is why most associations are refined to uses or containment relationships.

7.3   Association Implemented Through a Third-Party Class

As an example of the second method for implementing associations—using a third-party association class as opposed to a referential attribute—consider the companies for which a person has worked in the past. This might be the type of information one would find on a person's resume. If this one-to-many association were imple-

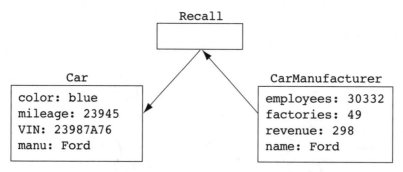

Figure 7.2 A third-party class using an association relationship.

mented as a referential attribute, then the attribute would need to be a list. An easier implementation is to create a separate third-party object for each company for which a person has worked (see Figure 7.3). These objects are instantiated from a third-party association class, which usually gets the name of the association as its name. Association classes are typically a collection of referential attributes that refer to the classes involved in the association.

Again, associations that are not capturing uses relationships always imply that some third party wishes to use the association in an indirect uses relationship. The third party was created due to some distribution of system intelligence requirement in a particular domain.

7.4 Deciding Between a Containment and an Association Relationship

Heuristic 7.1

> **When given a choice in an object-oriented design between a containment relationship and an association relationship, choose the containment relationship.**

This choice is not always available. The association examples that we have looked at must be association; they cannot be containment relationships. In an object-oriented design, it sometimes happens that we are given this choice. Consider the home heating system problem posed in Booch's object-oriented design text [7]. In Section 3.4, we examined the notion of rooms deciding that they need heat, informing a heat flow regulator, which turns on a furnace, etc. There is the additional requirement that once heat is available, when the furnace has hot water to flow through the pipes, the water valve to the room requiring heat must be opened. The key question is who should open the valve. Two possibilities come to mind:

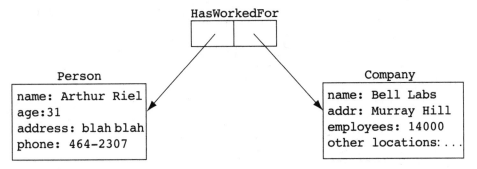

Figure 7.3 Implementing associations through third-party classes.

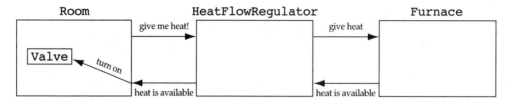

Figure 7.4 Home heating system with indirect uses relationship.

1. Each room contains its water valve.

2. The furnace contains all of the water valves.

In the first design, after a room decides it needs heat, it tells the heat flow regulator to get heat. The heat flow regulator then asks the furnace to provide heat; the furnace informs the heat flow regulator when heat is available; the heat flow regulator tells the room that heat is available; the room tells the valve to open; and, finally, the valve opens (see Figure 7.4).

This is an extremely roundabout design. Some designers argue that since the furnace knows when the valve can open, the furnace should tell the valve to open when heat is available. This implies that the furnace contains the valves. The design that follows from this premise is much cleaner and more direct, as Figure 7.5 shows.

How does the furnace know which valve to open when heat is available? Obviously, someone has to tell it. The heat flow regulator can pass the name of the room as an explicit argument, and each valve could contain the name of the room to which it is associated. The furnace could perform an easy search through the valve's room attribute until it finds a match. It is important to note that in this design the name of the room is a referential attribute of the valve class. What is the relationship between the `Valve` class and the `Room` class? In this design it is an association relationship. There is no direct uses relationship between the two classes; the furnace acts as the third-party class. These two designs bring up an interesting point. Should the room contain a valve, or should it be associated with a valve? The heuristic states that containment is the better design, but in this example we have seen that the association model gives us a cleaner design with more direct uses relationships. What is the problem with using association instead of containment?

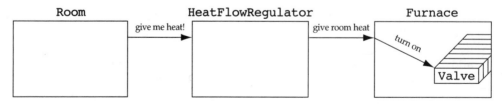

Figure 7.5 Another possible design for the home heating system.

Consider the task of constructing a new Room object. In the first design, the constructor for the room knows implicitly that it must build a valve since the containment relationship states that each room must have a valve. In the second design, users of the Room class must know by convention that constructing a new Room implies building a Valve object and giving it to the Furnace. Not only are developers required to follow this convention, but Rooms are now unnaturally dependent on, and aware of, the implementation of Furnaces. This is the key problem with choosing associations over containment. Association relationships build conventions into the design, and users of the classes need to know these details. The containment relationship creates implicit and hidden implementation details that users of the class do not need to know. Given this information, the first design is the better choice, despite the need for some roundabout uses relationships.

Glossary

Association An object-oriented relationship specifying that two classes have some relationship, but it is not an inheritance, containment, or uses relationship.

Descriptive attribute An attribute whose only purpose is to describe some feature of the objects that belong to the class.

Referential attribute An attribute whose purpose is to allow an object of a class to get access to an object of another class.

Simple association A term used in some object-oriented methodologies to describe an association that is not reducible to any of the other object-oriented relationships.

Heuristics Summary

Heuristic 7.1 When given a choice in an object-oriented design between a containment relationship and an association relationship, choose the containment relationship.

Chapter 8

Class-Specific Data and Behavior

8.1 Introduction to Class-Specific Versus Object-Specific Data and Behavior

When teaching an object-oriented design course, I often ask the question, "Is an object required when you wish to send a message?" Invariably, the response is "Of course, messages are sent to objects." Since the constructor of a class is one of its messages, how does one build the first object? It is clear that the constructor is a different sort of message. It does not require an object before it can be sent. (In the case of C++, the constructor is considered a normal message sent to an object that the standard allocator has created. For the purpose of this discussion, I consider my use of the term "constructor" to include standard allocation and initialization).

Another example of this phenomenon can be found in the design of an `Invoice` class. What pieces of data does each invoice object require? Some common data members of invoices include the billing address, the return address, line items, the total value, etc. Each invoice object must get its own copy of this data. In addition, each invoice has the behaviors of adding items, deleting items, and printing. These three operations require a target invoice object in order to execute. These data and behaviors are considered object-specific, since each object gets a unique copy of the data and only objects have access to the behaviors.

There is another piece of data that each invoice object must possess: a unique invoice number. Again, each invoice object must have its own copy. Who decides the value of this invoice number? There must be some counter that keeps track of the last invoice number. When an invoice object is constructed, this counter is incremented and the invoice number of the object is assigned the new value. Who owns this counter? Certainly not the invoice object, since there is only one invoice counter for all of the objects. The obvious choice is the `Invoice` class. In fact, whenever there is bookkeeping to be performed on the objects of the class, then that class should store the necessary data. In addition, we may want to know what the next invoice number is going to be. This should not be an object-specific behavior, since there may be no invoice objects at the time we wish to examine the next invoice number. It would be inconvenient, at best, to build an invoice object just to ask it the value of the next invoice number. Of course, there is also the problem that the action of getting that number will waste an invoice. The obvious entity to ask is the `Invoice` class. It knows the value of the next invoice number whether or not any invoice objects currently exist in the system.

The invoice counter is an example of class-specific data. A piece of class-specific data is often called a **class variable**. Class variables are used to store information concerning the objects, not an individual object, of the class. Whenever a developer is using global data within the methods of a class, he or she should determine if a class variable would be more appropriate.

The constructor and the `GetNextInvoiceNum`-type methods of the `Invoice` class are examples of class-specific behaviors. A class-specific behavior is often called a **class method**. A class method is used whenever behavior accesses only class variables within a class. If no object-specific data is being accessed, a class designer should ask himself if the operation really belongs to the class itself, as opposed to the objects of the class.

Heuristic 8.1

> **Do not use global data or functions to perform bookkeeping information on the objects of a class. Class variables or methods should be used instead.**

8.2 Using Metaclasses to Capture Class-Specific Data and Behavior

Languages use two main methods to implement the notion of class-specific versus object-specific data and functionality. The first and, in my opinion, the cleanest implementation is to keep these different types of data and behavior completely separate. In pure object-oriented languages (e.g., SmallTalk), everything is considered an object. Even a class is an object. If classes are objects, then what is the class for those objects? A class of a class is called a **metaclass**. The basic idea is that object-specific data and behavior should be placed in the class definition, while the class-specific data and behavior should be placed in the class's associated metaclass. This provides a clear separation of concerns. When talking about a specific object of the class, we examine the class definition. When talking about all of the objects instantiated by the class, we examine the metaclass. This separation of concerns can be best illustrated by Figure 8.1, which shows the `Invoice` class and its associated metaclass.

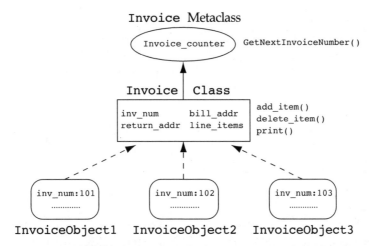

Figure 8.1 The Invoice class and its metaclass.

8.3 Using Language-Level Keywords to Implement Class- Versus Object-Specific Data and Behavior

In some multiparadigm languages such as C++, the implementation is to throw the class- and object-specific data and behavior in one bundle, namely, the class definition. There is no notion of a metaclass. The class-specific data and behavior are distinguished from the object-specific data and behavior via a language keyword. In the case of C++, the keyword is static. This implementation does not offer the same lexical separation that is apparent in the metaclass solution, yet it serves the necessary purpose of implementing class-specific data and behavior (see Figure 8.2).

8.4 Metaclasses à la C++

The object-oriented designer may hear the occasional C++ programmer mutter something about metaclasses. I have stated that the C++ language does not support the notion of metaclass, so what is he or she discussing? Again, in the object-oriented community, one must be very careful with vocabulary. When C++ programmers use the term "metaclass," they are referring to the **template** construct in C++. The relationship between the template construct in C++ and metaclasses can be best summarized in the following statement.

All C++ templates are metaclasses, but not all metaclasses are C++ templates.

Metaclasses are traditionally a place where class-specific data and behavior are declared/defined/stored. The notion of templates in C++ came about due to a problem

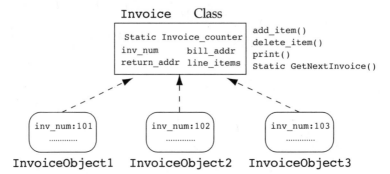

Figure 8.2 The `Invoice` class and metaclass implemented with keyword.

often encountered in strongly typed object-oriented languages. Consider the case where a designer wants a list of dogs called **x**, a list of airplanes called **y**, and a list of meals called **z**. What are the differences between the classes `Doglist`, `Airplane-list`, and `Meallist`? Upon inspection, the three classes differ only on the type of data stored in the list. The algorithms of the three lists are exactly the same. If fact, the code is identical except for the name of the type. Unfortunately, in a strongly typed language, the different type name is enough to require a whole new class definition along with all of its methods. Many developers considered this a waste of code and looked for a better solution. A common approach was to create one list class, called `ListOfAnything`. They then made the `Dog`, `Airplane`, and `Meal` classes inherit from the class `Anything` so that they would be allowed in the list (see Figure 8.3). This effectively turned C++ into a weakly typed language for that portion of their application.

While this solution will work, not all applications can use weak type checking at this point in the application. Our original requirements wanted the object **x** to be a list of dogs, **y** to be a list of airplanes, and **z** to be a list of meals. In this solution, the objects **x**, **y**, and **z** are all lists of anything, but by convention **x** has only dogs in it,

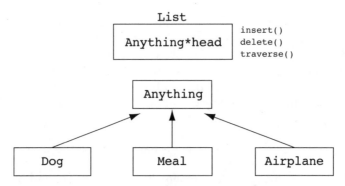

Figure 8.3 A generic `List` class.

y only airplanes, and z only meals. The obvious danger of programming by convention means that it is possible to accidentally put a dog onto the list object y. The control tower then accidentally tries to fly the dog off of a runway. Likewise, people may order a meal at a restaurant and accidentally get an airplane or dog on their plate. The whole point of strong type checking is to catch these errors at compile time, not at runtime.

The developers unhappy with the weak type-checking solution turned to C++'s preprocessor and created elaborate schemes to use it for creating the notion of a parameterized type. They were thwarted by the sheer ugliness of a macro spanning several hundred lines as well as many preprocessor's annoying habit of limiting the macro buffer size to some value like 4K. This implied that a class, with all of its messages and method definitions, had to be described in fewer than 4,000 characters. This was certainly not a good solution either.

Stroustrup's answer to the demand for easy parameterization of classes, maintaining the strong type checking inherent in C++, was the template mechanism. Templates are a language-level facility that uses one description to describe a family of classes. The relationship between the classes being captured in the template abstraction is that they differ on some data type or types that can be provided at compile time by the developer. Our solution to the list of dogs, airplanes, and meals problem posed above is to create a template called "list of your favorite data type." The list template is described with a formal parameter that takes the place of the data to be stored in the list (see Figure 8.4). The corresponding actual parameters are provided at compile time by the developer defining the objects x, y, and z. The template instantiates a new class whenever a new actual parameter is introduced. Since templates instantiate classes, they capture class-specific data and behaviors and therefore are technically metaclasses. However, the true notion of metaclass extends beyond the notion of templates to imply the capture of any class-specific data and behavior, not just the abstractions that templates cover.

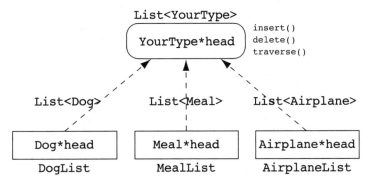

Figure 8.4 A list template.

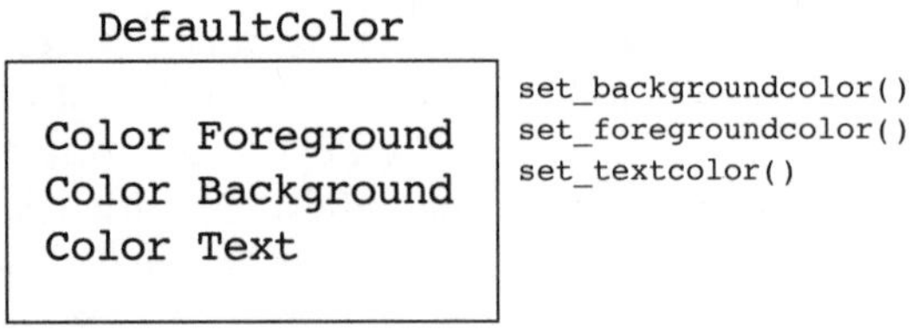

```
              DefaultColor
      ┌──────────────────────┬──────────────────────
      │                      │ set_backgroundcolor()
      │  Color Foreground    │ set_foregroundcolor()
      │  Color Background    │ set_textcolor()
      │  Color Text          │
      │                      │
      └──────────────────────┘
```

Figure 8.5 Example of a useful abstract class that lacks derived classes.

8.5 A Useful Abstract Class That Is Not a Base Class?

Recall in Chapter 5 that we discussed Heuristic 5.6, which states, "All abstract classes must be base classes in order to be useful." At that time, we observed that for all intents and purposes this was true, but we mentioned an anomalous case whose discussion we postponed. Consider a class composed of all class-specific data and methods. In our keyword implementation of class-specific data and behavior, this would amount to all static data and function members (a la C++). Such a class could be abstract, given that we would not define a constructor, yet the class would have some use in the system. This technically shows an abstract class from which no one inherits yet it is still useful. Why would anyone desire a class with no object-specific methods or data? I had never seen a need for such a class, but someone had mentioned this example in a design course long ago and I passed it along for the purists to ponder. Robert Martin, in the course of reviewing this book, provided a practical example for such a class wherein it is used to encapsulate and limit the scope for a collection of global data. This allows for better understandability of the application as well as the avoidance of **namespace pollution** (i.e., the cluttering of an application's global name space with duplicate names, causing link errors). I pass along his example for your review (see Figure 8.5).

Glossary

Class method   A method that is attached to a class as opposed to the objects of a class. Class methods cannot operate on object-specific data or invoke object-specific methods.

Class variable   A piece of class-specific data.

Metaclass   A class whose instances are classes.

Namespace pollution   The collision of names in the global name space of an executable file, often resulting in link errors.

Object data   The data of a class of which each object is to receive a unique copy.

Object method   A method that is attached to the objects of a class, that is, it requires an object of the associated class in order to execute.

Template   A C++ language mechanism that allows for the encapsulation of common code where the only distinction between the code modules is the name of a data or function member. Also called a generic or a parameterized class.

Heuristics Summary

Heuristic 8.1   Do not use global data or functions to perform bookkeeping information on the objects of a class. Class variables or methods should be used instead.

Chapter 9

Physical Object-Oriented Design

9.1 The Role of Logical and Physical Object-Oriented Design

When most people use the term "object-oriented design," they are typically referring to *logical* object-oriented design. There are actually two facets to object-oriented design: logical design and physical design. Logical design involves everything discussed thus far, including the discovery of classes, their protocols, their uses relationships, their containment relationships, and their inheritance relationships. In short, anything that relates to the key abstractions and mechanisms of an application can be categorized as logical design. Physical design involves the techniques used to map these abstract constructs onto given software and hardware platforms. Any implementation details based on target language(s), tools, networks and their protocols, databases, or hardware would be included in physical design. The main heuristic to keep in mind while examining physical design is that physical design should not corrupt the logical design.

A classic example can be found in the world of information management. Many software development teams in this domain are faced with management-directed mandates stating that a given relational database must be used for a particular system. (With good reason! Many MIS-domain companies have spent millions of dollars on this software and cannot justify an additional, equivalent expense to purchase object-oriented database software.) The fear is that these teams will analyze the mandated database and realize it is capable only of capturing the abstractions of data records and their associations. They then extrapolate this realization to state that their object-oriented design need not examine inheritance relationships since they are not directly modeled in the entity–relationship paradigm. The correct method of examining this problem states that logical design should ignore the shortcomings of the relational model (an implementation detail) but instead specify what they need from their database object. The needs can be implemented later in a layer of software sitting on top of the required relational database. The layer of software separating an object-oriented domain from an underlying, nonobject-oriented subsystem is often called a **wrapper**. We will discuss software wrappers in more detail later in this chapter.

The reader should not assume that the above discussion is an argument that a software developer should ignore physical design until logical design is complete. Many logical design decisions hinge on physical design information. These are not corruptions of a logical design in favor of physical design; they are simply logical design decisions based on physical design constraints. As an example, in my object-oriented analysis and design course, I used an example scenario from an object-oriented analysis and design book which discussed withdrawing $100 from an ATM. The scenario went roughly like this:

1. A user inserts an ATM card into a card reader.

2. The ATM detects that its card reader has a card and reads the account number off the card.

3. The ATM asks for a PIN number on its display screen.

4. The user enters her PIN number through the ATM's keypad.

5. The ATM then sends the account and PIN number to the bank, which verifies the user's identification.

6. The ATM then asks what the user wants to do.

7. The user uses the keypad to state that she wants to withdraw $100 from her checking account.

8. The ATM asks the bank to process the transaction.

9. The bank states that the transaction is valid.

10. The ATM gives the user $100 from her checking account.

I successfully used this scenario in six or seven classes that each consisted of 15 or 20 people. Everyone was perfectly happy with this scenario. The next class that I taught had an individual who worked for a large New York bank. He immediately objected to the scenario, saying that no ATM in the world worked this way. What was his objection? It turns out that each time we want to use the network (i.e., the ATM wants to talk to the bank, or vice versa), it costs us 50 cents. No ATM is going to spend 50 cents just to ask a bank if the account and PIN number are correct. The person stated that the ATM would check locally if the account and PIN number matched (stating that the account and PIN were electronically encoded on the back of the card). The ATM checked only to see if the person using the card knew what was electronically encoded on the back of the card. What if I created my own card with an account and PIN number; would the ATM let me in? Of course it would, but what danger would that cause? When a transaction is built and sent to the bank for processing, the account and PIN number are sent along as well. The bank can then verify everything with only one network access. In fact, most of today's systems do not even bother with local verification. They assume you are the owner of a card until you try to process a transaction. Travelers quickly learn this when they are in a distant city and they try to use a bank card that is not on the network of the ATM. You are allowed to get all the way through transaction creation. It is only when you try to process the transaction that the ATM spits out your card and informs you that you are not on the given network.

This is a case where logical design does not care which mechanism you choose, but physical design states that if you use a particular mechanism, your software system saves several tens of millions of dollars per year. In effect, physical design considerations force the developer to make a particular logical design choice. We see this in the real world very often. When AT&T first introduced the notion of debit cards for local pay telephones, I wondered why they were going through all of the trouble. After all, didn't they already have telephone access cards? Of course, the first answer that comes to mind is that AT&T gets your money before you make the call, saving the cost of billing (a logical design decision) and allowing them an interest-free loan. Even if these advantages are factored out via discounts, there is still an advantage to AT&T. The debit cards are local, whereas access cards require a network connection to verify the calling card. This physical design information states that debit cards are cheaper to process than calling cards. We can often think of physical design information as the data we need to add a cost factor to each method in a class. With logical design information alone, all messages are considered to be the same value.

Heuristic 9.1

> **Object-oriented designers should not allow physical design criteria to corrupt their logical designs. However, physical design criteria are often used in the decision-making process at logical design time.**

Consider the home heating system problem we have discussed previously. In design courses in which it is used, a frequent argument revolves around whether rooms demand heat from the heat flow regulator or if the heat flow regulator should ask rooms if they need heat. Figure 9.1 depicts these two options.

This particular logical design argument will go on forever. Given logical design information alone, the two designs are equivalent. A good tongue-in-cheek heuristic is if, during a logical design critique, two parties who know what they are talking about argue for a long length of time, it is a safe bet that the argument is irrelevant and a decision should be made with the flip of a coin. The key phrase here is "know what they are talking about." I have seen many longwinded arguments in a design critique that were very important but could not be resolved because both parties lacked the

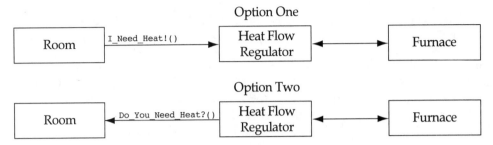

Figure 9.1 Heat flow regulator design choices.

necessary background to make a proper design decision. One need not look far to see these irrelevant arguments occurring. Most ANSI committees are plagued by long delays between the time they have a reasonable standard and when it is accepted. The reason is difficulty in getting everyone to agree on the small details. The large issues have large trade-offs, which are quickly decided.

How should our home heating system design be resolved? Often, physical design will state that one method is more expensive than the other. This information will coerce the logical design to accept the cheapest solution (see Figure 9.2). In the event that physical design criteria do not offer a solution, I generally add the method to the class which is the least complex. If they offer the same approximate complexity, then I flip a coin.

If this book were to be used as a text in an "Introduction to Software Development" course, then this chapter would be much larger than it is. As it turns out, many of the traditional physical design criteria used in action-oriented design are still applicable to object-oriented physical design. This chapter also happens to involve the same problems and the same solutions. Consider the fact that C programmers have always worried (or should have worried) about the fact that integers on different machines are different sizes. For example, on an IBM PC running DOS, integers are two bytes, but on a Sun workstation they are four bytes. This is a physical design

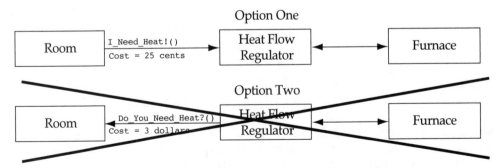

Figure 9.2 Physical design criteria and logical design.

issue that will carry over into the object-oriented paradigm; for example, C++ programmers have the same worries. The fact of the matter is that the solutions are the same and are not impacted by the object-oriented paradigm. This text will assume that the reader has some experience with software development and has faced the mundane problems. We will focus on those areas of physical design unique to the object-oriented paradigm, or at least those that have unique solutions under the object-oriented paradigm. These unique areas include the use of wrappers to isolate nonobject-oriented subsystems from object-oriented applications; persistence in an object-oriented system (i.e., object-oriented database management systems); memory management, including the copying and assigning of objects; minimal public interfaces for all classes in an object-oriented system; concurrency in an object-oriented system; and the mapping of object-oriented designs onto nonobject-oriented languages.

9.2   The Construction of Object-Oriented Wrappers

The notion of a software wrapper is not new, but like so many other concepts in the object-oriented paradigm, its name is new. In the past we referred to the notion of software layering. Consider the seven famous layers in a network architecture (e.g., the connection layer, the transport layer, the physical layer). They serve as a mechanism for separating levels of concern in networks, with each layer having control of a particular level of detail. If this architecture were defined today, I am sure it would be called the seven wrappers of a network architecture. Wrappers are simply layers of software written in an object-oriented fashion. There are many examples of the need for such a construct.

The first occasion when I become acquainted with the need for wrappers was at a software developers conference back in the mid-1980s. The conference featured a panel on the reusability of software. Each panelist was a representative of a particular programming language (C++, SmallTalk, Lisp/Flavors, and Eiffel) discussing patterns of reuse among the users of their language. After the panelists had delivered their position papers and a number of language-based questions had been answered, a gentleman approached the microphone and made the following statement (which I found to be one of the more enlightening):

> Each of you, in turn, has told me how to reuse C++ if I'm a C++ programmer, SmallTalk if I'm a SmallTalk programmer, Lisp/Flavors if I'm a Lisp/Flavors programmer, Eiffel if I'm an Eiffel programmer. Well, I'm someone who wants to be a C++ programmer but I happen to have a million lines of Fortran IV code which performs calculations on waveforms. How do I reuse my million lines of horrible, unmaintainable, nonextendible, *working* Fortran IV code in a C++ application? Don't ask me to rewrite the Fortran code, because no one understands how it works and the author left the company 15 years ago.

It was the first time I had considered the problem. Based on the panel's response, it was the first time for a lot of people. This brought up the subject of reusing nonobject-oriented code in an object-oriented application via a wrapper. The idea was to create a collection of classes that modeled the Fortran code in an object-oriented manner. The methods of these classes are function calls into the Fortran library. Of course, the new problem was to find this collection of classes. One technique of finding classes from a collection of existing functions is to examine the arguments passed into each function. Each record type argument is a good candidate for a class, since the corresponding function will end up a method with that record type passed as an implied first argument. Of course, Fortran IV does not even have the notion of record, so it was necessary to look for patterns of arguments being passed to a collection of functions within the library. For example, three integers followed by six real numbers followed by a character string might imply the numeric description of a waveform. Once the classes are found, they can be easily implemented through calls to the Fortran library (see Figure 9.3). If, at a later date, the company decides to rewrite the Fortran waveform engine in C++, the applications will be completely isolated from the Fortran. Object-oriented applications get to talk to the same object-oriented waveform engine. They are users of the engine and could care less how that engine is implemented.

Another example of the need for a wrapper brings me back to my early days of corporate education. Back in 1985/1986, I gave design and C++ courses to four different companies involved with telecommunications networks. Companies involved with telecommunications were among the first to jump into object-oriented programming. This was due to the fact that there exist national standards for telecommunications devices. They are documented in publications with statements like, "If you want to build a T-1 network, then it must have the following abstract behavior, but you are free to implement it as you wish." The objects in the domain of

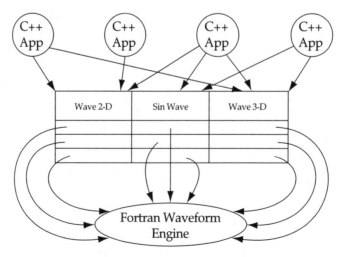

Figure 9.3 A C++ wrapper for a Fortran engine.

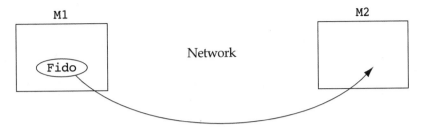

Figure 9.4 Moving `Fido` from `M1` to `M2`.

telecommunications were obvious; however, the architecture of the systems that used them were not so obvious. All four companies ran into the same interesting problem. How do we tell an object called `Fido` of the class `Dog` to move from machine `M1` to machine `M2` over a network? (See Figure 9.4.) In addition, we expect to be moving many objects of different classes from machine to machine.

Discussing this task was trivial during logical design. We simply send `Fido` the `Dog` the `move` message along with the machine object to which it is to move itself, e.g., `Fido.move(M2)`. Unfortunately, along comes physical design with the question, "What does a method like `move` look like?" This raises the interesting question of how we go about moving objects over networks. This network doesn't know about dogs, cats, tables, chairs, and T-1 objects. What do networks know about? At the lowest level they work with bits, then come bytes, and if we are lucky, packets of bytes. This brought up the need for an encoder, which turned a `Dog` (and any other object wishing to move from machine to machine) into a collection of packets, and a decoder, to decode the packets on the other machine (see Figure 9.5).

The problem with this solution is evident when we look at the internals of the decoder. It must check some field of the first packet to determine what object the packet stream is representing. Based on the value of this field, it will create the appropriate object. The companies involved with this design realized they were performing explicit case analysis on the type of an object, a violation of an important heuristic. They assumed their design was flawed and searched in vain for a better solution. Their design is not flawed in this example; the network is simply not object-oriented. Whenever an object-oriented application interfaces to a nonobject-oriented subsys-

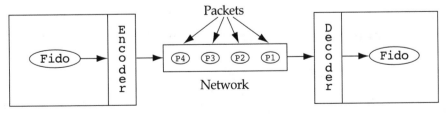

Figure 9.5 A solution to moving `Fido`.

tem, explicit case analysis is often the result. In this example, an object-oriented application is using a nonobject-oriented network. This network along with an encoder and a decoder can be viewed as an object-oriented network to the objects in the problem domain. Some will argue that the explicit case analysis still exists since only our view (i.e., partitioning) of the system has changed. However, the same argument can be made for polymorphism. Someone must perform an analysis on the exact type of the object. If users of the system need to perform the analysis, it is considered explicit case analysis; if the system performs the analysis, then it is considered implicit case analysis. At the time in question, there existed no object-oriented networks. Each of these companies was left to build its own object-oriented wrapper (i.e., encoder/decoder), which was difficult to maintain due to its explicit case analysis. In addition, the case analysis is dependent on the data types allowed across the network. The eventual solution is to build generic object-oriented networks that require only a description of the data in order to pass that data across the network in an object-oriented fashion.

An architecture for such a network has been proposed by the Object Management Group, and is known as **CORBA** (Common Object Request Broker Architecture) [13]. It addresses not only the problem of object-oriented networks but the need for objects to send remote messages to objects that live on other machines. Of course, we need not stop there. Why not let C++ objects send remote messages to SmallTalk objects which live on another machine? This creates truly seamless, distributed systems.

Another example of the explicit case analysis problem with respect to object-oriented systems interfacing with nonobject-oriented subsystems can be found in our previously explored fruit basket example. Consider an application that allows users interactively to build a custom fruit basket object by first prompting them for the number of fruit desired, followed by a prompt for each of the fruit as to type and other fields. In a menu-driven system, the application will have to perform explicit case analysis on the type of the fruit. This explicit case analysis is necessary due to the user interface's not being object-oriented. In a graphical user interface environment, we could envision a different icon for each type of fruit. The user would simply click a mouse over the appropriate icon in order to build that type of fruit object. One can argue that case analysis is still required. The code within the graphical user interface will check if the mouse was clicked between certain x and y coordinates. However, this case analysis is implicit since the user of the system is not performing it. It is all a matter of perception; where do the "system" and "outside the system" begin and end?

9.3   Persistence in an Object-Oriented System

In all of the preceding examples, we wanted to be sure that nonobject-oriented subsystems were placed in an object-oriented wrapper to ensure the consistent modeling of our object-oriented domain. One special type of wrapper is the database wrapper. Software developers quickly realized that relational databases were not sufficiently expressive to capture the detailed constructs of the object-oriented paradigm. While relational databases are able to capture data structures and their associations, they are inept at describing the bidirectional relationship between data and behavior, uses relationships, containment relationships, and inheritance. Many companies produced or acquired object-oriented database management systems with the goal that these subsystems would map more uniformly to the object-oriented problem model. These databases take a description of the logical design of the system and, from it, derive all the necessary information for mapping the logical design to flat files, with a possible intermediate mapping to a sophisticated database engine. An object-oriented database can be thought of as a wrapper for a relational database. The only task they eliminate from the object-oriented developer's job is the mapping of object-oriented constructs to something a relational database can understand. While this mapping is straightforward, it is an example of accidental complexity that should be eliminated. Much information is lost in the mapping to something less expressive, and there is always the chance of error when it is performed by a human.

Many information-management companies (banks, insurance companies, mailing-list brokers, etc.) have invested millions of dollars in relational database software. Is it worth the money to move to an object-oriented database system? Most of these companies insist that it is not, and I tend to agree with them. Why spend large sums of money on database software that is not as well tested as some of the large relational databases that are available? It is often cheaper for a company to build its own object-oriented wrapper for its relational database, taking advantage of the in-house experience and software.

Object-oriented databases are often used by developers building a system in which the database is an auxiliary subsystem not related to the main thrust of the system. For example, one company with which I worked was building a 3-D modeling tool. The tool would allow its users to save the 3-D model they designed. The obvious choice for designing this ability was to use an object-oriented database that could directly map the users' objects onto the flat files of the disk (see Figure 9.6). There is nothing wrong with an information-management application using an object-oriented database. It is just that these companies often have invested huge amounts of money in relational database software, and it should not go to waste. Most of this argument will disappear as soon as the large relational database vendors begin offering object-oriented extensions to their products. This is the general trend, with several third-party vendors already offering object-oriented database wrappers portable to a number of commercial relational databases.

There is a trend within information-management companies to reduce the use of mainframe computers to large data-storage devices with high-bandwidth networks. These data-storage devices are then attached to a collection of PCs or Unix workstations. The workstations or PCs handle all of the user interface work, collecting and displaying information interactively. The mainframe acts as a high-speed retrieval and processing center. Eventually, most of these companies will question why they are spending 10 million dollars on a mainframe when they can get the same use

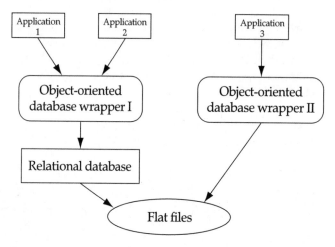

Figure 9.6 Architectures for object-oriented databases.

from 1 million dollars of specialized file server hardware. Companies with this architectural mixture of PCs and mainframes are often faced with an object-oriented PC application talking to an database living on the mainframe.

I dealt with an insurance company that was developing a worker's compensation claim system that had this particular problem. The first pass produced a logical design where many methods of the problem domain classes talked directly to the mainframe. I argued that the problem domain classes should not know anything about mainframes and their databases. All they know is that if they throw a claim number over a brick wall, a claim object will come back over the wall (see Figure 9.7). Where does it come from? Who cares! Maybe it is a brain-dead database on a mainframe, maybe it is from a local optical drive (because 15-gigabyte drives will be available for 8 dollars in 1998), or maybe a squirrel pulled it out of its nest. The point

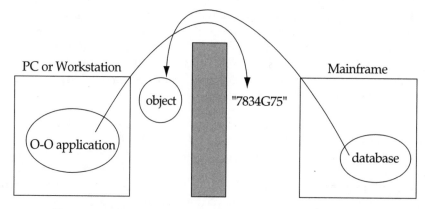

Figure 9.7 Hiding architectural details within wrappers.

is that we do not want our object-oriented domain polluted with nonobject-oriented details. We build a wrapper (the brick wall) and then use that wrapper. Buy an object-oriented database, and you are paying someone else to write the wrapper.

The discussion of object-oriented database management systems brings up the whole subject of **persistence**. Persistence means that objects can live after the power has been turned off. It is important to note that object-oriented databases and/or object-oriented wrappers for relational databases are only the most common form of one type of persistence, called **persistence in time**. Traditionally, this has meant storage to a static medium, which for most people implies a database. There is an alternative method for saving objects to a static medium besides using a centralized database (object-oriented or not). Each object can have local knowledge concerning how it should be saved to a disk. This is common in systems with relatively few persistent classes. This book was not stored in an object-oriented database. Each object making up the book—items such as chapters, paragraphs, sentences, words, frames, floating headers, floating footers, graphical objects drawn within frames, etc.—was told to store itself. Many people like to call this form of persistence **local persistence (in time)**. If a class has an output operation that produces a description of the object in a form that can be parsed and used to build the equivalent object (via some input operation), then the class has local persistence. The important distinction is in whether the storage algorithm is decentralized across all of the persistent classes or centralized in some subsystem (e.g., a database) that knows how to store objects of a class based on a description of that class.

There is a relatively new concept referred to as **persistence in space**. Persistence in space states that objects do not live after the power is turned off by saving themselves to static medium. Instead, they detect the power turning off and scurry across the network to a "safe" machine where they execute what they need or stay idle until their host machine's power returns, at which time they scurry back to the host. While this sounds a bit silly to some people, its uses go beyond the realm of writing distributed game programs. Many telecommunications companies are examining this form of persistence with the intent of applying its principles to routing algorithms. Routing algorithms are often very complex, unruly, and most interesting; they are centralized. The feeling is that decentralizing the routing algorithm will make them simpler. One can imagine a telephone packet finding a trunk line going down (or busy) and re-routing itself to a free trunk line. At this time, most of the work done in this field is in the research phase, with little practical application. It is expected to bring good results in decentralizing object-oriented applications across networked collections of machines.

9.4 Memory Management Issues in an Object-Oriented Application

Another interesting physical design area is that of memory management. There are two categories of languages when viewed from the method used to handle dynamic memory. There are those languages, like Lisp and SmallTalk, that support garbage collection. These systems periodically walk through memory, checking which used memory is no longer referenced by the resident applications. These pieces of memory are swept up for reuse on the environment's heap. The advantage of garbage collection is that application programmers do not have to worry about the allocation and deallocation of dynamic memory. The system does all the work for them. The disadvantage is that garbage collection reduces efficiency. Some systems arbitrarily suspend execution and perform their garbage collection for several seconds to several minutes, not the ideal for real-time systems. Others use some form of incremental garbage collection wherein the execution time slows down uniformly over the execution of an application without uncomfortable suspensions of execution. There is an added performance penalty in that access to an object is often indirect. Actual object addresses cannot be given to the user since the object may be physically moved during garbage collection.

The other language category includes nongarbage-collecting languages like C++. User programmers are given actual physical addresses of objects on the heap. For this reason, these languages cannot offer garbage collection since they cannot update all user-copied values of the physical addresses when garbage collecting. Any garbage-collection algorithms must be implemented by individual application programmers and usually employ the notion of memory handles to store the physical addresses in a memory location and give the address of that location to the users. This provides an extra level of indirection so that the garbage-collection algorithm is free to change the physical addresses so long as the indirect memory locations do not relocate. The advantage of these languages is the increased performance. The disadvantage is the increased chance of memory leakage and/or heap corruption in an application. Memory leakage occurs when a software developer allocates memory and forgets to free it. Users of C++ are especially prone to this error because C++ offers several default operations that cause memory leakage when not explicitly defined under certain, very common, conditions. The gory details of memory leakage in C++ are beyond the scope of a text on object-oriented design. However, due to its prevalence and the large numbers of C++ programmers, in Appendix B I have provided a paper that discusses these details. It is highly recommended that C++ programmers read the paper to familiarize themselves with the eight places that memory leakage occurs in C++ applications.

9.5   Minimal Public Interfaces for Reusable Components

In 1989 I constructed a commercial C++ class library along with two other developers. We first discussed the classes we would include in the library and came up with the usual assortment of data structures, mathematical entities, collection classes, and primitive data type mimics. Since we were shipping source code, we wanted our code to look consistent to the users of the library. This started us on the subject of coding standards and guidelines. One of the topics we explored was the construc-

tion of a minimal public interface that all classes in the library would implement
[14]. We discussed the types of operations we wanted, as well as their signatures and
abstract behavior. I believe that a minimal public interface should be established if
classes are to be reused. The minimal public interface gives users of a collection of
reusable classes a basis for understanding the collection's architecture. Users come
to expect a minimal functionality from anything they use in the collection.

A Minimal Public Interface for All Reusable Classes

Constructor.

All classes that have data members should have a constructor (initialization) message
that initializes that data. In addition, the class should be defined in such a way that
it is not possible for users of the class to create objects in an invalid state, namely, a
state for which one or more methods of the class are unprepared. Some languages
provide better support for this constraint than others. Languages that have automatic
calls to constructors (e.g., C++) are particularly useful in guaranteeing that the user
building an object of the class has passed through one of the constructors of that
class.

Destructor.

In general, only classes that need to clean up a portion of their object require a
destructor or cleanup function. However, often a class that does not require this
cleanup is extended in a way that does require cleanup. For this reason, it is common
to add empty destructors for extensibility.

Copying Objects.

The notion of all classes knowing how to make a copy of their objects seems reasonable. There is a bit of a problem in languages that distinguish containment by value
and containment by reference (e.g., C++). In these languages, what do we mean by
"copying"? Consider the Point objects shown in Figure 9.8. They have an example
of containment by reference (the color field). Is P2 a copy of P1? Is P3 a copy of
P1? What's the relationship between P2 and P3?

Before answering any of our questions, we need to consider the fact that containment
by reference implies two different types of copying. These are called **deep copy** and
shallow copy. A deep copy of an object is a copy of the entire structure, not just
copies of pointers. The original object and its deep copy do not share any memory
space. A shallow copy of an object is a copy of the first-level data members. If one
of the data members is a pointer, then only the pointer value is copied, not the

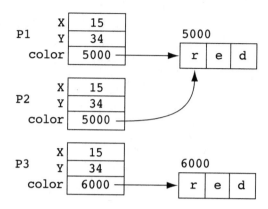

Figure 9.8 Shallow versus deep copying.

structure associated with it. The original object and its shallow copy share memory space.

Many real-world examples illustrate this distinction. If you go into a restaurant and tell the waiter/waitress that you want the meal that the person at the next table is eating, you are implying that you want a deep copy of that meal. A shallow copy of the meal would have the waiter/waitress put your fork in the other person's plate and walk away. In this application, a shallow copy of the meal is not adequate. On the other hand, if you are flying on a plane, you would hope that all of the air traffic controllers have a shallow copy of the air traffic map. It would not do any good for each air traffic controller to have a deep copy. Such a situation would imply that if air traffic controller X adds a new plane to the airport's air space, air traffic controllers Y and Z will not see it. This application clearly calls for shallow copying of the airport's air space.

In this example, P2 is a shallow copy of P1 because it shares the memory for the color string. P3 is a deep copy of P1 because it has its own memory for the color string. Technically speaking, P3 is a deep copy of P2 in that they are structurally equivalent but do not share memory. It is important to note that it is not possible to tell whether P1 is a shallow copy of P2 or P2 is a shallow copy of P1. That information is lost in this implementation of shallow copy. Some implementations add flags to the objects in order to determine the original from its shallow copies. Others use a technique called **reference counting** to make the difference between the two meaningless. We will explore the reference-counting technique later in this chapter.

Assigning Objects.

If each class understands how to copy its objects, then it must understand what it means to assign one of its objects to another of its objects. The only question is whether to use shallow or deep copy. We chose deep copy since it is the least likely to cause side effects to its implementations. In many languages, shallow copies are easiest to implement with some level of side effect. Users of the class should not be aware of whether or not it uses containment by reference in its implementation.

Equality Testing.

Given the differences between shallow and deep copying of objects, what does it mean for an object to be equal to another object? Since there exist two methods of copying objects, there must also exist two methods to test equality. We call these **equal** and **same**. The equal method tests for structural equivalence, while the same method tests for memory sharing. In our example, all three point objects are equal to one another since structurally they are equivalent. Only P1 and P2 are the same since they share data. P3 is not the same with either P1 or P2.

Print.

All classes should have a method that knows how to print out its objects in some format; many choose ASCII text. The need for this operation goes back to action-oriented programming, where many developers had `set` and `get` operations for each of their data structures. These are useful for debugging applications that use the class in question or for a minimal form of persistence (along with a parse method).

Parse.

All classes should have a parse method that knows how to initialize an object based on the output of the corresponding print method. Given a print method and a parse method that share output/input, the class can be said to have a form of minimal persistence. A user can tell an object of the class to print itself to a file and, at a later date, use the parse function to recreate that object from the description stored in the file. This is very useful for testing and debugging the use of a class in an application.

Self-Test.

Brad Cox [15] published an analogy between hardware reuse and software reuse. Hardware used to cost the earth until we decided to build everything from a set of standard, well-defined components. Now software costs the earth. In order to make software development cheap, we need to define an equivalent set of standard, well-defined components from which all of our software can be built. There are many problems with this analogy, including the fact that the economic models of hardware and software development are different. Hardware costs are all paid for during the development phase. The cost of manufacturing is insignificant compared to the up-front investment. In the case of software, the cost of development is often a small percentage of the cost of the software over its lifetime. Maintenance and extensibility are often the expenses parts of the software lifecycle. In fact, cheap development costs often imply more expensive maintenance in the future, because designers did not take the time to install extensibility hooks into their software.

Having said this, we still borrowed a little of this analogy after reasoning that hard-ware failure does not imply searching the smallest details to detect the problem. If you were to turn on your PC and it failed, you would not immediately start worrying that you had lost your all-important data on the hard drive. Nor would you drag out an oscilloscope and start checking individual chips until you found a defective one. The PC provides board-level diagnostics to at least attempt to pinpoint the area of the PC causing the problem. We feel that each class should have an equivalent, component-level test mechanism, which we named `self-test`. The `self-test` method is a class-specific method (as opposed to all others in the interface, which are object methods) that builds several objects of the class and exercises the public interface, checking for correct results. Some developers pointed out that if the con-structor of the class is flawed, we really cannot test much of the class's public inter-face. We agree. However, if you turn on your PC and nothing happens, you cannot really test much of the PC either. Having that little knowledge does give you much useful information. You do not worry about your hard disk failing, or memory fail-ing. You know to verify that the PC is plugged in, its switch is on, power is being supplied to the wall socket, etc. Likewise, if our `self-test` method fails outright, we know to check the constructor for problems. Like the PC analogy, there may or may not be many additional problems with the object in question.

This method proved invaluable in the porting of our library from one compiler/ platform to another. It was reassuring to have information like, "33 of our 40 classes passed their self-test, but seven need further examination for portability problems." Of course, the `self-test` function is only as good as the person who wrote it. Like all good testing procedures, it should be written by someone other than the developer of the class. If the developer thought to test something, then he or she probably did not make that mistake in the development of that class.

Several recent publications have been critical of minimal public interfaces, describing them as misguided efforts [16,17]. The authors of this material demonstrate classes whose semantics seem to break under each of the items listed in this minimal inter-face. I will avoid this particular argument and refuse to get too religious about the above interface. I invite the reader to check the provided reference, and he or she can be the final judge. I will leave you with the thought that many of the users of the class library that motivated the minimal interface found it useful as a learning hook into the library. Having used one class, they knew something about all of the other classes. The fact that there exist exceptions to the support of such an interface doesn't bother me or, presumably, other users of minimal interfaces.

9.6 Implementing Safe Shallow Copies

If we further consider our problems of copying objects whose classes possess containment by reference (i.e., shallow versus deep copying), we will find that we have a problem with shallow copying in languages that force us to perform our own memory management. How do we know when the object contained by reference can be destroyed safely? One method is to mark all shallow copies via a flag (see Figure 9.9) and develop a user-based constraint that states that shallow copies cannot live longer than the original. In this way, the original object is the only object that destroys the memory. The disadvantage is that it relies on a user to maintain the constraint. Programming by convention is a great source of errors.

A safer alternative to using a flag in the objects that share memory is to use a technique called **reference** or **use counting**. The idea of reference counting is to encapsulate the shared memory together with an integer counter. When a shallow copy of the object is created, it simply increments the reference counter. When an object is destroyed, it decrements the reference counter. If the counter goes to zero, then the object knows no one else is sharing the memory and so it can be freed (see Figure 9.10).

Let us consider the implementation of our air traffic control problem. How can our air traffic controllers share the same air traffic control memory? If all air traffic controllers in the world were looking at the same memory, then we would want to implement air traffic control memory as a class-specific piece of data. In that way, all air traffic controllers could share the object via the class. In the real world, let us assume that air traffic controllers in San Francisco are not interested in air traffic patterns over Madrid. However, all air traffic controllers in San Francisco are interested in sharing the same air traffic memory with their colleagues. Likewise, air traffic controllers in Madrid are interested in sharing their same memory. This is a case where groups of objects of the same class wish to share memory, but not all objects of that class want the same shared memory (see Figure 9.11). The best solution in

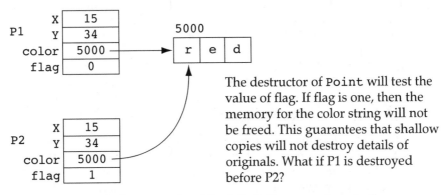

The destructor of Point will test the value of flag. If flag is one, then the memory for the color string will not be freed. This guarantees that shallow copies will not destroy details of originals. What if P1 is destroyed before P2?

Figure 9.9 An example of "safe" shallow copying via flags.

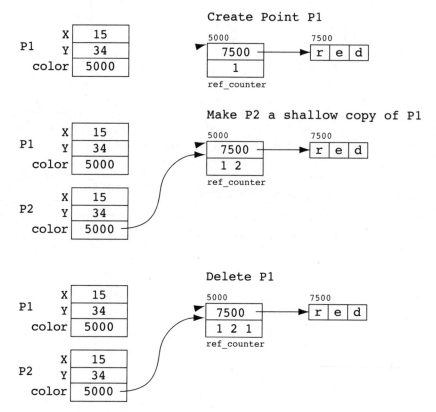

Figure 9.10 The reference counting of `Point` objects.

these situations is to use reference counting. Each air traffic controller accesses some air traffic control memory object that is shared with other air traffic controllers, but not all air traffic controllers share the same one.

Shallow copying, and therefore reference counting, is used whenever it is necessary for the system requirements (e.g., the air traffic control problem), or to save space and time. The space savings comes from eliminating the need to keep multiple copies of the data. The time savings comes from the reduced need to copy data. It is important to note that if a shallow copy or the original object changes the state of the shared data, then all objects involved in the sharing see the update. In the air traffic control problem, this is exactly what we want. In some domains, this cannot be tolerated, and deep copying, or **broadcasting**, is required.

The technique of broadcasting is used when an object is shared by a group of objects through containment by reference relationships with the constraint that state changes to the shared object must be reported to the entire group of objects. In the case of air traffic control, we might argue that one controller's changes to the air traffic control memory should be reported to all the other controllers. The air traffic memory

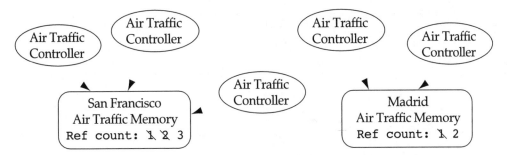

Figure 9.11 The air traffic control problem.

is the best object for broadcasting this message (see Figure 9.12). Of course, this implies that the air traffic memory (a contained object) knows about air traffic controllers (the containing objects), a violation of Heuristic 4.13. We can reduce the impact of this violation by stating that air traffic memory knows about a list of "things" that look at it but does not know the type of these things. The reuse restriction is changed from "anyone wishing to reuse air traffic memory objects must be air traffic controller objects (or their subclass)" to "anyone wishing to reuse air traffic memory objects must inherit from the `thing` class and implement the `state_modified()` message."

Heuristic 9.2

Do not change the state of an object without going through its public interface.

9.7 Concurrent Object-Oriented Programming

At a conference on parallel programming in the mid-1980s, a prominent researcher in the field stated that human beings will never be able to write parallel programs due to their complexity. The human brain, the researcher continued, can barely comprehend the complexity of sequential programming of large systems. Parallelism is out of the question. Of course, this made all of the parallel hardware people upset, since they were at the conference selling the opposite argument of the researcher. Developers then started thinking about parallelism in the real world. When I teach a course, I have no trouble understanding that there are 20 heartbeats running in parallel, a caterer taking away breakfast, a viewgraph projector turned on, several PCs in the room actively running game programs while those interacting with the game are listening to me (in parallel), the occasional car driving on the street below, and, if in New York, a window washer sitting on a small piece of wood some 400

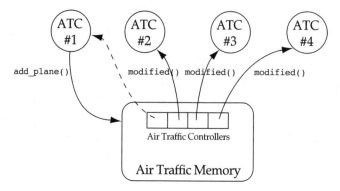

Figure 9.12 Broadcasting in the air traffic control domain.

feet above the street. All of these objects are executing methods in parallel, yet I have no problem understanding the complexity. Why not?

A number of researchers have discussed this question in workshops and published it in texts and research articles. Is the fact that the concurrency is locked inside of objects the key to understanding? Is it better to have the concurrency mechanisms outside, but surrounding the objects? Can we apply the notion of concurrent object-oriented programming to our common parallel programming problems and get better solutions? These are the types of questions being addressed today. There are two excellent texts on concurrent object-oriented programming [18,19].

I will not discuss concurrent object-oriented programming in any great detail in this text. I will say that concurrent object-oriented programming is hard—but only because concurrent programming is hard, not because the object-oriented paradigm adds any complexity to the problem. There is some vocabulary worth knowing. When studying concurrent object-oriented programming, you will invariably hear people discuss the notion of **passive objects** versus **active objects**. Passive objects belong to classes that fall into one of two categories (see Figure 9.13). The first category consists of classes that have not considered concurrency at all, in which case

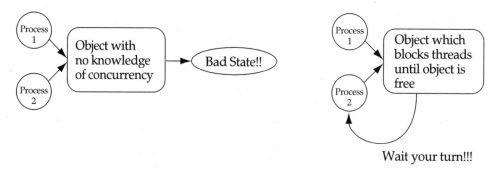

Figure 9.13 Examples of passive objects.

the semantics of the class are not guaranteed under multiple threads of control. The second category consists of classes that have considered multiple threads of control and have solved the problem through blocking. That is, when two or more threads of control want access to an object, the first thread gets control and the others wait on a queue. Some standard concurrency mechanism is used to control the queue, for example, semaphore, monitor, or guard. Active objects belong to classes that guarantee their semantics in the presence of multiple threads of control without the need for blocking (see Figure 9.14). Be careful when reading research articles on concurrent object-oriented programming. Many alternative definitions and uses for the terms "passive" and "active" exist.

9.8   Implementing Object-Oriented Designs in Nonobject-Oriented Languages

The final topic of interest in the area of physical design is how to go about implementing an object-oriented design in a nonobject-oriented language. This topic was of much greater interest in the late 1980s, when C++ was a moving target. At that time, many C programmers decided that they wanted to take advantage of object-oriented design but did not trust C++ for implementation. Many of them turned to object-oriented programming in C. Today C++ is fairly well defined with an ANSI committee adding on some final features. With this infrastructure in place, this topic becomes less interesting, although I have found a large number of developers who learn a lot about object-oriented programming by examining the implementation of its constructs using nonobject-oriented structures. I will summarize these details by examining each of the object-oriented constructs and how one might implement them in a nonobject-oriented language.

Overloaded Functions.

Most nonobject-oriented languages do not support the idea of two functions having the same name as long as their argument types differ (Prolog is one exception). The basic approach to handling this problem is to concatenate the name of the data type

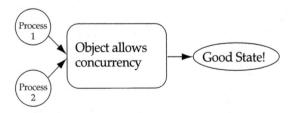

Figure 9.14   Example of an active object.

to the function name. This is how object-oriented languages implement overloaded functions. Either they mangle the name at compile time (e.g., C++), or they hash the name of the argument with the name of the function in order to find the address of the overloaded function (e.g., SmallTalk).

Class/Object.

A standard method of implementing the notion of class in a nonobject-oriented language is to encapsulate a data structure with its associated functions. This can be done by using a function module (if your language supports modules, e.g., Ada83, Modula-2) or in a file (e.g., C).

Data Hiding.

There is no way to establish data hiding in languages that do not support it except by convention, that is, programmers promise not to access particular data members of a record and/or functions associated with that data. There is an exception in the C programming language. The C language allows its users to define pointers to a data structure without ever defining the data structure itself. However, there are major restrictions on the use of that pointer. The user of the pointer cannot perform any pointer arithmetic or any dereference operation. The only thing he or she can do with the pointer is to pass it to functions. In this way, developers can define a structure (record) called `Dog` and place it in a file along with all of the functions that work with `Dog`s. One of these functions is a `get_Dog()` operation, which returns a pointer to a `Dog`. This file is compiled separately and given as object code to users of `Dog`s. Users of `Dog`s define a pointer to a `Dog` but are not allowed access to the internal details. They call `get_Dog()` to get one of these objects and proceed to pass it along to any function defined on `Dog`. They get to use `Dog` objects but never get to see any implementation details of the `Dog`.

Inheritance.

Inheritance is a difficult construct to fake. The implementation "trick" is exactly that used for implementing multiple inheritance in a single-inheritance language. The subclass (data structure) contains the superclass as its first data member. The user must then create a delegation function on the containing class for each function associated with the contained superclass. Like our multiple inheritance solution, this introduces accidental complexity in that we cannot just add a method to a superclass and have all of the subclasses inherit it. We must examine every class (data structure) that contains a modified class to determine if the modified class is really contained or if it is faking inheritance. If it is faking inheritance, then a delegation function must be added to the containing class. Many of the benefits of inheritance are lost in its implementation in a nonobject-oriented language.

Polymorphism.

Polymorphism is clearly the most difficult to implement in a nonobject-oriented language, with all solutions creating maintenance problems larger than the one we originally tried to avoid—explicit case analysis. The traditional approach to getting around polymorphism is to use pointers to functions (in languages that support them, e.g., C) to do something that used to be called generic programming. The idea is to bind the actual address to the function call at runtime by changing the value of a function pointer. Alternatives include performing the binding of a function call by forcing the user to call some function, perhaps named `bind`, which takes two string arguments: the type of the object making the call and the name of the function call. These two strings are hashed together to form an index, which, when used on a global hash table, returns the appropriate address of the desired function. For example, `bind(''Dog'', ''wag_tail'')` would hash to 142 (using some hash function which I neglect to provide). When index 142 is retrieved from a global hash table, the address of `Dog`'s `wag_tail()` function is returned and executed. This is similar to SmallTalk's implementation of polymorphism.

An alternative is to build, and unfortunately maintain, jump tables for every class that wants a polymorphic function(s). When an object is built, it gets a hidden pointer to the appropriate jump table. Users then execute the appropriate function by providing its index in the jump table. Since the user does not know at whose jump table a given object is pointing, the binding is considered dynamic. This is similar to the method C++ employs for implementing polymorphism.

It is important to note that in both cases, the bookkeeping normally done by a programming language is required by the programmer. This often produces more maintenance problems than the original explicit case analysis that the programmer set out to avoid.

Glossary

Active object   An object whose semantics are guaranteed under multiple threads of control.

Broadcasting   The act of an object sending messages to a collection of objects that contain it.

CORBA   An architecture that discusses the distribution of object-oriented systems across differing architectures. The acronym stands for Common Object Request Broker Architecture. This architecture is being developed by the Object Management Group (OMG).

Deep copy   The copying of an object in which the entire structure of the object is copied, not just its pointers and references.

Local persistence (in time)   The act of saving an object to a static medium where each class has knowledge of how to store and retrieve the object.

Logical object-oriented design   The area of object-oriented design dealing with finding classes, their protocols, and their relationships to one another (i.e., inheritance, containment, uses, and association).

OMG   The Object Management Group, a consortium of companies dedicated to standardizing distributed, persistent, object-oriented systems across a broad range of development platforms. The designers of CORBA.

Passive objects   Objects that belong to a class that either has not considered the possibility of multiple threads of control, or has considered the problem and solved it by blocking (i.e., allowing only one thread of control into the object at a time, forcing all other threads to wait).

Persistence   The quality of an object which allows it to live after the power has been turned off.

Persistence in space   The implementation of persistence where objects detect that a machine is powering down and scurry across the network to a safe machine where they can continue processing until their home machine is available.

Persistence in time   The implementation of persistence where objects are stored to some static medium from which they can be reloaded in the future. It usually implies a database.

Physical object-oriented design   The facet of object-oriented design dealing with hardware and software platforms and their impact on a logical object-oriented design.

Reference counting   A technique for developing safe shallow copies wherein the data to be shared is encapsulated with an integer counter that maintains the number of containing objects sharing the data.

Shallow copy   The copying of an object where only its addresses and references are copied. The original object and its copy share the objects representation.

Wrapper   A layer of software that hides some detail or subsystem of an application from the other subsystem(s).

Summary of Heuristics

Heuristic 9.1   Object-oriented designers should not allow physical design criteria to corrupt their logical designs. However, physical design criteria are often used in the decision-making process at logical design time.

Heuristic 9.2   Do not change the state of an object without going through its public interface.

Chapter 10

The Relationship Between Heuristics and Patterns

10.1 Heuristics Versus Patterns

At a workshop during OOPSLA '87, Kent Beck first brought up Christopher Alexander's text, *A Pattern Language* [20, 21]. In this text, Alexander attempts to capture the subconscious aesthetic qualities of architecture by using an invented pattern language. Beck suggested that we look for something similar to capture interesting patterns in good object-oriented design. Recently, a large amount of effort has been applied to this topic by Kent Beck, Richard Helm, Erich Gamma, Ralph Johnson, Bruce Anderson, James Coplien, Grady Booch, Frank Buschmann, Robert Martin, and many others. These researchers have examined patterns from many different angles, ranging from Anderson's "null object pattern," which examines a common solution to a multiparadigm language problem, to James Coplien's examination of corporate infrastructure patterns that lead to good product development.

All of this research has led me to wonder, "What is the exact relationship between the qualitative heuristics I have collected/developed and design patterns?" They are obviously related, in that the method I have used to find a good design heuristic is to find "trends" that various developers from different domains have followed. If these trends lead to designs that exhibit a desirable quality (e.g., easy to extend, easy to maintain, less complex to understand), then I try to generalize them to some rule. However, what occurs more often is a recurring trend that exhibits undesirable qualities. These need to be generalized to some design transformation pattern, namely, a pattern that captures the method by which a bad design is transformed into a good design.

Upon further examination, I have found that qualitative heuristics not only lead to a number of interesting patterns, but also exhibit some interesting properties between these patterns. A heuristic forms a gateway through which a designer can move from a bad design pattern to a good design pattern. The pattern description that captures this information consists of a source design pattern (the bad pattern), a motivating (i.e., violated) heuristic with its rationale, and a target design pattern (the good pattern). These transformation patterns (dare I call them metapatterns?) exhibit properties of transitivity and reflexivity.

An interesting problem that many of the patterns researchers have glossed over in their published literature is how a novice designer will know when a particular pattern should be applied. In some of the existing literature, the authors imply that a pattern can be applied intuitively by a design group that has been exposed to a catalog of patterns. When a pattern takes tens of pages of text to describe it, it is very unlikely that the designer will intuitively discover when the pattern is needed. Heuristics, on the other hand, are very easy to remember since their descriptions are rarely more than two sentences long. In fact, some preliminary research indicates that violations of at least two-thirds of the design heuristics described in this book could be automatically detected through the design information contained in an object-oriented case tool. As of the writing of this book, for example, at least two case tool vendors have discussed the addition of a heuristics engine to their tools. Once a designer realizes a heuristic is violated, he or she could look at a number of design transformation patterns associated with that heuristic. Each pattern would optimize the transformation for some attribute of design, for example, flexibility or minimization of classes. Some patterns may even take physical design trade-offs into consideration, such as efficiency considerations between polling and interrupt-driven architectures.

As a first example of a design transformation pattern, consider the following pattern, which I call the broadcast pattern. This pattern captures a common problem that occurs when a designer is required to share an object among a group of additional objects. The additional objects all contain the shared object by reference. The problem with this design pattern is that if one object updates the shared object, then all of the other containing objects have their state changed without a message being sent to their public interface. This can make program tracing more difficult. The solution is to have the contained object broadcast a state-change message to each of the containing objects, informing them of the update.

The Broadcast Pattern

Source Pattern.

It is common for an object-oriented design to require a number of objects to contain (by reference) the same object. This requirement may exist to save the space/time of maintaining multiple copies of an object, or to better implement referential integrity constraints that are complicated by multiple storage of the same entity, or to model in the real world an intrinsic part of the system.

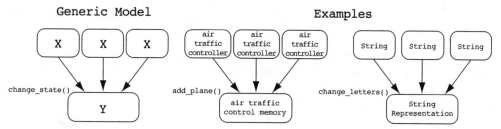

Motivating Heuristic.

The state of an object should not be modified except through a message sent to its public interface.

Rationale.

If an object outside the lexical scope of another object can change the second object's state, then the cost of maintaining the system is increased. This increase is similar to the problems associated with side effects due to public data in a class or, to a less extent, to global data.

Target Pattern.

When a group of objects contain the same object (by reference) in order to support better efficiency, easier maintenance of data integrity semantics, or the implementation of a system requirement, then the shared object should broadcast a state-change message to each of the containing objects whenever its state changes.

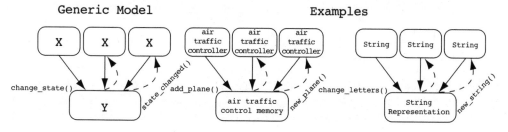

It is important to note that both the source and target patterns are shown as an abstract example along with two specializations of the abstract example in two different domains. This is to prove that the pattern is not just a domain-specific design/programming trick; it applies to numerous domains without regard to the specifics of the domain. Given that there are over 60 qualitative heuristics for object-oriented design, and that each heuristic denotes at least one transformation pattern, there are many of these patterns to document.

10.2 Transitivity Among Design Transformation Patterns

Consider the following transformation pattern, which I have named the interrupt pattern. It handles a common design problem that occurs in interrupt-driven architectures.

The Interrupt Pattern

Source Pattern.

Many systems have interrupt-driven devices or algorithms that, when modeled, result in a design in which the class representing the interrupting device needs to send a message to its containing class. Almost by definition, an interrupting device is interrupting something at a higher level in the system.

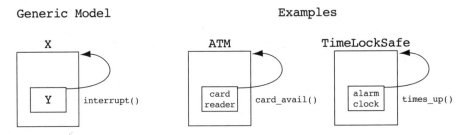

Motivating Heuristic.

Contained objects should never send a message to the objects that contain them.

Rationale.

If a contained object is dependent on the class that contains it, then it is not reusable. If the card reader of an automatic teller machine has knowledge that it is contained in an ATM, then it cannot be taken out of the ATM and used to build a security door. If an alarm clock is dependent on its containing bedroom, then we cannot take it out of the bedroom to build a time lock safe.

Target Pattern.

When a contained object must send a message to its containing class, then the containing class should be made more general through judicious use of inheritance. In this way, the contained object does not depend on the containing class, only on its base class. It is easier to require a reuser to inherit from some abstract class than to use a particular class (effectively ruining any chance of reuse outside of the original domain).

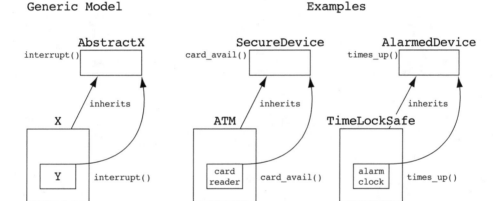

These patterns capture interesting design transformations and also have interesting properties of their own. The broadcast and interrupt patterns are transitive. The target of the broadcast pattern is equivalent to the source of the interrupt pattern. Used together, the two patterns improve the design in a two-step process. While this sounds weaker than transitivity, it actually states that "If there exists a design transformation pattern to take a design from A to B and there exists a design transformation pattern to take a design from B to C, then there exists a design transformation pattern to take A directly to C." We do not necessarily document this third pattern, just as we do not document an inheritance relationship achieved through transitivity. It is, nonetheless, a transitivity relationship. This transitivity can be continued through a third pattern, which takes the target of the interrupt pattern as its source.

The Interrupt-Polling Pattern

Source Pattern.

Designs that model interrupt-driven devices and algorithms often require the object modeling the interrupt-driven device to send a message to its containing class. This architecture is often made more flexible by having the containing class abstracted to some base class via inheritance.

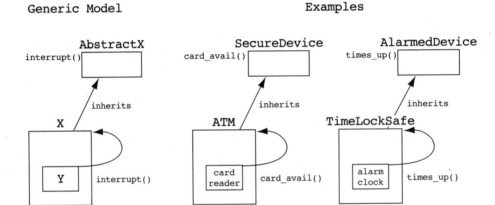

Motivating Heuristic.

A designer should minimize the number of collaborations in his or her design.

Rationale.

Each time a uses relationship is added to an object-oriented design, the complexity of the system increases. This complexity attacks the understanding of the system by its architects as well as harms the reusability of classes by increasing the dependency of the class sending the message.

Target Pattern.

The architecture of an object-oriented design should attempt to exploit the existing uses relationships rather than create new ones. The system should resort to a polling architecture rather than the interrupt-driven architecture of the source pattern. In this way, the containing class can poll the contained, interrupting object. The contained object has no dependency on its container, and we eliminate one uses relationship from the architecture.

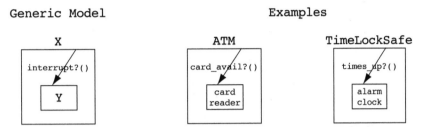

It is important to note that there are physical design trade-offs between the interrupt pattern and the interrupt-polling pattern. A particular application may not be able to afford the extra cost of polling in its particular domain. In this case, the designer is forced into a worse (i.e., more complex) logical design for physical design reasons. Most domains require such concessions from its designers for one reason or another, such as object designs interfacing to existing action-oriented systems, or languages that are not expressive enough to capture the necessary facets of design.

10.3   The Reflexive Property of Design Transformation Patterns

Transitivity is not the only property demonstrated by design transformation patterns. Some of the patterns illustrate the reflexive property. Consider the following two design transformation patterns, each of which takes the other pattern's target as its source. Those patterns that demonstrate the reflexive property show places in object-oriented design in which the designer must chose one of two architectures, each having advantages and disadvantages, but neither getting a decisive victory over the other.

The Generalization Pattern

Source Pattern.

A familiar use for inheritance is to specialize an existing class into a new customized class. We claim that the new derived class is a special type of the previously existing base class. In many of these cases, both the base and derived classes are concrete, that is, users of them can build objects.

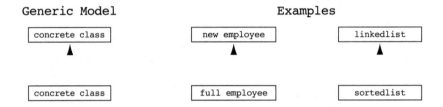

Motivating Heuristic.

Base classes should be abstract classes.

Rationale.

If a class inherits from a concrete class, there is fear that the concrete base class will change in a way in which the derived class does not want to follow. If this occurs, the architecture will not be able to support the change due to its inflexibility.

Target Pattern.

If a class is a special type of an existing concrete class, it should not inherit directly from that class. A better architecture is for both classes to inherit from a new abstract base class. In this way, if one, or both, of the concrete classes requires an extension, then the change can be effected in the derived class or the abstract base class (respectively).

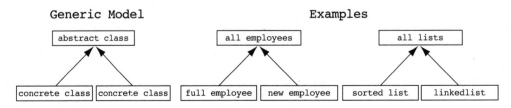

The Specialization Pattern

Source Pattern.

When two classes inherit from an abstract base class, sometimes one of the derived classes inherits all of its data and behavior from the abstract base class.

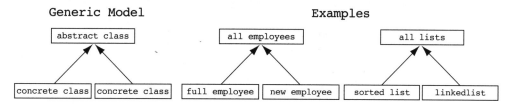

Motivating Heuristic.

Classes in an object-oriented design that do not add meaningful behavior should be eliminated as irrelevant classes.

Rationale.

A serious problem in designing object-oriented architectures is that if certain heuristics are not followed, then the developer can be forced to deal with a proliferation of classes. A leading cause of proliferation of classes is the acceptance of too many irrelevant classes.

Target Pattern.

If two classes inherit from the same abstract base class and one of the derived classes inherits all of its data and behavior from the abstract base class, then the hierarchy should be redesigned such that the second derived class inherits directly from the first derived class. This will result in the elimination of the abstract base class.

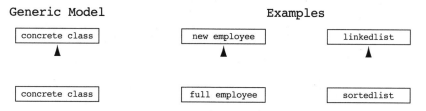

The reader may be tempted to argue that the generalization pattern is always the best choice since it offers maximum flexibility. This is true if there is only one case of this pattern in an architecture. What if there are 200 such cases? Do you want the overhead of maintaining 200 additional classes that add no meaningful behavior to your design? Do you want 200 maintenance time bombs waiting to go off due to poor flexibility of your design? Naturally, the designer wants neither of these. The designer will have to apply each of these patterns judiciously at each stage of design, taking into consideration the probability of a concrete base class getting additional information that the derived class would not want, as well as the need for flexibility. A designer working on a reusable framework, which is to be used by over 1,000 software architects in a company, is clearly more concerned with flexibility than an architect who works in a closed domain among a small group of developers.

10.4   Other Design Transformation Patterns

Many other design transformation patterns can be observed. The following descriptions examine several of the more useful patterns.

The Inverted Inheritance Pattern

Source Pattern.

Designers of inheritance hierarchies sometimes find themselves in a situation in which they are required to override base class methods in a derived class with a NOP method, that is, a method that does nothing.

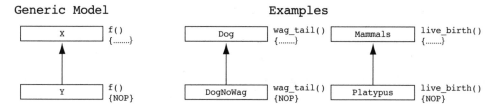

Motivating Heuristic.

Do not override base class methods in one or more derived classes with a NOP method.

Rationale.

If a derived class overrides a base class method with a NOP method, it is effectively saying that the derived class does not know that particular piece of behavior. If this is true, then the logic of the design is flawed. The designer is stating:

1. All Xs know how to f.

2. Y is a special type of X.

3. Y does not know how to f.

Logically, either all Xs do not know how to f, or Ys are not special types of Xs.

If this logic is allowed in specialization hierarchies, then anything can be made to be a special type of anything else. We can simply NOP all of the undesirable methods and add our choice of new ones. The solution to these design problems is to state that the derived class is not a special type of the base class. Both classes are derived classes of some undiscovered base class.

Target Pattern.

The inheritance hierarchy should be redefined such that both the base and derived classes inherit from some common base class.

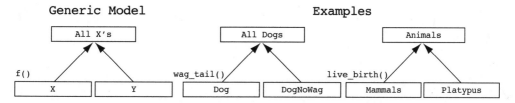

In some cases, this pattern can be further refined via the specialization pattern. These cases include those derived classes that do not have any additional messages beyond that of the base class.

The Lexical Scope Pattern

Source Pattern.

Some designs demonstrate a uses relationship between two classes contained within the same class, that is, the two classes share lexical scope.

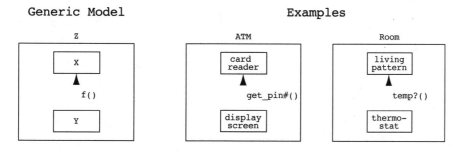

Motivational Heuristic.

Classes that are contained within the same class should not have a uses relationship between them.

Rationale.

A uses relationship between two classes contained within the same class is redundant. The containing class already has an implied uses between itself and each of the two contained classes. Any behavior needing a combined effort between the two contained classes should be conducted by the containing class to keep the contained classes free of extra dependencies. This simplifies the design and increases the reusability of the contained classes.

Target Pattern.

All coordination between two contained classes should be carried out by the containing class.

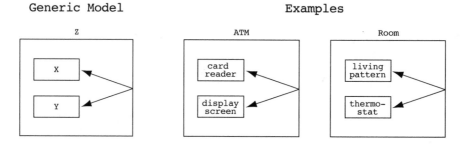

The One-Instance Pattern

Source Pattern.

There exist inheritance hierarchies in which each derived class has only one instance in a given domain, but each derived class has its own methods for the base class messages.

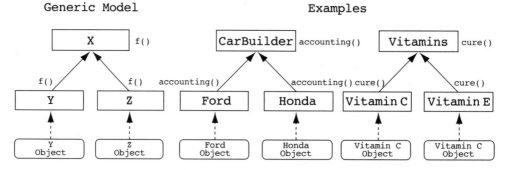

Motivational Heuristic.

Be wary of derived classes that possess only one instance. Be sure the derived classes are not objects of the base class.

Rationale.

Class designers often model objects, whose behaviors differ, as derived classes of some base class. Modeling objects as classes leads to class proliferation. What the designer really needs to do is generalize the objects into a new class. This is more complicated when the behavior of each object is different. The solution is to model the different behaviors as some data member (a formula) and a generic method (an interpreter of the formula). In any event, it makes no sense to have several related classes, each of which can instantiate only one object.

Target Pattern.

The derived classes need to be generalized into one class with a formula and an interpreter of that formula.

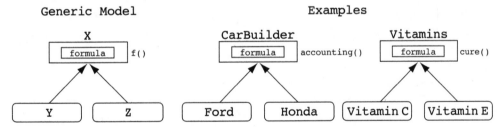

The Data-Hiding Pattern

Source Pattern.

A class designer will often argue that public data (in a class) is necessary in order to implement some feature of his or her application. This public data is used by the application directly, rather than going through the public interface of the class.

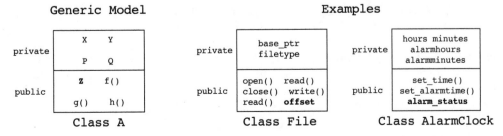

Motivating Heuristic.

A class should support strict data hiding of its implementation.

Rationale.

If a class has a public data member, it is not possible to find all of its dependencies without examining all of the application code. This examination becomes a management nightmare. Designers should ask themselves why they are making a particular data member public, what they are doing with the data member, and why the class that owns the data does not perform the behavior for them. In all cases, the public data member can be replaced by a public operation. In the worst case, the public operation returns a copy of the data in question (an accessor method). In the best case, the key abstraction represented by the class takes on the necessary higher-level behavior desired by the designers.

Target Pattern.

The class designers should endeavor to make all of the data private, reserving the public section of their classes for operations on that data.

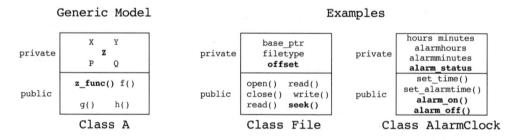

10.5   Future Research

This chapter raises more questions than the one it set out to explore, namely, "What is the relationship between heuristics and patterns?" I have shown that heuristics can be viewed as a motivation for transforming one design pattern into another, where the latter is an improvement over the former. I have also shown that these design transformation patterns possess interesting properties of transitivity and reflexivity. However, many interesting questions remain to be answered, and some interesting projects need to be carried out. These projects/questions include the following:

1. Over 60 design heuristics are available. All of their design transformation patterns need to be found, documented, and cataloged. Given that some heuristics could motivate more than one design transformation pattern, there are probably many of these design patterns.

2. Is there a good category science for these patterns? It may be possible to break them up based on the relationship (e.g., inheritance, containment) or the area of the object-oriented paradigm (e.g., analysis, domain analysis, physical design) with which they deal. Within these categories, they could be topologically sorted based on their property of transitivity. I have used the category notion for illustrating design heuristics, so it makes sense that this would apply to design transformation patterns as well.

3. Are there any other interesting relationships between, or properties of, design transformation patterns?

4. When a new-use case (i.e., scenario, requirement, business rule) is added to an existing object-oriented design, we know that it impacts the design. Are there patterns that capture this impact, and if so, what are the inputs/outputs of these patterns? I suspect they exist since, in many cases, designers get a "feel" for how much impact a given use case will have, which use case is going to be the most difficult to integrate, etc.

5. Karl Lieberherr [22] and the Demeter team at Northeastern University have done much research in mapping grammars into object-oriented designs. Are there interesting patterns in grammars, and if so, how do they relate to design transformation patterns? I suspect that there is much interesting work to be done in this area. One part of the Demeter team's research included reducing grammars into various minimalistic grammars in order to find a prototyping growth plan for an object-oriented design. As a grammar was allowed to become more complex, the object-oriented design also grew linearly more complex. Their latest work is in the area of adaptive software models, which is clearly related to design patterns.

6. Once a large number of design transformation patterns have been found, is it possible to automate the design optimization process? That is, can we develop a tool that would guide the user from a bad design to a better one? Such a tool would almost certainly require a scaling of properties of the design (e.g., flexibility, portability, efficiency, software/hardware constraints, importance of class minimization).

Chapter 11

The Use of Heuristics in Object-Oriented Design

11.1 The ATM Problem

When I originally set out to write a text on object-oriented design heuristics, I intended to devote a chapter on applying the heuristics to an actual design problem. As I got into the project, I realized that looking at actual applications could be a complete text on its own. However, my reviewers were almost unanimous in arguing for a complete example that moves away from meals, alarm clocks, fruit baskets, etc. Although I will argue that the heuristics are independent of domain and we should therefore select simple real-world domains for our exploration of them, it is very useful to see a full design of a computer science domain. Having come full circle in my thoughts on demonstrating the usefulness of heuristics in an actual design problem, I offer you the automatic teller machine problem as an exercise in designing an application. Although this example has been designed in several texts before this one, we will examine it from a very different and more interesting perspective. The published solutions include numerous heuristics violations, that, as I will show, detract from some beneficial facet of the resulting application. By examining both the ATM and the bank side of the software application, we can illustrate a useful design technique when systems span multiple address spaces (i.e., distributed systems) known as "design through proxies" [23].

Consider the following requirement specification for our design problem.

The ATM System Requirement Specification

An automated teller machine (ATM) is a machine through which bank customers can perform a number of the most common financial transactions. The machine consists of a card reader, a display screen, a cash dispenser slot, a deposit slot, a keypad, and a receipt printer (see Figure 11.1).

When the machine is idle, a greeting message is displayed. The keys and deposit slot will remain inactive until a bank card has been entered. When a bank card is inserted, the card reader attempts to read it. If the card cannot be read, the user is informed that the card is unreadable, and then the card is ejected.

If the card is readable, the card reader reads the account and PIN (personal identification number) numbers off the card and the user is asked to enter his or her PIN. The user is given feedback (in the form of asterisks, but not the specific digits entered) as to the number of digits entered at the numeric keypad. The PIN entered by the user is compared to the PIN on the ATM card. If the PIN is entered correctly, the user is shown the main menu (described below). Otherwise, the user is given up to two additional chances to enter the PIN correctly. Failure to do so on the third try causes the machine to keep the bank card. The user can retrieve the card only by dealing directly with an authorized bank employee.

The main menu contains a list of the transactions that can be performed. These transactions are as follows:

- Deposit funds to an account (required info.: checking/savings, amount);

- Withdraw funds from an account (required info.: checking/savings, amount);

- Transfer funds from one account to another (required info.: checking/savings, amount, other account number, other checking/savings);

- Query the balance of any account (required info.: checking/savings).

The user can select a transaction and specify all relevant information. When a transaction has been completed, the system returns to the main menu.

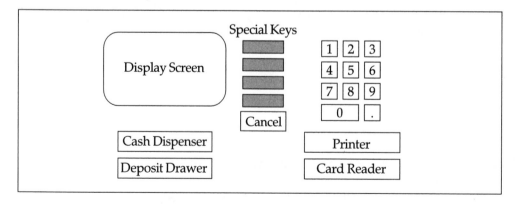

Figure 11.1 The ATM System.

At any time after reaching the main menu and before finishing a transaction (including before selecting a transaction), the user may press the Cancel key. The transaction being specified (if there is one) is cancelled, the user's card is returned, the receipt of all transactions is printed, and the machine once again becomes idle.

If a deposit transaction is selected, the user is asked to specify the account to which the funds are to be deposited to enter the amount of the deposit, and to insert a deposit envelope.

If a withdrawal transaction is selected, the user is asked to specify the account from which funds are to be withdrawn and the amount of the withdrawal. If the account contains sufficient funds, the funds are given to the user through the cash dispenser.

If a transfer of funds is selected, the user is asked to specify the account to which the funds are to be deposited, whether it is to checking or savings, and the amount of the transfer. If sufficient funds exist, the transfer is made.

If a balance inquiry is selected, the user is asked to specify the account whose balance is requested. The balance is not displayed on screen but is printed on the receipt.

All transactions are carried out cooperatively between the ATM and the bank. The bank holds all of the account information and must be consulted over the network at the appropriate time during the transaction. The bank is also responsible for updating the account information based on the transactions processed.

Two separate systems are being designed here. One is an application that runs on the ATM side of the system. The other application runs on the bank side of the system. We will assume we are building both.

11.2 Choosing a Methodology

In keeping with my promise in the Preface of this book not to create yet another design methodology, I will examine two competing views of object-oriented analysis and design and show that neither one, in its entirety, is optimal. The first view is defined by a camp of designers who feel that object-oriented analysis should be a data-driven process wherein the developer examines the requirements of the system, looking for associations, natural aggregations, and inheritance. The behavior (i.e., uses relationships) of the system is not assigned until design time. The idea is to produce a full object model without getting involved with assigning behavior. The Rumbaugh method [12] is the most popular of the data-driven models.

The second view is almost the opposite of data driven modeling. This view states that object-oriented analysis should focus on the behavior of the system. The designer is looking for classes and their uses relationships at analysis time. During design, some of these uses relationships are refined to containment relationships, and designers are expected to examine the system for inheritance. Booch, Jacobson, and

Weiner/Wilkerson/Wirfs-Brock [7, 3, 4, 9] are three of the better-known behavior-driven methodologies.

The problem with data-driven methodologies is that I do not believe a designer can find a complete object model without talking about behavior.

Question: "Why is A associated with B?"

Answer: "Because A needs B to do . . . ."

In systems with interesting behavior, many of the associations are due to behavioral needs. When this is the case, the designer is actually finding uses relationships, not just associations (a weaker relationship). A company with which I have worked in the past ran into this situation in designing a very large system. Some of the design groups became frustrated at trying to develop a full object model without talking about behavior. The result was a deliverable (the object model) that did not reflect the process undertaken to discover the information in that deliverable. When designers need to throw away information to fit what they have produced into a deliverable, then it is time to throw away the deliverable in favor of something that more accurately captures the process they are pursuing.

In some management information system (MIS) domains, the data-driven approach can work very well. This is due to the fact that there is no interesting behavior in these MIS applications. These applications are often grinding up an object model and spitting it out in a variety of forms. This is not to trivialize MIS applications. Many projects in this area are very complex; it is just that their behavior is trivial. All of the interest is in the static object model and possibly the user interface. As an example, consider a security reporting system for a brokerage house. All of the interesting design decisions revolve around the modeling of the data that captures the trading of securities and the graphic user interface to support that model. What is actually done with this data? It is printed in numerous reports, each of which uses the same model to generate information in a particular form for some government agency. The model itself has no interesting behavior between its classes. For systems like the ATM domain where the classes in the model have lots of interesting behavior between them, the data-driven approach cannot hope to give a complete object model without discussing the behavior of the system.

The behavior-driven methods share a different but equal problem. In large systems, where there will be many classes, a designer must take advantage of natural aggregations in the analysis model. If these natural aggregations are not considered, then every class in the system ends up at the top level of the design. This creates a very complex collaborations graph (the classes at the top level of design and their uses relationships). Attempts to find containment relationships by examining this graph will prove difficult. This problem is not visible in small systems where there may be only 15 or 20 classes, but attempts to apply this methodology to a system with 200 classes will demonstrate this weakness. The 200 classes may end up organized into 15 containment hierarchies. This is the level at which I want to examine the design,

15 classes rather than 200 classes. Of course, the data-driven model suffers from the fact that only natural aggregations can be found at analysis time. Most systems also use containment to distribute system intelligence within a containment hierarchy. This use of containment cannot be discovered without using the behavior of the system as a guide. The discovery of natural aggregations as well as manufactured containment for system intelligence distribution will be illustrated in the design of the ATM system.

Since I have argued against both data-driven and behavioral-driven design, what is a designer to do when creating a system from a requirement specification? I recommend a hybrid between the two. I always start with a data-driven modeling technique and then progress to a behavioral-driven design method. This allows me to simplify my design using natural aggregations and gives me the flexibility of discussing the behavior of the system at analysis time. It is my belief that starting with data-driven modeling will never hurt, so long as a designer realizes that it may not be possible to produce a full object model in many systems without discussing behavior.

11.3   A First Attempt at Producing an Object Model for the ATM

We begin by collecting all of the class candidates in our system. We are basically looking for nouns in the requirement specification. We will ignore the fact that the ATM (and its pieces) and the Bank (and its pieces) are in completely different address spaces on two different processors. We can ignore this fact during analysis time due to a design technique of using proxies, which we will explore when we start discussing the communication between items in the ATM application and items in the Bank application. Likewise, we ignore how objects are stored in our domain. The fact that accounts are in some central database within the bank is irrelevant. A good trick is to think of everything as living in memory. Later, in low-level design, we worry about the actual storage. We can get away with this trick because when an object of one class sends a message to an object of another class, that object will reside in memory. We can always "fake" this by hiding the actual access of the object within its class.

Given these assumptions, we can come up with the object model in Figure 11.2 by examining nouns in the domain and exploiting natural aggregations in the system. Natural aggregations result when tangible items are physically contained in another item; for example, ATMs contain card readers, banks contain accounts.

This first object model has captured the natural aggregations inherent in ATMs and Banks. Notice the lack of associations in this model. I argue that most of the associations in this system cannot be captured without examining the behavior of the system. Why are ATMs associated with Banks? They need a bank to process trans-

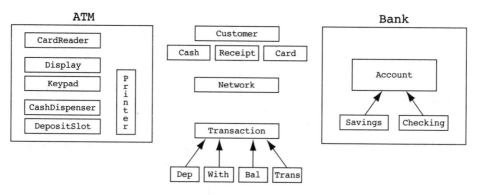

Figure 11.2 First object model of the ATM domain.

actions. Why are `Transactions` associated with `Accounts`? They need accounts to process themselves. The association exists only to satisfy some behavioral aspect of the system, that is, a uses relationship. This is in contrast to a system that lacks interesting behavior. Why are assignments associated with grades in an automated grading system? Because they just are; it is defined in the requirement specification.

One could argue that the inheritance relationships require behavior as well. After all, do the `Transaction` and `Account` classes have derived classes or are they concrete classes? The answer depends on whether or not the derived classes have interesting differences in behavior. If `Savings` and `Checking` accounts behave differently, then their design in our object model makes sense. If they do not behave differently, then `Savings` and `Checking` will end up irrelevant classes since all of their behavior will factor up to the `Account` class. There are two schools of thought on this subject. Data-driven analysis states that inheritance should be added up front and then eliminated during design time if the derived classes end up being irrelevant classes. Behavior-driven analysis states that inheritance is added at design time, only when commonality is found between two existing classes. Either view can be useful. We arbitrarily choose the first principle in this example, that is, we add inheritance wherever it is suspected and eliminate it at design time if necessary. (See Section 5.12 for a full discussion on the migration of either design choice to a correct design.)

11.4   Adding Behavior to Our Object Model

The first problem that many new designers face is one of understandability. Who starts everything in a decentralized system? In a centralized system, the flow of control is obvious. In a decentralized system, it is more hidden. In a decentralized system, the flow of control is started by something outside of the system. This something is either the main function of a C++ application, the SmallTalk environment, the CLOS environment, or more popularly, the constructor of a large containing class that wraps the entire system. The latter solution is often more useful because if the current system is to be reused as a component of a new larger system, it is a simple matter of adding operations to the large containing class. In the other solutions, some reengineering will have to be enacted in order to capture the desired information. Such a containing class is considered to be just outside the domain of the object-oriented model. In this example, we might define a class called `FinancialSystem` to wrap the entire object model. The constructor of this class builds `Bank` and `ATM` objects and wires them together with referential attributes. This is not the god class problem we spoke of earlier in this text, since the class is outside the system and is used only to build the top-level objects in our domain.

Now, let us examine as a first-use case the withdrawal of money from an ATM. Someone puts a card in the card reader, which detects that a card has been inserted and that it is a valid bank card and not an appropriately sized piece of plastic. Once this has been done, who sends a message to whom and what is the message? This is an important question to keep in mind. Invariably, designers will say, "Now we have to verify a PIN number." That is too vague. By forcing specific questions at specific places in design, a designer must justify exactly what he or she is doing. A common first choice at this stage of design is to have the card reader send a message to the display screen asking the display to put up an `Enter PIN:` prompt (see Figure 11.3). This is inevitably followed by a message from the card reader to the keypad to get a key or PIN number, etc.

This design violates Heuristic 4.14, which states that "objects that share lexical scope should not have uses relationships between them." Why not? We can examine our lexical scope pattern from Chapter 10 to answer that question. First, card readers have nothing to do with display screens except when in the domain of an ATM. We have now rendered the card reader unreusable in domains that do not possess a display screen. If I want to build a security door that also has a card reader, then I need to put a display screen in my security door. Second, and more important, I have added complexity to my design without motivation. The ATM already contains a card reader and display screen; therefore, it has implied uses relationships to them. The containing class can always accomplish any interaction between its pieces with the existing uses relationships. The added relationship is not required. In this example, the ATM should clearly handle the coordination between its pieces. We will see the reason a number of designers fall into this trap a little later in this design discussion.

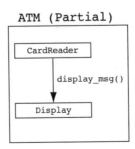

Figure 11.3 A Heuristic violating design.

It is important to note the relationship between heuristics and design patterns here. It is easy to determine when a heuristic is being violated. It is also easy to remember the heuristics since they are rarely more than two sentences of information. Patterns, on the other hand, can be quite long. I do not believe that designers will know intuitively when to select a particular pattern or how to combine them in interesting ways during the design process. Heuristics can provide the glue to help pull this information together.

Having gone this far in the design of the ATM system, a designer is tempted to state, "The card reader should inform the ATM that it has a card, then the ATM can send a message to its display screen to display a prompt" (see Figure 11.4).

The problem with this design is that the card reader is now aware of its container, a violation of a design heuristic whose intention is to make the contained class more reusable (Heuristic 4.13). We do not want card readers to be dependent on ATMs. Again, a solution around this problem can be found in the patterns from Chapter 10. Ideally, we can change the interrupt-driven nature of our design to a polling architecture. Why not let the ATM poll the card reader, asking it if it has a card? If the ATM has nothing else to do, then it can simply block on the card reader. If the ATM has other task, such as monitoring the bank for any interesting information it might be sending asynchronously, then the ATM should run the polling loop. Note that this last point is simply arguing where the polling should be performed, in the ATM or in the card reader.

There may be designs where an interrupt architecture cannot be turned into a polled architecture for physical design reasons, namely, time efficiency. In this case, we should at least make the card reader aware of a more general architecture, say a `SecureDevice` class. The ATM then inherits from the `SecureDevice` class, which has no data and a pure polymorphic `card_available()` method. The old restriction was that card readers could not be reused outside the domain of `ATM`. The new restriction is that card readers cannot be reused outside the domain of some `SecureDevice`. Since `SecureDevice` has no data and only a pure polymorphic method, it is an easy class from which to inherit. Yes, this solution can lead to multiple inheritance in some designs. Proponents of the technique of using callback functions to solve this problem can convince themselves that the proposed inheritance

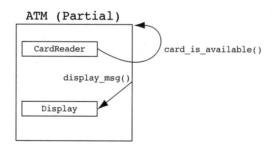

Figure 11.4 An interrupt-driven solution.

solution is a more strongly typed and less flexible solution than theirs. The callback function solution states that when a card reader is built, it is given the address of a function to call when a card becomes available. In the proposed inheritance solution, we restrict the address of the `callback` (polymorphic) function to a base class method pointer, which increases robustness.

Our ATM asks the card reader if it has a card, and eventually the answer is yes. The ATM then asks its display screen to put up the prompt for getting a PIN number. Now what happens? The naive designer will state that the ATM sends a `get_pin()` message to its keypad object. At first glance this sounds useful; however, the specification stated that after every key is pressed, an asterisk appears on the display screen. This may have looked trivial when first reading the specification, but it creates a complex issue in the design. The ATM is now forced to get a single key from the keypad, then tell its display to put up an asterisk, then get the second key pressed, put up an asterisk, ad nauseam. Many designers argue that the ATM is far too important an entity to be dealing with such picky issues. They wish to distribute the intelligence of the ATM to its pieces. Unfortunately, in order to distribute the intelligence of the system to the pieces of the ATM, it appears that the keypad will have to talk to the display screen (or vice versa). Designers often find themselves with this dilemma. A containing class (e.g., `ATM`) wants to distribute its intelligence to its pieces, but that intelligence is distributed over several of its objects. There is an interesting solution to this problem. What the designer needs is a new containing class, which sits between the original containing class and the pieces in question. Consider the role of the super keypad created in Figure 11.5.

The `ATM` can now simply tell its `SuperKeypad` object to fetch it a PIN number. It is oblivious to the details. In a large design project, this form of containment is useful for hiding the complexity of our model. We can go on with design, stating, that "The `ATM` gets a PIN number from the `SuperKeypad` and then it . . . ." How does the `SuperKeypad` get the PIN number? That is someone else's problem.

It is important to note that we had to place a `display_msg()` operation on the `SuperKeypad` because the `ATM` needs to put up its greeting message when first created and after every session with a customer. This operation simply passes through to the `display_msg()` operation on the display object. This constitutes

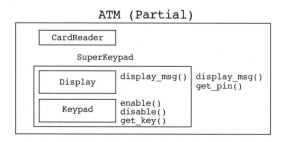

Figure 11.5 A partial `ATM` system design.

noncommunicating behavior on the part of the `SuperKeypad`, that is, behavior that uses a proper subset of the data members of `SuperKeypad`. The noncommunicating behavior acts as a counterforce in creating these third-party containing classes. Too much noncommunicating behavior suggests that the cohesiveness of the class is low, implying that the class needs to be dissolved into its two pieces. For example, if the public interface of the `SuperKeypad` class consisted solely of `display_msg()`, `enable()`, `disable()`, and `get_key()`, then it is a useless abstraction with very low cohesion in its data. It is operations like `get_pin()` that increase the cohesion of the class and make it a worthwhile addition to our system.

Containing classes of this type cannot be found by data-driven analysts. They can be found only by examining the behavior of the classes in a given system. Examining classes that have more than six data members is a good, mindless method for finding good candidates for this type of problem. This heuristic is useless for showing a designer where in these classes an intermediate containing class might be useful. For this second step, we need to discuss the behavior of the class with respect to its use cases.

The next step in our design revolves around verifying the PIN number given to us by the customer with the PIN on the card. Several popular and equivalent designs address this problem. Some designers state that the `ATM` should get a PIN number from the card reader (which gets it off of the card), get the PIN from the `SuperKeypad`, and compare them. Others state that the `ATM` should get a PIN number from the card reader, give it to the `SuperKeypad`, and let the `SuperKeypad` verify the user. These designers then argue whether the `ATM` or `SuperKeypad` should perform the looping of three chances before ordering the card confiscated. Still others argue that the `ATM` should get a PIN number from the `SuperKeypad` and give it to the card reader who then verifies the number. All of these solutions are valid. The arguments all revolve around the question of how the intelligence should be distributed. Since there is no quantitative metric for measuring complexity (and never will be), this issue is left for debate on qualitative, and therefore subjective, grounds. It is usually desirable to distribute the system intelligence away from a containing class, leaving it with just the coordination activities. However, it often happens that one of the pieces, such as the `SuperKeypad`, starts picking up too much behavior with respect to the containing class. We can then argue that we want some of the work pushed back onto the containing class. The debate of these three solutions can go on for quite some time during a design critique, with no party getting an upper edge on the other.

I have seen designers create a `PIN_Validator` object whose purpose is to get the two PIN numbers and verify them. The argument is that policy information is no longer encapsulated in a class like `ATM` or `SuperKeypad`, making them more reusable outside the domain. I claim that such controller classes consist only of behavior (often only one piece of behavior) and are the artificial separation of data and behavior. They violate the heuristic of keeping data and behavior in one place, as well as turning an operation into a class. What do `PIN_Validator` objects do? They validate PIN numbers. This is an operation, not an object abstraction. In addition, if we exploit controller classes, it is true that our other classes are more reusable outside the domain. But why? Because they are typically brain-dead chunks of data with a public interface of accessor methods. This is not object-oriented design; it is simply hiding our data structures behind a wall of `gets` and `sets` in one place and putting the behavior of that data elsewhere.

An interesting side issue to this design problem is the realization that the card reader must now know how to get PIN numbers. Is this something card readers do, in general? Of course not. A card reader, in general, reads the information off the back of a magnetically encoded card. We have just made our card reader less reusable by giving it knowledge of the ATM domain. We could put this policy of parsing information outside of the card reader, but this leaves the `ATM` as the candidate for implementing this parsing. The `ATM` argues that it is doing too much to warrant it handling the parsing. What is a designer to do about this problem? This is very similar to the problem we had with the ATM and its display screen and keypad. However, in this example, only one piece of the containing class is involved. We can use a wrapper around a physical card reader (the general, reusable component). The wrapper translates the general functionality of the physical card reader into the more ATM-specific requirements (see Figure 11.6). The physical card reader is reusable, and the card reader is domain-specific with the purpose of distributing system intelligence away from the ATM. The result is that everyone is happy!

This solution applies to numerous side arguments that erupt in critiquing this example. Should a display screen have a `display_msg()` operation, or should it have operations like `display_pinprompt()`, `display_mainmenu()`, etc.? Should a keypad have a `get_key()` operation or operations like `get_digit()`, `get_transactionnumber()`, etc.?

11.5 Explicit Case Analysis Due to Accidental Complexity

We now know that we have a verified PIN number on the back of a bank card. What is next? In general, `ATMs` would like to get a transaction object so that the bank can process it. How can an `ATM` get a transaction? A classic error is to have the `ATM` worry about putting up menus, enabling the keypad, getting a special key number, and mapping it to a specific transaction. This would add lots of noncommunicating behavior to the `SuperKeypad` class. Since the `SuperKeypad` class has everything it

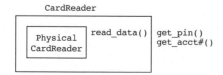

Figure 11.6 Using wrappers to gain reusable components.

needs to build a transaction (except maybe an account and PIN number), why not let it build the transaction for the ATM? The ATM could get the account and PIN number from the card reader and give them to the SuperKeypad, asking the SuperKeypad to get a transaction.

The SuperKeypad is then faced with the task of getting a transaction. It puts the main menu on the screen (assume the main menu labels key #1 as deposit, key #2 as withdraw, key #3 as balance, and key #4 as transfer), reads a key from the keypad, finds out that special key #2 was pressed, and then what? It is here that many designers assume they have made a mistake. In order to map the key to a transaction object, they are faced with an explicit case analysis. Several heuristics state/imply that explicit case analysis is a bad thing, since it implies that an addition to the system will result in changes to the existing code. This problem is common; whenever an object-oriented model bumps up against a nonobject-oriented system, explicit case analysis is often the result. Our design is not warped—our interface is! If we had an object-oriented interface, we would push a button and the desired constructor would run. Adding a new transaction would imply adding a new button with no change to the existing code. Some designers might argue that this is cheating since someone, somewhere is asking, "Did the user touch the screen between these X/Y-coordinates, or those X/Y-coordinates, etc.?" The important point is that the case analysis is pushed outside of our domain. If this sounds like a cheat, then polymorphism is a cheat. Someone, somewhere must be performing case analysis. Talk of jump tables and pointers to functions does not change the fact that it is case analysis. The only relevant question is, "Do you, the developer, need to perform the case analysis in your domain?" If the answer is no, then you can add new items to your system without modifying the existing code. (For a related discussion, see the object-oriented network section in Chapter 9, Section 9.2.)

There are two main solutions to consider in this mapping. Either we let the SuperKeypad collect the information for the transaction as part of its case statement and then build the appropriate transaction object with this information, or we immediately build the appropriate transaction object and let it polymorphically initialize itself. The disadvantage of the first design is that we are doing a large amount of work in each instance of the case statement. It is considered beneficial to minimize this work so that when a developer needs to add a new case, he or she will be modifying a minimal amount of existing code. The disadvantage of the second solution becomes obvious if we ask how a derived class knows how to collect information for filling in its data members. The derived classes of the transaction class will require a display screen and keypad to collect their information (or at least a SuperKeypad). This creates at least one more uses relationship in our system, adding complexity. The developer must now decide if the amount of work being performed in the case statement warrants a new uses relationship. This is very subjective given that there are no quantitative metrics for measuring complexity. My gut instinct in this example is to collect the information and then build the objects. The complexity of collecting information does not warrant a new uses relationship between Transaction and SuperKeypad. This must be decided on a case-by-case basis, and because of its subjective facet, it causes numerous, endless arguments during design critiques. Either solution to this problem results in a fully initialized transaction object (in this case, a `Withdraw` object) being returned to the `ATM`.

11.6   Messaging Objects in Different Address Spaces

At this point in the uses case, the `ATM` needs to send a message to the `Bank` object, asking it to process a transaction (passing the `Withdraw` transaction object as an explicit argument). It is here that the developer realizes that the `ATM` object lives in one address space (the `ATM` application) but the `Bank` lives in a different address space (the `Bank` application). I argued earlier that the `ATM` and `Bank` objects can be viewed as being in the same address space. This is due to a technique that employs proxies for the `ATM` and the `Bank` objects in each other's address spaces. The `ATM` cannot send a direct message to a `Bank`, so it sends a message to a `Bank` proxy that lives in the `ATM`'s address space (see Figure 11.7). This proxy packs up the request and transaction object and ships it across the network to an `ATM` proxy that lives in the `Bank`'s address space. The `ATM` proxy unpacks the request, reconstitutes the transaction object, and sends the process message to the real `Bank` object. The real `ATM` and `Bank` are completely unaware that they are really talking to proxies. This allows a designer to ignore the distributed facet of a distributed application during high-level design, leaving the gory details to low-level design proxy classes. The high-level of our design simply shows an `ATM` object sending a process message to a `Bank` object, when in reality our system is significantly more complex.

11.7   The Processing of the Transaction

Several different designs come to mind when a developer must decide how to process transactions. Often, the first design to come to mind is to ask the transaction for an account number, use the account number to find the account from the account list object, and then tell the account to process the transaction. The problem here is that

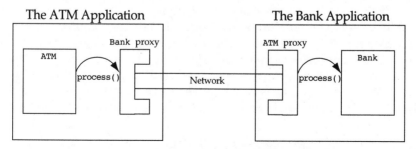

Figure 11.7 An `ATM` system design with rewrite proxies.

the account does not know how to process a transaction. The processing is dependent on the type of the transaction (in this case, `withdraw`). This implies the need to process the transaction object polymorphically, which brings us to our second design. The bank asks the transaction for its account number, uses the account number to find the account object from within the account list object, then sends the transaction object the process method (polymorphically), passing the account object as an explicit argument. This works great for `withdraw`, `balance query`, and `deposit`. `Transfer` presents an interesting problem in that it requires two account objects, a source account and a target account. Since the `Bank` is unaware of which transaction it has, determining the number of accounts that a transaction requires must be performed in a transaction-independent manner. One solution is for the transaction to give a list of account numbers when the `Bank` requests the account number from the transaction object. The `Bank` then hands this list to the `AccountList` object, which retrieves a list of account objects rather than just one. This list can then be handed to the transaction by the `Bank` when it sends the `process` method. A better alternative is to have the `Bank` simply tell its transaction object to process itself, handing it the whole list of accounts. In this way, the particular `process` method, which runs for a given transaction type, can be responsible for determining the selection of account object(s). It also allows us to keep related data and behavior closer together by eliminating the removal of the account number from the transaction object. Some designers may worry about efficiency at this point, arguing that sending one account object is cheaper than sending thousands. I would argue that we should corrupt the logical design for physical design concerns. In fact, physical design in this case will argue that the accounts are in a database. All we are sending to the `process` method is a database handle, a pointer. We save nothing by letting the `Bank` retrieve the account object(s). This fact helps justify heuristics that warn users not to worry too much about physical design issues, most notably efficiency, during logical design.

11.8   Returning to the Domain of the ATM

The actual processing of a transaction with respect to an account is fairly straightforward. Each transaction will check account information to ensure the viability of the transaction, update any information that can be updated (e.g., `withdraw`), and record any necessary audit trails that may be needed later (e.g., `deposit`). The transaction process method then returns `good` or `bad` to the `Bank`, which in turn returns this information to the ATM object. Recall that the actual sequence of events includes a return to an ATM proxy, which packages and ships the return value to a Bank proxy using a network. The `Bank` proxy then unpackages the return value and returns to the actual ATM object. As far as `Bank` and ATM are concerned, the proxies are the actual objects. The distributed processing has been buried in the implementation details.

The question now is, "What does an ATM do if the transaction is valid?" The problem here is that the ATM has the ability to do anything any transaction could want, but it does not know which transaction it has. The transaction knows (via a polymorphic call) what it needs to do but does not have the objects needed to do it. What do we do? The solution is for the ATM to tell a transaction to post-process itself (polymorphically), passing itself as an explicit argument to the method. The polymorphic call allows the flow control to figure out which transaction it has and what needs to be done; the ATM parameter allows the post-process method the ability to accomplish its goals. In this case, these goals involve dispensing cash to a customer. (It is helpful to note that each transaction also has a preprocess method; for example, deposits take an envelope using the deposit slot object, withdrawals check to be sure the cash dispenser has enough cash, etc.)

This solution bothers a lot of designers because we have a circular uses relationship. The ATM uses Transaction, and now Transaction uses ATM. While I feel uncomfortable with such a construct, it is the cost of eliminating explicit case analysis in the methods of the ATM. It is helpful to note that we are adding a new uses relationship between the Transaction and ATM classes, but this is no more of a concern than the addition of any other uses relationship. Avoid the temptation to say that we only need to pass the cash dispenser to the post-process method of the withdraw class. Keep in mind that the ATM does not know which transaction it has; if it were a balance query, it would require a printer, not a cash dispenser. I have seen solutions where the designer passes a number of ATM pieces to the polymorphic call, letting the actual method determine which of the pieces it will use. This solution is appropriate when we can guarantee that all of the transaction types use a proper subset of the ATM's pieces. If we want to be general and extensible, then we should pass the whole ATM to the method.

This often leads new designers to argue that the ATM now has a method in its public interface which will allow a user to dispense cash without any checking. Keep in mind that "allow a user" refers to a software developer, not an end user of the ATM machine. We are not arguing for a large red button on an ATM machine that, when pressed, mindlessly dispenses cash. This type of argument comes up very frequently when designers confuse software objects with the physical world. I have had attendees of courses worry about the fact that some BankSafe class has an open method. They ask, "How do I prevent a bank teller object from sending the safe object the open method, but allow the bank president object to send that method?" They feel a bit silly when I tell them to not code such a message send from within any method on the teller class. These are software objects; they cannot do things you do not code.

An interesting, related point to the confusion between users of classes and end users of systems came up in a course I was lecturing at a large telecommunications company. Should object-oriented languages support a feature by which a class can limit the access to certain parts of its public interface to a given list of classes? That is, should a BankSafe class be allowed to state that anyone can execute its close method, but only BankPresident, BankVicePresident, IRSOfficer, and Police objects can execute its open method? My initial reaction was to answer no. I argued that this would hinder software reuse in that I would need to modify the class definition if I decided that I wanted to send a restricted message to a class. I further argued that such restrictions were application semantic constraints that should be handled by the application designer. However, the company with which I was dealing was building a large application (millions of lines of code) consisting of an object-oriented framework and many applications to be built on top of it. They argued that within the classes of the framework were many operations in the public interface that were to be used exclusively by the other classes within the framework, not the applications. Other parts of the public interfaces of the framework classes were to be used by both the framework classes and the application writers. Due to the size of the development effort (hundreds of developers on two continents and in three countries), they argued that to convey the necessary aplication-level semantic constraints without language-level support was impossibly complex. Application developers were bound to make mistakes in their use of operations. I agree with this assessment. The trade-off is between communicating application-level semantic constraints versus ease of software reusability. They could have solved the problem by creating an object-oriented API (application interface) that mirrored the classes in the framework. For each class X in the framework, the API would have an APP_X that looked exactly like X except it would have a reduced interface. Each method in APP_X would simply delegate to the exact same method in X. The problem here is keeping each X and APP_X pair in sync with each other, another trade-off to play against the other two solutions.

11.9   Other Miscellaneous Issues

There are a number of loose ends to tie up in this design. Looking back on our first object model, we see a number of classes we have not examined. The first, and most interesting, is the Network class. We put it in our object model because it is clearly an interesting noun in our requirement specification. If we consider it a key abstraction, then we will use it when we decide to process a Transaction object, recognizing that the Network is an agent between the ATM object and the Bank object. In this scenario, we end up with the ATM object getting a transaction for the Super-Keypad, sending the Network object a process method with the Transaction object as an explicit argument. The Network object would then send the Bank a process method, again passing the Transaction object as an explicit argument. The Bank would process the Transaction as previously discussed, returning good or bad to the Network object. The Network object would then return this return value of good or bad to the ATM object. Most designers will quickly realize that the network is a useless agent between the ATM and Bank and that it should be eliminated in favor of a direct uses relationship. Later in design, when we discuss the ATM and Bank proxies, we realize that they are heavily dependent on the physical network. Not wanting these proxy classes to be tightly coupled with a particular network, we create a wrapper class called Network to isolate the physical network from the proxies that use it. This `Network` class is completely different from the first network we proposed. The first network was a candidate for a key abstraction, which we threw out of the system because it was a useless agent. The second network is an implementation class, which is of no interest to logical designers. We should consider implementation classes only during physical design.

Another implementation class is one that will wrap the particular storage of account objects, most likely some database. At high-level design, we consider the account object to live in some `AccountList` object in memory. In reality, the `AccountList` is really querying some database to get the necessary information to build an `Account` object in memory. Since we do not want our model dependent on the physical storage of accounts, we hide this information in some `Database` object. It is the `Database` object that contains all implementation-dependent information and translations.

A case study attesting to this type of architecture can be found in the insurance industry. In one application with which I had some contact, a group of designers were creating an insurance claim system on an IBM-compatible 486 machine. The actual claim records were stored in a relational database on a mainframe computer. In the first pass of design, the methods of the classes that made up the object-oriented model on the 486 side of the application were riddled with function calls to collect information on the IBM mainframe side of the application (e.g., network connects, SQL query calls). I asked a couple of the designers what they would do if I told them that the claim records would no longer be stored on a mainframe but would live on the local drive of the 486 machine. They quickly realized that a full system rewrite would be the result. Every class in their domain would be affected by this change. The solution was to create a database class with which the classes in the model could send a message to fetch a claim (given a claim number) and through some magic a claim object would be returned. The magic in their case was to run a network to a mainframe database and collect the necessary information to build a `Claim` object. If, at some later date, the database was to be stored on a local disk drive of the 486, the development team had a central location for any necessary changes. Their object-oriented model remained oblivious to the physical design change. The physical location of the records became the concern of one class, not the entire model.

What about the `Customer` class? It is true that the end user is providing external stimuli to the `ATM` domain, but the `ATM` domain never uses the customer class. This is the hallmark of a class outside the system. The `BankCard` and `Receipt` classes are also considered outside the system. They exist as tangible entities but do not provide useful service to the domain model. The `Cash` class could also be considered outside the system, but it is slightly different than the other three in that the amount of cash must be kept as a value within the cash dispenser. `Cash` is a good example of a class that has been reduced to an attribute of some other class, in this case the `CashDispenser`.

What about `Savings` and `Checking` account? Should these two entities be derived classes of `Account` or is the type of account simply an attribute of the `Account` class? The answer to this question is, "In this domain, do checking and savings accounts behave differently?" The answer, in this example, appears to be no; therefore `Checking` and `Savings` are simply values of a descriptive attribute of the `Account` class. Let us add a use case to the `ATM` domain that does distinguish the two types of accounts. Let us state that checking accounts bounce but savings accounts do not. That is, it is possible to send a `Checking` account object a `bounce` method, passing the number of days as an explicit argument to the method. This method returns the total amount of money in bounced checks the account has suffered during that time period. The FDIC would like to send the bank a bounce method with a number of days to find out how much money in bounced checks the bank has suffered. How do we implement such a method? The first attempt is to state that the `Bank` runs down its list of accounts, sending each account the `bounce` method. The problem here is that the `Savings` accounts in the list do not know what you mean. In fact, accounts in general do not know how to bounce. What can we do? We need to recognize that this is the "core the apple" problem we discussed in Chapter 5. In that example, we had a `FruitBasket` (the bank) that contained a list of different `Fruit` objects (the accounts). `Apples` (the checking account) had an extra method called `core` (bounce). The question in that example was, "How do we core the apples?" The solution in the `Fruit` domain was either to keep the `Apples` in a separate list within the `FruitBasket` (requiring case analysis on the type of an object) or to add a `core` method to the `Fruit` class, which does nothing by default (requiring the placement of derived class information in the base class). In our example, our choice is to keep a separate list of the `Checking` accounts within the `Bank` object or to place a `Bounce` method, which returns zero dollars on the `Account` class. We might be tempted by the latter solution because it is easier to implement, but when we consider physical design, we see that accessing an `Account` object is expensive (since the accounts are stored on a disk). This physical design information will argue that the first solution of keeping a separate list of checking accounts is much faster and often more preferable. For example, there may be 2 million accounts but only 800,000 are checking accounts. Why retrieve 2 million accounts when all we need to look at is 800,000? This example shows the interest in patterns and heuristics. Once you realize which problem you have via a heuristics violation, its related patterns offer you the necessary solutions for free.

And last, but not least, how do we handle the `Cancel` key? If we isolate `Cancel` to the period in which we collect information, then the `SuperKeypad` object can detect that the keystroke was the pressing of the `Cancel` button and will return `Cancel` to the `ATM` object, which in turn performs any necessary clean-up. If we wish to cancel after a transaction has been sent to the `Bank`, then things get a bit more complex. The `ATM` cannot block on the `Bank` proxy when it sends the process method. It simply returns and continues to poll the `SuperKeypad` for a `Cancel` return value and the `Bank` proxy for a `done` return value. If the `SuperKeypad` returns `Cancel` to any of the `ATM`'s queries, then the `ATM` must inform the `Bank` proxy that the end user has cancelled the transaction. The `Bank` will then be notified via its proxy and perform any necessary rollback of the transaction. In all cases, the `Cancel` option does not add much complexity to the design or its implementation.

11.10   Conclusion

It is my hope that this discussion has provided some insight into the mechanics of using design heuristics and patterns in the object-oriented analysis and design process. The reader should carefully note the way in which design heuristics allow a designer to reference a group of design patterns, one of which can be used to resolve the conflict implied by the violated heuristic. In addition, this discussion provides a good example of developing a distributed object-oriented design without considering the distributed qualities until after the logical design is complete. Early concerns with process distribution often force a development team to get bogged down in the details of a system. The judicious use of proxies allows the system architects to position all of their efforts at the top level of design, allowing the postponement of the system details. This postponement can dramatically simplify the design process of a distributed object-oriented system.

Appendix A

Heuristics Summary

Chapter 2 Classes and Objects: The Building Blocks of the Object-Oriented Paradigm

Heuristic 2.1 All data should be hidden within its class.

Heuristic 2.2 Users of a class must be dependent on its public interface, but a class should not be dependent on its users.

Heuristic 2.3 Minimize the number of messages in the protocol of a class.

Heuristic 2.4 Implement a minimal public interface that all classes understand [e.g., operations such as copy (deep versus shallow), equality testing, pretty printing, parsing from an ASCII description, etc.].

Heuristic 2.5 Do not put implementation details such as common-code private functions into the public interface of a class.

Heuristic 2.6 Do not clutter the public interface of a class with things that users of that class are not able to use or are not interested in using.

Heuristic 2.7 Classes should only exhibit nil or export coupling with other classes, that is, a class should only use operations in the public interface of another class or have nothing to do with that class.

Heuristic 2.8 A class should capture one and only one key abstraction.

Heuristic 2.9 Keep related data and behavior in one place.

Heuristic 2.10 Spin off nonrelated information into another class (i.e., noncommunicating behavior).

Heuristic 2.11 Be sure the abstractions that you model are classes and not simply the roles objects play.

Chapter 3   Topologies of Action-Oriented Versus Object-Oriented Applications

Heuristic 3.1   Distribute system intelligence horizontally as uniformly as possible, that is, the top-level classes in a design should share the work uniformly.

Heuristic 3.2   Do not create god classes/objects in your system. Be very suspicious of a class whose name contains `Driver`, `Manager`, `System`, or `Subsystem`.

Heuristic 3.3   Beware of classes that have many accessor methods defined in their public interface. Having many implies that related data and behavior are not being kept in one place.

Heuristic 3.4   Beware of classes that have too much noncommunicating behavior, that is, methods that operate on a proper subset of the data members of a class. God classes often exhibit a great deal of noncommunicating behavior.

Heuristic 3.5   In applications that consist of an object-oriented model interacting with a user interface, the model should never be dependent on the interface. The interface should be dependent on the model.

Heuristic 3.6   Model the real world whenever possible. (This heuristic is often violated for reasons of system intelligence distribution, avoidance of god classes, and the keeping of related data and behavior in one place.)

Heuristic 3.7   Eliminate irrelevant classes from your design.

Heuristic 3.8   Eliminate classes that are outside the system.

Heuristic 3.9   Do not turn an operation into a class. Be suspicious of any class whose name is a verb or is derived from a verb, especially those which have only one piece of meaningful behavior (i.e., do not count `sets`, `gets`, and `prints`). Ask if that piece of meaningful behavior needs to be migrated to some existing or undiscovered class.

Heuristic 3.10   Agent classes are often placed in the analysis model of an application. During design time, many agents are found to be irrelevant and should be removed.

Chapter 4   The Relationships Between Classes and Objects

Heuristic 4.1   Minimize the number of classes with which another class collaborates.

Heuristic 4.2   Minimize the number of message sends between a class and its collaborator.

Heuristic 4.3　Minimize the amount of collaboration between a class and its collaborator, that is, the number of different messages sent.

Heuristic 4.4　Minimize fanout in a class, that is, the product of the number of messages defined by the class and the messages they send.

Heuristic 4.5　If a class contains objects of another class, then the containing class should be sending messages to the contained objects, that is, the containment relationship should always imply a uses relationship.

Heuristic 4.6　Most of the methods defined on a class should be using most of the data members most of the time.

Heuristic 4.7　Classes should not contain more objects than a developer can fit in his or her short-term memory. A favorite value for this number is six.

Heuristic 4.8　Distribute system intelligence vertically down narrow and deep containment hierarchies.

Heuristic 4.9　When implementing semantic constraints, it is best to implement them in terms of the class definition. Often this will lead to a proliferation of classes, in which case the constraint must be implemented in the behavior of the class—usually, but not necessarily, in the constructor.

Heuristic 4.10　When implementing semantic constraints in the constructor of a class, place the constraint test in the constructor as far down a containment hierarchy as the domain allows.

Heuristic 4.11　The semantic information on which a constraint is based is best placed in a central, third-party object when that information is volatile.

Heuristic 4.12　The semantic information on which a constraint is based is best decentralized among the classes involved in the constraint when that information is stable.

Heuristic 4.13　A class must know what it contains, but it should never know who contains it.

Heuristic 4.14　Objects that share lexical scope—those contained in the same containing class—should not have uses relationships between them.

Chapter 5　The Inheritance Relationship

Heuristic 5.1　Inheritance should be used only to model a specialization hierarchy.

Heuristic 5.2　Derived classes must have knowledge of their base class by definition, but base classes should not know anything about their derived classes.

Heuristic 5.3   All data in a base class should be private; do not use protected data.

Heuristic 5.4   In theory, inheritance hierarchies should be deep—the deeper, the better.

Heuristic 5.5   In practice, inheritance hierarchies should be no deeper than an average person can keep in his or her short-term memory. A popular value for this depth is six.

Heuristic 5.6   All abstract classes must be base classes.

Heuristic 5.7   All base classes should be abstract classes.

Heuristic 5.8   Factor the commonality of data, behavior, and/or interface as high as possible in the inheritance hierarchy.

Heuristic 5.9   If two or more classes share only common data (no common behavior), then that common data should be placed in a class that will be contained by each sharing class.

Heuristic 5.10   If two or more classes have common data and behavior (i.e., methods), then those classes should each inherit from a common base class that captures those data and methods.

Heuristic 5.11   If two or more classes share only a common interface (i.e., messages, not methods), then they should inherit from a common base class only if they will be used polymorphically.

Heuristic 5.12   Explicit case analysis on the type of an object is usually an error. The designer should use polymorphism in most of these cases.

Heuristic 5.13   Explicit case analysis on the value of an attribute is often an error. The class should be decomposed into an inheritance hierarchy, where each value of the attribute is transformed into a derived class.

Heuristic 5.14   Do not model the dynamic semantics of a class through the use of the inheritance relationship. An attempt to model dynamic semantics with a static semantic relationship will lead to a toggling of types at runtime.

Heuristic 5.15   Do not turn objects of a class into derived classes of the class. Be very suspicious of any *derived* class for which there is only one instance.

Heuristic 5.16   If you think you need to create new classes at runtime, take a step back and realize that what you are trying to create are objects. Now generalize these objects into a class.

Heuristic 5.17   It should be illegal for a derived class to override a base class method with a NOP method, that is, a method that does nothing.

Heuristic 5.18 Do not confuse optional containment with the need for inheritance. Modeling optional containment with inheritance will lead to a proliferation of classes.

Heuristic 5.19 When building an inheritance hierarchy, try to construct reusable frameworks rather than reusable components.

Chapter 6 Multiple Inheritance

Heuristic 6.1 If you have an example of multiple inheritance in your design, assume you have made a mistake and then prove otherwise.

Heuristic 6.2 Whenever there is inheritance in an object-oriented design, ask yourself two questions:

1. Am I a special type of the thing from which I'm inheriting?

2. Is the thing from which I'm inheriting part of me?

Heuristic 6.3 Whenever you have found a multiple inheritance relationship in an object-oriented design, be sure that no base class is actually a derived class of another base class.

Chapter 7 The Association Relationship

Heuristic 7.1 When given a choice in an object-oriented design between a containment relationship and an association relationship, choose the containment relationship.

Chapter 8 Class-Specific Data and Behavior

Heuristic 8.1 Do not use global data or functions to perform bookkeeping information on the objects of a class. Class variables or methods should be used instead.

Chapter 9 Physical Object-Oriented Design

Heuristic 9.1 Object-oriented designers should not allow physical design criteria to corrupt their logical designs. However, physical design criteria often are used in the decision-making process at logical design time.

Heuristic 9.2 Do not change the state of an object without going through its public interface.

Appendix B

The Prevention
of Memory Leakage

One of the most dangerous pitfalls affecting the C++ community is that of **memory leakage**, or the unintentional nondeletion of dynamically allocated memory. A system inflicted with this problem will run correctly for some period of time, often weeks, with no discernable problem. It will then "seize up," that is, run out of heap space for no apparent reason. The operator typically reboots the application, which again runs problem-free. The danger of this situation is that it is not caught at compile, link, or test-run time. It is detected only after the product has been shipped to a number of clients.

While memory leakage has occurred in standard C applications, it is typically introduced into that environment when a developer dynamically allocates space and simply forgets to free it. The problem is accentuated in C++ because most memory leakage occurs through the compiler's implicit function calls, making detection dependent on the developer knowing the inner workings of C++. In the course of much C++ development, I have identified eight programming areas prone to C++ memory leakage. These range from the mundane and obvious, such as forgetting to delete space that was explicitly allocated, to the more esoteric reasons, such as confusing arrays of pointers with arrays of objects, forgetting to make a base class destructor virtual, missing copy constructors, missing overloaded assignment operators, missing size arguments to the delete function, and using a poor design when constructing overloaded operators. The following text details each of these problem areas and provides a C++ coded example for each. Developers armed with these examples will be able to relegate memory leakage to the class of pitfalls that are infrequently encountered and easily overcome.

Leak #1

Mismatched new/delete calls in the constructor and destructor of a class. The obvious case of C++ memory leakage occurs when a developer dynamically allocates memory via new and forgets to explicitly clean up that memory with a call to delete. This can occur when an object is created on the heap and not explicitly cleaned up or, more commonly, when the constructor of a class dynamically allocates memory but the destructor is either absent or not cleaning up the object correctly. An example of the former case is shown here.

Example Code for Leak #1

```
class Point {
   int x, y;
   char* color;
public:
   Point(int, int, char*);
};
// Note that the constructor allocates space
// for the ''color'' data member but there is
// no destructor to free this memory.

Point::Point(int new_x, int new_y, char* col)

{

   x = new_x;   y = new_y;
   color = new char[strlen(col)+1];
   strcpy(color, col);

}

// The proper destructor would look like:
Point::~Point()

{ delete color;

}
```

Leak #2

Nested object pointers that are not cleaned up properly. A less obvious pitfall exists when one object contains another object by reference instead of by value. In the example code shown here, a Meal object contains a Melon object by reference (i.e., a Meal contains a pointer to a Melon). This Melon is dynamically allocated in the Meal's constructor and therefore must be deallocated in its destructor. The confusion occurs when a developer thinks that the Melon's destructor is called automatically by the Meal's destructor. Automatic destructor calls will occur when one object contains another by value. In our example, this would translate to a Meal object that contains a Melon object (i.e., by value).

Example Code for Leak #2

```
#include <iostream.h>
class Melon {
```

```
 char* variety;
public:
 Melon(char* var);
 ~Melon();
 void print();

};

Melon::Melon(char* var)
{
 variety = new char[strlen(var)+1];
 strcpy(variety, var);
}

Melon::~Melon()
{
 delete variety;
}

void
Melon::print()
{
 cout << ''I'm a '' << variety << ''Melon\n'';
}
class Meal {
 char* restaurant;
 Melon* m;
public:
 Meal(char* var, char* res);
 ~Meal();
 void print();
};

Meal::Meal(char* var, char* res)
{
 m = new Melon(var);
 restaurant = new char[strlen(res)+1];
 strcpy(restaurant, res);
}

// Oops! Forgot to delete the contained Melon.
// This would not be necessary if Melon were a
// contained object as opposed to a pointer to an
// object.
Meal::~Meal()
{
 delete restaurant;
}
// The correct destructor would be defined
// as follows:
/* Meal::~Meal()
{
 delete restaurant;
 delete m;
} */
```

```
void
Meal::print()
{
 cout << ''I'm a Meal owned by '';
 m->print();
}

main()
{
 Mean m1(''Honeydew'', ''Four Seasons'');
 Meal m2(''Cantaloup'', ''Brook Manor Pub'');
 m1.print(); m2.print();
}
```

Leak #3

Deleting an array of objects without using the square brackets on `delete`. A common point of confusion for C++ novices involves the use of the square brackets on the `delete` function; for example, `delete[] p` versus `delete p`. This size argument is unnecessary for deleting a single object, a single primitive data type (e.g., `int`, `char`, `short`), or an array of a primitive type. It is required for deleting arrays of any object that has a destructor defined on it. Variable-sized objects are a particularly vulnerable category of objects affected by this constraint. A variable-sized object is an object that contains a pointer to dynamically allocated space. (Note: For a more detailed discussion of variable-sized classes/objects and their ramifications, see "Towards a Minimal Public Interface for C++ Classes" and "A Framework for Variable-Sized Classes," *The C++ Insider*, Vol. **1**, nos. 1 and 2, respectively.) The square brackets tell the compiler that the pointer is pointing to a vector of objects and that the destructor must be called along with the proper values for the object addresses (i.e., `&array[0]`, `&array[1]`, `&array[2]`, etc.). If the brackets are not provided, then the pointer is assumed to be pointing at one object. The additional objects in the array will not have their destructors called, resulting in memory leakage. If a number is placed between the square brackets and is larger than the size of the array, then the compiler will call the destructor on invalid objects (memory overflow), resulting in heap corruption. If a number between square brackets is smaller than the size of the array, the compiler will not call the necessary number of constructors, resulting in memory leakage.

In all cases of memory leakage due to missing square brackets, the space taken up by the class (`sizeof(class_name)`) is put back on the heap because of the nature of `new` and `delete`. For this reason, some C++ developers claim the `size` argument is unnecessary for classes that do not have destructors defined on them. This is a dangerous coding convention since many such classes become variable-sized or have destructors added as the application matures. For example, a `Point` class containing two integer data members (x and y) might get a dynamically allocated string called `color`, (see Figure B.1), or a `Meal` class might add a `melon` pointer or even a `melon` object.

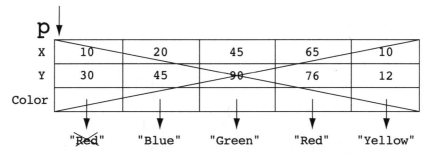

Figure B.1 Graphical representation of memory leak #3.

Some developers consider this memory leakage problem to be the worst because it cannot be eliminated by the class implementor since C++ is a multiparadigm language (i.e., it contains nonclass/object entities. In a pure system, an array class would handle the deletion correctly for all users. Of course, arrays could be made a C++ class for a given application, eliminating this particular memory leakage problem.

Example Code for Leak #3

```
// The following code demonstrates the
// memory leakage problems associated
// with deleting a dynamically allocated
// array of Point objects.

#include <iostream.h>
class Point {
  int x, y;
  char* color;
public:
  Point(int=0, int=0, char*=''Red'');
  ~Point();
};

{
  x = new_x;
  y = new_y;
  color = new char[strlen(col)+1];
  strcpy(color, col);
}

Point::~Point()
{
  delete color;
  cout << ''In the destructor\n'';
}
Point::Point(int new_x, int new_y, char* col)
```

```
main()
{
 Point *p = new Point[5];
 // Note the missing square brackets. This
 // statement is identical to ''delete[1] p;''.
 // It will call the destructor once with
 // the address of &p[0] as an argument. The
 // color string of the first Point object is
 // put back on the heap followed by the
 // memory occupied by the five Point objects.
 // The memory leaked is the color strings for
 // Points two through five (indices 1 to 4).

 delete p;
 // The correct statement is:
 // delete[] p; or delete[5] p;
}
```

Leak #4

Arrays of pointers to objects are not arrays of objects.   Another point of confusion related to the use of delete's square brackets is the fact that destroying arrays of object pointers is very different from destroying arrays of objects. As was shown in the preceding code, the square brackets on the delete function control the proper calls to each object's destructor when used for destroying arrays of objects. Some developers attempt to use the size argument as a method for controlling proper destructor calls for objects stored in arrays of pointers to objects. Adding a size argument to the delete call on an array of pointers to objects simply tells the compiler the number of pointers to destroy. Since pointers are considered primitive types in C++, this argument has no effect on destructor calls. The pointers are placed back on the heap, but all of the objects are kept in their allocated state. The result is memory leakage.

Example Code for Leak #4

```
#include <iostream.h>
class Point {
 int x, y;
 char* color;
 Point(int=0, int=0, char*=''Red'');
 ~Point();
};
Point::Point(int new_x, int new_y, char* col)
{
 x = new_x; y = new_y;
 color = new char[strlen(col)+1];
 strcpy(color, col);
}
```

```
Point::~Point()
{
 delete color;
}
main()
{
// The following line of code dynamically
// allocates an array of 10 pointers to
// Point objects (not the objects themselves).

 Point **p = new Point*[10];
 int i;
// The loop below allocates one Point object
// for each of the Point pointers.
 for (i=0; i<10; i++) {
  p[i] = new Point(i, i, ''Green'');
 }
// The following statement does not clean up
// the individual points, just their pointers. It
// results in the leakage of memory
// (10*sizeof(Point) + 60 bytes of space).
// Note: The 60 bytes are incurred for the
// storage of the string ''Green'' in each of the
// 10 objects.
   delete[] p; // or delete[10] p;
   // The correct code is as follows:
   /*
      for (i=0; i<10; i++) {
       delete p[i];
      }
      delete p;
   */
 }
```

Leak #5

Missing copy constructors. If the user of a C++ class attempts to invoke a constructor function that the implementor of that class has not defined, then the user expects to get an error from the compiler or, at a minimum, the linker. This is normally the case in C++, unless that constructor happens to be the **copy** constructor (also called the initialization constructor). The **copy** constructor is a constructor function whose sole argument is a reference to an object of the constructor's class. For example, the prototype of the **copy** constructor for the `Point` class looks like `Point(const Point&);`. If this constructor is not defined, then the compiler assumes its definition to be a memberwise copy of the data members (bitwise copy in C++ version 1.2). Unfortunately, memberwise (or bitwise) copying of a pointer is defined as copying the address from one location to another. The ramifications of this implicit pointer copying is that two objects will have pointers to the same dynamically allocated memory. When the first object is destroyed, its destructor will clean up the dynamically allocated memory associated with it. When the second object is destroyed, its destructor attempts to clean up the same memory. Deleting the same memory twice is considered an error and will probably corrupt the heap. A developer may argue that, by convention, no user of his or her class will call the copy constructor. Aside from the usual folly of *programming by convention*, there are issues dictating that a copy constructor be explicitly defined. Most calls to the copy constructor are not explicit calls. The copy constructor is called whenever one object is initialized to another of the same type, an object is passed by value as an argument to a function, or an object is returned by value from a function. This implicit behavior will cause memory leakage in variable-sized classes.

Example Code for Leak #5

```
#include <iostream.h>
class Point {
  int x, y;
  char* color;
public:
  Point(int, int, char*);
// Note the commented-out copy constructor.
// Point(const Point&);
  ~Point();
  Point duplicate(Point);
  void print();
};
Point::Point(int new_x, int new_y, char* col)
{
    x = new_x; y = new_y;
    color = new char[strlen(col)+1];
    strcpy(color, col);
}
// This is an example copy constructor for the
// Point class. Note that it is commented out
// of the application.
/*
Point::Point(const Point& rhs)
{
  x = rhs.x; y = rhs.y;
  color = new char[strlen(rhs.color)+1];
  strcpy(copy, rhs.color);
}
*/
Point::~Point()
{
  delete color;
}
// This function takes a Point object as an
// argument ''by value.'' That will cause an
// implicit call to the copy constructor.
// In addition, the C++ statement
// ''return(*this);'' will cause an implicit call to
```

```
// the copy constructor because
// the function returns a Point
// object by value.

Point
Point::duplicate(Point rhs)
{
 x = rhs.x;
 y = rhs.y;
 return(*this);
}

void
Point::print()
{
 cout << ''I'm a point at ('';
 <<x<<'', ''<<y<<'')\n'';
 cout << ''My color is''; <<color<<''.\n\n'';
}

main()
{
 Point p1(10, 10, ''Blue'');
 Point p2(15, 18, ''Green'');
// The following declaration causes an
// implicit call to the copy constructor;
 Point p3 = p2;
// Another way of writing the above
// declaration is:
// Point p3(p2);
 p1.print();
 p2.print();
 p3.print();
// The function ''duplicate'' takes a Point
// object by value and returns a local copy by
// value. The statement causes two implicit
// calls to the copy constructor.
 p1.duplicate(p2);
 p1.print();
 p2.print();
 p3.print();
}
```

Leak #6

Missing overloaded assignment operator.   The memory leakage problem associated with a missing overloaded assignment operator is similar to the problem associated with the missing copy constructor. When an operator is used on an object of a class, the compiler (or linker) will generate an error if that operator is not overloaded for that class. The C++ language makes an exception with the assignment operator. If the user does not specify its functionality, then C++ guesses that the user wants to

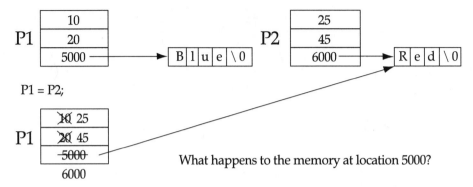

Figure B.2 Memory leakage due to a missing assignment operator.

perform a memberwise copy (bitwise copy in versions 1.2 and earlier). If the class is variable-sized, then the result is memory leakage. The actual leakage occurs when the object on the left-hand side of the assignment operator has its internal address overlayed with the internal address of the object on the right-hand side of the operator. The memory to which the left-hand side points is no longer referenced but is still allocated. In addition, the two `operand` objects point at the same dynamically allocated memory (see Figure B.2). This will probably cause heap corruption when the destructor for the class is invoked by each object (at some later execution time) and each invocation attempts to delete the same address.

Example Code for Leak #6

```
#include <iostream.h>
class Point {
  int x, y;
  char* color;
public:
  Point(int, int, char*);
  Point(const Point&);
  ~Point();
  void print();
// Note the commented-out operator=
// const Point& operator=(const Point& rhs);
};
Point::Point(int new_x, int new_y, char* col)
{
  x = new_x; y = new_y;
  color = new char[strlen(col)+1];
  strcpy(color, col);
}
Point::Point(const Point& rhs)
{
  x = rhs.x; y = rhs.y;
```

```
   color = new char[strlen(rhs.color)+1];
   strcpy(color, rhs.color);
Point::~Point()}
{
 delete color;
}

void
Point::print()
{
 cout << ''I'm a point at ('';
 cout << x <<'', '' << y << '')\n'';
 cout << ''My color is '' << color <<''.\n\n'';
}
// The following operation is a sample
// implementation of the overloaded assignment
// operator for the Point class. It is important that
// the function allow for assignment of one object
// to itself. The returned reference is marked
// constant so that the return value of overloaded
// operator= cannot be used as an lvalue.
// That is, (x=y) = z is illegal.
/*
const Point&
Point::opertor=(const Point& rhs)
{
 // Avoid assignment to self.
 if(this == &rhs) {
  return(*this);
 }
 x = rhs.x; y = rhs.y;
 delete color;
 color = new char[strlen(rhs.color)+1];
 strcpy(color, rhs.color);
 return(*this);
}
*/

main()
{

 Point p1(10, 10, ''Blue'');
 Point p2(15, 18, ''Green'');
 p1.print(); p2.print();
 p2 = p1;
 p1.print(); p2.print();
}
```

Leak #7

General confusion concerning the overloading of nonmodifying operators. A nonmodifying operator is an operator that does not affect any of its operands and evaluates to an object of the same type as the operands. Typical examples include the mathematical operators like addition (+), subtraction (−), multiplication (*), division (/), and modulus (%). Relational operators are not considered nonmodifying, because they always evaluate to type `boolean` regardless of the data types being compared. In addition, assignment operators (e.g., =, +=, <<=) are not nonmodifying, because these operators affect their left-hand-side operand.

Memory leakage associated with incorrectly implemented, nonmodifying operators is the type of problem that either is nonexistent in an application or appears in almost every class. This discrepancy is due to the fact that it revolves around invalid assumptions about overloaded operators. The main issue involved with the implementation of nonmodifying operators revolves around the return value. For the sake of efficiency, a C++ developer may decide to return the evaluated result by reference instead of by value. (Recall that returning an object by value will implicitly call the copy constructor, costing runtime.) A first attempt at designing such an operation might be to build the evaluated result in a temporary variable and return it by reference. The `Point` example in the code here illustrates the fact that returning a local object by reference is an error since the memory associated with the reference is returned to the stack upon exit from the function. The caller is left with a returned reference to an invalid, deallocated object.

Returning a Reference to a Stack Object

```
#include <iostream.h>
class Point {
  int x, y;
  char* color;
public:
  Point(int = 0, int = 0, char* = ''Red'');
  ~Point();
  Point(const Point&);
  void print();
  const Point& operator=(const Point&);
  const Point& operator+(const Point&);
};
void
Point::print()
{
  cout << ''I live at ('';
  cout <<x<<'', ''<<y<<'') and '';
  cout << ''I'm'' << color <<''.\n'';
}
const Point&
Point::operator=(const Point& rhs)
{
  x = rhs.x; y = rhs.y;
  delete color;
  color = new char[strlen(rhs.color)+1];
  strcpy(color, rhs.color);
}
```

```
// This function returns a hidden pointer
// (i.e., a reference) to a temporary Point
// object that will be destroyed upon return
// from the function.
const Point&
Point::operator+(const Point& rhs)
{
  Point temp;
  temp.x = x + rhs.x; temp.y = y + rhs.y;
  delete temp.color;
// Not exactly a good color-mixing scheme!
  temp.color = new char[strlen(color)+strlen(rhs.color)+1];
  sprintf(temp.color, ''%s%s'', color, rhs.color);
  return(temp);
main()}
{
  Point p1(10, 10, ''Blue'');
  Point p2(20, 60, ''Green'');
// The copy constructor is receiving a destroyed
// Point object as an argument since the operator+
// function returns a hidden pointer to the
// automatic variable temp. This variable had its
// destructor called upon exit from operator+.
  Point p3 = p1 + p2;

  p3.print();
}
```

Another attempt at a solution to this problem is to make the temporary `Point` object of internal static storage class. An internal static object is not created and destroyed upon entrance/exit from the function; it simply goes in and out of scope. This code will work fine, provided the operator is never used in a nested function call. Of course, one can imagine all sorts of uses for nesting addition operators. The C++ statement x+y+z is one of the more mundane yet valid examples. Because each call to `operator+` uses exactly the same temporary `Point` object, the nested calls will stomp the memory of each other.

Returning an Internal Static Object Reference

```
#include <iostream.h>
class Point {
  int x, y;
  char* color;
public:
  Point(int = 0, int = 0, char* = ''Red'');
  ~Point();
  Point(const Point&);
  void print();
  const Point& operator=(const Point&);
  const Point& operator+(const Point&);
};
```

```
const Point&
Point::operator+(const Point& rhs)
{
// Note the use of the internal static storage class
// for temp. Each caller to this function reads and
// writes exactly the same Point object.
  static Point temp;
  temp.x = x + rhs.x; temp.y = y + rhs.y;
  delete temp.color;
// Not exactly a good color-mixing scheme!
  temp.color = new char[strlen(color)+strlen(rhs.color)+1];
  sprintf(temp.color, ''%s%s'', color, rhs.color);
  return(temp);
}
```

Taking a step back to examine the relevant problems of each example, we realize that we need a completely separate Point object upon each invocation of the operator, yet its existence must include the scope of the operator's return value. The logical choice is to dynamically allocate the new Point object from within the overloaded operator and to return a Point reference to it.

Returning a Memory Leaking Dynamically Allocated Object

```
#include <iostream.h>
class Point {
  int x, y;
  char* color;
public:
  Point(int = 0, int = 0, char* = ''Red'');
  ~Point();
  Point(const Point&);
  void print();
  const Point& operator=(const Point&);
  const Point& operator+(const Point&);
};
const Point&
Point::operator+(const Point& rhs)
{
  Point *temp = new Point;
  temp->x = x + rhs.x;
  temp->y = y + rhs.y;

// This deletion is necessary due to the nature
// of calling the constructor for Point with
// zero arguments.
  delete temp->color;

// Not exactly a good color-mixing scheme!
  temp->color = new char[strlen(color)+
         strlen(rhs.color)+1];
  sprintf(temp->color, ''%s%s'', color, rhs.color);
```

```
    return(*temp);
}
```

The C++ developer writing this software tests it extensively (complete with nested calls) and finds that it works flawlessly. It is shipped to numerous clients, some of whom begin complaining of memory leakage problems. Where is this memory leakage? This problem is best illustrated by posing the question, "Where is the `temp` object, which is dynamically allocated upon each invocation of `Point::operator+`, cleaned up?" Its destructor is not called automatically since pointers never invoke an object's destructor implicitly. The caller cannot explicitly call the `Point` object's destructor since the address of the object is not available. Consider the C++ code `z = x + y;`. How does a user retrieve the address of the `temp` object?

The answer, of course, is that he or she cannot retrieve the address and, therefore, cannot destroy the `temp` object. The `temp` object created upon each invocation of `Point::operator+` is leaked from the application and cannot be retrieved.

Our initial premise, that we need to return a reference to a `Point` object from `Point::operator+`, was an error. As it turns out, nonmodifying operators must always return an object and not a reference to an object. The object returned is of the automatic storage class.

Correct Method for Leak #7

```
#include <iostream.h>

class Point {
  int x, y;
  char* color;
public:
  Point(int = 0, int = 0, char* = ''Red'');
  ~Point();
  Point(const Point&);
  void print();
  const Point& operator=(const Point&);
  const Point operator+(const Point&);
};

void
Point::print()
{
  cout << ''I live at ('';
  cout <<x<<'', ''<<y<<'') and'';
  cout << ''I'm'' << str(color) <<''.\n'';
}

const Point
Point::operator+(const Point& rhs)
{
  Point temp;
  temp.x = x + rhs.x; temp.y = y + rhs.y;
```

```
  delete temp.color;
// Not exactly a good color-mixing scheme!
  temp.color = new char[strlen(color)+
          strlen(rhs.color)+1];
  sprintf(temp.color, ''%s%s'', color, rhs.color);
  return(temp);
}

main()
{
 Point p1(10, 10, ''Blue'');
 Point p2(20, 60, ''Green'');
 Point p3 = p1 + p2;

 p3.print();
}
```

Leak #8

Forgetting to make the destructor of a base class virtual.   The eighth memory leakage error with which a C++ developer needs to be concerned involves the use of virtual destructors. Developers will often use inheritance to create a taxonomy of classes for the purpose of treating the very different `leaf` classes as a homogeneous set (e.g., treating the very different `apple`, `banana`, and `orange` objects as a homogeneous collection of `fruit`). This homogeneous collection of `fruit` is implemented as an array of `fruit` pointers, where each `fruit` pointer points at a particular type of `fruit` object (i.e., an `apple`, `banana`, or `orange` object). Eventually, the `delete` function must be called on each of the `fruit` pointers in order to destroy the `fruit` type to which it points. The main question is which destructor will be called when the statement, `delete basket[i]` is invoked at runtime (assume `basket` is the array of `fruit` pointers). If the destructor for `fruit`, namely, `Fruit::~Fruit()`, is not virtual, then each time the `delete` statement is invoked, it is calling the destructor for `fruit`. If the destructor for `fruit` is marked virtual (polymorphic), then the correct destructor for the particular type of fruit is invoked at runtime (i.e., `Apple` objects call `Apple::~Apple()`, `Banana` objects call `Banana::~Banana()`). If any of the `leaf` classes (in this example, apples, bananas, and oranges) contain pointers to dynamically allocated space, then a nonvirtual base class destructor (in this example, `Fruit::~Fruit`) will result in memory leakage, since the destructor for the `leaf` class is never called (see Figure B.3). The following example illustrates this problem, using `Fruit`, `Apple`, and `Banana`.

Code Example for Memory Leakage #8

```
#include <iostream.h>

class Fruit {
 double weight;
```

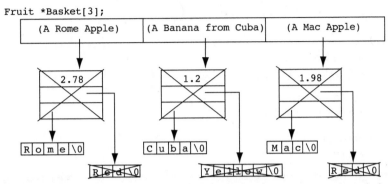

Figure B.3 Graphical example of memory leakage due to a nonvirtual destructor (memory for "Rome", "Cuba", and "Mac" is leaked off the heap).

```
  char* color;
protected:
  Fruit(double, char*);
  Fruit(const Fruit&);
public:
// Note the nonpolymorphic destructor
    ~Fruit();
// The correct destructor would look like:
// virtual ~Fruit();
  virtual void print();
};

Fruit::Fruit(double w, char* col)
{
  weight = w;
  color = new char[strlen(col)+1];
  strcpy(color, col);
}

Fruit::Fruit(const Fruit& rhs)
{

  weight = rhs.weight;
  color = new char[strlen(rhs.color)+1];
  strcpy(color, rhs.color);
}

Fruit::~Fruit()
{
  delete color;
}

void
Fruit::print()
{
  cout << ''\tFruit weight:'' << weight << ''\n'';
```

```cpp
  cout << ''\tFruit color:'' << color << ''\n'';
}

class Apple : public Fruit {
 char* variety;
public:
 Apple(double, char*, char*);
 Apple(const Apple&);
 ~Apple();
 void print();
};

Apple::Apple(double w, char* col, char* var) : Fruit(w, col)
{
 variety = new char[strlen(var)+1];
 strcpy(variety, var);
}

Apple::Apple(const Apple& rhs) : Fruit(rhs)
{
 variety = new char[strlen(rhs.variety)+1];
 strcpy(variety, rhs.variety);
}

Apple::~Apple()
{
 delete variety;
}

void
Apple::print()
{
 cout << ''Hi, I'm a'' << variety << ''Apple\n'';
 Fruit::print();
}
class Banana : public Fruit {
 char* export;
public:
 Banana(double, char*);
 Banana(const Banana&);
 ~Banana();
Banana::Banana(double w, char* exp): Fruit(w, ''Yellow'')
{
 export = new char[strlen(exp) + 1];
 strcpy(export, exp);
}

Banana::Banana(const Banana& rhs) : Fruit(rhs)
{
 export = new char[strlen(rhs.export)+1];
 strcpy(export, rhs.export);
}

Banana::~Banana()
```

```
{
 delete export;
}
void
Banana::print()
{
 cout << ''Hi, I'm a banana from '';
 cout << export << ''\n'';
}

main()
{
 Fruit *basket[20];
 int i, num;
 double weight;
 char color[128], variety[128], answer[128];
// The following code allows the user to
// interactively build a fruit basket of size
// 1 through 20.
 cout << ''How many fruit in the basket? '';
 cin >> num;
 if (num < 0 || num > 20)  num = 10;
 for (i=0; i<num; i++) {
  cout << ''A)pple or B)anana? '';
  cin >> answer;
  if (answer[0] == 'a' || answer[0] == 'A') {
   cout << ''Apple's weight: ''; cin >> weight;
   cout << ''Apple's color: ''; cin >> color;
   cout << ''Apple's variety: ''; cin >> variety;
   basket[i] = new Apple(weight, color, variety);
  }

  else {
   cout << ''Banana's weight: '';
   cin >> weight;
   cout << ''Banana's country: '';
   cin >> variety;
   basket[i] = new Banana(weight, variety);
  }
 }
 for (i=0; i<num; i++) {
  basket[i]->print();
 }

// If Fruit's destructor is not virtual,
// then this code will call Fruit's
// destructor num times. This will leak
// the memory used for the variety string in
// each Apple and the export string in each
// Banana.

 for (i=0; i<num; i++) {
  delete basket[i];
 }
}
```

Appendix C

Selected C++ Examples

For those who desire some concrete examples illustrating the abstractions discussed in this text, I have provided 21 C++ programs. Those examples of general interest are published in this appendix. The remainder is available from Addison-Wesley at World Wide Web URL http://www.aw.com/cp/riel.html. and via anonymous FTP from ftp.aw.com in the directory cp/riel. The examples and a brief description of each are provided in the following list.

Example	Chapter	Description
#1	2	The implementation of the AlarmClock class described in Section 2.1.
#2*	3	The implementation of the course-scheduling system described in Section 3.3. The solution without controller classes is illustrated here.
#3	3	The implementation of the home heating system described in Section 3.4 (poor design with accessor methods).
#4*	3	The implementation of the home heating system described in Section 3.4 (good design without accessor methods).
#5*	4	The implementation of the "car uses a gas station" example described in Section 4.3. The five methods for implementing the uses relationship are demonstrated.
#6	4	The implementation of the meal containment hierarchy as described in Section 4.6.
#7	5	The implementation of the fruit basket example described in Section 5.9.
#8	5	The implementation of the meal containment hierarchy with inheritance as described in Section 4.6. This is a more general solution of Example #6.
#9*	5	The implementation of the sorted linked list inheriting from the linked list example described in Section 5.10.

Example	Chapter	Description
#10*	5	The implementation of the `LinkedRing` class added to the linked list hierarchy of Example #9.
#11	5	The first solution to the "core the apple in the fruit basket" problem discussed in Section 5.19. This solution uses a NOP method in the base class.
#12	5	The second solution to the "core the apple in the fruit basket" problem discussed in Section 5.19. This solution uses a bookkeeping mechanism in the containing class.
#13	5	The third solution to the "core the apple in the fruit basket" problem discussed in Section 5.19. This solution uses a generic message handler, which is overridden in each derived class.
#14	6	The implementation of the wooden door example described in Section 6.3.
#15*	6	The implementation of the graduate student example described in Section 6.7. It illustrates the use of virtual, multiple inheritance in C++.
#16	8	The implementation of the `Invoice` class described in Section 8.3.
#17*	8	The implementation of the weak type-checking solution for constructing linked lists of dogs, linked lists of meals, and linked lists of airplanes; as described in Section 8.4.
#18*	8	The implementation of the template solution for constructing linked lists of dogs, linked lists of meals, and linked lists of airplanes; as described in Section 8.4.
#19*	9	The implementation of a minimal public interface in C++ on a reference-counting `String` class. This minimal interface is described in Section 9.5.
#20*	9	An example implementation of garbage collection in C++. The example examines a node class that hoards memory, and the memory handler that frees the space on demand.
#21*	11	The implementation of the automatic teller machine/bank example as designed in Chapter 11.

* This example is presented in this text. All others can be downloaded from the publisher via ftp.

Selected C++ Example #2

```
// Example #2

// This C++ example illustrates the checking of a student's
// course prerequisites without using controller classes.
// This puts policy information inside one of the classes
// involved in the policy, rendering it less reusable.
// I feel that controller classes add complexity to design
// with little or no benefits. While controller classes do allow
// their host classes to be more reusable outside of the current
// domain, they are reusable only because they don't do anything,
// that is, they have data and a bunch of get and set methods.
```

```
// In this example, in order to check prerequisites, the
// course offering will ask the student for his/her list of
// courses that he/she has taken. The course offering will
// ask the Course to verify that the student has the necessary
// prerequisites by passing the course list as an explicit
// argument. The Course object then makes the determination.

// This example has several examples of containment in its
// implementation. For those readers who do not yet understand
// containment, I recommend reading Chapter 4 before working
// through this example. Experienced readers will notice areas
// where inheritance would have been very useful. Most noticeably
// in the area of reference counting. I felt that the addition
// of inheritance would have caused too many forward references
// into the text. It was left out at the expense of some
// redundant abstraction.

// The efficiency-minded should be aware that this code
// was written for understanding, not speed. All methods are not
// inline. The one-liners could easily be made inline. Also,
// some of the conditional tests could be improved for speed
// at the cost of readability.

#include <iostream.h>
#include <string.h>
#include <stdlib.h>
#include <stdarg.h>

// Forward references to the list classes.
class CourseList;
class StudentList;
class OfferingList;


// Constants used within this program.

const int name_len = 30;
const int desc_len = 128;
const int course_len = 30;
const int student_len = 50;
const int small_strlen = 15;

// Courses have a name, description, duration, and a list
// of prerequisites. Since we expect Course objects to
// appear on many lists (e.g., Calculus I is a prerequisite of
// Calculus II, Calculus III, Physics I, etc.), we would like
// to implement shared shallow copies, i.e., we copy only
// pointers, not the entire course object. We accomplish
// this through a technique called reference counting. The
// class gets an integer counter, which maintains how many
// objects are sharing the particular course object. Anyone
// who points at the object must call the Course::attach_object()
// method, which increments the counter. When destroyed, the
// sharing object calls Course::detach_object() to decrement
```

```
// the counter. If detach_object() returns zero, then the
// caller knows that it is the last user of that Course
// object and it calls its destructor.

class Course {
private:
    char name[name_len];
    char description[desc_len];
    int duration;
    CourseList* prereq;
    int reference_count;
public:
    Course(char*, char*, int, int, ...);
    Course(const Course&);
    ~Course();
    int attach_object();
    int detach_object();
    void add_prereq(Course&);
    int check_prereq(CourseList&);
    void print();
    void short_print();
    int are_you(char*);
};


// Each key abstraction also has a corresponding list class
// to maintain the list operations. Readers with more
// experience would certainly argue for the use of C++ templates
// to handle the list classes. I felt that this was too much
// forward referencing, which would have rendered the example less
// readable.

class CourseList {
private:
    Course **courses;
    int size;
    int course_num;
public:
    CourseList(int);
    CourseList(CourseList&);
    ~CourseList();
    int add_item(Course&);
    Course* find_item(char*);
    int find_all(CourseList&);
    void print();
};


// This constructor for course takes a name, description,
// duration, and a variable list of prerequisites. Each
// prerequisite is added to the list using the CourseList::
// add_item() method.
Course::Course(char* n, char* d, int len, int pnum, ...)
```

```
{
    int i;
    va_list ap;

    strncpy(name, n, name_len);
    strncpy(description, d, desc_len);
    duration = len;
    prereq = new CourseList(course_len);
    reference_count = 1;
    if (pnum) {
        va_start(ap, pnum);
        for (i=0; i < pnum; i++) {
                    prereq->add_prereq(*va_arg(ap, Course*));
        }
        va_end(ap);
    }
}

// The copy constructor for course makes a copy of all the
// strings and calls the copy constructor for a CourseList.
Course::Course(const Course& rhs)
{
    strcpy(name, rhs.name);
    strcpy(description, rhs.description);
    duration = rhs.duration;
    prereq = new CourseList(*rhs.prereq);
    reference_count = rhs.reference_count;
}


// The destructor for Course deletes its prerequisites and
// checks to be sure that it is the last user that called
// delete on the course object. If not, an error message
// is displayed.
Course::~Course()
{
    delete prereq;
    if (reference_count > 1) {
        cout << ''Error: A course object destroyed with '';
        cout << reference_count << '' other objects referencing
                    it.\n'';
    }
}


// Each object that points at a Course object must call
// attach_object to register itself with the object.
int
Course::attach_object()
{
    return(++reference_count);
}
```

```
// Each object that called attach_object must call detach_object
// in its destructor (or other member function) to decrement
// the reference counter.
int
Course::detach_object()
{
     return(--reference_count);
}


// To add a prerequisite to the course, we call the add_item
// method of CourseList. This method returns zero on failure
// to add the Course (i.e., the list is full).
void
Course::add_prereq(Course& new_prereq)
{
     if (prereq->add_item(new_prereq) == 0) {
         cout << ''Error: Cannot add any new prerequisites.\n'';
     }
}


void
Course::print()
{
     cout << ''\n\nCourse: '' << name << ''\n'';
     cout << ''Description: '' << description << ''\n'';
     cout << ''Duration: '' << duration << ''\n'';
     cout << ''List of Prerequisites: '';
     prereq->print();
     cout << ''\n\n'';
}


// The short_print method is used in places where we only
// want to see the name and not all of the associated info
// of the Course.
void
Course::short_print()
{
     cout << name;
}



// This method is very important in the design of this
// system. The Course object receives a course list and
// checks its prerequisites against it, using the CourseList::
// find_all method. This method checks to see if all of the
// courses in the argument list are in the list to which the
// message was sent.
int
Course::check_prereq(CourseList& courses_taken)
```

```
{
    return(courses_taken.find_all(*prereq));
}


// This method checks to see if its name is equal to the
// name passed in. It is used for searching for a particular
// course from a list of Course objects (by name).
int
Course::are_you(char* guess_name)
{
    return(!strcmp(name, guess_name));
}


CourseList::CourseList(int sz)
{
    course_num = 0;
    courses = new Course*[size=sz];
}


// Note the use of reference counting in the CourseList copy
// constructor. Each course is simply pointed to, not copied.
// The attach_object method allows the incrementing of the
// reference counter. This reference counter keeps track of
// how many objects (CourseList or otherwise) are pointing to
// the Course object.
CourseList::CourseList(CourseList& rhs)
{
    int i;

    courses = new Course*[size=rhs.size];
    for (i=0; i < size; i++) {
        courses[i] = rhs.courses[i];
        courses[i]->attach_object();
    }
    course_num = rhs.course_num;
}


// The CourseList destructor detaches each object in the
// prerequisite list. If any of the detach_object method
// calls evaluates to zero, this course list is the
// last object using the course and its destructor must be
// called.
CourseList::~CourseList()
{
    int i;
    for (i=0; i < course_num; i++) {
        if (courses[i]->detach_object() == 1) {
                delete courses[i];
        }
    }
```

```
        delete courses;
}


// The add_item method checks to be sure the list still has
// room. A reasonable solution would be to increase the
// size of the list on demand. This adds a significant amount
// of code and complexity without enlightening the reader
// to the problem at hand. For that reason, lists are a fixed
// size at creation time. They report an error when full (by
// returning zero).
// If the list has room, then the course is added and it is
// attached to preserve the reference counting.
int
CourseList::add_item(Course& new_item)
{
    if (course_num == size) {
        return(0);
    }
    else {
        courses[course_num++] = &new_item;
        new_item.attach_object();
    }
    return(1);
}


// The course list searches its list for the course whose
// name matches that passed in by the user. If the course
// isn't found, this method returns the NULL pointer.
Course*
CourseList::find_item(char* guess_name)
{
    int i;

    for (i=0; i < course_num; i++) {
        if (courses[i]->are_you(guess_name)) {
                return(courses[i]);
        }
    }
    return(NULL);
}


// This method checks to be sure that all courses of the
// findlist are in the list to which the message was sent.
// Since courses are shallow copied in these lists, we need
// only check the addresses of the course objects and not
// the course names.
int
CourseList::find_all(CourseList& findlist)
{
    int i, j, found;
```

```
        for (i=0; i < findlist.course_num; i++) {
            found = 0;
            for (j=0; j < course_num && !found; j++) {
                    if (findlist.courses[i] == courses[j]) {
                            found=1;
                    }
            }
            if (!found) {
                    return(0);
            }
        }
        return(1);
}


void
CourseList::print()
{
        int i;

        cout << ''\n\n'';
        for (i=0; i < course_num; i++) {
            courses[i]->short_print();
            cout << '' '';
        }
        cout << ''\n\n'';
}
```

```
// Students have a name, social security number, and age. Like
// the Course objects, they also have a list of courses (the
// courses that the student has completed). Students are
// a reference-counting class just like the Course class. The
// reference counting works in exactly the same way as that of
// the Course. This will lead the experts to criticize the
// duplicate abstraction caused by the reference-counting
// mechanism. We could use inheritance to solve the problem
// but have not discussed this topic yet. The use of inheritance
// to eliminate duplicate abstractions will be examined in
// Chapter 5.
class Student {
private:
        char name[name_len];
        char ssn[small_strlen];
        int age;
        CourseList *courses;
        int reference_count;
public:
        Student(char*, char*, int, int, ...);
        Student(const Student&);
        ~Student();
        int attach_object();
        int detach_object();
        void add_course(Course&);
        CourseList& get_courses();
```

```cpp
        void print();
        void short_print();
        int are_you(char*);
};


// The StudentList mirrors the CourseList class except it is
// working on Student objects rather than Course objects.
class StudentList {
private:
        Student **students;
        int size;
        int student_num;
public:
        StudentList(int);
        StudentList(StudentList&);
        ~StudentList();
        int add_item(Student&);
        Student* find_item(char*);
        void print();
};


Student::Student(char* n, char* s, int a, int num, ...)
{
        int i;
        va_list ap;

        strncpy(name, n, name_len);
        strncpy(ssn, s, small_strlen);
        age = a;
        courses = new CourseList(course_len);
        reference_count = 1;
        if (num) {
            va_start(ap, num);
            for (i=0; i < num; i++) {
                        courses->add_item(*va_arg(ap, Course*));
            }
            va_end(ap);
        }
}


Student::Student(const Student& rhs)
{
        strcpy(name, rhs.name);
        strcpy(ssn, rhs.ssn);
        age = rhs.age;
        courses = new CourseList(*rhs.courses);
        reference_count = rhs.reference_count;
}

Student::~Student()
{
```

```
        delete courses;
}


int
Student::attach_object()
{
        return(++reference_count);
}


int
Student::detach_object()
{
        return(--reference_count);
}


void
Student::add_course(Course& c)
{
        if (courses->add_item(c) == 0) {
                cout << ''Cannot add any new courses to the Student.\n'';
        }
}

// Note the need for an accessor method. This method will
// be used by the CourseOffering class when it needs to
// check the prerequisites of a Student object. The Student
// is asked for its course list, which is then given to the
// course for processing. In general, accessor methods are
// bad in that they imply that this piece of data is not
// strongly related to the other data of this class or its
// methods. In general, ask why you are removing this data
// from its encapsulation, what you are doing with it, and
// why doesn't the class that owns the data do it for you.
// In this example, the class cannot perform the behavior itself
// because it needs data from both the Course and Student objects
// to make the decision.
CourseList&
Student::get_courses()
{
        return(*courses);
}


void
Student::print()
{
        cout << ''\n\nName: '' << name << ''\n'';
        cout << ''SSN: '' << ssn << ''\n'';
        cout << ''Age: '' << age << ''\n'';
        cout << ''Prerequisites: '';
        courses->print();
```

```cpp
        cout << ''\n\n'';
}


void
Student::short_print()
{
        cout << name;
}


int
Student::are_you(char* guess_name)
{
        return(!strcmp(name, guess_name));
}



StudentList::StudentList(int sz)
{
        student_num = 0;
        students = new Student*[size=sz];
}


StudentList::StudentList(StudentList& rhs)
{
        int i;

        students = new Student*[size=rhs.size];
        for (i=0; i < size; i++) {
            students[i] = rhs.students[i];
            students[i]->attach_object();
        }
        student_num = rhs.student_num;
}


StudentList::~StudentList()
{
        int i;
        for (i=0; i < student_num; i++) {
            if (students[i]->detach_object() == 1) {
                        delete students[i];
            }
        }
        delete students;
}


int
StudentList::add_item(Student& new_item)
{
```

```
        if (student_num == size) {
            return(0);
        }
        else {
            students[student_num++] = &new_item;
            new_item.attach_object();
        }
        return(1);
}


Student*
StudentList::find_item(char* guess_name)
{
        int i;

        for (i=0; i < student_num; i++) {
            if (students[i]->are_you(guess_name)) {
                        return(students[i]);
            }
        }
        return(NULL);
}


void
StudentList::print()
{
        int i;

        for (i=0; i < student_num; i++) {
            students[i]->short_print();
            cout << ' ';
        }
}


// The CourseOffering class captures the relationship of a
// course, in a room, on a particular date, with a particular
// group of students. It is not a reference-counting class,
// because we never share CourseOffering objects on multiple
// lists.
class CourseOffering {
private:
        Course* course;
        char room[small_strlen];
        char date[small_strlen];
        StudentList *attendees;
public:
        CourseOffering(Course&, char*, char*);
        CourseOffering(const CourseOffering&);
        ~CourseOffering();
        void add_student(Student&);
        void print();
```

```
        void short_print();
        int are_you(char*, char*);
};


// The CourseOffering list class is similar to the Student
// and Course list classes.
class OfferingList {
private:
        CourseOffering **offerings;
        int size;
        int offering_num;
public:
        OfferingList(int);
        OfferingList(OfferingList&);
        ~OfferingList();
        int add_item(CourseOffering&);
        CourseOffering* find_item(char*, char*);
        void print();
};


CourseOffering::CourseOffering(Course& c, char* r, char* d)
{
        course = &c;
        course->attach_object();
        strncpy(room, r, small_strlen);
        strncpy(date, d, small_strlen);
        attendees = new StudentList(student_len);
}


CourseOffering::CourseOffering(const CourseOffering& rhs)
{
        course = rhs.course;
        course->attach_object();
        strcpy(room, rhs.room);
        strcpy(date, rhs.date);
        attendees = new StudentList(*rhs.attendees);
}


CourseOffering::~CourseOffering()
{
        if (course->detach_object() == 1) {
            delete course;
        }
        delete attendees;
}


// The course offering must ensure that a new student has
// the necessary prerequisites. It does this by getting
// the list of courses the student has taken from the Student
```

```
// and gives it to the check_prereq method of the course.
// The course can determine if the prerequisites are met,
// since the course has the list of prerequisites and the
// Student has given, via the CourseOffering object's call
// to get_courses, the list of courses.
void
CourseOffering::add_student(Student& new_student)
{
    if (course->check_prereq(new_student.get_courses())) {
        attendees->add_item(new_student);
        cout << ''Student added to course.\n'';
    }
    else {
        cout << ''Admission refused: Student does not have the '';
        cout << ''necessary prerequisites.\n'';
    }
}


void
CourseOffering::print()
{
    cout << ''\n\nThe course offering for '';
    course->short_print();
    cout << '' will be held in room '' << room << '' starting on '';
    cout << date << ''\n'';
    cout << ''Current attendees include: '';
    attendees->print();
    cout << ''\n\n'';
}


void
CourseOffering::short_print()
{
    course->short_print();
    cout << ''('' << date << '')'';
}


// The name of the course is not enough when comparing course
// offerings. We must also test the dates.
int
CourseOffering::are_you(char* guess_name, char* guess_date)
{
    return(!strcmp(guess_date, date) &&
               course->are_you(guess_name));
}


OfferingList::OfferingList(int sz)
{
    offering_num = 0;
```

```
        offerings = new CourseOffering*[size=sz];
}


OfferingList::OfferingList(OfferingList& rhs)
{
    int i;

    offerings = new CourseOffering*[size=rhs.size];
    for (i=0; i < size; i++) {
        offerings[i] = rhs.offerings[i];
    }
    offering_num = rhs.offering_num;
}


OfferingList::~OfferingList()
{
    int i;
    for (i=0; i < offering_num; i++) {
        delete offerings[i];
    }
    delete offerings;
}


int
OfferingList::add_item(CourseOffering& new_item)
{
    if (offering_num == size) {
        return(0);
    }
    else {
        offerings[offering_num++] = &new_item;
    }
    return(1);
}


CourseOffering*
OfferingList::find_item(char* guess_name, char* date)
{
    int i;

    for (i=0; i < offering_num; i++) {
        if (offerings[i]->are_you(guess_name, date)) {
                return(offerings[i]);
        }
    }
    return(NULL);
}


void
```

```
OfferingList::print()
{
    int i;

    for (i=0; i < offering_num; i++) {
        offerings[i]->short_print();
        cout << '' '';
    }
}


// The main program is a simple menu-driven system for creating
// courses, course offerings, students; listing courses,
// students, and offerings; adding courses to students,
// students to courses, and prerequisites to courses. It can
// be used to test the public interfaces of the classes in
// this application.
void
main()
{
    CourseList courses(50);
    StudentList students(50);
    OfferingList offerings(50);
    Course *course1, *course2;
    Student *student;
    CourseOffering *offer1;
    int duration, age, choice;
    char answer[128], name[40], description[128],
                course_name[50];
    char ssn[20], date[20], room[20];
    char c;

    do {
        cout << ''What would you like to do? \n'';
        cout << ''  1) Build a new course\n'';
        cout << ''  2) Build a new student\n'';
        cout << ''  3) Build a new course offering\n'';
        cout << ''  4) List courses\n'';
        cout << ''  5) List students\n'';
        cout << ''  6) List offerings\n'';
        cout << ''  7) Add a prerequisite to a course\n'';
        cout << ''  8) Add a course to a student\n'';
        cout << ''  9) Add a student to a course offering\n'';
        cout << '' 10) Detailed info on a course\n'';
        cout << '' 11) Detailed info on a student\n'';
        cout << '' 12) Detailed info on an offering\n'';
        cout << ''  q) Quit\n'';
        cout << ''\nYour Choice: '';
        cin.getline(answer, 128);
        choice = atoi(answer);
        switch (choice) {
                case 1:
                        cout << ''Enter Name: '';
                        cin.getline(name, 40);
```

```
                        cout << ''Enter Description: '';
                        cin.getline(description, 128);
                        cout << ''Enter Length of Course: '';
                        cin >> duration;
                        courses.add_item(*new Course(name,
                          description, duration, 0));
                        cin.get(c);
                        break;
            case 2:
                        cout << ''Enter name: '';
                        cin.getline(name, 40);
                        cout << ''Enter ssn: '';
                        cin.getline(ssn, 20);
                        cout << ''Enter age: '';
                        cin >> age;
                        students.add_item(*new Student
                          (name, ssn, age, 0));
                        cin.get(c);
                        break;
            case 3:
                        cout << ''Enter course: '';
                        cin.getline(course_name, 50);
                        course1 = courses.find_item(course_name);
                        if (course1 == NULL) {
                                cout << ''Sorry, Cannot
                          find that course.\n'';
                                break;
                        }
                        cout << ''Enter room: '';
                        cin.getline(room, 20);
                        cout << ''Enter date: '';
                        cin.getline(date, 20);
                        offerings.add_item(*new
                          CourseOffering(*course1,
                          room, date));
                        break;
            case 4:
                        cout << ''\nList of courses: \n'';
                        courses.print();
                        cout << ''\n\n'';
                        break;
            case 5:
                        cout << ''\nList of students: \n'';
                        students.print();
                        cout << ''\n\n'';
                        break;
            case 6:
                        cout << ''\nList of Offerings: \n'';
                        offerings.print();
                        cout << ''\n\n'';
                        break;
            case 7:
                        cout << ''To which course? '';
                        cin.getline(course_name, 50);
                        course1 = courses.find_item
```

```
            (course_name);
            if (course1 == NULL) {
                    cout << ''Sorry, Cannot
             find that course.\n'';
                    break;
            }
            cout << ''Which prerequisite? '';
            cin.getline(course_name, 50);
            course2 = courses.find_item
             (course_name);
            if (course2 == NULL) {
                    cout << ''Sorry, Cannot
             find that course.\n'';
                    break;
            }
            course1->add_prereq(*course2);
            break;
    case 8:
            cout << ''To Which Student? '';
            cin.getline(name, 40);
            student = students.find_item(name);
            if (student == NULL) {
                    cout << ''Sorry, Cannot
             find that student.\n'';
                    break;
            }
            cout << ''Which Course? '';
            cin.getline(course_name, 50);
            course1 = courses.find_item
             (course_name);
            if (course1 == NULL) {
                    cout << ''Sorry, Cannot
             find that course.\n'';
                    break;
            }
            student->add_course(*course1);
            break;
    case 9:
            cout << ''To which course? '';
            cin.getline(course_name, 50);
            cout << ''On which date? '';
            cin.getline(date, 20);
            offer1 = offerings.find_item
             (course_name, date);
            if (offer1 == NULL) {
                    cout << ''Sorry, Cannot
             find that course offering.\n'';
                    break;
            }
            cout << ''Which Student? '';
            cin.getline(name, 40);
            student = students.find_item(name);
            if (student == NULL) {
                    cout << ''Sorry, Cannot
```

```
                                  find that student.\n'';
                                          break;
                              }
                              offer1->add_student(*student);
                              break;
                  case 10:
                              cout << ''On Which Course? '';
                              cin.getline(course_name, 50);
                              course1 = courses.find_item
                                (course_name);
                              if (course1 == NULL) {
                                          cout << ''Sorry, Cannot
                                find that course.\n'';
                                          break;
                              }
                              course1->print();
                              break;
                  case 11:
                              cout << ''On Which Student? '';
                              cin.getline(name, 40);
                              student = students.find_item(name);
                              if (student == NULL) {
                                          cout << ''Sorry, Cannot
                                find that student.\n'';
                                          break;
                              }
                              student->print();
                              break;
                  case 12:
                              cout << ''On Which Course? '';
                              cin.getline(course_name, 50);
                              cout << ''Which date? '';
                              cin.getline(date, 20);
                              offer1 = offerings.find_item
                                (course_name, date);
                              if (offer1 == NULL) {
                                          cout << ''Sorry, Cannot
                                find that course offering.\n'';
                                          break;
                              }
                              offer1->print();
                              break;
                  }
                  } while (answer[0] >= '1' &&
                    answer[0] <= '9');
                  }
```

Selected C++ Example #4

```
// Example #4

// This C++ example illustrates the better method for implementing
// a fragment of the home heating system example described in
```

```
// Booch's OOA/D book. This better solution pushes higher-level
// functionality onto the Room class, making the heat flow
// regulator less god-like.

// This example illustrates several examples of containment. If
// you are unfamiliar with the concept of containment, please read
// Chapter 4 before working through this example.

#include <iostream.h>
#include <stdlib.h>
#include <string.h>

// Constants used in this example.

const int name_len = 50;
const int large_strlen = 128;
const int room_len = 20;


// These sensor classes are identical to those in the previous
// example. See the comments on the classes in that example for
// further information.
class DesiredTempActuator {
public:
     int get_temp();
};

// Returns a random number from 50 to 90
int
DesiredTempActuator::get_temp()
{
     return(random(41) + 50);
}


class ActualTempSensor {
public:
     int get_temp();
};

int
ActualTempSensor::get_temp()
{
     return(random(41) + 50);
}


class OccupancySensor {
public:
     int anyone_in_room();
};


// Returns a random value (0 or 1)
```

```
int
OccupancySensor::anyone_in_room()
{
      return(random(2) % 2);
}
```

```
// The Room class contains a desired temperature input device, a
// temperature sensor, and an occupancy sensor (all by value). It
// has a name attribute for descriptive information.
// Note that the accessor methods have been eliminated in favor of
// a ''do_you_need_heat()'' method.
class Room {
      char name[name_len];
      DesiredTempActuator dtemp;
      ActualTempSensor atemp;
      OccupancySensor occ;
public:
      Room(char*);
      int do_you_need_heat();
};
```

```
Room::Room(char* n)
{
      strncpy(name, n, name_len);
}
```

```
// The Room object determines if it needs heat by calculating its
// working temperature (desired - actual) and checking if anyone
// is in the room. The room needs heat if the actual temperature
// is less than the desired temperature and someone is in the room,
// OR if no one is in the room and the actual temperature is more than
// five degrees less than the desired temperature.
// The method returns one if heat is needed and zero if not.
int
Room::do_you_need_heat()
{
      int working_temp, occupied;

      working_temp = dtemp.get_temp() - atemp.get_temp();
      occupied = occ.anyone_in_room();
      cout << ''The '' << name << '' has a working temp of '' <<
working_temp;
      cout << '' and '' << (occupied ? ''someone in the room.\n'' :
''no one in the room.\n'');
      if (working_temp > 5 || working_temp > 0 && occupied) {
            return(1);
      }
      return(0);
}
```

```
// Our furnace does little in this implementation of a design
// fragment because it is relatively uninteresting to illustrate
// the problem of poorly related data and behavior.
class Furnace {
public:
    void provide_heat();
    void turnoff();
};

void
Furnace::provide_heat()
{
    cout << ''Furnace Running\n'';
}

void
Furnace::turnoff()
{
    cout << ''Furnace Turned Off\n'';
}
```

```
// The heat flow regulator does not contain a list of rooms and a
// furnace. It is associated with them. There is a very large
// difference between stating that a class contains an object by
// reference, or a class is associated with an object. See
// Chapter 7 for an indepth discussion on this subject.
class HeatFlowRegulator {
    Room *house[room_len];
    Furnace *heater;
    int room_num;
public:
    HeatFlowRegulator(Furnace*, int, Room**);
    int loop();
};
```

```
// This constructor is identical to the one of the previous
// example.
HeatFlowRegulator::HeatFlowRegulator(Furnace* f, int num, Room
**rooms)
{
    int i;

    heater = f;
    room_num = num;
    for (i=0; i < room_num; i++) {
        house[i] = rooms[i];
    }
}
```

```
// The looping of the heat flow regulator is to check each room to see
```

```
// if it needs heat. In order to do this, the regulator simply asks
// the room if it needs heat. The work of figuring out if heat is
// needed has been pushed onto the Room class, which contains the
// necessary information.
int
HeatFlowRegulator::loop()
{
    int anyone_need_heat=0, i;

    for (i=0; i < room_num; i++) {
        anyone_need_heat += house[i]->do_you_need_heat();
    }
    if (anyone_need_heat)
        heater->provide_heat();
    else
        heater->turnoff();
    return(anyone_need_heat);
}


void
main()
{
    int room_num, i, retval;
    Furnace our_furnace;
    Room *rooms[room_len];
    char buffer[large_strlen];

    cout << ''How many rooms in your house? '';
    cin >> room_num;
    cin.get();
    if (room_num > room_len)
        room_num = room_len;
    for (i=0; i < room_num; i++) {
        cout << ''What is the name of room['' << (i+1) << '']? '';
        cin.getline(buffer, large_strlen, '\n');
        rooms[i] = new Room(buffer);
    }

    HeatFlowRegulator h(&our_furnace, room_num, rooms);

    do {
        retval = h.loop();
        cout << retval << '' rooms required heat!\n'';
        cout << ''Continue? '';
        cin.getline(buffer, large_strlen, '\n');
    } while (buffer[0] == 'y');
}
```

Selected C++ Example #5

```
// Example #5
// This example with its five parts will illustrate how a
```

```
// uses relationship may be implemented. The most common
// method of implementing the uses relationship is via
// containment. Containment relationships always imply
// uses, but uses do not always imply containment. The second
// example illustrates uses via containment. How does a Meal
// know the name of its Melon object when it wants to use
// it? Answer: It knows its name because it contains it, i.e.,
// Meals contain Melons.
// This brings up an interesting point. In a design
// discussion, if a member of the design team states that
// some class X uses class Y, always ask, ''How does the X
// object know the name of the Y object?''. While the answer is
// often, ''Because X contains the Y object,'' there are five
// other possibilities. We will discuss these in the context
// of a car using a gas station.

// How does the Car object know the name of the GasStation
// object? It clearly doesn't contain it; Cars do not contain
// GasStations.

// The first, and most popular, method is that the Car object
// is given the GasStation object as an explicit parameter to
// its method. This is illustrated by the Car1 class.

// The second method is for all Car objects to go to the
// same global GasStation. They know its name by hardcoding
// it into the Car's method(s). Some consider this to be
// a special case of the first method since global variables
// are really implicit parameters. Because it has a different
// form, we implement it in the class Car2.

// The third method is for the wealthy. When their Car runs
// out of gasoline, they build a GasStation, pump gas, and
// tear down the gas station. While this is ridiculous in
// the domain of cars and gas stations, it is appropriate in
// many domains. The Car3 class captures this method of using
// local objects.

// The fourth method is that when a car is born, god gives
// it its gas station for later use. Each car has a one-to-one
// association with its gas station. We will talk more about
// associations in Chapter 7, but this serves as a good example
// of the implementation of associations. Do not confuse
// an association with containment by reference. The
// relationships are very different at design time, however,
// C++ does not distinguish them. The class Car4 implements
// this feature.

// The fifth method is for the Car class to ask a third-party
// object for a gas station. Of course, this only postpones
// the problem. How did we know the name of the third-party
// object? It must be one of the other five methods: i.e.,
// containment, passed as an argument, a global object,
// a local object, an association, or ... ask a fourth-
```

```
// party object ... (ad nauseum).
// The Car5 class illustrates this implementation of uses by
// asking a contained map object for a gas station.

#include <iostream.h>

// The GasStation is the same class in all five methods of
// implementing uses relationships. The only interest is how
// we gain knowledge of the name of a particular gas station
// we want to use. Our gas station has a constructor; it
// can take gas deliveries, it can change its price (no grades
// of gasoline here, for simplification), and most
// importantly, it can dispense gasoline to anyone willing
// to pay. In our case, Car objects.
class GasStation {
private:
     double quantityOfGas;
     double price;
public:
     GasStation(double, double quantity=0.0);
     void take_gas_delivery(double);
     void change_price(double);
     double give_gasoline(double);
};

GasStation::GasStation(double start_price, double quantity)
{
     quantityOfGas = quantity;
     price = start_price;
}

void
GasStation::take_gas_delivery(double quantity)
{
     quantityOfGas += quantity;
}

void
GasStation::change_price(double new_price)
{
     price = new_price;
}

double
GasStation::give_gasoline(double amount)
{
     double gas_purchased;

     gas_purchased = amount / price;
     quantityOfGas -= gas_purchased;
     if (quantityOfGas < 0) {
         gas_purchased += quantityOfGas;
         quantityOfGas = 0.0;
     }
```

```
        return(gas_purchased);
}



// The Car1 class implements the first method of implementing
// a uses relationship which is not containment. The Car's
// get_gasoline method takes not only money, but also a
// GasStation object, as an argument.
class Car1 {
private:
        double milesPerGallon;
        double fuelCapacity;
        double gasInTank;
        double mileage;
public:
        Car1(double, double, double=0.0, double=0.0);
        void get_gasoline(GasStation&, double);
        void drive(double);
        void print();
};


Car1::Car1(double mpg, double capacity, double starting_gas,
                        double miles)
{
        milesPerGallon = mpg;
        fuelCapacity = capacity;
        gasInTank = starting_gas;
        mileage = miles;
}


// The drive method computes the gasoline needed to travel the
// desired distance. It then checks to see if there is enough
// gasoline in the car. If not, a message is printed to the user and
// the car moves as far as it can. If the car has less than 10% of its
// remaining capacity, a warning is printed to the user.
void
Car1::drive(double miles)
{
        double gas_needed;

        gas_needed = miles / milesPerGallon;
        if (gas_needed > gasInTank) {
            mileage += gasInTank * milesPerGallon;
            cerr << ''You ran out of gasoline after travelling '';
            cerr << gasInTank * milesPerGallon << '' miles.\n'';
            gasInTank = 0.0;
        }
        else {
            mileage += miles;
            gasInTank -= gas_needed;
            if (gasInTank < 0.1 * fuelCapacity) {
```

```
                              cerr << ''Warning: You have only enough gas
to go '';
                              cerr << GasInTank * miles_per_gallon << ''
miles.\n'';
          }
      }
}
```

```
// The get_gasoline method is the most interesting. In this
// implementation the Car class knows the name of its gas station
// because it is passed into the method. The gas station is used to
// get the gasoline, and a number of checks are made to be sure the
// gas station wasn't out of gas or that the user didn't spill some
// gas. Of course, this implementation could be made more
// elaborate but this will suffice to demonstrate the
// implementation of ''Car uses GasStation.''
void
Car1::get_gasoline(GasStation& myGasStation, double money)
{
    double gas_received;

    gas_received = myGasStation.give_gasoline(money);
    if (gas_received == 0) {
        cerr << ''Sorry the gas station was out of gas.\n'';
    }
    else {
        gasInTank += gas_received;
        if (gasInTank > fuelCapacity) {
                cerr << ''You spilled '' << (gasInTank -
fuelCapacity);
                cerr << '' gallons of gas on the ground.\n'';
                gasInTank = fuelCapacity;
        }
    }
}
```

```
void
Car1::print()
{
    cout << ''The car gets '' << miles_per_gallon;
    cout << '' miles per gallon.\nIt currently has '';
    cout << gasInTank << '' gallons of gasoline on board.\n'';
    cout << ''Its maximum fuel capacity is '' << fuelCapacity;
    cout << '' gallons\nand it has '' << mileage << '' miles.\n''
}
```

```
// The Car2 class demonstrates the implementation of a uses
// relationship through a global GasStation object. In this case,
// all Car2 objects go to the same GasStation, in this case
// ''Global_GasStation.'' Some designers consider this a special
```

```
// case of implementing the uses relationship through a parameter
// (e.g., Car1), but since it looks different in implementation, I
// felt it should be included.

GasStation Global_GasStation(1.25, 10000);
class Car2 {
private:
      double milesPerGallon;
      double fuelCapacity;
      double gasInTank;
      double mileage;
public:
      Car2(double, double, double=0.0, double=0.0);
      void get_gasoline(double);
      void drive(double);
      void print();
};


Car2::Car2(double mpg, double capacity, double starting_gas,
                      double miles)
{
      milesPerGallon = mpg;
      fuelCapacity = capacity;
      gasInTank = starting_gas;
      mileage = miles;
}


void
Car2::drive(double miles)
{
      double gas_needed;

      gas_needed = miles / milesPerGallon;
      if (gas_needed > gasInTank) {
          mileage += gasInTank * milesPerGallon;
          cerr << ''You ran out of gasoline after travelling '';
          cerr << gasInTank * milesPerGallon << '' miles.\n'';
          gasInTank = 0.0;
      }
      else {
          mileage += miles;
          gasInTank -= gas_needed;
          if (gasInTank < 0.1 * fuelCapacity) {
                     cerr << ''Warning: You have only enough gas
to go '';
                     cerr << GasInTank * milesPerGallon << ''
miles.\n'';
          }
      }
}
```

```cpp
// Note the use of the Global_GasStation object to get the gasoline.
void
Car2::get_gasoline(double money)
{
     double gas_received;

     gas_received = Global_GasStation.give_gasoline(money);
     if (gas_received == 0) {
         cerr << ''Sorry the gas station was out of gas.\n'';
     }
     else {
         gasInTank += gas_received;
         if (gasInTank > fuelCapacity) {
                 cerr << ''You spilled '' << (gasInTank -
fuelCapacity);
                 cerr << '' gallons of gas on the ground.\n'';
                 gasInTank = fuelCapacity;
         }
     }
}


void
Car2::print()
{
     cout << ''The car gets '' << milesPerGallon;
     cout << '' miles per gallon.\nIt currently has '';
     cout << gasInTank << '' gallons of gasoline on board.\n'';
     cout << ''Its maximum fuel capacity is '' << fuelCapacity;
     cout << '' gallons\nand it has '' << mileage << '' miles.\n'';
}


// The Car3 class implements its uses relationship through a local
// object that is built ''on-the-fly'' at runtime. Whenever the
// get_gasoline() method is called on Car3 objects, the method
// builds itself a gas station, uses the gas station, and then
// destroys it. This is inefficient but is used in some
// implementations.
class Car3 {
private:
     double milesPerGallon;
     double fuelCapacity;
     double gasInTank;
     double mileage;
public:
     Car3(double, double, double=0.0, double=0.0);
     void get_gasoline(double);
     void drive(double);
     void print();
};
```

```cpp
Car3::Car3(double mpg, double capacity, double starting_gas,
                        double miles)
{
    milesPerGallon = mpg;
    fuelCapacity = capacity;
    gasInTank = starting_gas;
    mileage = miles;
}


void
Car3::drive(double miles)
{
    double gas_needed;

    gas_needed = miles / milesPerGallon;
    if (gas_needed > gasInTank) {
        mileage += gasInTank * milesPerGallon;
        cerr << ''You ran out of gasoline after travelling '';
        cerr << gasInTank * milesPerGallon << '' miles.\n'';
        gasInTank = 0.0;
    }
    else {
        mileage += miles;
        gasInTank -= gas_needed;
        if (gasInTank < 0.1 * fuelCapacity) {
                    cerr << ''Warning: You have only enough gas
to go '';
                    cerr << gasInTank * milesPerGallon <<
'' miles.\n'';
        }
    }
}


// Note the creation and use of local_station in order to get
// gasoline for the car. While a bit silly in the domain of cars and
// gas stations, there are domains where the use of a local object
// as part of the implementation of a method is perfectly
// appropriate.
void
Car3::get_gasoline(double money)
{
    double gas_received;
    GasStation local_station(1.25, 1000);

    gas_received = local_station.give_gasoline(money);
    if (gas_received == 0) {
        cerr << ''Sorry the gas station was out of gas.\n'';
    }
    else {
        gasInTank += gas_received;
        if (gasInTank > fuelCapacity) {
```

```
                        cerr << ''You spilled '' << (gasInTank -
    fuelCapacity);

                        cerr << '' gallons of gas on the ground.\n'';
                        gasInTank = fuelCapacity;
                }
            }
    }


    void
    Car3::print()
    {
        cout << ''The car gets '' << milesPerGallon;
        cout << '' miles per gallon.\nIt currently has '';
        cout << gasInTank << '' gallons of gasoline on board.\n'';
        cout << ''Its maximum fuel capacity is '' << fuelCapacity;
        cout << ''gallons\nand it has'' << mileage << ''miles.\n'';
    }


    // The Car4 class uses a different twist in implementing its uses
    // relationship. When each Car4 object is built, it is told who its
    // gas station is. This gas station is stored in the Car4 object for
    // later use. In this case, the class will make a copy of the gas
    // station, which is safer because it avoids problems of the gas
    // station given to the Car4 object being destroyed before the Car4
    // object. If data sharing is desired, then only the pointer,
    // and not the stuff to which it points, should be copied. For an
    // example of this form of shallow copying which also provides a
    // safety mechanism, see the Air Traffic Controller example in
    // Chapter 9 (Example #3). Do not confuse association with
    // containment by reference. While the Car4 class does have a
    // pointer to a GasStation as a data member, this is not containment
    // by reference, it is association through a referential attribute.
    // While C++ does not let us distinguish these two relationships,
    // the distinction is available AND important to designers. If this
    // were containment, we could ignore GasStations at some high
    // level of design. The fact that it is assocation means we cannot.
    class Car4 {
    private:
        double milesPerGallon;
        double fuelCapacity;
        double gasInTank;
        double mileage;
        GasStation* myStation;
    public:
        Car4(GasStation*, double, double, double=0.0, double=0.0);
        ~Car4();
        void get_gasoline(double);
        void drive(double);
        void print();
    };
```

```
// Note the constructor copying the GasStation passed to it using
// the default copy constructor for GasStation. (Note: GasStation
// is a fixed-sized class so the default copy constructor does not
// cause any memory leakage/heap corruption problems. See Appendix B
// for a more thorough explanation of memory leakage/heap corruption
// problems of copy constructors/assignment operators.
Car4::Car4(GasStation* station, double mpg, double capacity,
                         double starting_gas, double miles)
{
    myStation = new GasStation(*station);
    milesPerGallon = mpg;
    fuelCapacity = capacity;
    gasInTank = starting_gas;
    mileage = miles;
}


Car4::~Car4()
{
    delete myStation;
}


void
Car4::drive(double miles)
{
    double gas_needed;

    gas_needed = miles / milesPerGallon;
    if (gas_needed > gasInTank) {
        mileage += gasInTank * milesPerGallon;
        cerr << ''You ran out of gasoline after travelling '';
        cerr << gasInTank * milesPerGallon << '' miles.\n'';
        gasInTank = 0.0;
    }
    else {
        mileage += miles;
        gasInTank -= gas_needed;
        if (gasInTank < 0.1 * fuelCapacity) {
                    cerr << ''Warning: You have only enough gas
to go '';
                    cerr << gasInTank * milesPerGallon <<
'' miles.\n'';
        }
    }
}


// Note the use of the referential attribute in the get_gasoline method.
void
Car4::get_gasoline(double money)
{
    double gas_received;
```

```
        gas_received = myStation->give_gasoline(money);
        if (gas_received == 0) {
            cerr << ''Sorry the gas station was out of gas.\n'';
        }
        else {
            gasInTank += gas_received;
            if (gasInTank > fuelCapacity) {
                    cerr << ''You spilled '' << (gasInTank -
fuelCapacity);
                    cerr << '' gallons of gas on the ground.\n'';
                    gasInTank = fuelCapacity;
            }
        }
}


void
Car4::print()
{
    cout << ''The car gets '' << milesPerGallon;
    cout << '' miles per gallon.\nIt currently has '';
    cout << gasInTank << '' gallons of gasoline on board.\n'';
    cout << ''Its maximum fuel capacity is '' << fuelCapacity;
    cout << '' gallons\nand it has '' << mileage << '' miles.\n'';
}



// The Car5 class implements its uses relationship by asking a
// third-party class, in this case a Map object. Of course, asking
// a third-party only postpones the answer to the question, ''How
// does a class know the name of the object it wishes to use?'' We
// will have to use one of the other five methods of implementing
// uses. In this case, I chose containment, i.e., Car5 contains a
// Map object.

// We first implement our Map class. I have chosen a naive algorithm
// for finding a GasStation on a Map. Each Map object has four
// quadrants and a car has an x,y location. The map takes the x-
// and y-coordinates of a car and returns one of four stations.
// While it is true that this is naive (the attentive will notice
// that a Map has no way of getting gasoline deliveries to its
// GasStations), it is sufficient to demonstrate uses.
class Map {
private:
    GasStation* quadrant[4];
public:
    Map();
    ~Map();
    GasStation* get_station(int, int);
};

// The constructor for Map simply builds the four GasStations, one
// for each quadrant.
```

```
Map::Map()
{
    quadrant[0] = new GasStation(1.45, 1000);
    quadrant[1] = new GasStation(1.30, 200);
    quadrant[2] = new GasStation(2.10, 10000);
    quadrant[3] = new GasStation(1.10, 678);
}

Map::~Map()
{
    int i;

    for (i=0; i < 4; i++) {
        delete quadrant[i];
    }
}


// When a Car5 object asks the Map for a station, it gives the Map its
// x- and y-coordinates. The Map returns the appropriate
// GasStation.
GasStation*
Map::get_station(int x, int y)
{
    if (x > 0) {
        if (y > 0)
                return(quadrant[0]);
        else
                return(quadrant[3]);
    }
    else {
        if (y > 0)
                return(quadrant[1]);
        else
                return(quadrant[2]);
    }
}


// The Car5 class contains the Map by value. Even if it contained it
// by reference, this would still be a containment relationship.
// It would not be association through a referential attribute
// like the Car4 class. The difference is significant at design time.
// I can state that Maps are not as important a class in this domain
// as Car5 and GasStation objects because the former is contained in
// a top-level class and does not have to be discussed at high-level
// design time.
class Car5 {
private:
    int loc_x, loc_y;
    double milesPerGallon;
    double fuelCapacity;
    double gasInTank;
    double mileage;
```

```
        Map myMap;
public:
        Car5(int, int, double, double, double=0.0, double=0.0);
        void get_gasoline(double);
        void drive(double);
        void print();
};

// The constructor for Map is called automatically before the
// constructor for each Car5 object. The destructor for Map will
// likewise be called whenever a Car5 object is destroyed.
Car5::Car5(int x, int y, double mpg, double capacity,
                            double starting_gas, double miles)
{
        loc_x = x;
        loc_y = y;
        milesPerGallon = mpg;
        fuelCapacity = capacity;
        gasInTank = starting_gas;
        mileage = miles;
}


void
Car5::drive(double miles)
{
        double gas_needed;

        gas_needed = miles / milesPerGallon;
        if (gas_needed > gasInTank) {
            mileage += gasInTank * milesPerGallon;
            cerr << ''You ran out of gasoline after travelling '';
            cerr << gasInTank * milesPerGallon << '' miles.\n'';
            gasInTank = 0.0;
        }
        else {
            mileage += miles;
            gasInTank -= gas_needed;
            if (gasInTank < 0.1 * fuelCapacity) {
                        cerr << ''Warning: You have only enough gas
to go '';
                        cerr << gasInTank * milesPerGallon <<
''miles.\n'';
                }
        }
}


// Note the use of the contained, third-party object called MyMap to
// get a GasStation for use by the get_gasoline method.
void
Car5::get_gasoline(double money)
{
        double gas_received;
```

```
        GasStation *myStation = myMap.get_station(loc_x, loc_y);

        gas_received = myStation->give_gasoline(money);
        if (gas_received == 0) {
            cerr << ''Sorry the gas station was out of gas.\n'';
        }
        else {
            gasInTank += gas_received;
            if (gasInTank > fuelCapacity) {
                    cerr << ''You spilled '' << (gasInTank -
    fuelCapacity);
                    cerr << '' gallons of gas on the ground.\n'';
                    gasInTank = fuelCapacity;
            }
        }
}


void
Car5::print()
{
        cout << ''The car at location ('' << loc_x << '', '' << loc_y <<
'') gets '';
        cout << milesPerGallon << '' miles per gallon.\nIt currently
has '';
        cout << gasInTank << '' gallons of gasoline on board.\n'';
        cout << ''Its maximum fuel capacity is '' << fuelCapacity;
        cout << '' gallons\nand it has '' << mileage << '' miles.\n''
}


void
main()
{
// The following code tests the Car1 class:
        GasStation g1(1.18, 300), g2(1.45, 2300);
        Car1 mycar1(22, 18, 10);

        mycar1.print();
        mycar1.drive(200);
        mycar1.print();
        mycar1.drive(100);
        mycar1.print();
        mycar1.get_gasoline(g1, 15.00);
        mycar1.print();

// The following code tests the Car2 class:

        Car2 mycar2(30, 20, 3);

        mycar2.print();
        mycar2.drive(200);
        mycar2.print();
        mycar2.get_gasoline(20.00);
```

```
    mycar2.print();
    mycar2.get_gasoline(10.00);
    mycar2.print();


// The following code tests the Car3 class:

    Car3 mycar3(9, 13, 5);

    mycar3.print();
    mycar3.drive(38);
    mycar3.print();
    mycar3.get_gasoline(10.00);
    mycar3.print();
    mycar3.drive(150);
    mycar3.print();

// The following code tests the Car4 class:

    Car4 mycar4(&g2, 18, 25, 12);

    mycar4.print();
    mycar4.get_gasoline(15.00);
    mycar4.print();
    mycar4.drive(150);
    mycar4.print();
    mycar4.get_gasoline(3.69);
    mycar4.print();

// The following code tests the Car5 class:

    Car5 mycar5(10, -34, 35, 18, 15);

    mycar5.print();
    mycar5.drive(250);
    mycar5.print();
    mycar5.drive(250);
    mycar5.print();
    mycar5.get_gasoline(10.00);
    mycar5.print();
    mycar5.get_gasoline(20.00);
    mycar5.print();
}
```

Selected C++ Example #9

```
// Example #9

// This example illustrates the reuse of a linked list
// abstraction in the development of a sorted linked list.
// The linked list has insert and remove methods, which are
// monomorphic. They make use of two polymorphic, protected
```

```
// find functions to implemement the differences between the
// two abstractions. Example 4b will illustrate the problem
// with software reuse through inheritance by introducing a
// linked ring class to the design. None of this linked list's
// code will be reusable when we introduce the linked ring
// (the bad news). But with the introduction of a new
// protected abstraction for testing the end of a list, it will
// be able to reuse the abstraction (the good news).

#include <iostream.h>
#include <new.h>

// We show that this class is a good candidate for
// parameterization. We will turn it into a template in
// the selected C++ examples of Chapter 8.
typedef int DATUM;

// The linked list class contains a local, protected data
// type for the nodes. It is protected instead of private
// because the sorted linked list needs access to the type.
// The linked list class also provides two protected polymorphic
// methods for finding (insert and remove, respectively), which
// are used by the insert and remove methods. These will be
// overridden in the derived class ''sorted linked list.''
// The protected get_head method allows the hiding of the
// head pointer's implementation within the base class ''linked
// list'' while still allowing the derived class to access the
// abstraction.
class LinkedList {
protected:
     struct Node {
          DATUM data;
          Node* next;
     public:
          Node(const DATUM&);
     };
     virtual Node* ifind(const DATUM&) const;
     virtual Node* rfind(const DATUM&) const;
     Node* get_head() const;
private:
     Node* head;
     int length;
public:
     LinkedList();
     ~LinkedList();
     int insert(const DATUM&);
     int remove(const DATUM&);
     void traverse() const;
     virtual char* type();
     void test();
};


LinkedList::Node*
```

```
LinkedList::get_head() const
{
     return(head);
}


LinkedList::Node*
LinkedList::ifind(const DATUM&) const
{
     Node* temp = head;

     if (temp == NULL) {
         return(NULL);
     }
     while (temp->next != NULL) {
         temp = temp->next;
     }
     return(temp);
}

// The remove find method returns three possible values. A
// return of -1 implies that the object to be removed is at
// the head of the list, NULL implies the item is not in
// the list, any other value implies the pointer returned
// is a pointer to the preceding node in the list.
LinkedList::Node*
LinkedList::rfind(const DATUM& bad_item) const
{
     Node* found = head, *pre_found = (Node*) -1;


     while (found != NULL) {
         if (found->data == bad_item) {
                 return(pre_found);
         }
         pre_found = found;
         found = found->next;
     }
     return(NULL);
}



LinkedList::Node::Node(const DATUM& new_data)
{
     data = new_data;
     next = NULL;
}


LinkedList::LinkedList()
{
     head = NULL;
     length = 0;
```

```
        }


LinkedList::~LinkedList()
{
      Node* temp;

      while (head != NULL) {
           temp = head;
           head = head->next;
           delete temp;
      }
}


int
LinkedList::insert(const DATUM& new_item)
{
      Node* temp = ifind(new_item);
      Node* new_node = new Node(new_item);

      if (temp == NULL) {
           new_node->next = head;
           head = new_node;
      }
      else {
           new_node->next = temp->next;
           temp->next = new_node;
      }
      return(++length);
}


int
LinkedList::remove(const DATUM& bad_item)
{
      Node* found = rfind(bad_item);
      Node* temp;

      if (found == NULL) {
           return(0);
      }
      else if (found == (Node*) -1) {
           length--;
           temp = head;
           head = head->next;
           delete temp;
           return(1);
      }
      else {
           length--;
           temp = found->next;
           found->next = found->next->next;
           delete temp;
```

```
                return(1);
        }
}


void
LinkedList::traverse() const
{
        Node* temp = head;

        cout << ''('';
        while (temp != NULL) {
                cout << temp->data << '' '';
                temp = temp->next;
        }
        cout << '')\n'';
}

char*
LinkedList::type()
{
        return(''LinkedList'');
}


// Note the major reuse of the LinkedList abstraction in this
// class. The SortedLinkedList need only redefine three
// protected polymorphic methods from the LinkedList.
class SortedLinkedList : public LinkedList {
protected:
        Node* ifind(const DATUM&) const;
        Node* rfind(const DATUM&) const;
public:
        char* type();
};


LinkedList::Node*
SortedLinkedList::ifind(const DATUM& new_item) const
{
        Node *found = get_head(), *pre_found = NULL;

        while (found != NULL && found->data < new_item) {
                pre_found = found;
                found = found->next;
        }
        return(pre_found);
}


LinkedList::Node*
SortedLinkedList::rfind(const DATUM& bad_item) const
{
        Node* found = get_head(), *pre_found = (Node*) -1;
```

```
        while (found != NULL && found->data <= bad_item) {
            if (found->data == bad_item) {
                        return(pre_found);
            }
            pre_found = found;
            found = found->next;
        }
        return(NULL);
    }

char*
SortedLinkedList::type()
{
        return(''SortedLinkedList'');
}


void
main()
{
        LinkedList x;
        SortedLinkedList y;

        cout << ''Testing the LinkedList\n'';
        x.test();
        cout << ''\n\nTesting the SortedLinkedList\n'';
        y.test();
}


void
LinkedList::test()
{
        char c = 'a';
        int size;
        DATUM num;

        while (c != 'q') {
            cout << ''Your '' << type() << '' looks like: '';
            traverse();
            cout << ''What's your pleasure i)nsert, d)elete, q)uit? '';
            cin >> c;
            if (c == 'i') {
                        cout << ''Number to insert: '';
                        cin >> num;
                        size = insert(num);
                        cout << ''Number of elements on the '' << type();
                        cout << '' is '' << size << ''\n.'';
            }
            else if (c == 'd') {
```

```
                                   cout << ''Number to delete: '';
                                   cin >> num;
                                   size = remove(num);
                                   if (size == 0) {
                                           cout << ''Couldn't find the number \''
        << num;
                                           cout << ''\'' in the '' << type() <<
        ''.\n'';
                                   }
                                   else {
                                           cout << ''Found and deleted the num-
        ber \'' << num;
                                           cout << ''\'' from the '' << type() <<
        ''.\n'';
                                   }
                           }
                   }
           }
```

Selected C++ Example #10

```
        // Example #10

        // This example illustrates the necessary changes to Example
        // #4a when adding a LinkedRing as a new derived class of
        // LinkedList.


        #include <iostream.h>
        #include <new.h>

        typedef int DATUM;

        // The LinkedRing class requires that we abstract out the
        // test for the end of a list into a separate, protected
        // polymorphic ''at_end()'' method. Since, in a LinkedRing,
        // the beginning and end tests of a list are equivalent (i.e.,
        // the pointer you have is equal to the head), the loops in
        // the linked list methods had to be inverted from while to
        // do-while. In addition to these changes, we had to add a
        // protected polymorphic method to handle the different
        // initialization of a node's next pointer. LinkedList assigns
        // it to NULL, while a LinkedRing assigns it to itself (to make
        // a ring of one node).

        // Requiring a change to the base class when a new derived
        // class is added to an existing hierarchy occurs more often
        // than not. This certainly has caused some reusability
        // problems when inheritance is involved.
        class LinkedList {
        protected:
                struct Node {
```

```
            DATUM data;
            Node* next;
        public:
            Node(const DATUM&);
        };
        virtual Node* ifind(const DATUM&) const;
        virtual Node* rfind(const DATUM&) const;
        virtual int at_end(const Node*) const;
        virtual void set_next(Node*);
        void cleanup();
        Node* get_head() const;
private:
        Node* head;
        int length;
public:
        LinkedList();
        ~LinkedList();
        int insert(const DATUM&);
        int remove(const DATUM&);
        void traverse() const;
        virtual char* type();
        void test();
};


// The at_end method for the LinkedList simply checks the
// current_ptr against NULL.
int
LinkedList::at_end(const Node* current_ptr) const
{
        return(current_ptr == NULL);
}

// The set_next method is used to distinguish the LinkedList
// versus LinkedRing behavior of creating nodes. The
// LinkedList wants a NULL next pointer, while the LinkedRing
// wants the next point to reference the object that owns
// it.
void
LinkedList::set_next(Node* new_node)

{
        new_node->next = NULL;
}


LinkedList::Node*
LinkedList::get_head() const
{
        return(head);
}


LinkedList::Node*
```

```
LinkedList::ifind(const DATUM&) const
{
     Node* temp = head;

     if (temp == NULL) {
          return(NULL);
     }
     while (!at_end(temp->next)) {
          temp = temp->next;
     }
     return(temp);
}

// The remove find method returns three possible values. A
// return of -1 implies that the object to be removed is at
// the head of the list, NULL implies the item is not in
// the list, any other value implies the pointer returned
// is a pointer to the preceding node in the list.
LinkedList::Node*
LinkedList::rfind(const DATUM& bad_item) const
{
     Node* found = head, *pre_found = (Node*) -1;

     if (head != NULL) {
          do {
                    if (found->data == bad_item) {
                              return(pre_found);
                    }
                    pre_found = found;
                    found = found->next;
          } while (!at_end(found));
     }
     return(NULL);
}



LinkedList::Node::Node(const DATUM& new_data)
{
     data = new_data;
     next = NULL;
}


LinkedList::LinkedList()
{
     head = NULL;
     length = 0;
}


LinkedList::~LinkedList()
{
     if (head != NULL)
```

```
                cleanup();
        }


        void
        LinkedList::cleanup()
        {
            Node *temp, *current_ptr = head;
            do {
                temp = current_ptr;
                current_ptr = current_ptr->next;
                delete temp;
            } while (!at_end(current_ptr));
            head = NULL;
        }


        int
        LinkedList::insert(const DATUM& new_item)
        {
            Node* temp = ifind(new_item);
            Node* new_node = new Node(new_item);


            if (head == NULL) {            // Insertion into an empty list
                set_next(new_node);
                head = new_node;
            }
            else if (temp == NULL) {       // Insertion at the head
                new_node->next = head;
                head = new_node;
            }
            else {                         // All others
                new_node->next = temp->next;
                temp->next = new_node;
            }
            return(++length);
        }


        // Remove gets more complicated because LinkedRings are a
        // pain when you need to remove their head node. This
        // method does not remove the head node until it is the last
        // thing in the list. It will copy the second node's data
        // into the head node and delete the second node instead.
        int
        LinkedList::remove(const DATUM& bad_item)
        {
            Node* found = rfind(bad_item);
            Node* temp;

            if (found == NULL) {           // The item is not in the list.
                return(0);
            }
```

```cpp
// The item is in the list, so decrement the count. Then check
// if it is the head, which we want to delete. If it is, then
// check if it is the last item in the list. If so, then
// simply get rid of it. If not, we need to copy the second
// node's data and throw away the second node (to preserve the
// last node in the list's next pointer to the head).
    length--;
    if (found == (Node*) -1) {
        if (!at_end(head->next)) {
                head->data = head->next->data;
                temp = head->next;
                head->next = head->next->next;
                delete temp;
        }
        else {
                delete head;
                head = NULL;
        }
        return(1);
    }
    else {
        temp = found->next;
        found->next = found->next->next;
        delete temp;
        return(1);
    }
}


void
LinkedList::traverse() const
{
    Node* temp = head;

    cout << ''('';
    if (head != NULL) {
        do {
                cout << temp->data << '' '';
                temp = temp->next;
        } while (!at_end(temp));
    }
    cout << '')\n'';
}


char*
LinkedList::type()
{
    return(''LinkedList'');
}


// Note the major reuse of the LinkedList abstraction in this
```

```
// class. The SortedLinkedList need only redefine three
// protected polymorphic methods from the LinkedList.
class SortedLinkedList : public LinkedList {
protected:
     Node* ifind(const DATUM&) const;
     Node* rfind(const DATUM&) const;
public:
     char* type();
};


LinkedList::Node*
SortedLinkedList::ifind(const DATUM& new_item) const
{
     Node *found = get_head(), *pre_found = NULL;

     while (found != NULL && found->data < new_item) {
          pre_found = found;
          found = found->next;
     }
     return(pre_found);
}


LinkedList::Node*
SortedLinkedList::rfind(const DATUM& bad_item) const
{
     Node* found = get_head(), *pre_found = (Node*) -1;


     while (found != NULL && found->data <= bad_item) {
          if (found->data == bad_item) {
                    return(pre_found);
          }
          pre_found = found;
          found = found->next;
     }
     return(NULL);
}

char*
SortedLinkedList::type()
{
     return(''SortedLinkedList'');
}


class LinkedRing : public LinkedList {
protected:
     int at_end(const Node*) const;
     void set_next(Node*);
public:
     ~LinkedRing();
     char* type();
```

```cpp
};


LinkedRing::~LinkedRing()
{
    if (get_head() != NULL)
        cleanup();
}


// The at_end method of a LinkedRing checks if the current
// pointer is equal to the head pointer.
int
LinkedRing::at_end(const Node* current_ptr) const
{
    return(current_ptr == get_head());
}

void
LinkedRing::set_next(Node* new_node)
{
    new_node->next = new_node;
}

char*
LinkedRing::type()
{
    return(''LinkedRing'');
}



void
main()
{
    LinkedList x;
    SortedLinkedList y;
    LinkedRing z;

    cout << ''Testing the LinkedList.\n'';
    x.test();
    cout << ''\n\nTesting the SortedLinkedList.\n'';
    y.test();
    cout << ''\n\nTesting the LinkedRing.\n'';
    z.test();
}

void
LinkedList::test()
{
    char c = 'a';
    DATUM num;
    int size;
```

```
        while (c != 'q') {
            cout << ''Your '' << type() << '' looks like: '';
            traverse();
            cout << ''What's your pleasure i)nsert, d)elete, q)uit? '';
            cin >> c;
            if (c == 'i') {
                    cout << ''Number to insert: '';
                    cin >> num;
                    size = insert(num);
                    cout << ''Number of elements on the '' << type();
                    cout << '' is '' << size << ''.\n'';
            }
            else if (c == 'd') {
                    cout << ''Number to delete: '';
                    cin >> num;
                    size = remove(num);
                    if (size == 0) {
                            cout << ''Couldn't find the number
\'''' << num;
                            cout << ''\'' in the '' << type() <<
''.\n'';
                    }
                    else {
                            cout << ''Found and deleted the
number \'''' << num;
                            cout << ''\'' from the '' << type()
<< ''.\n'';
                    }
            }
        }
}
```

Selected C++ Example #15

```
// Example #15
// This C++ example illustrates the use of virtual multiple
// inheritance to force data and constructor sharing of a
// common base class. The example comes from the graduate
// student problem posed in Chapter 6.

#include <iostream.h>
#include <string.h>

// Constants used in this example.

const int name_len = 50;
const int ssn_len = 12;
const int course_len = 20;
const int student_len = 50;


// The Person class is the common base class, which both
```

```
// the student and instructor classes inherit. It would
// be inherited twice in the graduate student class if it
// were not for virtual inheritance at both the student and
// instructor levels.

// Note the protected accessor methods. The assumption is
// that one or more derived classes of Person need access
// to name and social security number. These methods are a
// bit dangerous in that they give pointers to the internals
// of Person. The fact that they are constant does not help
// much, since a user could cast the return value to a
// regular char pointer. The only safe way to protect the
// state of the Person class would be to force the user to
// pass the Person object a buffer. The Person object would
// then copy the name/ssn into the required buffer; e.g.,
//          void get_name(char* buf);
//          void get_ssn(char* buf);
// This copying is quite expensive. I would use the above
// forms if I were making these public accessors. Since they
// are protected, I'm willing to gamble that I do not have
// pathological implementors of derived classes. The choice
// depends on your level of paranoia.

// The copy constructor is not required here, since Person
// is a fixed-size class. I place it here for readability
// since it will be called further down the hierarchy.

class Person {
      char name[name_len];
      char ssn[ssn_len];
protected:
      const char* get_name() { return(name); }
      const char* get_ssn() { return(ssn); }
      Person();
public:
      Person(char*, char*);
      Person(Person&);
      void print();
};


// The first uncomfortable item we need to deal with is
// the requirement that the Person constructor possess this
// constructor, which, in fact, will never be called. We
// want to be able to initialize a graduate student given
// only a student object and a salary. This requires us to
// have a protected constructor for the Instructor class,
// which takes a salary (only) as an argument. Such a
// constructor will have an implied call to this constructor
// (see the protected instructor constructor below), but
// since the Instructor virtually inherits from Person, this
// constructor will never be called. Without it, however,
// the example will not compile.
// We also want to build a graduate student from only an
```

```
// Instructor. This requires a protected student
// constructor that takes no arguments. The same problem that
// occurs with the instructor constructor occurs here.
Person::Person()
{
}

Person::Person(char* n, char* social_num)
{
     strncpy(name, n, name_len);
     strncpy(ssn, social_num, ssn_len);
}

Person::Person(Person& rhs)
{
     strcpy(name, rhs.name);
     strcpy(ssn, rhs.ssn);
}

void
Person::print()
{
     cout << ''Hi! My name and SSN is '' << name;
     cout << '' '' << ssn << ''.\n'';
}


// The Student class contains a list of courses, each of
// which contains a name and a grade.
class Course {
     char name[name_len];
     int grade;
public:
     Course(char*, int);
     Course(Course&);
     void print(const char*);
};


Course::Course(char* n, int g)
{
     strncpy(name, n, name_len);
     grade = g;
}


Course::Course(Course& rhs)
{
     strcpy(name, rhs.name);
     grade = rhs.grade;
}


void
```

```
Course::print(const char* student)
{
     cout << student << '' received a '' << grade;
     cout << '' in the course '' << name << ''\n'';
}
```

```
// The Student class virtually inherits from Person. The
// Student class is advertising that it is willing to share
// its Person base object with any other Person base object
// in a multiple inheriting derived class (the GradStudent, in
// this case). This virtual keyword has nothing to do with
// polymorphism. In fact, there is no polymorphism in this
// example. The behavior of Student is defined to be the same
// regardless of the virtual keyword; its implementation
// changes, however. Virtual inheritance will affect only the
// children of the virtually inheriting class.
class Student : virtual public Person {
     Course* course_list[course_len];
     double GPA;
     int grade_sum;
     int course_num;
protected:
     Student();
public:
     Student(char*, char*);
     Student(Student&);
     ~Student();
     int add_course(char*, int);
     void print();
};
```

```
// This protected constructor is called only indirectly from
// the graduate student constructor. The implied call to a
// Person constructor, which is callable with zero arguments,
// necessitates the protected Person constructor above. But,
// since this constructor is never called directly, that
// person constructor will never be executed. The result is
// a required constructor that can never be called.
Student::Student()
{
     int i;

     GPA = 0.0;
     grade_sum = course_num = 0;
     for (i=0; i < course_len; i++) {
          course_list[i] = NULL;
     }
}
```

```
// If this constructor is called directly, i.e., someone is
// building a Student, then it will call the Person
// constructor. If it is called indirectly from a GradStudent
// constructor, then the Person constructor will not be called.
```

```cpp
// The GradStudent constructor will be responsible for the
// call to the Person constructor.
Student::Student(char* name, char* ssn) : Person(name, ssn)
{
    int i;

    GPA = 0.0;
    grade_sum = course_num = 0;
    for (i=0; i < course_len; i++) {
        course_list[i] = NULL;
    }
}


Student::Student(Student& rhs) : Person(rhs)
{
    int i;

    GPA = rhs.GPA;
    grade_sum = rhs.grade_sum;
    course_num = rhs.course_num;
    for (i=0; i < course_num; i++) {
        course_list[i] = new Course(*rhs.course_list[i]);
    }
}


Student::~Student()
{
    int i;

    for (i=0; i < course_num; i++) {
        delete course_list[i];
    }
}


int
Student::add_course(char* name, int grade)
{
    course_list[course_num++] = new Course(name, grade);
    grade_sum += grade;
    GPA = grade_sum / course_num;
    return(course_num);
}


void
Student::print()
{
    int i;

    cout << ''Student Name: '' << get_name() << ''\n'';
    cout << ''Social Security Number: '' << get_ssn() << ''\n'';
```

```
        cout << ''Courses: \n'';
        for (i=0; i < course_num; i++) {
            cout << ''\t'';
            course_list[i]->print(get_name());
        }
        if (course_num) {
            cout << ''Grade Point Average: '' << GPA << ''\n'';
        }
        cout << ''\n\n'';
}


// The Instructor class must also virtually inherit if the
// Person object is to be shared at the GradStudent level.
// All base classes wishing to share a common base class
// in a multiple inheriting derived class must virtually
// inherit.
class Instructor : virtual public Person {
        double salary;
        Student* students[student_len];
        int student_num;
protected:
        Instructor(double);
public:
        Instructor(char*, char*, double);
        Instructor(Instructor&);
        ~Instructor();
        int add_student(Student&);
        void print();
};

// This protected constructor has an implied call to a Person
// constructor callable with zero arguments. This required
// us to define such a constructor above. But since this
// constructor is protected, it will only be called by derived
// constructors. When called indirectly, this constructor will
// NOT call Person's constructor. The result is a needed
// constructor for compiling, which is never really called.
Instructor::Instructor(double sal)
{
        int i;

        salary = sal;
        student_num = 0;
        for (i=0; i < student_len; i++) {
            students[i] = NULL;
        }
}


Instructor::Instructor(char* name, char* ssn, double pay)

        : Person(name, ssn)
{
        int i;
```

```
        student_num = 0;
        salary = pay;
        for (i=0; i < student_len; i++) {
            students[i] = NULL;
        }
}


Instructor::Instructor(Instructor& rhs) : Person(rhs)
{
        int i;

        salary = rhs.salary;
        student_num = rhs.student_num;
        for (i=0; i < rhs.student_num; i++) {
            students[i] = new Student(*rhs.students[i]);
        }
}


Instructor::~Instructor()
{
        int i;

        for (i=0; i < student_num; i++) {
            delete students[i];
        }
}

int
Instructor::add_student(Student& new_student)
{
        students[student_num++] = new Student(new_student);
        return(student_num);
}

void
Instructor::print()
{
        int i;

        cout << ''Instructor Name: '' << get_name() << ''\n'';
        cout << ''Salary: '' << salary << ''\n'';
        if (student_num) {
            cout << ''Cost per Student: '' << salary/student_num <<
''\n'';
        }
        cout << ''Students: \n'';
        for (i=0; i < student_num; i++) {
            students[i]->print();
        }
        cout << ''\n\n'';
}
```

```
// The Grad_student class multiple inherits from Instructor
// and Student. Since they both virtually inherit from
// the Person class, they will share the same Person object.
// Also, their constructors will not call the Person
// constructor. The Grad_student is responsible for that
// initialization, as we will see below.
// The Grad_student class has three constructors: one that
// builds a graduate student from a name, social security
// number, and salary; one that builds a graduate student
// from a student object and a salary; and a third that
// builds a graduate student from an instructor.
class Grad_student : public Instructor, public Student {
public:
    Grad_student(char*, char*, double);
    Grad_student(Student&, double);
    Grad_student(Instructor&);
    void print();
};


// This constructor requires three additional constructor
// calls. The first constructor to be called will be
// the Person constructor, which takes a name and social
// security number. (Because all virtually inheriting base
// classes are called first.) The second constructor will
// be the Instructor constructor because it was the first
// class to be inherited in the class definition above. (Note:
// The order that constructor calls appear in the constructor
// definition is irrelevant. The importance is the order of
// the class definition.) Lastly, a call to the protected
// Student constructor callable with zero arguments is made.
// It is important to note that neither the Student or
// Instructor constructors will call their Person constructor.
// They would have made these calls if they were called
// directly.
Grad_student::Grad_student(char* name, char* ssn, double salary)
            : Instructor(salary), Person (name, ssn)
{
}


// This constructor calls Person's copy constructor, followed
// by Instructor's constructor, which takes a salary, followed
// by Student's copy constructor.
Grad_student::Grad_student(Student& rhs, double salary)
            : Student(rhs), Instructor(salary),Person(rhs)
{
}


// This constructor calls Person's copy constructor, followed
// by Instructor's copy constructor, followed by Student's
// protected constructor callable with zero arguments.
Grad_student::Grad_student(Instructor& rhs)
                                : Instructor(rhs), Person(rhs)
```

```
{
}

// The graduate student must resolve ambiguity on the print
// method between Student and Instructor. In this case it
// chooses a boring solution. It could have been more
// elaborate by calling each base class method. It is useful
// to note that there is no ambiguity on the call to get_name()
// even though it can be inherited via student or instructor.
// The compiler recognizes that both paths give it the same
// function.
void
Grad_student::print()
{
    cout << ''I'm just a grad student named: '';
    cout << get_name() << ''\n'';
// Could have printed both like:
//   Student::print();
//   Instructor::print();
}

void
main()
{
    Student x(''Arthur J. Riel'', ''038-48-9922'');
    Student y(''John Doe'', ''234-78-9988'');

    x.print();
    x.add_course(''Biology 101'', 94);
    x.add_course(''Physics 307'', 35);
    x.add_course(''Computer Science 101'', 98);
    x.add_course(''Advanced C++'', 78);
    x.print();

    y.add_course(''Biology 207'', 87);
    y.add_course(''Organic Chemistry'', 67);
    y.add_course(''English 109'', 100);

    Student z = x;
    z.add_course(''Introduction to Latin'', 89);
    z.add_course(''Running for Fun'', 84);
    z.add_course(''Basket Weaving 101'', 100);

    Instructor loco(''Chris Roth'', ''934-76-4365'', 29400);

    loco.add_student(x);
    loco.add_student(y);
    loco.add_student(z);

    loco.print();

// Build a graduate student from a student.
```

```
      Grad_student g1(x, 14800);

// Build a graduate student from scratch.
      Grad_student g2(''Bob Miller'', ''888-44-7765'', 34900L);


// Build a graduate student from an instructor.
      Grad_student g3(loco);

      g3.add_course(''Post-Doc 101'', 82);
      g3.add_student(x);

   cout << ''\n\nPrinting Grad Student g1 as a student\n'';
   ((Student*) &g1)->print();
   cout << ''Printing Grad Student g1 as a Instructor\n'';
   ((Instructor*) &g1)->print();
   cout << ''Printing Grad Student g1 as a grad student\n'';
   g1.print();

   cout << ''\n\nPrinting Grad Student g2 as a student\n'';
   ((Student*) &g2)->print();
   cout << ''Printing Grad Student g2 as a Instructor\n'';
   ((Instructor*) &g2)->print();
   cout << ''Printing Grad Student g2 as a grad student\n'';
   g2.print();

   cout << ''\n\nPrinting Grad Student g3 as a student\n'';
   ((Student*) &g3)->print();
   cout << ''Printing Grad Student g3 as a Instructor\n'';
   ((Instructor*) &g3)->print();
   cout << ''Printing Grad Student g3 as a grad student\n'';
   g3.print();
}
```

Selected C++ Example #17

```
// Example #17

// This example code shows the attempt to implement three
// different lists (meal lists, airplane lists, and dog lists)
// with one implementation of the list code. The general approach
// is to use inheritance to weaken the type-checking mechanism
// of C++ by making all data types that want to be in a list
// inherit from a common base class (in this case the class
// ListItem). The common base class captures any necessary
// operations that the LinkedList class might need (in this
// case, print() and type()). The problem with weak type
// checking is that a wrong derived object might end up on
// the wrong list. The benefits of mixed list and strong
// type checking are captured in the next example, which
// reimplements this code with C++ templates.
```

```
// This example could be extended to include type checking.
// The algorithm for doing this is to have each LinkedList
// object remember the data type of the first argument inserted.
// Once this is recorded all other insertions will check the
// type of the object being added to the list with the stored
// value. Of course, this algorithm makes it impossible to
// have mixed data type lists anywhere in the application.

#include <iostream.h>
#include <new.h>

// ListItem is the class responsible for weakening the type
// checking of C++. We make all of our list element classes
// inherit from this common base class. The LinkedList will
// be of pointers to this base class. Note that all ListItems
// must know how to give their type and print themselves.
class ListItem {
public:
      virtual void print(ostream& o = cout) = 0;
      virtual const char* type() = 0;
};


// The derived classes Dog, Meal, and Airplane are only
// skeleton classes to simplify their implementation.
class Dog : public ListItem {
public:
      void bark();
      void bite();
      void print(ostream& o = cout);
      const char* type();
};

void
Dog::bark()
{
      cout << ''Bow Wow\n'';
}

void
Dog::bite()
{
      cout << ''Ouch!!!\n'';
}

void
Dog::print(ostream& o)
{
      o << ''I am a dog!\n'';
}

const char*
Dog::type()
{
```

```
        return(''Dog'');
}


class Meal : public ListItem {
public:
        void eat();
        void print(ostream& o = cout);
        const char* type();
};

void
Meal::eat()
{
        cout << ''Crunch ... Munch ... Crunch ...\n'';
}

void
Meal::print(ostream& o)
{
        o << ''I'm a meal\n'';
}


const char*
Meal::type()
{
        return(''Meal'');
}


class Airplane : public ListItem {
public:
        void fly();
        void print(ostream& o = cout);
        const char* type();
};

void
Airplane::fly()
{
        cout << ''Va-a-a--room!!!\n'';
}


void
Airplane::print(ostream& o)
{
        o << ''I'm an airplane!\n'';
}


const char*
Airplane::type()
```

```
{
     return(''Airplane'');
}


typedef ListItem* DATUM;


class LinkedList {
     struct Node {
          DATUM data;
          Node* next;
     public:
          Node(DATUM&);
     };

     Node* head;
     int len;
public:
     LinkedList();
     ~LinkedList();
     int insert(DATUM&);
     DATUM remove();
     void traverse() const;
     int length();
};

LinkedList::Node::Node(DATUM& new_data)
{
     data = new_data;
     next = NULL;
}


LinkedList::LinkedList()
{
     head = NULL;
     len = 0;
}


LinkedList::~LinkedList()
{
     Node* temp;

     while (head != NULL) {
          temp = head;
          head = head->next;
          delete temp;
     }
}
```

```cpp
int
LinkedList::insert(DATUM& new_item)
{
    Node* temp = head;

    if (temp == NULL) {
        head = new Node(new_item);
    }
    else {
        while (temp->next != NULL) {
                    temp = temp->next;
        }
        temp->next = new Node(new_item);
    }
    return(++len);
}


// The remove method needs something to return if the list
// is empty. We deal with this problem by creating a dummy
// DATUM as an internal variable within the remove method.
DATUM
LinkedList::remove()
{
    Node* temp = head;
    static DATUM bad_item;
    DATUM retval;

    if (temp == NULL) {
        return(bad_item);
    }
    else {
        retval = head->data;
        head = head->next;
        len--;
        delete temp;
        return(retval);
    }
}


// Notice that the traverse method sends a message to the
// data in each node to print itself. This sets up a requirement
// that any data type that wants to be in a LinkedList needs
// a print method (this constraint is enforced in the base
// class ''ListItem''). An even more important consideration is
// the fact that the syntax is different if DATUM is a pointer
// or nonpointer. Nonpointers would use a dot, and not
// an arrow, operator. This problem carries over to templates
// as well. It is common to see templates advertise which types
// they can, and cannot, handle.
void
LinkedList::traverse() const
{
```

```
        Node* temp = head;

        cout << ''(\n'';
        while (temp != NULL) {
            temp->data->print();
            cout << ''\n'';
            temp = temp->next;
        }
        cout << '')\n\n'';
}


int
LinkedList::length()
{
        return(len);
}


void
main()
{
        LinkedList MealList, AirplaneList, DogList;
        Meal *meal1 = new Meal, *meal2 = new Meal, *meal3 = new Meal;
        Dog *dog1 = new Dog, *dog2 = new Dog, *dog3 = new Dog;
        Airplane *air1 = new Airplane, *air2 = new Airplane, *air3 =
new Airplane;

// At first glance everything seems to work nicely.
        MealList.insert(meal1);
        MealList.insert(meal2);
        MealList.insert(meal3);
        Meal* aMeal = (Meal*) MealList.remove();
        aMeal->eat();

        AirplaneList.insert(air1);
        AirplaneList.insert(air2);
        AirplaneList.insert(air3);

        DogList.insert(dog1);
        DogList.insert(dog2);
        DogList.insert(dog3);

        MealList.traverse();
        AirplaneList.traverse();
        DogList.traverse();

// Until we see some of the nasty side effects of weak type
// checking. This code accidentally flies a dog off the
// runway at the airport.

        AirplaneList.insert(dog2);
        DATUM anItem;
        while (AirplaneList.length() != 0) {
```

```
        anItem = AirplaneList.remove();
        cout << ''My real type is '' << anItem->type() << ''\n'';
        cout << ''I can fly...watch...\n'';
        ((Airplane*) anItem)->fly();
    }
    delete meal1;
    delete meal2;
    delete meal3;
    delete dog1;
    delete dog2;
    delete dog3;
    delete air1;
    delete air2;
    delete air3;
}
```

Selected C++ Example #18

```
// Example #18

// This example code shows the attempt to implement three
// different lists (meal lists, airplane lists, and dog lists)
// with one implementation of the list code. The general approach
// is to use C++ templates to capture the common structure
// that all LinkedLists share. The template is then used to
// generate the three different lists. The advantage of templates
// over weakened type checking via inheritance (Example #17) is
// that mistakes of flying dogs off runways cannot occur (due to
// the maintenance of strong type checking by templates). The
// disadvantage is that we pay for the class/method code for each
// new data type that wishes to have a list instantiation.

#include <iostream.h>
#include <new.h>


// The derived classes Dog, Meal, and Airplane are only
// skeleton classes, to simplify their implementation.
class Dog {
public:
    void bark();
    void bite();
    void print(ostream& o = cout);
};

void
Dog::bark()
{
    cout << ''Bow Wow\n'';
}

void
```

```
Dog::bite()
{
     cout << ''Ouch!!!\n'';
}

void
Dog::print(ostream& o)
{
     o << ''I am a dog!\n'';
}

class Meal {
public:
     void eat();
     void print(ostream& o = cout);
};

void
Meal::eat()
{
   cout << ''Crunch ... Munch ... Crunch ...\n'';
}

void
Meal::print(ostream& o)
{
     o << ''I'm a meal\n'';
}

class Airplane {
public:
     void fly();
     void print(ostream& o = cout);
};

void
Airplane::fly()
{
     cout << ''Va-a-a--room!!!\n'';
}


void
Airplane::print(ostream& o)
{
     o << ''I'm an airplane!\n'';
}

// Borland wouldn't accept nested templates, so the Node class is
// placed outside the scope of the LinkedList.
template <class DATUM>
struct Node {
     DATUM data;
     Node* next;
```

```cpp
public:
      Node(DATUM&);
};

template <class DATUM>
class LinkedList {
      Node<DATUM>* head;
      int len;
public:
      LinkedList();
      ~LinkedList();
      int insert(DATUM&);
      DATUM remove();
      void traverse() const;
      int length();
};


template <class DATUM>
Node<DATUM>::Node(DATUM& new_item)
{
      data = new_item;
      next = NULL;
}


template <class DATUM>
LinkedList<DATUM>::LinkedList()
{
      head = NULL;
      len = 0;
}

template <class DATUM>
LinkedList<DATUM>::~LinkedList()
{
      Node<DATUM>* temp;

      while (head != NULL) {
            temp = head;
            head = head->next;
            delete temp;
      }
}


template <class DATUM>
int
LinkedList<DATUM>::insert(DATUM& new_item)
{
      Node<DATUM>* temp = head;

      if (temp == NULL) {
            head = new Node<DATUM>(new_item);
```

```
        }
        else {
            while (temp->next != NULL) {
                        temp = temp->next;
            }
            temp->next = new Node<DATUM>(new_item);
        }
        return(++len);
}


template <class DATUM>
DATUM
LinkedList<DATUM>::remove()
{
        Node<DATUM>* temp = head;
        static DATUM bad_item;
        DATUM retval;

        if (temp == NULL) {
            return(bad_item);
        }
        else {
            retval = head->data;
            head = head->next;
            len--;
            delete temp;
            return(retval);
        }
}


// Notice that the traverse method sends a message to the
// data in each node to print itself. This sets up a requirement
// that any data type that wants to be in a LinkedList needs
// a print method. An even more important consideration is
// the fact that the syntax is different if DATUM is a pointer
// or nonpointer. Nonpointers would use a dot, and not
// an arrow, operator. The template requires its DATUM to be
// a pointer (in this example), and that the DATUM possess a
// print method.
template <class DATUM>
void
LinkedList<DATUM>::traverse() const
{
        Node<DATUM>* temp = head;

        cout << ''(\n'';
        while (temp != NULL) {
            temp->data->print();
            cout << ''\n'';
            temp = temp->next;
        }
        cout << '')\n\n'';
```

```
}

template <class DATUM>
int
LinkedList<DATUM>::length()
{
    return(len);
}


void
main()
{
    LinkedList<Meal*> MealList;
    LinkedList<Airplane*> AirplaneList;
    LinkedList<Dog*> DogList;

// The following template expansion would generate errors due to
// the traverse method requiring a pointer data type (or at least
// a data type that supports the ''->'' operator).
//
//      LinkedList<Dog> x;
//

    Meal *meal1 = new Meal, *meal2 = new Meal, *meal3 = new Meal;
    Dog *dog1 = new Dog, *dog2 = new Dog, *dog3 = new Dog;
    Airplane *air1 = new Airplane, *air2 = new Airplane, *air3 =
                    new Airplane;

// At first glance everything seems to work nicely.
    MealList.insert(meal1);
    MealList.insert(meal2);
    MealList.insert(meal3);
    Meal* aMeal = (Meal*) MealList.remove();
    aMeal->eat();
    char c;
    cin >> c;

    AirplaneList.insert(air1);
    AirplaneList.insert(air2);
    AirplaneList.insert(air3);

    DogList.insert(dog1);
    DogList.insert(dog2);
    DogList.insert(dog3);

    MealList.traverse();
    AirplaneList.traverse();
    DogList.traverse();

    cin >> c;

// The following line of code would generate compiler errors due to
```

```
//   the preservation of strong type checking by the C++ template
//   mechanism.
//
//              AirplaneList.insert(dog2);


     delete meal1;
     delete meal2;
     delete meal3;
     delete dog1;
     delete dog2;
     delete dog3;
     delete air1;
     delete air2;
     delete air3;
}
```

Selected C++ Example #19

```
// Chapter 9 Example #1
// This C++ example illustrates a minimal public interface
// implementation for a reference-counted String class. The
// minimal interface used is the one described in Chapter 9
// of this text. The code is actually three different files,
// string.hxx (the header file), string.inl (the inline
// function file included into the header file), and string.cpp
// (the C++ methods file). The three files are provided to
// illustrate the code organization as well as the details of
// the interface. Extra methods/operators are shown in the
// class definition but are not provided in the source code
// (for brevity).

// String.hxx
// This file contains the class definition for the class String.
#ifndef _STRING_
#define _STRING_
#include <iostream.h>
#include <string.h>

// The external definition of the global string that contains the
// name of this class's name, i.e., String.
extern char* String_type;

class String {
   struct StringRep {
           char* s;
           int ref_cnt;
           StringRep(const char*);
      };
      StringRep *str;
      void disconnect_self();
public:
```

```
        // Constructors and Destructors
        String(const char*);
        String(const String&);
        ~String();

        // Required functions for each class
        const char* type() const;
        String& shallow_copy(const String&);
        String& deep_copy(const String&);
        String* shallow_copy() const;
        String* deep_copy() const;
        int equal(const String&) const;
        int same(const String&) const;

        // Additional member functions
        String& upper_case();
        String& lower_case();
        String& upper_case(const String&);
        String& lower_case(const String&);
        String& reverse();
        int length() const;

        // Required operators
        String& operator=(const String&);
        int operator==(const String&) const;
        int operator!=(const String&) const;
        friend ostream& operator<<(ostream&, const String&);
        friend istream& operator>>(istream&, String&);

        // Additional operators
        String& operator=(const char*);
        String operator+(const String&) const;
        String& operator+=(const String&);
        int operator<(const String&) const;
        int operator>(const String&) const;
        int operator<=(const String&) const;
        int operator>=(const String&) const;
        String operator~() const;
        char& operator[](int index) const;

        // Required self-test function.
        static void test();
};

#include ''string.inl''
#endif

// String.inl
// This file contains all the inline function definitions used by
// the class String.

// The function that returns the type of the class String is
// implemented as an inline function, which returns the global
// type string of this class. This global variable contains the
```

```
// constant String, is defined in String.cxx, and is used to
// facilitate fast testing of the type of an object. For example,
//        if (o.type() == String_type) {
// as opposed to
//        if (!strcmp(o.type(), ''String'')) {

inline const char*
String::type() const
{
     return(String_type);
}


// The constructor for String, which takes a character pointer as
// an argument, creates a new StringRep structure on the heap
// and allocates space within it for the String's characters.
// These characters are copied into the allocated space, and the
// reference counter is assigned to one.
inline
String::String(const char* s)
{
     str = new StringRep(s);
}


// The destructor for the String class must disconnect the String
// object from its StringRep implementation. The disconnect_self
// function is a private function that decrements the reference
// counter and, if it goes to zero, cleans up the object.
inline
String::~String()
{
     disconnect_self();
}


// The shallow copy function for the String class, which takes
// zero arguments, is implemented as an inline function call to
// the copy constructor for Strings. The object that calls this
// constructor is allocated space on the heap. The source of the
// copy is the current object, which called the shallow copy
// function in the first place.
inline String*
String::shallow_copy() const
{
     return(new String(*this));
}


// The deep copy function for the String class, which takes zero
// arguments, is implemented as an inline function call to the
// constructor for Strings that takes a character pointer as an
// argument. This heap object encapsulates the character array
// in the current object (i.e., *this).
```

```cpp
inline String*
String::deep_copy() const
{
     return(new String(str->s));
}


// The equal function for the String class is implemented as an
// inline function call to the standard C library function
// ''strcmp,'' which tests the equality of two strings.
inline int
String::equal(const String& rhs) const
{
     return(!strcmp(str->s, rhs.str->s));
}


// The ''same'' function for the String class is implemented as an
// inline function that tests the StringRep pointers to ensure
// that they are the same. If they are the same, then the two
// String objects are the exact same object or shallow copies of
// each other.
inline int
String::same(const String& rhs) const
{
     return(str == rhs.str);
}


// The overloaded equivalence operator is implemented as an
// inline function call to the equal function defined on the
// class String. This function returns one if the two strings are
// equivalent (i.e., contain the same characters) and zero
// otherwise. For testing exact equality, see the function
// ''same()'' above.
inline int
String::operator==(const String& rhs) const
{
     return(equal(rhs));
}


// The overloaded nonequivalence operator is implemented as
// an inline function call to the equal function defined on the
// class String. The return value of the equal function is
// inverted before being returned. This operator returns one if
// the strings are not equal and zero otherwise.
inline int
String::operator!=(const String& rhs) const
{
     return(!equal(rhs));
}
```

```
// String.cxx
// This file contains the member functions for the class String.
#include ''string.hxx''
char* String_type = ''String'';

// The constructor for StringRep is used as a support function in
// several of the member functions for Strings. It takes a
// character pointer as an argument, allocates space for it,
// copies the characters into this allocated space, and assigns
// its reference count to one.

String::StringRep::StringRep(const char* old_s)
{
    if (old_s != NULL) {
        s = new char[strlen(old_s)+1];
        strcpy(s, old_s);
    }
    else {
        s = NULL;
    }
    ref_cnt = 1;
}


// The disconnect_self function is a private function that will
// separate a String object from its internal StringRep node.
// This process involves decrementing the reference counter in
// the StringRep node and, if it is zero (indicating that the
// String disconnecting itself is the last object pointing to the
// StringRep), the String object cleans up the StringRep object.
void
String::disconnect_self()
{
    if (--str->ref_cnt == 0) {
        delete str->s;
        delete str;
    }
}


// The copy constructor for the String class will increment the
// ref_cnt field of the String on the right-hand side of the
// initialization, i.e., the argument rhs. The StringRep pointer
// of the new object is then initialized to point at the existing
// StringRep (to which rhs is also pointing).
String::String(const String& rhs)
{
    rhs.str->ref_cnt++;
    str = rhs.str;
}


// The shallow copy function for Strings will simply assign the
// pointer to the StringRep object to point at the StringRep of
```

```
// the object on the right-hand side. The String object on the
// left-hand side of the function call (i.e., this) must first
// disconnect itself from its StringRep.

String&
String::shallow_copy(const String& rhs)
{
    disconnect_self();
    str = rhs.str;
    str->ref_cnt++;
    return(*this);
}


// The deep copy function for the String class (which takes an
// additional argument) first disconnects the node from its
// current StringRep and then creates a new StringRep,
// assigning that StringRep to the value of the character array
// stored in the StringRep of the rhs String object. This
// function returns a reference to the String object on the left-
// hand side (i.e., *this) to facilitate nested function calls.
String&
String::deep_copy(const String& rhs)
{
    if (!same(rhs)) {
        disconnect_self();
        str = new StringRep(rhs.str->s);
    }
    return(*this);
}


// The overloaded operator= function for the String class must
// first disconnect the String object on the left-hand side from
// its associated StringRep. It then assigns the StringRep pointer
// in that object to point at the StringRep object in the String
// object on the right-hand side of the assignment operator.
// This function returns a reference to the String object on the
// right-hand side in order to facilitate nested function calls.

String&
String::operator=(const String& rhs)
{
    if (!same(rhs)) {
        disconnect_self();
        str = rhs.str;
        str->ref_cnt++;
    }
    return(*this);
}


// The overloaded assignment operator for the String class, which
// takes a character pointer as an argument, first disconnects
```

```
// the string from its StringRep data member. It then creates a
// new StringRep structure and encapsulates the argument array
// of characters (i.e., rhs) into it.
String&
String::operator=(const char* rhs)
{
    disconnect_self();
    str = new StringRep(rhs);
    return(*this);
}



// The overloaded input and output operators for Strings simply
// read in the character array using standard C++ functions.
// The overloaded input operator will first disconnect the existing
// String from its associated StringRep object.
ostream&
operator<<(ostream& o, const String& rhs)
{
    o << rhs.str->s;
    return(o);
}


istream&
operator>>(istream& i, String& rhs)
{
    char buf[512];
    rhs.disconnect_self();
    i >> buf;
    rhs.str = new String::StringRep(buf);
    return(i);
}
```

Selected C++ Example #20

```
// Chapter 9 Example #2
// This C++ example illustrates the implementation of garbage
// collection in C++. Garbage collection in C++ typically
// revolves around a memory handler function that ''knows''
// which classes in the system are hoarding memory. The memory
// handler knows which classes are hoarding memory because the
// author of the application overloaded the new and delete
// functions for the class in question.
// In this example, we have a LinkedList class, which contains
// Node objects. The Node class has overloaded its standard
// allocator and deallocator (i.e., operators new and delete)
// to hoard recyclable nodes on a freelist (a class variable).
// The Node class has a free_garbage class method, which users
// of the class can call. In this example, our memory handler,
// called free_garbage, detects that memory has run out and
```

```
// tells the Node class to put the memory back.

#include <iostream.h>
#include <new.h>
#include <stdlib.h>
#include <string.h>

typedef int DATUM;

// The memory handler for the application.
void garbage_collect();


// Notice that the Node class is granting friendship to the
// LinkedList class. Granting friendship to a class or method
// is typically considered bad style since it weakens data
// hiding. In this example, it is allowed since the Node class
// is really an internal implementation detail of the LinkedList.
// To force the LinkedList class to use accessor methods for
// each access would overly convolute the code of the LinkedList
// with items such as ''head->set_next(head->get_next())''
// instead of the much more readable ''head = head->next''.
class Node {
      DATUM data;
      Node* next;
      static Node* freelist;
      friend class LinkedList;
public:
      Node(DATUM&);
      void* operator new(size_t);
      void operator delete(void*);
      static int free_garbage();
      static void print_freelist();
};

// The definition of the class variable ''freelist'' attached
// to the Node class.
Node* Node::freelist = NULL;


// The overloaded new operator (the standard allocator) will
// first try to recycle a node before going to the heap and
// getting one the expensive way.

void*
Node::operator new(size_t sz)
{
      Node* p;

// First try to get a node off the freelist.
      if (freelist != NULL) {
            p = freelist;
            freelist = freelist->next;
      }
```

```cpp
        else {
// If that doesn't work, get one the old-fashioned, expensive
// way by making a trip to the heap.
            p = (Node*) new char[sz];
        }
        return(p);
}


// Be sure that ''delete 0'' works properly (a NOP),
// then add the node to the freelist for later recycling.
void
Node::operator delete(void* p)
{
        if (p != NULL) {
            ((Node*) p)->next = freelist;
            freelist = (Node*) p;
        }
}

// The constructor for Node simply initializes the two data
// members, regardless of whether or not it is a recycled node.
Node::Node(DATUM& new_data)
{
        data = new_data;
        next = NULL;
}


// This class method is used for diagnostics. It prints the
// current addresses out on the Node's freelist.
void
Node::print_freelist()
{
        Node* temp = freelist;

        cout << ''Freelist: '';
        while (temp != NULL) {
            cout << temp << '' '';
            temp = temp->next;
        }
        cout << ''\n'';
}

// This class function will throw away the freelist of
// nodes if a garbage-collection handler function
// requests it. Since nodes have an overloaded delete
// operator, the global delete must be called. Note the use
// of the scope resolution operator. This function returns
// the number of bytes it put back on the heap.
int
Node::free_garbage()
{
        Node* temp;
```

```
        int counter = 0;
        while (freelist != NULL) {
            temp = freelist;
            freelist = freelist->next;

// Must use global delete to prevent infinite
// recursion between deleting a node off of the
// freelist and the overloaded delete operator putting
// the node back on the freelist.
            ::delete temp;
            counter++;
        }
        return(counter*sizeof(Node));
}


// The LinkedList class is a user of Nodes. Its constructor
// and destructor call the overloaded new and delete of the
// Node class. Use of LinkedList objects results in a Freelist
// of Node objects stashed away in the Node class.
class LinkedList {
        Node* head;
        int length;
public:
        LinkedList();
        LinkedList(DATUM);
        ~LinkedList();
        int insert(DATUM);
        int remove(DATUM);
        void traverse() const;
};

LinkedList::LinkedList()
{
        head = NULL;
        length = 0;
}

LinkedList::LinkedList(DATUM first_item)
{
        head = new Node(first_item);
        length = 1;
}

LinkedList::~LinkedList()
{
        Node* temp;

        while (head != NULL) {
            temp = head;
            head = head->next;
            delete temp;
        }
}
```

```cpp
int
LinkedList::insert(DATUM new_item)
{
    Node* temp = head;

    if (temp == NULL) {
        head = new Node(new_item);
    }
    else {
        while (temp->next != NULL) {
            temp = temp->next;
        }
        temp->next = new Node(new_item);
    }
    return(++length);
}


int
LinkedList::remove(DATUM bad_item)
{
    Node* temp = head;

    if (temp == NULL) {
        return(0);
    }
    if (head->data == bad_item) {
        head = head->next;
        length--;
        delete temp;
    }
    else {
        while (temp->next != NULL &&
                    temp->next->data != bad_item) {
            temp = temp->next;
        }
        if (temp->next == NULL) {
            return(0);
        }
        else {
            Node* p = temp->next;
            temp->next = temp->next->next;
            length--;
            delete p;
        }
    }
    return(1);
}


void
LinkedList::traverse() const
```

```
{
    Node* temp = head;

    cout << ''('';
    while (temp != NULL) {
        cout << temp->data << '' '';
        temp = temp->next;
    }
    cout << '')\n'';
}


// The main function first installs our memory handler.
// It then works with a number of LinkedList objects, which
// results in a freelist of nodes. We attempt to allocate
// an unallocatable amount of memory. The new operator for
// the array of characters is called. It calls the equivalent
// of malloc, which fails. New detects the failure and checks if
// there is a memory handler. There is one installed
// (garbage_collect), so we execute it and try malloc again,
// hoping for success. The hope is that the garbage collector
// will free enough memory so that the second attempt by new
// to allocate the memory is successful. In this example, the
// second attempt fails. The memory handler detects that no
// additional space has been freed and thus exits from the
// application, preventing infinite attempts to free memory even
// when there is none to free.
void
main()
{
    set_new_handler(garbage_collect);

    LinkedList a;
    LinkedList b(100);

    a.traverse();  b.traverse();
    a.insert(1);   a.insert(2);
    a.insert(3);   a.insert(4);
    a.insert(5);   a.insert(6);
    b.insert(200); b.insert(300);
    b.insert(400); b.insert(500);
    b.insert(600); b.insert(700);

    a.traverse(); b.traverse();
    Node::print_freelist();

    a.remove(1);  b.remove(100);
    a.traverse(); b.traverse();
    a.remove(6);  b.remove(700);
    a.traverse(); b.traverse();
    a.remove(4);  b.remove(400);
    a.traverse(); b.traverse();

    Node::print_freelist();
```

```
        a.insert(99);  a.insert(199);
        b.insert(-45); b.insert(-44);
        a.traverse();  b.traverse();

        Node::print_freelist();

        char* big_buf = NULL;
```

```
// This block is impossible to retrieve. New will fail and will
// call our handler, which tells the Node class to free
// its horded nodes. The call to new still fails, so we exit
// the application.
```

```
        big_buf = new char[65530L];
        strcpy(big_buf, ''Arthur Riel'');
        cout << ''big_buf = '' << big_buf <<''.\n'';
}
```

```
// The garbage-collection routine is a cornerstone in this
// example. It possesses knowledge of what element of the
// application is hoarding memory. When the heap is out of
// space, this routine tells the hoarders to put their memory
// back on the heap. If this routine cannot find any memory to
// free, it bails out.
void
garbage_collect()
{
        int space_freed;
```

```
// Get some space freed on the heap by telling the hoarding
// Node class to put its memory back.
        space_freed = Node::free_garbage();
```

```
// If there's nothing to free, simply fail. Otherwise,
// return and let new try again.
        if (!space_freed) {
            cerr << ''Fatal Memory Error!!!\n'';
            exit(-1);
        }
}
```

Selected C++ Example #21

Overview Notes. The following C++ example is an implementation of the ATM/ Bank distributed process discussed in Chapter 11. It is a simulation in that there is no physical network between the two sides of the application. Each side was tested independently by simulating the network action through strings with the appropriate fields. The reader may replace four message sends in the Network class with their favorite byte-transfer mechanism system calls and have a fully distributed system through remote proxies. The actual mechanism used is irrelevant, as this code will demonstrate. Several points of interest in this code in which the reader may be particularly interested are itemized below. This code should not be examined until the reader has become familiarized with the design discussion of Chapter 11.

- This code is not particularly concerned with bells and whistles, although many are included. Undoubtedly, more could have been added. Items such as checking for corrupted input data files are fairly minimal. Any bells and whistles that were part of the function specification have been included, however. Physical network timeouts were not addressed in this code. They would normally be implemented via alarm signals on each of the processes. The Cancel key would also be implemented in this way. Leaving out these asynchronous events left the code in a cleaner state and therefore made it easier to understand. Their implementation is not conceptually difficult given this code, but it is a bit tedious.

- The reader should be sure to examine the relationship between the `Card-Reader` and `PhysicalCardReader` classes in `atm.hpp` and `atm.cpp`. This is a good example of a wrapper class for software reuse. The comments surrounding these two classes discuss this reuse at length.

- The reader should also be sure to examine the role of the `SuperKeypad` class in allowing the containing `ATM` class to distribute its intelligence without adding uses relationships between its pieces. This type of abstraction is extremely useful to object-oriented designers and is discussed fully in the text portion of Chapter 11. It also is an example of a flaw in the data-driven methodologies. These methodologies can not detect these classes without considering behavior. However, it is useful to discover these classes early in analysis and design for purposes of controlling the complexity of the design.

- The reader should carefully examine the role that the `BankProxy` (`atm.hpp/atm.cpp`), the `ATMProxy` (`bank.hpp/bank.cpp`), and the `Network` (`network.hpp/network.cpp`) classes play in hiding the details of distributed programming during design time. The use of remote proxies can clearly encapsulate the complex interprocess communication issues within distributed applications. This subject is discussed in Chapters 9 and 11.

- Lastly, efficiency issues were not a high priority. For those real-time programmers who wish to question why I send a four-byte ASCII field to report a `Good/Bad` status over the network instead of a single-byte (or bit), keep in mind this code is meant to teach design. Besides, four bytes make for a more extensible system!

The ATM Side of the Application

```
// ATMMain.cpp: The main driving routine for the ATM side of the
// application. This main function initializes the Card Slot
// directory (to simulate the card slot of the card reader), and ATM
// Slot directory (to simulate the ATM slot where the ATM puts the
// cards it eats. These are initialized from two command line
// arguments, which are passed in to the main program. It then
// builds a network object, which would require some parameter to
// initialize a particular byte-transmission mechanism in the
// real world. For this simulation, the user will type in strings to
// simulate information transmitted over a network of some kind.
// The main method then builds BankProxy around the network and
// uses it to create an ATM object. It then activates the ATM
// object, which sits in an infinite loop waiting for bank cards.

#include <iostream.h>

#include ''network.hpp''
#include ''atm.hpp''
#include ''trans.hpp''

int
main(int argc, char** argv)
{
     if (argc != 3) {
          cout << ''Usage: '' << argv[0] << '' CardSlots ATMSlots\n'';
          return(1);
     }

  Network *network = new Network;
     BankProxy* MyBank = new BankProxy(network);
     ATM *a1 = new ATM(MyBank, ''ATM1'', 8500.00);

     strcpy(CardSlots, argv[1]);
     strcpy(ATMSlots, argv[2]);

     a1->activate();

     delete MyBank;
     delete a1;
     return(0);
}
```

The Atm.hpp File

```
// Atm.hpp: This is the header file for the main classes, which
// reside solely on the ATM side of the application.

#ifndef __ATM__
#define __ATM__
```

```
// Files that deal with transactions will often define an ATM_SIDE
// or BANK_SIDE macro to describe which application space they are
// in. The transaction code gets compiled into each application,
// but some methods are only appropriate for one address space or
// the other.


#include <iostream.h>
#include <stdlib.h>
#include ''consts.hpp''

// Forward references
class Transaction;
class TransactionList;
class Network;


// These two pointers provide the path for the Card
// Reader's directory, which simulates where a card is
// inserted, and the ATM's directory, where eaten cards
// are placed. Normally these would be hardware addresses,
// but for our simulation they are going to be directories
// in a file system. A person copies a BankCard file
// into the CardSlots directory to simulate inserting
// a card into the ATM and the ATM removes the file to
// simulate ejecting the card. The ATM moves the file to its
// internal directory to simulate eating a card. The Bank
// Card file is a one-line ASCII file that consists of seven
// numeric characters representing the account number and
// a four-digit PIN number. The bank card itself is the
// same name as the physical card reader's ''name'' data member.
// These two directory strings are assigned in the main driver
// function to the first two command line arguments passed
// in.

extern char CardSlots[];
extern char ATMSlots[];

// The following two constant strings are used for
// portability in simulating ejecting and eating cards.

extern const char* file_delete_format;
extern const char* file_move_format;

// The relationship between the PhysicalCardReader
// and the CardReader is that the CardReader is a
// wrapper class for the PhysicalCardReader. The
// latter is very reusable in that it reads only raw
// data off of a card. The CardReader is specific to
// the domain of ATM and therefore is not reusable. It is
// responsible for distributing the system intelligence
// from the ATM to its pieces (in this case, the CardReader).

class PhysicalCardReader {
```

```
        char name[small_string];
public:
    PhysicalCardReader(char* n);
        int readinfo(char* buf);
        void eject_card();
        void eat_card();
};


// The following classes model the physical pieces of the ATM
// class. They include CardReader, Display, Keypad, DepositSlot,
// CashDispenser, and ReceiptPrinter. Of particular interest is
// the SuperKeypad. This class exists solely due to an analysis of
// the behavior of the system. This analysis indicated much
// cohesion between the Keypad and DisplayScreen. Cohesion is one
// metric for determining when two or more classes need
// encapsulation inside of a containing class. It is useful to note
// that a pure data driven analysis methodology would be unable to
// detect such classes since they are motivated by behavior and do
// not exist in the real-world model.
class CardReader {
        PhysicalCardReader cardReader;
    int validcard;
        char account[small_string];
        char pin[small_string];
public:
        CardReader(char* n);
        int read_card();
        int get_account(char*);
        int get_pin(char*);
        void eject_card();
        void eat_card();
};

class Keypad {
        int enabled;
public:
        Keypad();
        void enable();
        void disable();
        char getkey();
};

class DisplayScreen {
public:
        void display_msg(const char*);
};

class SuperKeypad {
        Keypad *keypad;
        DisplayScreen *display;
public:
        SuperKeypad();
        ~SuperKeypad();
```

```cpp
        void display_msg(const char*);
        int verify_pin(const char* pin_to_verify);
        Transaction* get_transaction(char* account, char* pin);
};


class CashDispenser {
        int cash_on_hand;
public:
        CashDispenser(int initial_cash);
        int enough_cash(int amount);
        int dispense(int amount);
};

class DepositSlot {
public:
        int retrieve_envelope();
};

class ReceiptPrinter {
public:
        void print(TransactionList* translist);
};


// The BankProxy class is the representative of the Bank class in
// the ATM's address space. It is a wrapper class for the Network,
// which is itself a wrapper for the exact byte-transfer mechanism
// (pipes, in this example).
class BankProxy {
    Network* network;
public:
    BankProxy(Network* n);
    int process(Transaction*);
};


class ATM {
        BankProxy* bank;
        CardReader* cardReader;
        SuperKeypad* superKeypad;
        CashDispenser* cashDispenser;
        DepositSlot* depositSlot;
        ReceiptPrinter* receiptPrinter;
        TransactionList* translist;
public:
        ATM(BankProxy* b, char* name, int cash);
        ~ATM();
        void activate();
        int retrieve_envelope();
        int enough_cash(double amount);
        int dispense_cash(double amount);
};
```

```
#endif
```

The Atm.cpp File

```
// Atm.cpp: The source file of the main classes composing the ATM
// side of the application. It consists of all method and global
// data definitions required by these classes.

#include <stdio.h>
#include <iostream.h>
#include <string.h>
#include <math.h>

#include ''network.hpp''
#include ''atm.hpp''
#include ''trans.hpp''

// Definition of the two card slots in the ATM system, the
// card reader's slot, where a user inserts his or her card,
// and the ATM's slot into which eaten cards are taken.
// These are simulated in this system by directories in the
// file system. The two path names are given to the ATM application
// as its first two command-line arguments.

char CardSlots[large_string];
char ATMSlots[large_string];

// The definition of the two format strings for simulating
// the ejecting and eating of bank cards. Can be changed to
// the equivalent Unix commands for portability.

const char* file_delete_format = ''del %s\\%s'';
const char* file_move_format = ''copy %s\\%s %s\\%s.%d'';


// The checking of an account name determines that it consists of
// numeric digits. (Note: The actual account on the Bank side of the
// application sees seven digits plus a terminating S or C for
// savings and checking, respectively).
int
bad_account(char* account)
{
    while (*account != '\0') {
        if (*account < '0' || *account > '9') {
            return(1);
        }
        account++;
    }
    return(0);
}
```

```
// For now PIN numbers and account numbers use the same algorithm.
// They may drift in the future.
int
bad_pin(char* pin)
{
    return(bad_account(pin));
}


// Each PhysicalCardReader has a name, which it uses as the name of
// the BankCard file when it is inserted into CardSlot directory.
// This naming would not be necessary in a real system, since the
// hardware would take care of this naming problem. It appears in
// this application only for simplifying the simulation.
PhysicalCardReader::PhysicalCardReader(char* n)
{
    strcpy(name, n);
}


// The readinfo method tries to open a file in the CardSlots
// directory with the name of the card reader. This name
// would not be needed in a real system. The encoded data
// would be read off the card reader's hardware. The method
// returns a one if the card cannot be read, zero if it
// was read successfully. The buf argument is filled in
// with the first line of the file on success. It is assumed
// to contain a seven-digit numeric string (account number)
// followed by a four-digit numeric string (pin number).

int
PhysicalCardReader::readinfo(char* buf)
{
    FILE* fd;

    sprintf(buf, ''%s/%s'', CardSlots, name);
    if ((fd = fopen(buf, ''r'')) == NULL) {
        return(1);
    }
    fgets(buf, large_string, fd);
    fclose(fd);
    return(0);
}


// The simulation for eject cards is to remove the file from the card
// slot directory. In a real ATM system, this method would be a call
// to a hardware driver.
void PhysicalCardReader::eject_card()
{
    char buf[large_string];

    sprintf(buf, file_delete_format, CardSlots, name);
    system(buf);
}
```

```
// The simulation for eating cards is to move the BankCard file from
// the CardSlot directory to the ATM slot directory. In a real ATM
// system, this method would be a call to a hardware driver.
void
PhysicalCardReader::eat_card()
{
      char buf[large_string];
      static int count=1;

      sprintf(buf, file_move_format, CardSlots, name, ATMSlots,
name, count++);
      system(buf);
}


// The constructor for CardReader calls the constructor of its
// PhysicalCardReader.
CardReader::CardReader(char* name) : cardReader(name)
{
      validcard = 0;
      account[0] = pin[0] = '\0';
}


// The read_card method checks to see if there is a card in
// the slot. If there isn't, it returns 1. If there is and
// it isn't readable, then the card is rejected and a 1 is
// returned. If the data on the card is readable, then the account
// and PIN number are read from the card (account is assumed to be
// a seven-character numeric string, the PIN a four-digit numeric
// string). If the data cannot be parsed (the card is not a valid
// bank card), then a 1 is returned and the card is ejected.

int
CardReader::read_card()
{
      char buf[large_string];

      validcard = 0;
      switch (cardReader.readinfo(buf)) {
           case -1: // If the card couldn't be read, then eject it.

                        cardReader.eject_card();
                        return(1);
           case 1:  // If there is no card, then report it to ATM.
                        return(1);
           case 0:  // We have the information, parse it.
                        // If the account number is bad, return 1 and
                          eject.
                        sscanf(buf, ''%7s'', account);
                        account[7] = '\0';
                        if (bad_account(account)) {
                                  cardReader.eject_card();
                                  return(1);
```

```
                              }

                              // If the PIN number is bad, return 1 and
                              //    eject.
                              sscanf(&buf[7], ''%4s'', pin);
                              pin[4] = '\0';
                              if (bad_pin(pin)) {
                                        cardReader.eject_card();
                                        return(1);
                              }
                    }
          validcard = 1;
          return(0);
    }


    // The accessor methods are required for verifying a user-
    // supplied PIN number and building transactions. These are
    // valid since there is a design situation facing policy between
    // two separate key abstractions, i.e., the SuperKeypad and
    // the CardReader. Both return 0 on success, 1 on failure.

    int
    CardReader::get_account(char* acc)
    {
          if (validcard) {
                strcpy(acc, account);
          }
          return(!validcard);
    }


    int
    CardReader::get_pin(char* p)
    {
          if (validcard) {
                strcpy(p, pin);
          }
          return(!validcard);
    }


    // The following two methods simply delegate to their wrapped
    // PhysicalCardReader class and execute its methods.
    void
    CardReader::eject_card()
    {
          cardReader.eject_card();
    }


    void
    CardReader::eat_card()
```

```
{
      cardReader.eat_card();
}




Keypad::Keypad()
{
      enabled = 0;
}

void
Keypad::enable()
{
      fflush(stdin);
      enabled = 1;
}


void
Keypad::disable()
{
      enabled = 0;
}
```

```
// The getkey method reads a single character from the Keypad
// (in the simulation, the hardware is assumed to be the standard
// input). We assume the newline character to be the Enter key,
// implying that all input has been received. The method returns
// the character read on success, NULL terminator if the keypad
// is not enabled.
char
Keypad::getkey()
{
      return(enabled ? getchar() : '\0');
}


void
DisplayScreen::display_msg(const char* msg)
{
      cout << ''@ATM Display@ '' << msg;
}


SuperKeypad::SuperKeypad()
{
      keypad = new Keypad;
      display = new DisplayScreen;
}

SuperKeypad::~SuperKeypad()
{
```

```
        delete keypad;
        delete display;
}


// This method delegates to its contained display screen. Such
// noncommunicating behavior is an argument for splitting the
// SuperKeypad class. However, the verify_pin() and
// get_transaction() methods provide more than enough cohesion
// of data to justify the SuperKeypad's existence.
void
SuperKeypad::display_msg(const char* msg)
{
        display->display_msg(msg);
}



// The verify_pin method enables the keypad, prompts the user
// for a PIN number, and checks it against the user-supplied
// PIN number. The method returns zero on success, nonzero
// on failure.
int
SuperKeypad::verify_pin(const char* pin_to_verify)
{
        char pin[small_string];
        int i = 0;

        keypad->enable();
        display->display_msg(''Enter Pin Number: '');
        while (((pin[i++] = keypad->getkey()) != EnterKey)
                ;
        pin[i] = '\0';
        keypad->disable();
        return(strncmp(pin, pin_to_verify, 4));
}



// Note the case analysis on the type of transaction. This case
// analysis is necessary since our object-oriented design has
// bumped up against an action-oriented (text-menu driven) user
// interface as per our discussion in Chapter 9. At least this case
// analysis is restricted to one point in the design (one method)
// and hidden in the SuperKeypad class. Any classes higher in the
// system are oblivious to the case analysis.
Transaction*
SuperKeypad::get_transaction(char* account, char* pin)
{
        int i = 0;
        char amount_str[small_string], trans_type;
        char target_account[small_string];
        double amount;

        keypad->enable();
        do {
            display->display_msg(''Select a Transaction\n'');
```

```
                    display->display_msg(''\tW)ithdrawal\n'');
                    display->display_msg(''\tD)eposit\n'');
                    display->display_msg(''\tB)alance\n'');
                    display->display_msg(''\tT)ransfer\n'');
                    display->display_msg(''\tQ)uit\n'');
                    trans_type = keypad->getkey();
                    while (keypad->getkey() != EnterKey)
                              ;
            } while (trans_type != 'W' && trans_type != 'D' &&
                    trans_type != 'B' && trans_type != 'T' && trans_type
                    != 'Q');

            if (trans_type == 'Q') {
                return(NULL);
            }
            display->display_msg(''Enter Account Type (S/C): '');
            account[7] = keypad->getkey();
            account[8] = '\0';
            while (keypad->getkey() != EnterKey)
                  ;

            if (trans_type != 'B') {
                display->display_msg(''Enter Amount: '');
                while ((amount_str[i++] = keypad->getkey())  !=
                EnterKey)
                          ;
                amount_str[i-1] = '\0';
                amount = atof(amount_str);
            }
            if (trans_type == 'T') {
                display->display_msg(''Enter Target Account Number:'');
                i=0;
                while ((target_account[i++] = keypad->getkey()) !=
                EnterKey)
                          ;
                target_account[i-1] = '\0';
                display->display_msg(''Enter Target Account Type (S/
C): '');
                target_account[7] = keypad->getkey();
                target_account[8] = '\0';
                while (keypad->getkey() != EnterKey)
                          ;
            }
            switch (trans_type) {
                case 'W':
                            return(new Withdraw(account, pin, amount));
                case 'D':
                            return(new Deposit(account, pin, amount));
                case 'B':
                            return(new Balance(account, pin));
                case 'T':
```

```
                              return(new Transfer(account, pin,
                              target_account, amount));
                  default:
                              cerr << ''Unknown type in get_transaction
                              switch statement\n'';
                              return(NULL);
            }
}


CashDispenser::CashDispenser(int initial_cash)
{
      cash_on_hand = initial_cash;
}


int
CashDispenser::enough_cash(int amount)
{
      return(amount <= cash_on_hand);
}

// We can give out only multiples of $10. The reader may want to
// elaborate on this class by giving it fixed numbers of $20 bills,
// $10's, $5's, etc. Some ATMs allow for the dispensing of stamps,
// theater tickets, etc., as well. Many warn the user that they are
// out of $10 bills and will dispense only multiples of $20. All of
// these items can be added to this class without impact on the rest
// of the system.
int
CashDispenser::dispense(int amount)
{
      amount -= amount % 10;
      if (enough_cash(amount)) {
            cout << ''@CashDispenser@ Giving the user '' << amount
<< '' cash\n'';
            return(0);
      }
      return(1);
}


int
DepositSlot::retrieve_envelope()
{
      cout << ''@DepositSlot@ Getting an envelope from the
user\n'';
      return(0);
}


// The receipt printer simulates the printing of receipts by
// creating a Receipts file in the current working directory.
// Again, the reader can elaborate on this class, adding a number
```

```
// of error checks, paper availability, etc. Like the cash
// dispenser, this is left as an exercise // to the reader since it
// adds no pedagogical benefit to this example.
void
ReceiptPrinter::print(TransactionList* translist)
{
    FILE* fd;

    cout << ''@ReceiptPrinter@ Your receipt is as follows: \n'';
    if ((fd = fopen(''receipt'', ''w'')) == NULL) {
        fd = stdout;
    }
      translist->print(fd);
    if (fd != stdout) {
        fclose(fd);
    }
}
```

```
// The BankProxy is an extremely important class. It is the
// representative of the Bank class within the ATM application. It
// is merely a wrapper for the Network class, which is a wrapper
// itself for which transport mechanism a distributed process is
// going to use for communication. In this example, I chose to
// simulate the network, but readers are free to use any network
// or byte-transfer mechanism they wish. The application is
// completely independent of this mechanism. (Note: Changes in the
// byte-transfer mechanism affect only the Network class's
// implementation.)
BankProxy::BankProxy(Network* n)
{
    network = n;
}
```

```
// When a BankProxy needs to process a transaction, it asks its
// Network object to send it. Assuming the send works correctly,
// the method then asks the Network for a response, which takes the
// form of a status integer (0, 1, indicating success or failure on
// part of the real Bank class living in the bank's application
// space). If other Transaction application-specific data is
// required, then it is sent to the appropriate transaction's
// update message. This is to allow the Bank to update the state of
// a transaction in the ATM's application space from changes
// generated from the Bank's application space. Currently, only
// the Balance derived transaction uses this method to update its
// balance from the account in the Bank's application space.
int
BankProxy::process(Transaction* t)
{
    int status, count;
    char other_info[small_string];
```

```
    if (network->send(t)) {
      return(1);
    }
    count = network->receive(status, other_info);
    if (count) {
      t->update(other_info, count);
    }
      return(status);
}
```

```
// A new ATM object is given its Bank Proxy, a name to be handed down
// to its PhysicalCardReader (only needed for simulation), and its
// initial cash.
ATM::ATM(BankProxy* b, char* name, int cash)
{
      bank = new BankProxy(*b);
      cardReader = new CardReader(name);
      superKeypad = new SuperKeypad;
      cashDispenser = new CashDispenser(cash);
      depositSlot = new DepositSlot;
      receiptPrinter = new ReceiptPrinter;
      translist = new TransactionList(max_transaction_atm);
}
```

```
ATM::~ATM()
{
      delete bank;
      delete cardReader;
      delete superKeypad;
      delete cashDispenser;
      delete depositSlot;
      delete receiptPrinter;
      delete translist;
}
```

```
// The activate method for the ATM class is the main driver for the
// ATM objects. This method puts up the welcome message and waits
// for a card to become available (in simulation, a card becomes
// available when a user copies a file with the PhysicalCard-
// Reader's name into the CardSlots directory). When a card is
// available, the ATM retrieves the account and PIN number from the
// CardReader. It then asks its SuperKeypad to verify the PIN.
// The SuperKeypad verifies the PIN by getting a PIN number from the
// user and ensuring that it equals the one from the card. The
// actual check will be done by the Bank, which ensures that the PIN
// is equal to the one stored in the Account object.
// Once the PIN is verified, this method asks the SuperKeypad to
// collect and build a transaction. It preprocesses the
// transaction (handling things like getting envelopes for
// deposits, checking the cash dispenser to ensure enough cash is
// available for a withdrawal, etc.). If preprocessing was
// successful, it then asks its BankProxy to process the
```

```
// transaction. This method packages up the transaction, ships it
// over the network to the Bank's application, and collects a
// response from the Bank's application via the network. Notice
// the transparent nature of the interprocess communication. At
// design time we were able to completely ignore this distributed
// processing. Assuming the processing went well, we then execute
// a postprocess, which performs tasks like giving the user his or
// her money, etc. This method repeats the processing of the
// transaction until the user selects Quit, which requires the
// SuperKeypad::get_transaction method to return NULL. At this
// time the receipt printer generates a receipt and ejects the
// card.
void
ATM::activate()
{
      char account[small_string], pin[small_string];
      int count = 1, verified;
      Transaction* trans;

      while (1) {
             superKeypad->display_msg(''Welcome  to  the  Bank  of
Heuristics!!!\n'');
             superKeypad->display_msg(''Please Insert Your Card In
the Card Reader\n'');
// Get a card.
             while (cardReader->read_card() != 0) {
                            ;
             }
             cardReader->get_account(account);
             cardReader->get_pin(pin);
// Try three times to verify the PIN number.
             do {
                           verified = superKeypad->verify_pin(pin);
             } while (verified != 0 && count++ < 3);
// If it couldn't be verified, then eat the card.
             if (verified != 0) {
                           superKeypad->display_msg(''Sorry,    three
strikes and you're out!!!\n'');
                           cardReader->eat_card();
             }
             else {
// Otherwise, keep getting Transactions until the user asks to
// quit.
// while ((trans = superKeypad->get_transaction(account, pin))
// != NULL) {
// Preprocess the transaction, if necessary. The default is to do
// nothing.
// if (trans->preprocess(this) == 0) {
// If preprocessing was successful, then process the Transaction.
// If the Bank says the Transaction is valid, then add it to the
// current list (for the receipt) and carry out any postprocessing.
// if (bank->process(trans) == 0)
// { translist->add_trans(trans);
// trans->postprocess(this);
```

```
                    }
// If problems occur, display an appropriate message and continue.
                else {
                    superKeypad->display_msg(''The Bank Refuses Your
Transaction!\n'');
                    superKeypad->display_msg(''Contact   your   Bank
Representative.\n'');
                    delete trans;
                }
                                }
                                else {
                superKeypad->display_msg(''This ATM is unable to
                comply with your'');
                superKeypad->display_msg('' request at this
                time.\n'');
delete trans;
                                        }
                        }
// When we're done, print the receipt, clean up the Transaction
// list, and eject the card. We're now ready to loop for another
// user.
                    receiptPrinter->print(translist);
                    translist->cleanup();
                    cardReader->eject_card();
            }
        }
    }


// These are methods used by derived types of Transaction,
// specifically, in their pre-/post-process methods.
int
ATM::retrieve_envelope()
{
        return(depositSlot->retrieve_envelope());
}

int
ATM::enough_cash(double amount)
{
        return(cashDispenser->enough_cash((int) amount));
}


int
ATM::dispense_cash(double amount)
{
        return(cashDispenser->dispense((int) amount));
}
```

The Bank Side of the Application

```cpp
// Bankmain.cpp: The main driver function for the Bank side of the
// application. This main method builds a network, creates a bank,
// initializing its accounts to the data in a user-provided file,
// and builds an ATM proxy, which is then activated. The ATM proxy
// will listen on the network for a data packet. When it arrives,
// this packet is parsed to build an appropriate transaction. The
// Bank is then asked to process the transaction, and the results
// are shipped back to the sender. In this simulation, the network
// is really a user typing in packets with the appropriate format.
// The reader can replace these calls to getline with any
// appropriate byte-transfer mechanism.

#include <iostream.h>
#include ''bank.hpp''
#include ''trans.hpp''

main(int argc, char** argv)
{
    if (argc != 2) {
        cout << ''Usage: '' << argv[0] << '' AccountsFile\n'';
        return(1);
    }

    Network* network = new Network;
    Bank* mybank = new Bank(100, argv[1]);
    ATMProxy* atm = new ATMProxy(mybank, network);

    atm->activate();

    delete mybank;
    delete atm;
    return(0);
}
```

The Bank.hpp File

```cpp
// Bank.hpp: This is the header file for the main classes that
// exist solely on the Bank side of the application.

#ifndef __BANK__
#define __BANK__

#define BANK_SIDE

#include ''consts.hpp''
#include ''trans.hpp''
#include ''network.hpp''

// Forward class declarations.
```

```
class Bank;

// The Account class contains the account number, the PIN number,
// and the balance. While Accounts seem to have a type on the ATM
// side of the application, this type becomes a suffix letter (S or
// C) on the account number on the Bank side of the application.
// The get_balance method is used by Balance::process, which must
// be able to get its current balance from the account for return to
// the ATM user.
class Account {
     char account_name[small_string];
     char pin[small_string];
     double balance;
public:
   Account(char* acc_name, char* p, double amount = 0.0);
   double get_balance();
// The verify_account method checks that the account name and PIN
// number passed in are equal to that of the account.
   int verify_account(char* acc_name, char* p);
// The check_balance method ensures that the account balance is at
// least ''amount'' in value. The modify_balance will add the
// amount argument to the balance of the account. Deposits modify
// with a positive amount, Withdrawals modify with a negative
// amount, and transfers do both.
   int check_balance(double amount);
   void modify_balance(double amount);
// The equal method checks if the account name passed in is equal to
// that of the account. This is used by the find_account method of
// the AccountList class.
   int equal(char* acc_name);
   void print(FILE*);
   };


class AccountList {
     Account** accountList;
     int accountnum;
     unsigned size;
public:
     AccountList(unsigned sz);
     AccountList(unsigned sz, const char* AccountFile);
     ~AccountList();
     Account* find_account(char* acc_num);
     int add_account(Account* a);
     void print(FILE* fd);
};


// The ATMProxy is a very important class in the design of this
// application. It is the representative of the real ATM within the
// Bank application's address space. While its counterpart, the
// BankProxy in the ATM application, is mostly reactive, the
// BankProxy is proactive. It must know who its Bank object is so it
// can send it messages whenever the network delivers a request to
```

```
// process a transaction. The Network class is a wrapper for an
// appropriate byte-delivery mechanism (files, pipes, sockets,
// TCP\IP, a squirrel with the information on a piece of paper so it
// can type it in with its nose, etc.). The activate method is the
// main driver of the Bank application. The Bank acts as a general
// server for this class.
class ATMProxy {
    Bank* bank;
  Network* network;
public:
    ATMProxy(Bank* b, Network* n);
    void activate();
};


// The Bank is constructed from a data file of accounts. In a
// real-world bank application, the bank would undoubtedly have
// many more responsibilities. The big one for this application is
// the processing of transactions.
class Bank {
    AccountList* accountList;
    TransactionList* transList;
public:
    Bank(unsigned sz, const char* accounts_file);
    ~Bank();
    int  add_account(char*  account_num,  char*  pin,  double
balance = 0.0);
    int process(Transaction* t);
};

#endif
```

The Bank.cpp File

```
// Bank.cpp: The source file for the main classes of the Bank side of
// the application. It contains all of the method and global data
// definitions these classes need.

#include <iostream.h>
#include <stdio.h>
#include <stdlib.h>
#include <string.h>

#include ''bank.hpp''


Account::Account(char* acc_name, char* p, double amount)
{
    strcpy(account_name, acc_name);
    strcpy(pin, p);
    balance = amount;
}
```

```
// Currently used solely by the Balance::get_balance method for
// retrieving the account balance for the users of the ATM that
// request it.
double
Account::get_balance()
{
    return(balance);
}


// This method verifies that the account name and PIN number of a
// transaction match the account. This method would be more
// sophisticated in the real world. There is no doubt that, at a
// minimum, an encryption algorithm would be employed on the PIN
// number. The friendly Bank of Heuristics can easily leave it out
// for demonstration purposes.
int
Account::verify_account(char* acc_name, char* p)
{
        return(!strncmp(account_name, acc_name, 7) &&
!strncmp(pin, p, 4));
}


int
Account::check_balance(double amount)
{
        return(amount <= balance);
}


// Note: Withdraw objects modify with negative amounts, while
// Deposit objects use positive amounts. Tranfers use one of each.
void
Account::modify_balance(double amount)
{
        balance += amount;
}

// This method is used by the find_account method of the AccountList
// class.
int
Account::equal(char* acc_name)
{
        return(!strncmp(account_name, acc_name, 7));
}


void
Account::print(FILE* fd)
{
        fprintf(fd, ''%s %s %4.2lf\n'', account_name, pin, balance);
}
```

```
AccountList::AccountList(unsigned sz)
{
    accountList = new Account*[size = sz];
    accountnum = 0;
}


// The AccountFile is assumed to consist of an arbitrary
// number of lines, each of which is a seven-numeric-character
// string, a space, a four-digit PIN number, a space, and
// an initial balance.

AccountList::AccountList(unsigned sz, const char* AccountFile)
{
    FILE* fd;
    char buffer[large_string];
    char* account_num, *pin, *amount;

    accountList = new Account*[size = sz];
    accountnum = 0;

    if ((fd = fopen(AccountFile, ''r'')) == NULL) {
        cerr << ''AccountList Error: Cannot read \'' ''<<
AccountFile;
        cerr << ''\'' to initialize accounts.\n'';
    }
    while (fgets(buffer, large_string, fd) != NULL) {
        account_num = &buffer[0];
        pin = &buffer[8];
        amount = &buffer[13];
        buffer[12] = buffer[7] = '\0';
        if   (add_account(new   Account(account_num,   pin,
atof(amount)))) {
                    cerr << ''AccountList Error: Ran out of
space for the AccountList.\n'';
                    break;
        }
    }
    fclose(fd);
}


AccountList::~AccountList()
{
    int i;

    for (i=0; i < accountnum; i++) {
        delete accountList[i];
    }
    delete accountList;
}
```

```
Account*
AccountList::find_account(char* acc_name)
{
    int i;
      for (i=0; i < accountnum; i++) {
            if (accountList[i]->equal(acc_name)) {
                        return(accountList[i]);
            }
      }
      return(NULL);
}


int
AccountList::add_account(Account* a)
{
      if (accountnum < size) {
            accountList[accountnum++] = a;
            return(0);
      }
      else {
            return(1);
      }
}

void
AccountList::print(FILE* fd)
{
      int i;

      for (i=0; i < accountnum; i++) {
            accountList[i]->print(fd);
      }
}


ATMProxy::ATMProxy(Bank* b, Network* n)
{
      bank = b;
    network = n;
}


// This method drives the entire Bank side of the application. The
// ATMProxy waits for a transaction to be taken off the network.
// When such an object comes through the network, the method gives
// it to the Bank to process and then ships the return status back to
// the caller. If a NULL transaction is received, it is determined
// to be a Quit, and the Bank application terminates.
void
ATMProxy::activate()
{
    Transaction* t;
```

```
    int status;

    while (1) {
        if ((t = network->receive()) == NULL) {
            break;
        }
        status = bank->process(t);
        network->send(status, t);
    }
}



Bank::Bank(unsigned sz, const char* accounts_file)
{
    accountList = new AccountList(sz, accounts_file);
    transList = new TransactionList(max_transaction_bank);
};


Bank::~Bank()
{
    cout << ''Bank is being destroyed!!!\n'';
    accountList->print(stdout);
    transList->print(stdout);
        delete accountList;
        delete transList;
}


int
Bank::add_account(char* account_num, char* pin, double balance)
{
    return(accountList->add_account(new Account(account_num,
pin, balance)));
}


// When a bank processes a transaction, it first adds the
// transaction to its daily list of transactions. It then asks the
// transaction (polymorphically) to process itself. The bank
// hands its whole AccountList to the transaction since the bank
// does not know which, or how many, accounts the transaction
// requires. In this simulation, all of the accounts live in memory.
// In a real-world implementation, the accounts would live in a
// database. This change would impact only the implementation
// of the AccountList class and is irrelevant to any other code in
// our system. This is very beneficial since it implies that, at design
// time, we can pretend all objects live in memory. If in reality
// they live on disk in some database, then one of our classes, a
// wrapper, will isolate that fact from the rest of our application.
int
Bank::process(Transaction* t)
```

```
    {
        transList->add_trans(t);
        return(t->process(accountList));
    }
```

The Common Classes

```
// Consts.hpp: This header file for the ATM system captures a few
// constant definitions.
#ifndef __CONSTS__
#define __CONSTS__

const int max_transaction_atm = 20;
const int max_transaction_bank = 1000;
const int max_accounts = 100;
const int small_string = 16;
const int large_string = 128;
const char EnterKey = '\n';

#endif
```

The Trans.hpp File

```
// Trans.hpp: This header file contains the definition of the
// classes that make up the Transaction portion of this
// application. The Transaction classes are interesting in that
// they span both sides of the application, i.e., they are used by
// both Bank classes and ATM classes. In fact, the transactions
// used by the Bank classes do not need to look anything like the
// transactions used by the ATM classes. In this implementation, I
// have chosen to make them one in the same. The different public
// interfaces are supported via #ifdef's using ATM_SIDE and
// BANK_SIDE macros to differentiate them.

#ifndef __TRANS__
#define __TRANS__

#include <stdio.h>
#include <iostream.h>
#include <string.h>
#include <math.h>
#include <time.h>

#include ''consts.hpp''

// Forward references
class Account;
class AccountList;
class ATM;

// A TimeStamp object encapsulates the data and time of a
```

```
// transaction. Its current implementation is that of a string
// produced via the time and ctime library routines. The reader
// should feel free to come up with something more elaborate.
class TimeStamp {
     char date_time[small_string*2];
public:
     TimeStamp();
     void print(FILE*);
};


// All transactions have a TimeStamp, one account name, its PIN
// number, and an amount. (Note: While Balance transactions do not
// need an amount, they use it to carry back the balance value.)
// Recall that protected accessor methods are perfectly
// appropriate. The packetize method is used to turn the object
// into a string suitable for shipping across the network. It
// requires every transaction (derived classes included) to know
// the format of this string, but the alternative is to have the
// Transaction class grant friendship to the network or at least
// provide a collection of accessor methods. The latter tends to be
// problematic in that all classes gain access to the abstract
// implementation of the Transaction class. This format knowledge
// does not imply that a network needs to ship the format as is. It
// implies only that they must use it to produce the final packets
// they will ship.
class Transaction {
     TimeStamp timeStamp;
     char source_account[small_string];
     char pin[small_string];
     double amount;
protected:
     Transaction(char* account, char* p, double a);
   char* get_source_account();
     double get_amount();
   void set_amount(double new_amount);
public:
   virtual void print(FILE*);
   virtual char* type() = 0;
// Only ATM classes use the preprocess, postprocess, and update
// methods. The Transaction class for the Bank side of the
// application never compiles them into the object code.
   #ifdef ATM_SIDE
   virtual int preprocess(ATM*);
   virtual void postprocess(ATM*);
   virtual void update(char* info, int count);
   virtual void packetize(char* buf);
#endif
// The process and verify_account methods are used only by the
// classes on the Bank's side of the application. The Transaction
// class for the ATM side of the application never compiles them
// into the object code.
#ifdef BANK_SIDE
     virtual int process(AccountList* accounts) = 0;
```

```
      int verify_account(Account*);
      virtual void packetize(int status, char* buf);
#endif
};

// The following four classes are the derived classes of the
// abstract Transaction class: Deposit, Withdraw, Balance, and
// Transfer.

class Deposit : public Transaction {
public:
      Deposit(char* account, char* p, double a);
       void print(FILE*);
             char* type();
#ifdef ATM_SIDE
      int preprocess(ATM*);
#endif
#ifdef BANK_SIDE
      int process(AccountList* accounts);
#endif
};


class Withdraw : public Transaction {
public:
      Withdraw(char* account, char* p, double a);
            char* type();
#ifdef ATM_SIDE
      int preprocess(ATM*);
      void postprocess(ATM*);
#endif
#ifdef BANK_SIDE
      int process(AccountList* accounts);
#endif
      void print(FILE*);
};


class Balance : public Transaction {
      double balance;
public:
      Balance(char* account, char* p);
       void print(FILE*);
            char* type();
#ifdef ATM_SIDE
      void update(char* info, int count);
#endif
#ifdef BANK_SIDE
      int process(AccountList* accounts);
#endif
};

// The Transfer class adds the additional data member of
// target_account since the money needs to be transferred
```

```
// someplace.
class Transfer : public Transaction {
    char target_account[small_string];
public:
    Transfer(char* s_account, char* p, char* t_account, double
a);
    void print(FILE*);
    char* type();
#ifdef ATM_SIDE
    void packetize(char* buf);
#endif

#ifdef BANK_SIDE
    int process(AccountList* accounts);
#endif
};


class TransactionList {
    Transaction** TransList;
    int transnum;
    unsigned size;
public:
    TransactionList(unsigned sz);
    ~TransactionList();
    int add_trans(Transaction*);
    void print(FILE*);
    void cleanup();
};


#endif
```

The Trans.cpp File

```
// Trans.cpp: The source code for the Transaction classes. The
// Transaction classes are interesting since they appear on both
// sides of the application. The Transaction objects on each side
// of the application could be completely different definitions.
// For convenience, they were made the same in this example. The
// parts of the public interface unique to one side of the
// application are restricted through the use of the BANK_SIDE or
// ATM_SIDE macros.

#define BANK_SIDE

#ifdef ATM_SIDE
#include ''atm.hpp''
#endif

#ifdef BANK_SIDE
#include ''bank.hpp''
```

```
#endif

#include ''trans.hpp''

// The TimeStamp constructor uses the time and ctime standard C
// library functions to create a simple string capturing data and
// time.
TimeStamp::TimeStamp()
{
     time_t timer;

     time(&timer);
     strcpy(date_time, ctime(&timer));
}

void
TimeStamp::print(FILE* fd)
{
     fprintf(fd, ''%s'', date_time);
}


Transaction::Transaction(char* account, char* p, double a)
{
     strcpy(source_account, account);
     strcpy(pin, p);
     amount = a;
}

// These are protected accessor methods for use by the four derived
// classes of the Transaction class.
char*
Transaction::get_source_account()
{
   return(source_account);
}


double
Transaction::get_amount()
{
     return(amount);
}


void
Transaction::set_amount(double new_amount)
{
   amount = new_amount;
}


void
Transaction::print(FILE* fd)
```

```
{
     timeStamp.print(fd);
     fprintf(fd, ''\tAccount: %s\tAmount: %4.2lf\n'',
      source_account,
        amount);
}


#ifdef ATM_SIDE
```

```
// If the application is the ATM side, then define the preprocess,
// postprocess, and update methods to do nothing. The packetize
// method is responsible for building a string, which consists of a
// type field (four characters), the source account (seven
// characters), a space, a PIN number (four characters), a space,
// an amount (nine characters), a space, and a NULL terminator.
// This string is suitable for shipping across a network, or it can
// be transformed into something that can be shipped across a
// network.
```

```
int
Transaction::preprocess(ATM*)
{
     return(0);
}

void
Transaction::postprocess(ATM*)
{
}


void
Transaction::update(char* info, int count)
{
}

void
Transaction::packetize(char* buf)
{
   char type_buf[small_string];
   strcpy(type_buf, type());
   type_buf[4] = '\0';

   sprintf(buf, ''%s%s %s %4.2lf'', type_buf, source_account,
pin, amount);
}
#endif
```

```
// If this is the Bank side of the application, include a
// verify_account method, which checks if an account's name and
// PIN match that of the Transaction.
```

```
#ifdef BANK_SIDE
```

```
int
Transaction::verify_account(Account* a)
{
    return(a->verify_account(source_account, pin));
}


void
Transaction::packetize(int status, char* buf)
{
    sprintf(buf, ''%4d %4.2lf'', status, amount);
    cout << ''Bank packetized network object: \'''' << buf <<
''\''\n'';
}

#endif


Deposit::Deposit(char* account, char* p, double a) :
    Transaction(account, p, a)
{
}


void
Deposit::print(FILE* fd)
{
        fprintf(fd, ''Deposit: '');
        Transaction::print(fd);
}


char*
Deposit::type()
{
    return(''Deposit'');
}


// Preprocessing deposits requires grabbing an envelope. Nothing
// can go wrong with this in the simulation, but in the world of
// hardware we would have to consider timeouts, jammed envelopes,
// etc. In the real world, the DepositSlot::retrieve_envelope
// method would be implemented to handle these cases.
#ifdef ATM_SIDE

int
Deposit::preprocess(ATM* a)
{
        return(a->retrieve_envelope());
}

#endif
```

```
// Processing a Deposit transaction involves getting the source
// account, verifying it, and then modifying the balance to reflect
// the deposited amount. This is a bit of a simplification from the
// real world, where a ''shadow'' account might be updated but a
// human needs to retrieve the envelope and check to be sure that
// money was actually included. This method suits our purposes,
// which is to show the design and implementation of a distributed
// process.
#ifdef BANK_SIDE

int
Deposit::process(AccountList* accounts)
{
    Account* account = accounts->find_account(get_source_account());

    if (account == NULL) {
        return(1);
    }
    if (!Transaction::verify_account(account)) {
        return(1);
    }
    account->modify_balance(get_amount());
    return(0);
}

#endif


Withdraw::Withdraw(char* account, char* p, double a) :
    Transaction(account, p, a)
{
}


void
Withdraw::print(FILE* fd)
{
    fprintf(fd, ''Withdraw: '');
    Transaction::print(fd);
}

char*
Withdraw::type()
{
    return(''Withdraw'');
}


// Preprocessing a withdrawal involves checking the cash
// dispenser to be sure the ATM has enough cash. Postprocessing
// gives the user the cash.
#ifdef ATM_SIDE
```

```
int
Withdraw::preprocess(ATM* a)
{
      return(!a->enough_cash(get_amount()));
}

void
Withdraw::postprocess(ATM* a)
{
    a->dispense_cash(get_amount());
}

#endif


// The processing of a Withdraw transaction requires finding the
// source account, verifying the account, ensuring there is enough
// cash in the account, and, only then, reducing the amount of money
// in the account.
#ifdef BANK_SIDE

int
Withdraw::process(AccountList* accounts)
{
    Account* account = accounts->find_account(get_source_account());

    if (account == NULL || !account->check_balance
(get_amount()))
{
      return(1);
    }
    if (!Transaction::verify_account(account)) {
      return(1);
    }
    account->modify_balance(-get_amount());
    return(0);
}

#endif


Balance::Balance(char* account, char* p) : Transaction(account,
p, 0.0)
{
}

void
Balance::print(FILE* fd)
{
      fprintf(fd, ''Balance: '');
      Transaction::print(fd);
}

char*
```

```cpp
Balance::type()
{
    return(''Balance'');
}


// Processing a Balance involves finding the source account and
// copying its balance into the Amount field of the Transaction
// object. This assumes the account name and PIN were verified.
#ifdef BANK_SIDE

int
Balance::process(AccountList* accounts)
{
    Account* account = accounts->find_account(get_source_account());

    if (account == NULL) {
        return(1);
    }
    if (!Transaction::verify_account(account)) {
        return(1);
    }
    set_amount(account->get_balance());
    return(0);
}

#endif

// The update method for Balance (on the ATM side of the
// application) is used to copy the retrieved balance back into the
// corresponding Transaction object on the ATM side.
#ifdef ATM_SIDE
void
Balance::update(char* info, int count)
{
    set_amount(atof(info));
}

#endif


Transfer::Transfer(char* s_account, char* p, char* t_account,
double a)
        : Transaction(s_account, p, a)
{
        strcpy(target_account, t_account);
}


void
Transfer::print(FILE* fd)
{
        fprintf(fd, ''Transfer: '');
        Transaction::print(fd);
```

```
    fprintf(fd, ''\tTarget Account: %s\n\n'', target_
    account);
}


char*
Transfer::type()
{
    return(''Transfer'');
}

// Packetizing a transfer implies including the target account at
// the end of the packet.
#ifdef ATM_SIDE

void
Transfer::packetize(char* buf)
{
    Transaction::packetize(buf);
    strcat(buf, '' '');
    strcat(buf, target_account);
}

#endif

// Processing a Transfer object requires that we retrieve the
// source and target accounts, verify the source account, ensure
// that the source account has enough money for the transfer, and
// only then update the balances of the source (by subtracting the
// amount) and the target (by adding the equivalent amount).

#ifdef BANK_SIDE

int
Transfer::process(AccountList* accounts)
{
    Account* src_account = accounts->find_account
      (get_source_account());
    Account* tar_account = accounts->find_account(target_account);

    if (src_account == NULL || tar_account == NULL) {
        return(1);
    }
    if (!Transaction::verify_account(src_account)) {
        return(1);
    }
    if (!src_account->check_balance(get_amount())) {
        return(1);
    }
    src_account->modify_balance(-get_amount());
    tar_account->modify_balance(get_amount());
    return(0);
}
```

```
#endif


TransactionList::TransactionList(unsigned sz)
{
     transnum = 0;
     TransList = new Transaction*[size=sz];
}

TransactionList::~TransactionList()
{
     cleanup();
     delete TransList;
}

int
TransactionList::add_trans(Transaction* t)
{
     if (transnum < size) {
         TransList[transnum++] = t;
         return(0);
     }
     return(1);
}

void
TransactionList::cleanup()
{
     int i;
     for (i=0; i < transnum; i++) {
         delete TransList[i];
     }
}


void
TransactionList::print(FILE* fd)
{
     int i;
     for (i=0; i < transnum; i++) {
         TransList[i]->print(fd);
     }
}
```

The Network.hpp File

```
// Network.hpp: The header file for the network implementation
// class. While not a first-class citizen in this design (i.e., a key
// abstraction), it is a very important implementation class. This
// class is a basic wrapper for the physical network, whatever it,
// happens to be (a pipe, sockets, a LAN, a WAN, a telephone, two
// soup cans). The data of the Network class can be filled in with the
```

```
// reader's favorite mechanism. The methods of the class clearly
// state where a send buffer or receive buffer needs to be placed.
// This code has a simulation so that both sides of the application
// can be tested.

#ifndef __NETWORK__
#define __NETWORK__

#include <iostream.h>
#include <stdlib.h>
#include <string.h>
#include ''consts.hpp''

#define BANK_SIDE

class Transaction;

class Network {
// The user's favorite byte-transmission method goes here. See the
// implementation of the four methods to determine where the send
// and receives for this method need to go.
public:
#ifdef ATM_SIDE
    int send(Transaction* t);
    int receive(int& status, char* buf);
#endif
#ifdef BANK_SIDE
    Transaction* receive();
    void send(int status, Transaction* t);
#endif
};


#endif
```

The Network.cpp File

```
// Network.cpp: The implementation of the Network class for this
// application. The Network class, like the Transaction class, is
// used on both sides of the application. It uses ATM_SIDE and
// BANK_SIDE macros to distinguish which side is being compiled.
// Each side of the network class has both a send and receive pair,
// which match the formats of the corresponding application side.

#include ''network.hpp''
#include ''trans.hpp''

// The send method, which takes a Transaction, is used by the ATM
// side of the application to send a transaction to the Bank side of
// the application. It asks the Transaction to packetize itself.
// The Transaction will build a string in its argument address
// which has the format of a four-character type field (first four
```

```
// letters of the class's name, a seven-digit source account field,
// a space, a four-digit PIN number, a space, a nine-digit
// floating-point field (stored in ASCII), and a NULL terminator).
// Some transactions may add additional info to the end of the
// record, e.g., the Transfer transaction adds the target account
// to the end of the string for later retrieval by the Network::
// receive() method below (which takes zero arguments).
// In this simulation, the method simply prints the packet it would
// send through the reader's favorite mechanism.

#ifdef ATM_SIDE
int
Network::send(Transaction* t)
{
    char buffer[large_string];

    t->packetize(buffer);
    cout << ''@Network Simulation@ Sending from the ATM to the
Bank: \'''' << buffer;
    cout << ''\''\n'';
// The reader would now send this string through there favorite
// byte sending mechanism.
    return(0);
}

// The receive method for the Network class on the ATM side of the
// application waits for a buffer to be sent from the Bank. This
// buffer is expected to have the return status (0 or 1) in the first
// four bytes, followed by any transaction-specific information in
// the remaining characters. It is assumed that a space separates
// the status from the additional info. If the fifth character is a
// NULL terminator, then there is no additional info. The method
// returns the number of bytes existing, aside from the status
// field.
int
Network::receive(int& status, char* buf)
{
    char buffer[large_string];

// The reader would place his or her favorite byte-exchange
// mechanism here and ask it to receive a byte string from the Bank
// side of the application. This byte string is assumed to be a
// four-character status field followed by an indeterminant number
// of transaction-specific information. In this simulation, the
// balance of the account is passed as additional information.

    cout << ''@Network Simulation@ Enter Status (4 characters), a
space, '';
    cout << ''and the account balance: '';
    cin.getline(buffer, large_string, '\n');
    if (buffer[4] == '\0') {
        status = atoi(buffer);
        buf[0] = '\0';
        return(0);
```

```
        }
        else if (buffer[4] == ' ') {
            buffer[4] = '\0';
            status = atoi(buffer);
            strcpy(buf, &buffer[5]);
            return(strlen(&buffer[5]));
        }
        else {
            cout << ''@Network Simulation@ Bad packet received at the
ATM!!!\n'';
            status = 1;
        }
        return(0);
}

#endif

#ifdef BANK_SIDE
// The receive method on the Bank side of the application receives
// a string of the byte-transfer mechanism (in this case, a string
// typed by the user). The string is then parsed by the Network
// class, and an appropriate Transaction object is built. The
// explicit case analysis on the type of the transaction is
// necessary due to the absence of an object-oriented network. The
// Network class provides the object-oriented interface so that
// the rest of our model sees nothing but objects. The case analysis
// is hidden within this method.

Transaction*
Network::receive()
{
    char buffer[large_string];

    // The reader may replace this call to getline with any
    // appropriate byte-transfer mechanism.
    cout << ''@Network Simulation@ Enter type (4 characters), '';
    cout << ''an account (7 digits), \n'';
    cout << ''@Network Simulation@ a space, a pin (4 characters), a
space, '';
    cout << ''and an amount: \n'';
    cin.getline(buffer, large_string);

// We parse the string by turning the whitespace into NULL
// terminators. We then build the appropriate object denoted by
// the first four characters of the buffer. This is the inverse
// routine for the send method on the ATM side of the application.

    buffer[11] = buffer[16] = buffer[26] = '\0';
    if (!strncmp(buffer, ''With'', 4)) {
        return(new Withdraw(&buffer[4], &buffer[12], atof
(&buffer[17])));
    }
    else if (!strncmp(buffer, ''Depo'', 4)) {
        return(new Deposit(&buffer[4], &buffer[12], atof
```

```cpp
(&buffer[17])));
   }
   else if (!strncmp(buffer, ''Bala'', 4)) {
     return(new Balance(&buffer[4], &buffer[12]));
   }
   else if (!strncmp(buffer, ''Tran'', 4)) {
     return(new Transfer(&buffer[4], &buffer[12], &buffer
[27], atof(&buffer[17])));
   }
   else {
     cout << ''@Bank Application@ Unknown packet type!!!\n'';
   }
   return(NULL);
}

// The send method of the Bank side of the application uses the
// transaction to packetize the data. The buffer created will be a
// four-digit status field, followed by a space, and the amount of
// the transaction. This amount is then given to the Balance
// transaction on the other side of the application (the ATM side).
void
Network::send(int status, Transaction* t)
{
    char buffer[large_string];

    t->packetize(status, buffer);
// The reader can replace this output with the appropriate
// byte-transfer mechanism.
    cout << ''@Network Simulation@ Packet Sent to ATM: \'''' <<
buffer << ''\''\n'';
}

#endif
```

Bibliography

[1] Brooks, Frederick. "Conceptual Essence of Software Engineering or There is No Silver Bullet," *IEEE Computer*, October 1987.

[2] Brooks, Frederick. *The Mythical Man-Month*, Reading, MA: Addison-Wesley, 1975.

[3] Jacobson, Ivar, Magnus Christerson, Patrik Jonsson, and Gunnar Övergaard. *Object-Oriented Software Engineering: A Use Case Driven Approach*, revised, Reading, MA: ACM Press/Addison-Wesley, 1995.

[4] Jacobson, Ivar, Maria Ericsson, Agneta Jacobson. *The Object Advantage: Business Process Re-Engineering with Object Technology*, Addison-Wesley, 1995.

[5] Jacobson, Ivar. "The Confused World of OOA & OOD," *J. Object-Oriented Programming*, Sigs Publications, September 1995.

[6] Wirfs-Brock, Rebecca. "Responsibility Driven Design: How Designs Differ," *Report on Object Analysis & Design*, Sigs Publications, November–December 1994.

[7] Booch, Grady. *Object-Oriented Design with Applications*, Redwood City, CA: Benjamin/Cummings, 1991.

[8] Foote, Brian, and Ralph Johnson. "Designing Reusable Classes," *J. Object-Oriented Programming*, Sigs Publications, June 1988.

[9] Wirfs-Brock, Rebecca, B. Wilkerson, and L. Wiener. *Designing Object-Oriented Software*, Englewood Cliffs, NJ: Prentice-Hall, 1990.

[10] Meyer, Bertrand. *Object-Oriented Software Construction*, Englewood Cliffs, NJ: Prentice-Hall, 1989.

[11] Coplien, James. *Advanced C++ Programming Styles and Idioms*, Reading, MA: Addison-Wesley, 1995.

[12] Rumbaugh, James, Michael Blaha, William Premerlani, Frederick Eddy. *Object-Oriented Modeling and Design*, Englewood Cliffs, NJ: Prentice-Hall, 1991.

[13] Ben-Natan, R. *CORBA: A Guide to Common Object Request Broker*, New York, McGraw-Hill, 1995.

[14] Riel, Arthur, and John Carter. "Towards a Minimal Public Interface for C++," *The C++ Insider*, 1990.

[15] Cox, Brad, and Andrew Novobilski. *Object-Oriented Programming: An Evolutionary Approach*, 2nd ed., Reading, MA: Addison-Wesley, 1991.

[16] Carroll, M. D., and M. A. Ellis. *Designing and Coding Reusable C++*, Reading, MA: Addison-Wesley, 1995.

[17] Carroll, M. D., and M. A. Ellis. "Designing and Coding Reusable C++," *J. Object-Oriented Programming*, Sigs Publications, November 1994.

[18] Agha, G., and C. Hewitt. "Actors: A Conceptual Foundation for Concurrent Object-Oriented Programming," in *Research Directions in Object-Oriented Programming*, ed. B. Schriver and P. Wegner, Cambridge, MA: The MIT Press, 1987.

[19] Yonezawa, A., and M. Tokoro, eds. *Object-Oriented Concurrent Programming*, Cambridge, MA: The MIT Press, 1987.

[20] Alexander, Christopher. *A Pattern Language*, Oxford: Oxford Press, 1978.

[21] Alexander, Christopher. *A Timeless Way of Building*, Oxford: Oxford Press, 1979.

[22] Lieberherr, Karl J. "Adaptive Object-Oriented Software: The Demeter Method with Propagation Patterns," Boston, MA: PWS Publishing, 1995.

[23] Gamma, Erich, Richard Helm, Ralph Johnson, and John Vlissides. *Design Patterns: Elements of Reusable Object-Oriented Software*, Reading, MA: Addison-Wesley, 1995.

Other Books Used for Reference in This Text

1. Ellis, M., and Bjarne Stroustrup. *The Annotated C++ Reference Manual*, Reading, MA: Addison-Wesley, 1990.

2. Lippman, S. *The C++ Primer*, 2nd ed., Reading, MA: Addison-Wesley, 1991.

3. Meyers, Scott. *Effective C++: Fifty Specific Ways to Improve Your Programs and Designs*, Reading, MA: Addison-Wesley, 1992.

4. Booch, Grady. *Object-Oriented Analysis and Design with Applications*, 2nd ed., Redwood City, CA: Benjamin/Cummings, 1994.

5. Budd, T. *An Introduction to Object-Oriented Programming*, Reading, MA: Addison-Wesley, 1991.

6. De Champeaux, Dennis, Douglas Lea, and Penelope Faure. *Object-Oriented Systems Development*, Reading, MA: Addison-Wesley, 1993.

7. Coleman, Derek. *Object-Oriented Development: The Fusion Method*, Englewood Cliffs, NJ: Prentice-Hall, 1994.

8. Firesmith, D. *Object-Oriented Requirements Analysis and Logical Design: A Software Engineering Approach*, New York, NY: Wiley, 1993.

9. McGregor, J., and David Sykes. *Object-Oriented Software Development: Engineering Software for Reuse*, Van Nostrand Reinhold, 1992.

10. Pinson, Louis, and Richard Wiener. *Applications of Object-Oriented Programming*, Reading, MA: Addison-Wesley, 1990.

Index

A

Abstract classes
    can't instantiate objects, 22–23
    facilitate construction of inheritance
        hierarchies, 23
    place constructor in public interface, 18
Abstract data type (ADT), 23
Access area
    private, 77
    protected, 77
    public, 77
Accessed global variable types, 30
Accessor methods
    created by get and set functions, 33–34
Accidental complexity, 3–4, 9
    explicit case analysis due to, 209–11
Accidental multiple inheritance, 134
Account class, in ATM example, 215–16
Action-oriented
    applications, 29
    applications, heuristics, 220
    programming, 7, 9
    programming iterative software
        development model and, 3
    software development, 29
    topology, 30
Active objects vs. passive objects, 178
Address spaces, messaging objects in different
    spaces, 211
Agents classes, 46
Aggregations
    natural, defined, 203
    natural, in behavior-driven models, 202–3
Anderson, Bruce, 183
A Pattern Language (Alexander), 183
Applications
    analysis, 11
    design, 11
    implementation, 11
Assembly-language mnemonics, 1–2

Assigning objects, 172–73
Association relationship, 143
Association relationship (object-based), 53
Associations
    heuristics, 223
    implemented through a referential
        attribute, 144
    implemented through a third-party class,
        146–7
    vs. relationships, 202, 204
ATM system requirement specification, 199–201
Attribute, 66–67
Automated teller machine (ATM) problem,
    199–217
    Account class, 215–16
    Cancel key, 216
    card reader, 208–9
    choosing methodology for, 201–3
    Customer class, 215
    explicit case analysis, 209–11
    messaging objects in different address
        spaces, 211
    miscellaneous issues, 214–16
    Network class, 214–15
    object model for, 203–9
    PIN_Validator, 208
    requirement specification, 199–201
    returning domain to ATM, 212–14
    SuperKeypad, 208–10
    SuperKeypad in, 216
    transaction processing, 211–12

B

Base class
    functionality, 77
    as superclass, 76
Beck, Kent, 183
Behavior
    and data relationship, 12
    of the entity, 12

Behavior (*Continued*)
  of its class, 12
    noncommunicating, 208, 209
Behavioral form cause
  object-oriented paradigm, 32
Behavior-driven models, 201–3
    inheritance relationships in, 204
Benefits of data hiding, 14
Bidirectional relationship between data and
  behavior
    cornerstone of object-oriented paradigm,
      12
Booch, Grady, 37, 143, 147, 183, 201
Broadcasting or deep copying, 176
Brooks, Frederick, 3, 8, 137
Buschmann, Frank, 183
Buzzwords, 2–3

C

Callback function, 206–7, 207
CallProcessingBlock, a large global data
    structure, 39
Cancel key, in ATM problem, 216
Card readers, 208–9
Categorization hierarchy
    taxonomy of classes involved, 80
Centralized control mechanism, 29
Centralized system, 204
    created, 20
Circular uses relationships, 213
Class
    as concept, 12
    coupling and cohesion between/within
      classes, 18
    data type objects are variable, 13
    denotes behavior of entity, 12
    as generalization of object, 12
    implemented as record definition, 13
    implies a set of attributes, 12
    interface complexity reduced, 17
    method, 152
    objects constructed, 16
    point user affected, 15
    variable, 152
Class-based relationship, 71
Classes
    in behavior-driven models, 201, 202–3
    containing, 205, 206, 207–8
    controller, 208
    external, 215
    heuristics, 219, 223

implementation, 215
    proxy, 214–15
    restrictions on, 213–14
    wrapper, 214–15
Collaboration between two classes, 58
Collection of all states of a class's objects, 21
Commonality between two classes
    generalization, 75
Common-code private function created, 17
Compiled language at compile time, 15
Compiled time message, 15
Complexity
    accidental, 3–4, 9
    essential, 3–4, 9
Components
    system-specific classes, 123
Compositional mixins are object-oriented
    structures, 138
Concept, 12
    known as class, 12
"Conceptual Essence of Software Engineering
    or There Is No Silver Bullet" (Brooks),
    3, 8
Concrete classes
    to instantiate objects, 23
Concurrent object-oriented programming,
    178
Constructor
    message that initializes data, 171
Constructor of the class
    initialization of the object-oriented
      paradigm, 16
Construct users, 12
Container class, 60
Containing classes
    creating, 207–8
    defined, 205
    reusability of, 206
Containment
    hierarchies, 202–3
    by reference, 71
    relationship (object-based), 53, 60
    by value, 71
    via data members, 85
Control essential complexity, 29
Controller classes, 35, 208
Coplien, James, 107, 183
CORBA (Common Object Request Broker
    Architecture), 166
"Core the apple" problem, 216
Coupling between classes
    covert coupling, 19
    export coupling, 19
    nil coupling, 19

Coupling between classes (*Continued*)
    overt coupling, 19
    surreptitious coupling, 19
Cox, Brad, 173
Customer class, in ATM example, 215

D

DAG multiple inheritance, 140
Data
    behavior relationship bidirectional, 12
    definition functional dependencies, 13
    dependencies, 30
    to functions dependencies, 13
    hidden within its class, 13
    hiding, benefits of, 14
    modifications mapping of, 13
    types local variable declarations, 13
    types parameters, 13
    types return values, 13
Database wrapper, 166–67
Data-driven models, 201–3
    inheritance relationships in, 204
Data-hiding pattern, 195–96
Decentralization
    of software, 29
Decentralized
    architecture, 2
    systems, 204
Decomposition of system
    decentralized clumps of data, 31
Deep copy, 171
Deep copying or broadcasting, 176
Delegation functions, 136
Demeter team at Northeastern University, 198
Dependencies of functionality on data, 31
Dependency types
    data to functions, 13
    functions to data, 13
Derived class
    as subclass, 76
Descriptive attributes, 72, 144
Design methodology
    behavior-driven, 201–3
    choosing, 201–3
    data-driven, 201–3
Design of optional components
    containment by reference, 117
    inheritance, 117
Design patterns, 33
    heuristics and, 206, 216
"Design through proxies", 199

Destructor of a base class virtual, 240
Destructor of the class
    clean-up mechanism of object-oriented
        paradigm, 16, 171
    initialization, 16
Development
    milestones, 6
Dictionary class
    require ability to add and find words, 20
Different-language prototyping, 6–7, 9
Directed acyclic graph (DAG), 139
Display_msgO operation, 207–8
Domain analysis, 123
Dynamic binding or polymorphism, 95
Dynamic semantics of class
    states of class's object, 21–22
Dynamic semantic wrapper, 107

E

Equal equality testing, 173
Essential complexity, 3, 4, 9
Evolutionists, attitudes toward object-oriented
    programming, 1–3
Execution of object's behavior
    sending message, 15
Explicit case analysis, due to accidental
    complexity, 209–11

F

Fat interface solution, 122
File system with design-language-level
    mechanism, 32
Formal parameter types, 30
Framework, 137
    contains base class by reference, 123
Functional decomposition, 29
Functionality
    dependent on public data, 14
Function call
    implied first argument, 15
Functions to data dependencies, 13

G

Gamma, Erich, 183
Generalization
    commonality between two classes, 75, 92

Generalization (*Continued*)
    pattern, 190
Get and set functions
    accessor methods, 33
God class problem
    behavior form, 32
    data form, 32
    poorly distributed system intelligence, 32

H

Hash table, 21
Helm, Richard, 183
Heuristic 4.14, 205
Heuristics
    design patterns and, 206
    in object-oriented design, 199–217

I

Identity as facet of object, 12
Implementation
    classes, 215
    constructs hidden, 12
    coupling allows give-away, 19
    of the device, 11
    of function, 13, 30
    of message is method, 15
    vs. public interface, 11
Implementors of class, 15
Implementor's view of object, 13
Implied dependencies between
    implementations, 19
Implied first argument is self object, 15
Information hiding, 13
Inheritance
    class-based relationship, 76
    hierarchies vs. attributes, 103–4
    for implementation, 85
    is transitive, 80
    relationship, 75
    relationship (class-based), 53
    relationships, heuristics, 221–23
    relationships, multiple, heuristics, 223
    relationships in behavior-driven models,
        204
    relationships in data-driven models, 204
    reusability mechanism, 76
Initialization parameters, 163
Inline functions, 63

Instantiated object, 12
Instantiation relationship
    notion of class and object, 12
Insurance industry, claim system, 215
Interclass overloading, 15
Interpretated language at runtime, 15
Interrupt
    architecture, 206
    pattern, 186
Intraclass overloading, 15
Inverted inheritance pattern, 192–93
Irrelevant classes eliminated, 42
Iterative model, of software development, 5–6,
    10

J

Jacobson, Ivar, 35, 47, 143, 201
Johnson, Ralph, 183

K

Key abstraction
    main entity, 19
    map only one class, 20

L

Languages
    multiparadigm, 7, 9
    for prototyping, same- vs. different, 6–7,
        9, 10
    pure object-oriented, 7, 10
Learning curve, 29
Legacy system, 39
Lexical scope
    pattern, 193–94
    relationships and, 205
Lieberherr, Karl, 197
Limiting of access is
    information hiding, 13
LinkedList class, 17
Linked list implementations, 21
List of messages is protocol, 15
Local persistence in time, 182
Local variable
    declarations, 13
    types, 30

Logical object-oriented design, 50, 159
Loose coupling between classes, 18

M

Management information system (MIS)
    applications, data-driven modeling in,
        202
Mapping, transactions, 210
Mapping of data modifications
    to functionality, 13
Martin, Robert, 156, 183
Memory leakage, 225
Memory management, 169–70
Message
    argument types, 15
    class to which it is attached, 15
    function name, 15
    list is protocol, 15
    name of object behavior, 15
    name or prototype, 15
    return type, 15
    synchronous or asynchronous, 15
Messaging objects, in different address spaces,
    211
Metaclass, 152
Method is message implementation, 15
Methods subset, 20
Milestones, iterative, 63
Minimal public interface, 17, 171
    consists of functionality expected from
        every class, 17
MIS (management information science)
    accidental complexity in, 3–4
Mismatched new/delete calls, 225
Missing
    copy constructors, 231
    overloaded assignment operator, 233–34
Mixins are inheritance hierarchies, 137
Modeling
    behavior-driven, 201–3
    data-driven, 201–3
Models of software development
    iterative, 5–6, 10
    waterfall, 4–5, 10
Monomorphic or statically bound, 95
Multiparadigm programming languages, 7, 9
Multiple inheritance
    heuristics, 223
    relationship, 131
Mythical Man-Month, The (Brooks), 3, 31

N

Name or prototype of object behavior is
    message, 15
Namespace pollution, 156
Natural aggregations
    in behavior-driven models, 202–3
    defined, 203
Nested object pointers, 226
Network class, in ATM problem, 214–15
Network wrapper class, 47
Noncommunicating behavior, 208, 209
Nonobject–oriented language, 179
Notion of class and object relationship
    instantiation relationship, 12
Notion of data and behavior, 12

O

Object
    attributes of its class, 12
    behavior of its class, 13
    data, 156
    instance of class, 12
    method, 157
    own identity, 12
    published interface of its class, 13
    using subset of its class's behavior, 24
    values for attributes, 12
    variables of class data type, 13
Object-based relationship, 72
Object models, for automated teller machine
    (ATM) problem, 203–9
Object-oriented
    applications, 29
    languages, pure, 7, 9
    paradigm concepts for application, 11
    programming, 164
    programming accidental complexity, 3
    programming as evolutionary vs.
        revolutionary, 1–3
    programming motivation for, 1–9
    programming same- vs. different-
        language prototyping, 7
    programming value of, 9
    programming vocabulary of, 2–3
    systems, 166
    wrappers, 163
Object-oriented applications, heuristics, 220
Object-oriented design
    automated teller machine (ATM) problem,
        199–217

Object-oriented design (*Continued*)
heuristics in, 199–217
Object-oriented design, physical, heuristics, 223
Objects
has local state at runtime, 21
heuristics, 219
messaging,in different address spaces,
211
OMG Object Management Group network,
166
One class is special type of class
specialization, 75
One instance pattern, 194–95
Operators or overloaded functions, 15
Overloaded functions or operators, 15
Overloaded plus operator, 17
Overloading of nonmodifying operators,
238–40
Overriding method, 79

P

Page-Jones, Meiler, 45
Parameters, 13
Parse method, 173
Passive objects vs. active objects, 178
Patterns, heuristics and, 206, 216
Persistance, 169
in space, 169
in time, 169
Physical object-oriented design, 50, 159
heuristics, 223
PIN numbers, 208–9
PIN_Validator, ATM problem, 208
Polar coordinates change
affects user of class point, 15
Policy, 35
Polled architecture, 206
Polymorphic calls, 213
Polymorphism or dynamic binding, 95
Private and protected inheritance
are containment relationship, 85
Private inheritance, 85
Program by convention, 20
Programming by convention, 232
Proliferation of classes problem, 32
Protected
access function, 82–83
inheritance, 85
Protocol is list of messages, 15
Prototyping
different-language, 6–7, 9
same-language, 6–7, 10
value of, 6
Proxies, 211, 212, 216
Proxy classes, 214–15
Public data, 14
Public inheritance, 85
Public interface
dependent on associated data, 31
vs. implementation, 11
Published interface of its class, 13
Pure object-oriented languages, 7, 9
Pure polymorphism
no default definition in the base class,
97

R

Record definition
class implemented by, 13
Reference
or use counting, 175
Reference counting, 172
Referential attribute, 54, 144
Reflexive property of design transformation
patterns, 189
Relational database technology, accidental and
essential complexity in, 3–4
Relationship between uses and containment,
69–70
Relationships
in behavior-driven modeling, 201–2
circular uses, 213
heuristics, 220–21
lexical scope and, 205
vs. associations, 202, 204
Returning
an internal static object reference, 237–38
a memory leaking dynamically allocated
object, 238–39
a reference to a stack object, 236–37
Return values, 13
Reusability
class not dependent on its users, 16
class restrictions and, 213–14
minimize messages in protocol of class,
17
of software, 8
users dependent on public interface, 16
Revolutionists, attitudes toward object-oriented
programming, 1, 2
Role vs. classes, 24
Rumbaugh, James, 143, 201

S

Same equality testing, 173
Same-language prototyping, 6–7, 10
SecureDevice class, 206
Self object implied first argument of method, 15
Self-test, 174
Semantic constraints between classes, 64–66
Semantics documented in a state-transition
    diagram, 22
Sending a message
    execution of object's behavior, 15
Shallow copy, 171
Simple associations, 143
Software
    buying, 7–8
    reusing, 8
Software development
    accidental and essential complexity in, 3–4
    as art vs. science, 8
    as evolutionary, 1–3
    iterative model, 5–6, 10
    milestones, 6
    waterfall model, 4–5, 10
Software prototypes *see also* prototyping, 6, 10
Specialization
    hierarchy, 78
    one class is special type of another class, 75
    pattern, 191
State-transition diagram, 22
Statically bound or monomorphic, 95
Static semantics, 22
Stroustrup, Bjarne, 76–77, 155
Subclass
    as derived class, 76
    inherits from another class, 76
Subset
    of data members, 20
    of methods, 20
Subtyping for combination
    used to define new class, 135
Superclass
    as base class, 76
    inherited by another class, 76
SuperKeypad
    ATM problem, 208–10
    in ATM problem, 216
Symbolic functional decomposition, 29
System analysis
    finds key abstractions, 123

T

Template, 153
Tight cohesion within classes, 18
Transaction processing, ATM problem,
    211–12
Transactions, mapping, 210
Transitivity of inheritance, 80
True polymorphism, 95

U

Underlying data structures, 29
Understandability of message, 15
Unidirectional relationship between code and
    data, 31
Unlearning curve, 2
Use counting or reference, 175–76
Use of protected section of a base class, 81
Use of separate entity and controller classes,
    48–49
User interfaces display internals of model,
    36
Users of the construct, 12
Users view
    of interface, 13
Uses relationship (object-based), 53–60

V

Vague classes creating a centralized system,
    20

W

Waterfall model, of software development,
    4–5, 10
Weiner, Wilkerson and Wirfs-Brock, 103–4,
    201–202
Wirfs-Brock, Rebecca, 36, 143
Wrapper, 4, 160, 209
Wrapper classes, 214–15